CHEAP EATS

IN LONDON

timeout.com

Published by Time Out Guides Ltd, a wholly owned subsidiary of Time Out Group Ltd.
Time Out and the Time Out logo are trademarks of Time Out Group Ltd.

© Time Out Group Ltd 2009
Previous editions 2003, 2004, 2005, 2007

10 9 8 7 6 5 4 3 2 1

This edition first published in Great Britain in 2009 by Ebury Publishing
A Random House Group Company
20 Vauxhall Bridge Road, London SW1V 2SA

Random House Australia Pty Limited 20 Alfred Street, Milsons Point, Sydney,
New South Wales 2061, Australia
Random House New Zealand Limited 18 Poland Road, Glenfield, Auckland 10, New Zealand
Random House South Africa (Pty) Limited Isle of Houghton, Corner Boundary Road
& Carse O'Gowrie, Houghton 2198, South Africa

Random House UK Limited Reg. No. 954009

Distributed in USA by Publishers Group West
1700 Fourth Street, Berkeley, California 94710

Distributed in Canada by Publishers Group Canada
250A Carlton Street, Toronto, Ontario M5A 2L1

For further distribution details, see www.timeout.com

ISBN: 978-1-84670-074-3

A CIP catalogue record for this book is available from the British Library

Printed and bound by Firmengruppe APPL, aprinta druck, Wemding, Germany

The Random House Group Limited supports The Forest Stewardship Council (FSC), the leading
international forest certification organisation. All our titles that are printed on Greenpeace
approved FSC certified paper carry the FSC logo. Our paper procurement policy can be found
at http://www.rbooks.co.uk/environment.

Time Out carbon-offsets all its flights with Trees for Cities (www.treesforcities.org).

Edited and designed by
Time Out Guides Limited
Universal House
251 Tottenham Court Road
London W1T 7AB
Tel + 44 (0) 20 7813 3000
Fax + 44 (0) 20 7813 6001
Email guides@timeout.com
www.timeout.com

Contributors
Reviews in this guide were written by Edoardo Albert, Shane Armstrong, Will Aspinall,
Julian Bell, Claire Boobbyer, Joanna Booth, Manoj Brahmbhatt, Nuala Calvi, Jessica
Cargill Thompson, Tom Collins, Simon Collis, Simon Coppock, Radhika Dandeniya, Hannah
Davies, Guy Dimond, Thea Downie, Dominic Earle, Orlando Einsiedel, Will Fulford-Jones,
Nicola Homer, Emma Howarth, Emily Kerrigan, Jenny Kleeman, Harriet Long, Stephen
Magnus, Jim Merrett, Charmaine Mok, Anne-Alexis Moody, Kate Mossman, Jenni Muir,
Spencer Murphy, Anna Norman, Tamasine Osher, Natasha Polyviou, Ros Sales, Farah
Shafiq, Cyrus Shahrad, Jez Smadja, Dan Susman, Kate Tanner, Maisie Tomlinson, Adnan
& Sana Van Dal, Ellie Watts-Russell, Patrick Welch, Natalie Whittle, Elizabeth Winding.
Features Cyrus Shahrad, Pete Watts.

The Editor would like to thank all contributors to the *Time Out London Eating & Drinking*
guide 2009, whose works forms the basis for parts of this book.

Maps JS Graphics (john@jsgraphics.co.uk).
London Underground map supplied by Transport for London.

Photography pages 3, 34, 35, 93, 129, 167, 168, 176, 183, 185, 187, 190, 192/193,
195, 199, 202, 203, 209, 212, 217, 223, 226, 227, 237, 238/239, 243, 245, 246, 261
Jitka Hynkova; pages 10, 12, 13, 14, 17, 66, 73, 173 Ming Tang-Evans; pages 19, 46, 52,
53, 60, 76, 87, 96, 104, 107, 108/109, 111, 126/127, 130, 136/137, 140, 145, 149,
154/155, 158, 229, 233, 247, 249, 252 Michelle Grant; pages 21, 66 Heloise Bergman;
pages 28, 29, 30, 31, 56 Rob Greig; pages 41, 81, 91, 101, 197, 201 Britta Jaschinski;
pages 115, 122 Jonathan Perugia; page 117 Michael Franke; page 151 Rolf Marriott;
page 180 Alys Tomlinson; pages 256, 257 Marzena Zoladz.

Cover photograph by Nerida Howard. Taken at Cumin (020 7794 5616/www.cumin.co.uk).

About the guide

What is cheap?

Cheap is, of course, relative – London is one of the world's most expensive cities, after all. And yet hidden among its many fine and fancy restaurants is a galaxy of lower-priced eateries. So arm yourself with a £20 note and a hearty appetite, and tuck in.

In all of the **more than 500** places reviewed within this guide you should be able to get two courses (starter + main or main + dessert), plus half a bottle of house wine (or a couple of beers) plus service (we've assumed ten per cent when it is not automatically added) for no more than **£20 per person**.

Where restaurants allow you to bring your own booze, we've estimated the cost as £5 for a bottle of wine from an off-licence plus any corkage charged by the restaurant. In places that don't allow any alcohol, we've assumed you'll have a couple of soft drinks.

We have indicated in the relevant reviews those restaurants where only certain items on the menu fall within the 'budget' category.

Average

In the listings for each restaurant, you'll see one to three £ signs. These indicate average per person prices as follows:

£	= under £14
££	= £14-£17
£££	= £17-£20

Meal deals

At the end of each area chapter you'll find a section headed 'Meal deals'. The restaurants listed here would normally be too expensive to qualify as 'cheap eats', but offer menus at certain times or on certain days that would bring in a meal at less than £20 per person.

In the area

After 'Meal deals' comes 'In the area', which gives basic listings of branches that appear within that area but are affiliated to places that are reviewed elsewhere in the guide. Look in the index to find the review of the main branch.

Stars

Those restaurants that our reviewers particularly like are marked ★ in this guide. These are not necessarily the cheapest places, but all are outstanding in some way.

New

Those restaurants added since the last edition are marked NEW. These aren't necessarily new businesses, but are new to the guide.

Telephone numbers

All phone numbers listed in this guide assume you are calling from within London. From elsewhere in the UK, prefix each number with **020**. From abroad, dial your international access code, then **44** for the UK, and then **20** for London.

Unbiased reviews

The reviews in *Cheap Eats in London* are based on the experiences of Time Out restaurant reviewers. Restaurants and cafés are always visited anonymously, and Time Out pays the bill. No payment or PR invitation of any kind has secured or influenced a review. The editors select which places are listed in this guide, and are not influenced in any way by the wishes of the restaurants themselves. Restaurants cannot volunteer or pay to be listed; we list only those we consider to be worthy of inclusion. Advertising and sponsorship has no effect whatsoever on editorial content. An advertiser may receive a bad review, or no review at all.

Disclaimer

While every effort has been made to ensure the accuracy of information within this guide, the publishers cannot accept responsibility for any errors it may contain. Details can change, and it's always advisable to phone to check before setting out.

Contents

uk | ireland | holland | australia | uae | belgium | new zealand
denmark | turkey | usa | cyprus | egypt | switzerland | greece

Mex and the city

South American street food has
the capital under wraps. About time,
says **Pete Watts**.

In retrospect, the most surprising thing isn't that it happened,
but that it was so long coming. A few years ago, any visitor to
southern American states like Texas would have noticed that
the type of food dominant over there was almost impossible
to find in London – and we're not talking about grits.

For decades, the capital's only Mexican restaurants were
plastic atrocities selling greasy fajitas smothered in shrink-
wrapped cheese, which were served with comedy oversized
sombreros and washed down with cheap tequila. No wonder
the cuisine had such a bad rep.

But all that has changed. Three years ago, when lawyer-
turned-restauranteur Ben Fordham first considered opening
a cheap and cheerful burrito bar in London, there was only
one competitor: the **Daddy Donkey** stall on Leather Lane.
Fordham's **Benito's Hat** (*see p51*) has now opened for
business, and already there are two other burrito dispensers

within a few hundred yards, plus roughly a dozen more throughout the city. A Mexican revolution is sweeping the capital – or Tex-Mexican, if you want to be precise. Indeed, purists see these restaurants as an abomination thanks to their reliance on the burrito, an American invention that critics feel turns a complex national cuisine into a bastardised hybrid – regardless of the authenticity of the marinades or salsas, or the freshness of the ingredients.

Mercifully, such opinions hold increasingly less sway across London. 'In the three years it has taken us to get here, things have changed a lot,' says Fordham. 'In a way that's great news because Mexican food has a better name, and competition is good – it pushes us to keep quality up and prices down, which in turn keeps customers happy – but it also makes things tougher because we have to try and stand out.'

Burrito brothers

Benito's Hat now forms a point in a tortilla chip-shaped triangle of Mexican outlets on Fitzrovia's Goodge Street. That's more by accident than design, explains Fordham, who was inspired to open his restaurant while studying law in Austin, Texas, a noted hotspot for Tex-Mex cuisine. 'This site took ages to come up, and when we started I had no idea that **Freebird** (a trailer operating at a number of London locations) and **El Burrito** (see p51) were nearby. El Burrito opened pretty much the day before we signed the lease, which was devastating for a while, although eventually I saw that it could work to our advantage by raising the profile of Mexican food locally.'

There is now a good relationship between the three ventures, all of which serve decent burritos for under a fiver (and one of which is promoted, day in, day out, by a youth dressed in an ill-fitting donkey outfit). They've even been known to help each other out with produce should one get let down by a supplier.

Which brings us to another of the challenges facing the burrito-peddling pioneers: sourcing ingredients. It's a subject that Fordham – who learned the basics at cookery school in Oaxaca, Mexico before teaming up with Mexican chef Felipe Fuentes Cruz to open his restaurant – takes very seriously. 'We have a few specialist suppliers for dried chillies, but

we've also found an amazing farm in Bedfordshire that grows fresh tomatillos, which as far as I'm aware nobody else has in central London. They're like small green tomatoes with a husk; in Texas they're common and very cheap, but they're impossible to find here.'

That's another upside to the growth in the Tex-Mex market: more restaurants means more suppliers. 'In supermarkets the Mexican food aisles seem to be growing,' says Fordham, 'but there's still the issue of educating the masses. A lot of people walk straight out when they hear we don't do chicken fajitas – even though they don't really know what a fajita is – just because that's what they're used to getting when they go to the places handing out the novelty sombreros and cheap tequila shots.'

Thankfully, customers now have plenty of alternatives when it comes to quality Mexican food in the capital. As well as the Goodge Street trinity, there's **Mucho Mas** on Upper Street, which has since spawned a second restaurant, **Chilango** on Fleet Street; **Tortilla**, with branches on Upper Street and Southwark Street; and **Mexicali** (*see p81*), with branches in Soho, Fulham and Notting Hill.

Growing pains

Which raises another issue: that of expansion. Some London ventures already own three restaurants, but the market is still awaiting its break-out chain. And with that comes the threat of giant American burrito outlets such as Chipotle, partly owned by McDonald's, which may be eyeing up the English market with a view to moving in.

Wahaca

'I've heard that they're starting to look,' says Fordham. 'It's a relatively recession-proof business model, but it's still a scary time to be making big investments. The other worry is that they will come over and try to take control of one of the British businesses already up and running, once they get four or five restaurants under their belt.'

The market is also changing from the other end, with the opening of high-profile restaurants such as **Wahaca** (*see p43*), a sit-down, mid-range Mexican in Covent Garden run by *MasterChef* winner Thomasina Miers; a second branch is situated in the Westfield shopping centre in Shepherd's Bush.

'Wahaca has done a huge amount to raise the reputation of Mexican food, and has really helped change people's opinions,' says Fordham. 'It's a slightly different concept – a bigger menu, sit-down table service – but it's nice that there's room for that kind of thing, as well as higher-end places such as **Green & Rod** and **Mestizo**, which are real quality restaurants. The landscape is changing rapidly.'

Chilango *142 Fleet Street, EC4A 2BP (7353 6761/www.chilango. co.uk)*. **Map** p270.
Daddy Donkey *100-101 Leather Lane Market, EC1N 7TE (07968 953644/www.daddy donkey.co.uk)*. **Map** p270.
Freebird *Exmouth Market, EC2.* **Map** p270.
Green & Red *51 Bethnal Green Road, E1 6LA (7749 9670/ www.greenred.co.uk)*.
Mestizo *103 Hampstead Road, NW1 3EL (7387 4064/www. mestizomx.com)*. **Map** p266.
Mucho Mas *27 Upper Street, N1 0PN (7704 2123/www.mucho- mas.co.uk)*. **Map** p299.
Tortilla *www.tortilla.co.uk. 13 Upper Street, N1 9LQ (7833 3103/)*. **Map** p299. *Unit 11A, 106 Southwark Street, SE1 0TA (7620 0285)*. **Map** p289.

A good grilling

Cyrus Shahrad forgoes dodgy döners to discover the capital's true kebab kings

Few foods are as ritually maligned as the humble kebab; the image of inebriated urbanites staggering up the high street, shredded meat spilling from the pitta pockets that they clutch as if for dear life, is one ingrained in the public imagination. Nor is the kebab's reputation for health-ruining entirely unfounded. Granted, a pre-prandial 12-pint tipple hardly helps, but a 2009 survey found that the average high-street kebab contained no less than 98 per cent of an adult's daily recommended salt intake and a staggering 148 per cent of his or her allowance of saturated fat. And that was before the addition of chilli or garlic sauce.

All the same, there are strong arguments in favour of this most misunderstood of late-night snacks. Not least of these is the fact that the murky marriage of booze and kebab is a British creation – in Turkey, döners are traditionally eaten for lunch, and in a state of sobriety in which most Londoners wouldn't dare enter their local kebab joint, let alone dine off the spoils. The Turkish equivalent is also decidedly lighter, with marinated strips of grilled meat instead of the mysterious minced 'elephant foot' so loved and loathed on these shores, fresh salad instead of a token scrap of sweaty lettuce, and a healthy helping of yoghurt where we would normally heap glutinous chilli or garlic sauces.

Turkish delights

Those looking for proof will find plenty of Turkish eateries across the capital offering an authentic window into the kebab as developed over the centuries by the Ottoman Empire. **Anatolia Ocakbaşı** (*see p190*) is one of those that does döners properly, marinating strips of lamb before slow-grilling them on the spit, then serving the shreds in quality pide with a thick, buttery tomato sauce and a range of vegetables. Those willing to embark on something of a kebab safari will find more than mere döner on the menu: **Antepliler** (*see p214*) on Green Lanes – north London's very own Little Istanbul – serves a sumptuous sogon kebab featuring meatballs served with sweet grilled shallots and pomegranate sauce; **Yildiz** (*see p216*) is known for halep kebabs that mix tender cayenne-spiced lamb with strips of fresh bread and a rich tomato and mushroom sauce. Other decent Turkish spots include central stalwart **Efes**, its walls dotted with framed pictures of 35 years' worth of celebrity customers and its output in quality grilled meats undiminished over the decades; **Izgara** in Edgware, which has a good line in fish and vegetarian dishes; and **Maedah Grill** (*see p179*) in Whitechapel.

Bakko *172-174 Muswell Hill Broadway, N10 3SA (8883 1111/ www.bakko.co.uk).*
Efes *80-82 Great Titchfield Street, W1W 7QT (7636 1953).* Map p266.
Hafez *5 Hereford Road, W2 4AB (7221 3167).* Map p280.
Iran Restaurant *59 Edgware Road, W2 2HZ (7723 1344).* Map p276.
Izgara *165-167 Station Road, Edgware, Middx HA8 7JU (8951 4460).*
Kebab Kid *90 New King's Road, SW6 4LU (7731 0427).*
Lazeez *253 Acton High Street, W3 9BY (8752 0078).*
Pomegranate *139 Upper Street, N1 1QP (7704 1102).* Map p299.

The latter is rather incongruously located amid one of London's most notable Indian and Pakistani communities, and most culinary tourists on the surrounding streets will be here to sample grilled offerings of a different kind. No local restaurant exudes such legendary magnetism as **Tayyabs** (*see p184*); opened as a basic Pakistani-Punjabi café in 1975, it now resembles a nightclub thanks to its racing green exterior, neon blue sign, gold-leaf VIP room and queues snaking nightly up the street. Starters here include delicious seekh kebabs and shami kebabs, the former featuring ground spiced lamb grilled on skewers, the latter comprising minced mutton and chickpea patties. The nearby **Lahore Kebab House** (*see p183*) has a similarly strong reputation, though the queues are more manageable for those in a hurry.

Middle Eastern promise

If east London contains many of the capital's top Indian restaurants, then westward lies its Middle East. Iranians in particular pride themselves on the quality of their grilled meats – kebab shops punctuate Tehran's streets with the frequency that pubs do London's – and few who sample them are left in any doubt of their culinary prowess. Lamb kebabs are the focus of attention, either minced and seasoned (koobideh) or filleted (bargh); chicken kebabs are marinated in lemon, saffron and onion (joojeh), and are also delicious, although they're seen as a cheap alternative by Iranian diners. All tend to be served either with grilled tomatoes and saffron rice that is then optionally loaded with butter and sumac, or simply wrapped in Iranian bread hot from the clay oven and eaten with side helpings of masto khiar (a cucumber and yohgurt dip) and bitter sabzi greens. **Mahdi** (*see p99*), in Hammersmith, is among the finest of the mid-range options (there's no such thing as a luxury Iranian restaurant in London), and serves some of the largest portions we've seen in the capital – expect to be feasting on leftovers the following day. **Hafez** in Bayswater is a more intimate affair popular with local Iranian families, especially during Iranian New Year (Nourouz), while the helpfully named **Iran Restaurant** offers a more upmarket alternative in the environs of the Edgware Road.

Maedah Grill

All of which can seem rather odd given the Edgware Road's obvious Arabic rather than Persian heritage – from the print on its newspapers to the punters whiling away afternoons, evenings and early mornings over shared shishas on the heated terraces of its numerous coffee shops. Kebabs here tend to be of the Lebanese variety – whether that's a quick pitstop lunch of a snatched shawarma sandwich (a döner-style wrap typically loaded with houmous), or a sit-down meal of hot and cold meze followed by the likes of kofta kebab (seasoned minced lamb) or shish taouk (charcoal-grilled chicken kebab with garlic sauce). **Abu Ali** and **Al-Dar** (for both, *see p46*) are popular with locals, although the best Lebanese kebabs we've eaten recently are at **Lazeez** in Acton.

There's no limit to how far true kebab connoisseurs can take their culinary world tour, sampling Kurdish kuzu shish kebabs at **Bakko** in Muswell Hill, for example, or Greek chicken souvlakia on a bed of red onion and rocket at Islington's **Pomegranate**. And it wouldn't be fair to say that there's no such thing as a decent late-night kebab joint; **Kebab Kid** on the New King's Road is admittedly popular with drunken hordes come closing time, but the number of cab drivers filling up tummies instead of tanks (the street outside resembles a taxi rank in the small hours) is proof that you don't need to be bladdered to enjoy the sustenance on offer – and with proper shawarmas and shish kebabs cooked to order from prime cuts of meat from Smithfield Market, its not hard to imagine why.

CENTRAL

Barbican

Carnevale

135 Whitecross Street, EC1Y
8JL (7250 3452/www.carnevale
restaurant.co.uk). Barbican tube/
Old Street tube/rail/55 bus. **Lunch**
served noon-3.30pm Mon-Fri.
Dinner served 5.30-10.30pm
Mon-Sat. **Average £££. Set**
meal (lunch Mon-Fri, 5.30-7pm
Mon-Sat) £13.50 2-3 courses.
Map p271. Vegetarian

Defiantly non-corporate despite its
City postcode, this combination deli,
lunchtime takeaway spot and
compact vegetarian restaurant offers
interesting salads (such as beetroot,
watercress, walnut and honey),
imaginative sandwiches (smoked
mozzarella and aubergine in piadina,
an Italian flatbread) and hot
takeaways (risotto with plum
tomatoes, wild garlic leaves and
parmesan). It's less atmospheric in
the evening (gentler lighting might
help) and the miniature courtyard
housing three tables is cute but far
too cramped. The Med-influenced
menu hits the occasional flat note –
nutty-textured veggie sausages were
too sweet and the colcannon wasn't
heated through – but a simple
butternut squash and saffron risotto
was tasty and generously portioned.

Fish Central

149-155 Central Street, EC1V 8AP
(7253 4970/www.fishcentral.co.uk).
Old Street tube/rail/55 bus. **Lunch**
served 11am-2.30pm Mon-Sat.
Dinner served 5-10.30pm Mon-
Thur; 5-11pm Fri, Sat. **Average**
££. **Map** p270. Fish & chips

In 40 or so years since it opened, Fish
Central has expanded from a simple
chippie into a grandmaster of
oceanic eating, its smart interior
mixing etched glass with pale tones
of white and mint, its enthusiastic
stream of locals mingling media and
financial bigwigs with students and
residents of the nearby estates. In
addition to the core menu of cod,
haddock, plaice, skate and rock
salmon, there are specials such as
grilled swordfish with paella, and
deep-fried hake. Desserts are equal
parts homely and adventurous (fruit
salad came with a banana leaf and
mango sorbet). The first-floor room
is often hired out for parties.

Pham Sushi

159 Whitecross Street, EC1Y 8JL
(7251 6336/www.phamsushi.co.uk).
Old Street tube/rail/55 bus. **Lunch**
served noon-2.30pm Mon-Fri.
Dinner served 5-10pm Mon-Sat.
Average ££. **Map** p271. Japanese

Pham Sushi's interior feels tired and
lacking in TLC – expect framed
woodcut prints, off-white walls and
functional high-backed chairs – but
while the decor is nothing to fawn
over, the food certainly is. We found
the place packed on a drizzly
Monday night, something that
quickly made sense as we tucked
into top-quality california rolls,
nigiri and sashimi, the carefully
assembled creations featuring thick,
fresh cuts of raw fish and perfectly
cooked rice. The menu spans a wide
range of noodle dishes, tempura,
teriyaki steaks and the like (you can
order everything to take away), all
authentically prepared by an all-
Japanese team with ingredients
imported from the homeland. In a
city of expensive sushi chains, Pham
Sushi is something of a standout –
albeit one in need of a makeover.

Bloomsbury

★ Bea's of
Bloomsbury NEW

44 Theobalds Road, WC1X 8NW
(7242 8330/www.beasofbloomsbury.
com). Chancery Lane or Holborn
tube. **Meals served** 8am-6pm Mon-
Fri; 10.30am-4pm Sat. **Average** ££.
Map p267. Café

Bea's of Bloomsbury

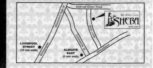

Bea Vo's plush daytime café is a saviour of special occasions thanks to its range of multi-tiered cakes, many displayed in the window. Three steps in the rear lead to a sky-lit open kitchen catering to more conventional feeding needs. Roasted vegetables featured in both a couscous and halloumi salad and a flatbread sandwich. Shredded duck salad with pomegranate and salty 'kimchi' cucumber was deliciously savoury and satisfying. A constant stream of cakes seemed to come from the kitchen: brownies with peanut butter, coconut, praline or mixed nuts; chocolate, blood-orange or raspberry meringues; swirly-topped cupcakes. The coffee is excellent and teas come from Jing, but best of all is Bea's own-recipe chai latte, surely London's best.

Bi-Won

24 Coptic Street, WC1A 1NT (7580 2660). Holborn or Tottenham Court Road tube. **Meals served** noon-11pm daily. **Average** ££. **Set meal** £17-£25 per person (minimum 2). **Map** p267. Korean
Bi Won's bright, wood-lined dining room makes a fine place to recharge the batteries after trawling around the treasures of the British Museum, and we've yet to sample a dish here that hasn't hit the mark – from tolsot bibimbap (rice, meat and vegetables cooked in a stone pot, enlivened by added pine nuts) to jajangmyun (thin Chinese-style noodles rolled in sweet soy sauce). The crowning glory are the kimchi chigae, a bubbling stew packed with thin slices of belly pork, green onions, tofu and fermented cabbage, and with a powerful chilli kick: it's undoubtedly one of the best quick lunches in the West End.

★ Savoir Faire NEW

42 New Oxford Street, WC1A 1EP (7436 0707/www.savoir.co.uk). Holborn or Tottenham Court Road
tube. **Meals served** noon-4pm, 5-10.30pm Mon-Sat; noon-10.30pm Sun. **Average** £££. **Set lunch** £9.90 2 courses. **Set dinner** (5-7.30pm) £11.50 2 courses; £16.90 2 courses. **Map** p267. French
The affection with which devotees regard this family-run bistro is understandable: in an area teeming with expensive and underwhelming restaurants, anywhere serving two courses of quality French food for £16.90 is worth getting to know well. There's a ramshackle feel to the interior, the two floors decorated with bawdy wall drawings and bills for West End musicals, the clutter of closely packed tables managing to suit both riotous groups and romantic one-on-ones. Warm sliced baguette was served before a chicken liver starter that was generous, tender and perfectly pink on the inside; beef bourguignon featured an intensely stormy sauce and an abundance of melting meat, while a lean rib-eye steak was cooked to order and came with a stack of creamy potatoes dauphinoise. Staff are friendly and enthusiastic about the food they serve.

Tas

22 Bloomsbury Street, WC1B 3QJ (7637 4555/www.tasrestaurant. com). Holborn or Tottenham Court Road tube. **Meals served** noon-11.30pm Mon-Sat; noon-10.30pm Sun. **Average** ££. **Set meal** £8.95 2 courses. **Set meze** £8.45-£9.95 per person (minimum 2). **Map** p267. Turkish
Its corner site beside the British Museum allows plenty of light through the large windows of this branch of the Tas chain; there's also a spacious basement dining area and pavement tables. The restaurant was very busy on our visit, and service was blindingly fast. Dishes were brought to the table on enormous trays, accompanied by folding stands. Patlıcan salatası was

a superior starter: creamy, smoky aubergine with fresh mint leaves. A main course of pirasali köfte featured minced lamb kebab on a bed of pan-fried leeks with tomato; the combination worked well and wasn't over-flavoured. Rebelling against a long Turkish tradition of combining simple flavours, Tas chefs prefer to blend intense flavours rather than risk blandness – a tactic that tends to pay off.

Ultimate Burger

34 New Oxford Street, WC1A 1AP (7436 6641/www.ultimate burger.co.uk). Holborn or Tottenham Court Road tube. **Meals served** noon-11pm Mon-Sat; noon-10pm Sun. **Average ££. Map** p267. Burgers Space is in short supply at Ultimate Burger, where even after squeezing between densely packed tables and inching on to one of the angular stools, you'll still have to watch your head thanks to some annoyingly dangled light fittings. Nor are engineering problems consigned to aesthetics alone: burgers look the business thanks to shiny sesame-seed buns, fat slices of tomato and lawns of green leaf, but their sheer girth makes them difficult to eat. A slick of grease spurted from our bacon cheeseburger, over-puffy onion rings left behind blobs of yellow goo, and a banana milkshake became ice-cream as we reached the bottom of its metal pitcher, rendering it impossible to drink. Ultimate seems to be struggling to live up to its name.

Wagamama

4A Streatham Street, WC1A 1JB (7323 9223/www.wagamama.com). Holborn or Tottenham Court Road tube. **Meals served** noon-11pm Mon-Sat; noon-10pm Sun. **Average ££. Map** p267. Oriental How much you enjoy the international eating phenomenon that is super-successful Wagamama will depend largely on your feelings about canteen-style dining (visitors to this branch – Wagamama's first – share long bench tables in a huge panelled dining room not unlike a school refectory). That said, it's hard to question the quality of the food thanks to the use of high-end ingredients, a practice that raises the chain above many of its imitators. We were impressed by the cut of the chargrilled steak, served on a bed of soba tossed with pak choi and sweet soy sauce. We also got a kick from the ebi raisukaree: perfectly cooked tiger prawns in a Thai-influenced coconut soup that burst into life with a squeeze of fresh lime.

Meal deals

Cigala *54 Lambs Conduit Street, WC1N 3LW (7405 1717/www. cigala.co.uk).* Set meal (Mon-Fri) £15-£18 2-3 courses. **Map** p267. Spanish

In the area

Abeno *47 Museum Street, WC1A 1LY (7405 3211).* Branch of Abeno Too. **Map** p267.
ASK *48 Grafton Way, W1T 5DZ (7388 8108).* **Map** p266.
ASK *74 Southampton Row, WC1B 4AR (7405 2876).* **Map** p267.
Busaba Eathai *22 Store Street, WC1E 7DS (7299 7900).* **Map** p266.
Carluccio's Caffè *The Brunswick, WC1N 1AF (7833 4100).* **Map** p267.
Giraffe *The Brunswick, WC1N 3AG (7812 1336).* **Map** p267.
Nando's *The Brunswick, WC1N 1AE (7713 0351).* **Map** p267.
Pâtisserie Valerie *The Brunswick, WC1N 1AF (7833 4906).* **Map** p267.
Pizza Express *30 Coptic Street, WC1A 1NS (7636 3232).* **Map** p267.
Ristorante Paradiso *35 Store Street, WC1E 7BS (7255 2554).* Branch of Pizza Paradiso. **Map** p266.
Yo! Sushi *The Brunswick, WC1N 1AE (7833 1884).* **Map** p267.

Chinatown

★ Baozi Inn NEW

*25 Newport Court, WC2H 7JS
(7287 6877). Leicester Square tube.*
Meals served 11am-10pm Mon,
Wed-Fri, Sun; 11.30am-10.30pm
Tue, Sat. **Average** ££. **No credit
cards. Map** p268. Chinese
The decor, inspired by Beijing's
hutongs (narrow alleys) circa 1952,
favours kitsch over culture, but the
Beijing and Chengdu-style street
snacks served here are 100%
authentic. The eponymous baozi –
steamed bread filled with pork or
vegetables, typical of northern China
– can be accompanied by a bowl of
slightly sweet millet porridge for an
inexpensive yet hearty meal.
Delicately spiced flowering bean
curd is composed of silky own-made
tofu, while dan dan noodles, a
Chengdu classic, is prepared from
noodles that are handmade on the
premises daily. Counter the heat of
the latter's ground-pork sauce with
a salad of springy poached peanuts
with celery, carrots and tofu skins.
Service is affable and efficient,
provided you can catch the waiters'
attention over the Chinese opera
roaring on the stereo.

Café de Hong Kong

*47-49 Charing Cross Road, WC2H
0AN (7534 9898). Leicester Square
or Piccadilly Circus tube.* **Meals
served** 11am-11pm Mon-Sat;
11am-10.30pm Sun. **Average**
££. **Map** p268. Chinese
The central location and quick-fix
menu of this multi-level Chinese
diner suggests a preoccupation with
convenience over quality, but don't
be fooled: cheesy Cantonese pop
blares constantly, the lighting is
garish and the plastic booths can be
uncomfortable, but the food here is
anything but cringeworthy. All the
Hong Kong favourites are present,
from full-flavoured spag bol to

creamy condensed milk on thick
toast. A big steaming portion of
roast duck noodles is comfort in a
bowl, as is the fail-safe option of
wok-fried beef ho fun. The long list
of bubble teas is formidable, but we
rate the thick, aromatic sesame
variation – its flavour is nothing
short of ambrosial. Just don't expect
the royal treatment from staff and
you won't leave disappointed.

Café TPT

*21 Wardour Street, W1D 6PN
(7734 7980). Leicester Square
or Piccadilly Circus tube.* **Meals
served** noon-1am daily. **Average**
££. **Set meal** £5.90-£19.50 per
person (minimum 2). **Map** p268.
Chinese
Eating at Café TPT is as fast and
cheap an experience as you'd expect
from a place named after the tai pai
tong, a type of open-air food stall
popular in Hong Kong, but the
surroundings are more comfortable
than the folding wooden tables and
stools of its namesake. Opt for a
home-style soup (usually a hearty
pork bone and vegetable broth), a
meal-on-a-plate (choose from rice or
noodle dishes with roast meats), or
one of the phenomenal desserts: the
mango and pomelo sago with
coconut milk is as good as it gets this
side of the Orient, while the silken
tofu in ginger syrup is served in a
traditional wooden vessel. Service is
brusque but well meaning.

Corean Chilli NEW

*51 Charing Cross Road, WC2H 0NE
(7734 6737). Leicester Square tube.*
Meals served noon-midnight daily.
Average ££. **Set meal** (noon-5pm)
£5-£6. **Map** p268. Korean
With its low ceilings, large red
lampshades and walls mixing
chipped granite with mock concrete
blocks, Corean Chilli feels like a
cross between an underground car
park and the sort of place the
characters of a Korean martial arts

comic might hang out. Korean and Chinese students take advantage of cheap lunch specials (served until 5pm), many with only a book for company. We found dried pollock soup a pleasant surprise – a light broth full of sliced radish, tofu and flavoursome strips of fish – but jeyuk deopbap (spicy fried belly pork) was flat and lacking in flavour. The handy location within sight of Leicester Square tube makes this a good choice for a weekday lunch or a quick bite after work.

★ Golden Dragon

28-29 Gerrard Street, W1D 6JW (7734 2763). Leicester Square or Piccadilly Circus tube. **Meals served** noon-11.30pm Mon-Thur; noon-midnight Fri, Sat; 11am-11pm Sun. **Dim sum served** noon-4.45pm Mon-Sat; 11am-4.45pm Sun. **Average** ££. **Set meal** £13.50-£40 per person (minimum 2). **Map** p268. Chinese
Tradition reigns supreme in Golden Dragon's grand dining room: the air-conditioning hums, chairs are metal-framed, tablecloths pink, and two fierce dragons leap from the rear wall. Staff are plentiful and efficient – ruthlessly so when clearing plates – while the mix of Chinese couples, office workers and tourists are understandably thrilled when their food arrives quickly, correctly prepared and packed with fresh ingredients. Successes on our last visit were many and memorable: the succulent, texturally varied filling of the stuffed mixed meat dumplings; the tangy gravy and tender flesh of the baby squid in curry sauce; and above all the immaculate freshness of the Chinese broccoli in garlic. Yet another sign of Chinatown's slow but steady return to form.

Harbour City

46 Gerrard Street, W1D 5QH (7287 1526/7439 7859). Leicester Square or Piccadilly Circus tube. **Meals served** noon-11.30pm Mon-Thur;

noon-midnight Fri, Sat; 11am-10.30pm Sun. **Dim sum served** noon-5pm Mon-Sat; 11am-5pm Sun. **Average** ££. **Set meal** £13.50-£15.50 per person (minimum 2); £15.50-£16 per person (minimum 4); £16.50-£21.50 per person (minimum 6). **Map** p268.
Chinese
This Chinatown stalwart may be something of an eyesore, its bustling ground floor overly bright and garish (bag a table on the more atmospheric first floor if possible), but the food remains affordable and authentic. A starter of deep-fried pork dumplings did little to stir the senses, but another of roll-your-own seafood lettuce wraps was a revelation, the leaves crisp and the egg-fried filling a rich mince of prawn, cod, squid and assorted vegetables. Main courses of sweet and sour fish, and honey and lemon chicken managed to be big on flavour without any artificial aftertaste, the former packed with flaky pieces of cod, the latter benefiting from a gloriously moreish glaze. Service was attentive without being intrusive.

Hing Loon

25 Lisle Street, WC2H 7BA (7437 3602). Leicester Square or Piccadilly Circus tube. **Meals served** noon-11.30pm Mon-Thur; noon-midnight Fri, Sat; noon-11pm Sun. **Average** £. **Set lunch** £4.50 2 courses. **Set dinner** £5.80-£9.50 per person (minimum 2). **Map** p268. Chinese
The two-course set lunch at this tiny, two-floor caff is a bargain at £4.50, but dishes lean towards Anglo-Chinese favourites such as sweet-and-sour pork and sweetcorn soup. Instead, we suggest consulting the 'economic meals' menu pasted on the front window, where larger-than-life bowls of noodles (the beef brisket was particularly tender, though the soup could have had more flavour) and plates of rice (try the crispy pork belly) are the hidden gems. Squid

with chilli and salt and a steaming pork and bean hotpot featured generous helpings of seafood and meat respectively, but vegetarians are also well catered for: a substantial dish of crunchy bamboo shoots, baby sweetcorn and juicy shiitake mushrooms was a plate-licking delight.

★ Imperial China

White Bear Yard, 25A Lisle Street, WC2H 7BA (7734 3388/www. imperial-china.co.uk). Leicester Square or Piccadilly Circus tube. **Meals served** noon-11.30pm Mon-Sat; 11.30am-10.30pm Sun. **Dim sum served** noon-5pm daily. **Average ££. Set meal** £16.50-£31.50 per person (minimum 2). **Map** p268. Chinese

On the far side of the red wooden footbridge fronting this palatial restaurant you'll find seating scattered throughout a handsome, wood-panelled room with low lighting. A recent visit revealed an evening menu as enjoyable as the daytime dim sum. The daily house soup was a clean, savoury broth stewed from chicken bones, served with a plate of poached peanuts and black-eyed beans sprinkled with soy sauce. Enormous steamed scallops with vermicelli noodles and shiitake mushrooms slid down deliciously, while a stir-fried dish of pork with crunchy lotus roots in nanru (fermented red bean curd) sauce was every bit as flavoursome as we'd hoped. Service is spot-on, even when students and chatty Chinese couples pack the place out on weekends.

Joy King Lau

3 Leicester Street, WC2H 7BL (7437 1132). Leicester Square or Piccadilly Circus tube. **Meals served** noon-11.30pm Mon-Sat; 11am-10.30pm Sun. **Dim sum served** noon-4.45pm daily. **Average ££. Set meal** £10-£35 per person (minimum 2). **Map** p269. Chinese

Baozi Inn. See p25.

Its menu may be comprehensive enough to serve as a culinary dictionary of sorts, but Joy King Lau is best known for the dim sum that draws mostly Chinese punters to its narrow ground-floor dining room, its wall panels backlit lime and pink in an attempt to offset the drab green carpet and lack of natural light. Dim sum highlights on our visit included tender squid rings in mild curry sauce, juicy char siu croquettes, prawn and chive dumplings, and spongy, slithery fish maw stuffed with springy minced prawn. Even better were the sweet dim sum: feather-light hot sponge cake (butter ma-lai ko) and crisp, deep-fried custard buns. Staff zip around purposefully, in a fairly friendly manner, and the atmosphere is always family-friendly.

Leong's Legends NEW

4 Macclesfield Street, W1D 6AX (7287 0288). Leicester Square or Piccadilly Circus tube. **Dim sum served** noon-5pm, **meals served** noon-11pm daily. **Average ££.** **Map** p268. Chinese

Screens and single low-lying lamps over each table create a sense of intimacy at this popular Taiwanese newcomer. The impressive menu includes plenty of non-Taiwanese food – pork slices with minced garlic and chilli (suan ni bai rou) is a cold appetiser from Sichuan – but visitors shouldn't miss the chance to sample homeland rarities like the moist omelette filled with briny baby oysters and stalks of garland chrysanthemum, a staple street food of the night markets of Taipei. The short list of dim sum includes delicious xiao long bao (soup-filled dumplings) and pretty pastries of succulent shredded turnip. A service charge is cheekily sneaked on to the bill as 'SC'. Even so, we like this place – it's different from anything else out there.

Little Lamb NEW

*72 Shaftesbury Avenue, W1D 6NA
(7287 8078). Piccadilly Circus tube.*
Meals served noon-10.30pm Mon-
Thur, Sun; noon-11pm Fri, Sat.
Average ££. Set meal £20 per
person (minimum 2). **Map** p268.
Chinese

The image of 13-century Mongolian
soldiers brewing a meaty broth in
their helmets before battle feels a
million miles away from this
diminutive restaurant, its tables set
with Kenwood hobs and its interior
a few ethnic prints away from a
greasy spoon. Dining is based
around an enormous metal pot –
filled with either a red chilli broth or
a pale herbal tonic – into which
customers dip meat, fish and
vegetables ordered plate by plate.
Some were delicious, with enormous
chunks of squid and thinly sliced
lamb absorbing the best of the fiery
mixture. Others, including rather
flavourless chicken dumplings, were
less successful, but the childish
amusement of plunging, losing and
later finding food in a bubbling
broth tends to outweigh any such
culinary shortcomings.

New World

*1 Gerrard Place, W1D 5PA (7734
0396). Leicester Square or Piccadilly
Circus tube.* **Meals served** 11am-
11.45pm Mon-Sat; 11am-11pm Sun.
Dim sum served 11am-6pm daily.
Average ££. Set meal £10.50-
£14.50 per person (minimum 2).
Map p268. Chinese

New World remains resolutely,
reliably old school, its dull red carpet
and metal-framed chairs horribly
outdated yet somehow adding to the
utilitarian charm. Dim sum trolleys
still circulate here, their steamed or
deep-fried snacks of varying quality.
Yam croquettes had a juicy minced
pork filling covered by smooth yam
paste and a coating of crisp fragility.
Also highly satisfactory were the
char siu pork puffs encased in
heavenly pastry and the fresh,
crunchy gai lan (Chinese broccoli).
But stodginess can raise its stolid
head, most evidently in the cold

Little Lamb

lotus seed buns coated in sesame seeds. It's best to dine here early, before food has spent too long on the trolley; lunchtimes tend to brim with authentic bustle.

★ Red 'N' Hot NEW

59 Charing Cross Road, WC2H 0NE (7734 8796/www.rednhot group.com). Leicester Square tube. **Meals served** noon-10pm Mon-Thur, Sun; noon-11pm Fri, Sat. **Average £££. Set meals** £18-£22 per person (minimum 2). **Map** p268. Chinese

Even the most courageous fire-eater could meet his match at Red 'N' Hot, where authentic Sichuan cuisine comes spiced to the point of spontaneous combustion. Black faux marble tables and red upholstered chairs make an oddly tranquil setting in which to explore the limits of chilli power, unleashed on everything from lungs and intestines to frogs' legs and tripe. We settled for a dish of dry-fried king prawns (plenty of them) in cumin and dried chillis (plenty of them,

too), infernal enough to have us sweating profusely despite its displaying just one pepper out of three on the menu's temperature scale. Intensity notwithstanding, it was a delicious and disarmingly subtle dish, as was a similarly searing side of aubergines with red and green peppers.

Tokyo Diner

2 Newport Place, WC2H 7JJ (7287 8777/www.tokyodiner.com). Leicester Square tube. **Meals served** noon-midnight daily. **Average ££. Set lunch** (noon-6pm) £6.50-£11.60. **Map** p268. Japanese

Straddling a corner of Chinatown that's been Japanese since 1992, Tokyo Diner seems unaffected by passing time, its pale yellow walls having acquired a patina of homely authenticity and sparsely decorated with the occasional framed print, dog-eared maps and shelves loaded with simple Japanese ceramics. The menu is surprisingly expansive, ranging from a small selection of sushi and some bargainous bento boxes to the perpetually popular curries. We plumped for a bowl of salmon don garnished with omelette and shredded cucumber, the heat of the rice over time altering the colour and texture of the raw fish, and a cool aubergine agé bitashi (deep-fried slices marinated in soy) topped with a thick slice of lotus root.

Meal deals

London Hong Kong
6-7 Lisle Street, WC2H 7BG (7287 0352/www.london-hk.co.uk). Dim sum (noon-5pm) £2-£3. **Map** p269. Chinese
New China *48 Gerrard Street, W1D 5QL (7287 9889).* Set meal £12.50-£16.50 per person (minimum 2). **Map** p268. Chinese

In the area

Pizza Express *29 Wardour Street, W1D 6PS (7437 7215).* **Map** p269.

City

Grazing NEW

*19-21 Great Tower Street, EC3R
5AR (7283 2932/www.grazingfood.
com). Monument or Tower Hill
tube/Fenchurch Street rail.* **Meals
served** 7am-4pm Mon-Fri. **Average**
££. **No credit cards**. **Map** p271.
Café

There's an unashamedly meaty
outlook at Grazing, the owners of
which are justifiably proud of their
products' provenance. This is
probably the only place in town
where you can pick up a haggis and
fried egg sandwich on the way to
work, while more conventional
butties feature grilled bacon from
the renowned Denhay Farm in
Bridport, Dorset, and healthier
breakfast options come in the form
of build-your-own muesli bars. By
lunchtime, Donald Russell's
Aberdeenshire beef rolls are the big
draw, although filled yorkshire
pudding specials make for a
tempting alternative. Small wonder,
then, that Grazing is as popular
with site-workers scanning the *Sun*
as it is with besuited City folk
spilling ketchup on their ties.

Konditor & Cook NEW

*30 St Mary Axe, EC3A 8BF (0845
262 3030/www.konditorandcook.
co.uk). Liverpool Street tube/rail.*
Meals served 7.30am-6.30pm Mon-
Fri. **Average** ££. **Map** p271. Café

The Gherkin outlet of the cake-
making café chain is larger than
most, and while its ground-floor
location means that those hoping for
sweeping City views will be sadly
disappointed, the airy interior and
slats satisfyingly criss-crossing the
large windows are pure Norman
Foster. City workers clearly love the
place; it's packed with suits on
weekday lunchtimes. Customers can
choose from the daily changing hot
meals (melanzane parmigiana was

naughtily cheesy, but delicious all
the same), or ready-made salads and
sandwiches from the cold counter.
And this wouldn't be a Konditor &
Cook without a fabulous display of
cakes: they're all laid out to tempt
you as you pay for your food and
order coffee at the till.

★ Passage Café NEW

*12 Jerusalem Passage, EC1V 4JP
(3217 0090/www.thepassagecafe.
com). Farringdon tube/rail.* **Meals
served** 11am-11pm Mon-Fri.
Average ££. **Map** p271. Brasserie

A mere slip of a venue with barely
room for 20 diners it may be, but the
Passage is the sort of place that
could hold its own in provincial
France; in central London, and at
these prices, it's nothing short of a
miracle. Caff-style furnishings are
lent a bistro feel by deep orange and
white walls, wooden flooring and
Gallic paintings. From the specials
menu we sampled luxuriously thick
cream of white asparagus and leek
soup (garnished with parsley and a
twirl of olive oil), then a (barely)
baked salmon fillet with chunky
sautéed potatoes and a crisp rocket
salad. A list of Belgian beers, cidres
bouchées and interesting wines
further heightened our admiration.
This is high-quality brasserie food
served at caff prices.

The Place Below

*St Mary-le-Bow, Cheapside, EC2V
6AU (7329 0789/www.theplace
below.co.uk). St Paul's tube/Bank
tube/DLR.* **Breakfast served**
7.30-11am, **lunch served** 11.30am-
2.15pm, **snacks served** 2.30-3pm
Mon-Fri. **Average** ££. **Unlicensed**.
Corkage no charge. **Map** p271.
Vegetarian

Dining meets the divine at this
subterranean café below Bow Bells
church (St Mary-le-Bow) in the
Square Mile. Quiches, salads and
filling breakfasts are dished out
canteen-style, as are interesting

soups, 'healthbowls' of rice and puy lentils in a tamari soy sauce and sesame dressing, imaginative ciabatta sandwiches (sweet potato, olive tapenade and goat's cheese) and hot dishes such as leek and lentil bake served with patatas bravas. The setting is key here, the cool, cavernous crypt offering a respite to overstressed City folk and older patrons who appreciate the calm atmosphere and simple, satisfying food. Prices are dropped either side of peak serving times (11.30am-noon and 1.30-2.30pm).

Pod NEW

5 Lloyds Avenue, EC3N 3AE (3174 0038/www.podfood.co.uk). Aldgate or Tower Hill tube. **Meals served** 7am-4.30pm Mon-Fri. **Average** £. **Map** p271. Café
There's a rather corporate feel to Pod: its healthy menu may be nourishing for the body, but its uninspired decor and lamentable easy-listening soundtrack leaves the soul wanting more. Still, if you're looking to pick up a simple, warming lunch then you'll find a healthy selection of soups, curries, stews, salads and sandwiches. For breakfast, choose from porridge served with the likes of goji berries or bananas, scrambled eggs on toast, and sausage or bacon sandwiches. A fridge cabinet holds a plentiful supply of yoghurts and there are fruit and granola combos aplenty, plus a good range of fortifying juices. Coffees and croissants are also passable. Not a destination venue by any means, but a decent alternative to the usual suspects if you happen to be in the area.

Meal deals

Barcelona Tapas Bar y Restaurante *13 Well Court, off Bow Lane, EC4M 9DN (7329 5111).* Tapas £3.25-£11.95. **Map** p271. Spanish

Barcelona Tapas Bar y Restaurante *15 St Botolph Street, entrance at 1 Middlesex Street, EC3A 7DT (7377 5222).* Tapas £3.25-£11.95. **Map** p271. Spanish

Barcelona Tapas Bar y Restaurante *24 Lime Street, EC3M 7HS (7929 2389).* Tapas £3.25-£11.95. **Map** p271. Spanish

Haz *9 Cutler Street, E1 7DJ (7929 7923).* Set meal £9.25 2 courses; set meze £13.45. **Map** p271. Turkish

Missouri Angel *America Square, 14 Crosswall, EC3N 2LJ (7481 8422/www.missourigrill.com).* Set dinner (Mon-Fri) £12 2 courses. **Map** p271. North American

In the area

Gourmet Burger Kitchen *Condor House, St Paul's Churchyard, EC4M 8AL (7248 9199).* **Map** p270.

Leon *12 Ludgate Circus, EC4M 7LQ (7489 1580).* **Map** p270.

Leon *86 Cannon Street, EC4N 6HT (7623 9699).* **Map** p271.

Napket *34 Royal Exchange, EC3V 3LP (7621 1831).* **Map** p271.

Paul *6 Bow Lane, EC4M 9EB (7489 7925).* **Map** p271.

Paul *147 Fleet Street, EC4A 2BU (7353 5874).* **Map** p270.

Paul *Kiosk, Tower of London, EC3N 4AB (3166 6985).* **Map** p271.

Paul *60-61 Leadenhall Market, EC3V 1LT (7929 2100).* **Map** p271.

Paul *Paternoster Square, EC4M 7DX (7329 4705).* **Map** p270.

Paul *New Street Square, EC4A 3BF (7353 3648).* **Map** p270.

Ping Pong *Bow Bells House, 1 Bread Street, EC4M 9BE (7651 0880).* **Map** p270.

Ping Pong *3 Appold Street, EC2A 2AF (7422 0780).* **Map** p271.

Pizza Express *1 Byward Street, EC3R 7QN (7626 5025).* **Map** p271.

Pizza Express *1 New Fetter Lane, EC4A 1AN (7583 8880).* **Map** p270.

Pizza Express *2 Salisbury House, London Wall, EC2Y 5HN (7588 7262).* **Map** p271.

Pizza Express *Condor House, St Paul's Churchyard, EC4M 8AY (7248 9464).* **Map** p270.

Pizza Express *8 Russia Row, EC2V 8BL (7600 2232).* **Map** p270.
Pizza Express *7-9 St Bride Street, EC4A 4AS (7583 5126).* **Map** p270.
Pizza Express *20-22 Leadenhall Market, EC3V 1LR (7283 5113).* **Map** p271.
Pizza Express *125 Alban Gate, London Wall, EC2Y 5AS (7600 8880).* **Map** p270.
Pod *162 London Wall, EC2M 5QD (7256 5506).* **Map** p271.
Pod *10 Devonshire Square, EC2M 4YP (3174 0108).* **Map** p271.
Rocket *6 Adams Court, Old Broad Street, EC2N 1DX (7628 0808).* **Map** p271.
S&M Café *50 Long Lane, EC1A 9EJ (7606 6591).* **Map** p270.
S&M Café *28 Leadenhall Market, EC3V 1LR (7626 6646).* **Map** p271.
Strada *4 St Paul's Churchyard, EC4M 8AY (7248 7178).* **Map** p270.
Wagamama *1A Ropemaker Street, EC2Y 9AW (7588 2688).* **Map** p271.
Wagamama *4 Great St Thomas Apostle, EC4V 2BH (7248 5766).* **Map** p271.
Wagamama *22 Old Broad Street, EC3N 1HQ (7256 9992).* **Map** p271.
Wagamama *109 Fleet Street, EC4A 2AB (7583 7889).* **Map** p270.
Wagamama *Tower Place, off Lower Thames Street, EC3R 4EB (7283 5897).* **Map** p271.
Yo! Sushi *5-14 St Paul's Churchyard, EC4M 8AY (7248 8726).* **Map** p270.

Clerkenwell & Farringdon

Clerkenwell Kitchen NEW

27-31 Clerkenwell Close, EC1R 0AT (7101 9959/www.theclerkenwell kitchen.co.uk). Angel tube/Farringdon tube/rail. **Meals served** 8am-5pm Mon-Wed, Fri; 8am-11pm Thur. **Average** ££. **Map** p270. Café
The architectural seating and arty light fittings of the Clerkenwell

Kitchen mask an affection for serving delicious, fresh, seasonal food at fair prices. The open kitchen serves breakfast (anything from muesli to mammoth bacon and egg constructions), while at lunchtime you can get a takeaway (soup, perhaps, or a creamy courgette and parmesan tart with a lentil, mint and beetroot salad). Alternatively, sit down for the full works: each day there are six dishes offered, such as honey-roasted gammon, roasted carrots and parsley sauce, or fish stew with squid, mussels, chorizo and croûtons. Your fellow diners will most likely be as sleek and stylish as the surroundings; many of them hail from nearby architectural practices and workshops.

De Santis

11-13 Old Street, EC1V 9HL (7689 5577). Barbican tube/Old Street tube/rail/55 bus. **Meals served** 8.30am-11pm Mon-Fri. **Average** ££. **Map** p270. Café
An off-shoot of the renowned paninoteca in Milan, De Santis feels genuinely Milanese – from the clean lines of its smartly modern interior

Grazing. See p32.

to its authentic Italian menu, extensive wine list and clientele of creative media types who rely on the place for breakfast, lunch and dinner. An ability to turn out the perfect panino with bread baked daily on the premises makes De Santis a popular lunch spot, with more than 40 fillings ranging from cured meats like speck and bresaola to seafood and vegetarian options. There's also an excellent selection of soups and salads, plus pasta and risotto dishes with bold Italian character. The charismatic owner's insistence on using only top-drawer olive oil and ingredients from renowned producers proves that quality is a priority.

★ Kipferl

70 Long Lane, EC1A 9EJ (7796 2229/www.kipferl.co.uk). Barbican tube. **Meals served** 8am-5pm Mon-Fri; 9am-5pm Sat. **Average** ££. **Map** p270. Austrian

Thoughtful use of space has made this small, square gem of an Austrian café feel thoroughly modern: light, airy and uncrowded. An L-shaped counter juts into the room, displaying freshly made open sandwiches on rye, a gorgeous strudel crammed with wafer-thin slices of apple and almond, and stacks of vanilla kipferl (a traditional Austrian biscuit). The meat and cheese counter offers debreziner, käsekrainer and wiener sausages, while a corner has shelves laden with imported Austrian food and drink – wines, beers, Staud's pickles, pumpkin-seed oils and baskets of fresh bread. Lunch specials change daily and might include frittaten soup (fine strips of savoury pancake in a clear broth), cold pasta salads or hot sausages. The coffee is consistently superb.

Kurz & Lang

1 St John Street, EC1M 4AA (7253 6623/www.kurzandlang. com). Farringdon tube/rail. **Meals served** 11am-11pm Mon-Thur, Sun; 11am-7am Fri-Sun. **Average** ££. **Map** p270. German

You could do far worse than grab a wurst at this miniscule joint specialising in German sausages. You'll find the whole family here: bratwurst, rindswurst (pure beef

sausages), currywurst – even short Nürnberger-style wursts filled with punchy herbs. Roll up at the counter and order from a concise menu with three set meals – the popular classic includes a wurst of your choice, served with healthy heapings of hot sauerkraut (properly sautéed with peppercorns and niblets of bacon), buttery potato cubes and bread (add 30p to upgrade to the pretzel menu). We only wish the default were two wursts per serving, as the generous helpings of sauerkraut and potato can get a bit boring once you've finished with the sausage.

★ Little Bay

171 Farringdon Road, EC1R 3AL (7278 1234/www.little-bay.co.uk). Farringdon tube/rail. **Meals served** noon-midnight Mon-Sat; noon-11pm Sun. **Average** ££. **Map** p270. International

Years have passed since Little Bay's inventive, affordable cuisine was talk of the town, but the restaurant has proved remarkably resilient. The decor is more kitsch than ever (oh, the crimes that can be committed with a roll of turquoise velour and a staple gun), but our last visit proved that they're still serious about their food. Roast vegetable tarte tatin arrived as a pretty pinwheel with rocket and parmesan, while lamb steak was cooked to order and came with a lovely melange of baked Mediterranean vegetables and mash. The chips fried in goose fat are legendary, while desserts of the hip-sticking variety include a chocolate fondant that we found satisfyingly dark, if not strictly molten. Dine before 7pm and it's even cheaper.

Piada NEW

12-14 St John Street, EC1M 4AY (7253 0472/www.piada.co.uk). Farringdon tube/rail. **Meals served** 7am-4pm Mon-Fri. **Average** ££. **Map** p270. Café

A suitably simple black, white and red interior serves as a backdrop to this streamlined operation based around the piada, a crisp Italian flatbread infused with olive oil, packed with flavourful ingredients and then toasted on a griddle. The menu lists 16 combinations ('zero' to 'sedici', but without a 13), from the pleasantly rustic matching of mortadella and mozzarella to more sophisticated pairings (bacon, courgette and mozzarella, or chicken, brie and sun-dried tomato); the sweet variation loaded with Nutella is the only one not served with rocket. Generous bowls of soup make for a satisfying alternative, and impeccably frothed coffees and dense, clean-cut brownies encourage lingering at the handful of tables. Staff are friendly and the vibe upbeat. A superb alternative to the usual suspects when it comes to sandwich culture in the capital.

La Porchetta

84-86 Rosebery Avenue, EC1R 4QY (7837 6060). Angel tube/Farringdon tube/rail. **Meals served** noon-11pm Mon-Thur, Sun; noon-11.30pm Fri, Sat. **Average** ££. **Map** p270. Pizza & pasta

Members of this small group feel more like local trattorias than parts of a chain. The homely Farringdon branch seems full with only a few diners; tables are quite close together, so waiting staff need to be on the svelte side. La Porchetta prides itself on having a child-friendly vibe, and the casual but slightly chaotic atmosphere makes this branch a good family option in an area distinctly short on them. Foodwise, there's much to choose from: an appealing range of no-frills Italian standards that look and taste distinctly home-made – although we've found the pastas decidedly less convincing than pizzas in the past. Service can be a little slow, but that just gives you more time to watch the drama unfold around you. The basement area is ideal for groups and parties.

Real Greek
140-142 St John Street, EC1V 4UA (7253 7234/www.therealgreek.com). Farringdon tube/rail. **Meals served** noon-11pm Mon-Sat. **Average** ££. **Set meze** £10.50 per person (minimum 2). **Map** p270. Greek
Forget vine-strewn taverna clichés: the Clerkenwell branch of this popular mini-chain is stylishly contemporary. An enormous bar dominates the industrial-chic space – all exposed piping, dark wood and striking floor-to-ceiling windows – surrounded by bar stools, high benches and small tables for more intimate dining. Portions are on the small side, but the mezédes are fresh and intensely flavourful. Dishes of creamy white taramosalata, squeaky saganáki cheese, hot flatbread and tender octopus were real winners, as was a fine Cretan Xerolithia vilana wine. The well-priced souvláki menu provides spot-on sustenance for boozers (this is as much a bar as a restaurant), and service is friendly and relaxed. A genuine success, although we've known quality and service to slip during visits to the Real Greek's more touristy locations.

Santoré NEW
59-61 Exmouth Market, EC1R 4QL (7812 1488). Angel tube/Farringdon tube/rail/19, 38, 341 bus. **Lunch served** noon-3pm, **dinner served** 5.30-11pm Mon-Sat. **Average** ££. **Set lunch** £8.95 2 courses. **Set meal** (5.30-7.30pm) £12.95 2 courses. **Map** p270. Pizza & pasta
Friendly, helpful service and quality food has allowed Santoré to stand its ground on a strip teeming with aspiring eateries – although the large windows and outdoors-in ambience can make the place feel a little chilly. The antipasti selection complements the usual mixture of olives and hams with interesting additions like a tasty omelette and two tarts, one crab and one tomato. Pizzas spun in the open kitchen at the rear, are delicious, with choices ranging from the classics (funghi, margharita) to speciality Neapolitan numbers. Of the meat and fish dishes, we loved the fish stew: a tomato broth crammed with fresh mussels, clams and prawns. All this was accompanied by an enjoyable house red from the varied wine list.

Meal deals

Ambassador *55 Exmouth Market, EC1R 4QL (7837 0009/www.theambassadorcafe.co.uk).* Set lunch (Mon-Fri) £12.50 2 courses, £16 3 courses. **Map** p270. Modern European
Cicada *132-136 St John Street, EC1V 4JT (7608 1550/www.ricker restaurants.com).* Dim sum £3.50-£6. **Map** p270. Oriental
Potemkin *144 Clerkenwell Road, EC1R 5DP (7278 6661/www.potemkin.co.uk).* Set lunch (Mon-Fri) £10 2 courses. **Map** p270. Russian
Quality Chop House *92-94 Farringdon Road, EC1R 3EA (7837 5093).* Set meal (lunch Mon-Fri, Sun, 6-7.45pm Mon-Sat) £9.95 2 courses. **Map** p270. British
Tinseltown *44-46 St John Street, EC1M 4DT (7689 2424).* Set lunch (11am-5pm Mon-Fri) £5.99 1 course incl soft drink. **Map** p270. Café

In the area
Carluccio's Caffè *12 West Smithfield, EC1A 9JR (7329 5904).* **Map** p270.
Konditor & Cook *46 Gray's Inn Road, WC1X 8LR (7404 6300).* **Map** p270.
Pho *86 St John Street, EC1M 4EH (7253 7624).* **Map** p270.
Pizza Express *1 Clerkenwell Road, EC1M 5PA (7253 7770).* **Map** p270.
Pizza Express *26 Cowcross Street, EC1M 6DQ (7490 8025).* **Map** p270.

Strada *8-10 Exmouth Market,*
EC1R 4QA (7278 0800). **Map** p270.
Tas *37 Farringdon Road, EC1M*
3JB (7430 9721). **Map** p270.
Yo! Sushi *95 Farringdon Road,*
EC1R 3BT (7841 0785). **Map** p270.

Covent Garden

Abeno Too

17-18 Great Newport Street, WC2H
7JE (7379 1160). Leicester Square
tube. **Meals served** noon-11pm
Mon-Sat; noon-10.30pm Sun.
Average ££. **Set lunch** £7.80-
£12.80. **Map** p272. Japanese
This cheerful little restaurant is
London's only dedicated provider of
okonomiyaki ('your choice'). These
are hearty Japanese pancakes
cooked to order at hot plates set into
the booth tables, which separate the
central horseshoe bar from large
windows perfect for people-
watching. The batter and cabbage
base is flavoured with ginger and
spring onions before being loaded
with ingredients – from healthy
handfuls of chunky vegetables to
seafood, pork and other assorted
titbits. Popular menu combinations
include the flavoursome 'Tokyo
mix', which features pork, squid and
prawn, and a veggie variation that
fuses tofu, corn and extra spring
onion. Don't dismiss the desserts:
own-made matcha ice-cream with
rice dumpling pancake, whipped
cream, aduki beans and maple syrup
is well worth trying.

Assa

53 St Giles High Street, WC2H
8LH (7240 8256). Tottenham Court
Road tube. **Lunch served** noon-
3pm Mon-Sat. **Dinner served**
5pm-midnight daily. **Average** ££.
Set lunch £4.50-£5.50 1 course.
Map p267. Korean
Its location may be less than cheerful
and its interior far from auspicious
– a culturally neutral clutter of

functional tables and chairs broken
only by a South Korean flag painted
on the ceiling – but the food at Assa
is as authentic as it is delicious. A set
lunch of vegetables in a stone pot,
for example, comprised a hot bowl
of rice with assorted vegetables, an
unexpected helping of minced beef
and a raw egg yolk, the flavours
melding deliciously as the contents
were cooked by the container. A
range of hotpots cater to pairs – we
loved the rich chilli kick of the
bubbling beef and kimchee broth.
Service can be erratic, but it's a small
price to pay in more ways than one.

★ Bistro 1

33 Southampton Street, WC2E
7HE (7379 7585/www.bistro1.co.uk).
Covent Garden tube. **Open** noon-
11.30pm Mon-Sat; noon-10.30pm
Sun. **Average** ££. **Set lunch**
£6.90 2 courses, £7.90 3 courses.
Set dinner £9.90 2 courses, £10.90
3 courses. **Map** p273. Mediterranean
It's hard to find fault with this
colourful, unpretentious restaurant
a short hop from Covent Garden
market. Tourists drift in and out, but
there's a great deal of hand-shaking
and joking between affable staff
members and a clutch of obvious
regulars. Not even the dated interior
can detract from the charm, the
tables crammed together and the
apricot walls replete with bizarre
framed caricatures. The food is
decent: a starter of feta salad came
with generous slices of crumbly
cheese and a delicious (albeit
unadvertised) pesto dressing, while
a perfectly grilled salmon fillet on a
bed of creamed spinach was let
down only by a congealing saffron
sauce. Still, with two courses for
£6.90 (three for £7.90), it hardly
seems worth mentioning.

Bullet NEW

3rd floor, Snow & Rock, 4 Mercer
Street, WC2H 9QA (7836 4922/
www.bullet-coffee.com). Covent

Garden tube/Charing Cross tube/ rail. **Meals served** 10am-6pm Mon-Wed, Sat; 10am-7pm Thur; 11.30am-4.30pm Sun. **Average** ££. **Map** p272. Café

The need to scale three flights of stairs to access Bullet seems appropriate given its location in extreme sports shop Snow & Rock, but it's worth the effort for the coffee alone, made from own-sourced fairtrade beans. The food menu is limited, and on our visit one of two main choices (beef lasagne and quiche) was finished. A selection of baguettes and bagels was available for toasting, and we couldn't resist the anzac biscuits (made from oats and golden syrup, and identical to those sent by Australian women to their men in World War I). Still, we'd have preferred some healthier options: the only nod to the 'health and fitness' nature of the shop was a bowl of fresh fruit.

★ Café Pasta

184 Shaftesbury Avenue, WC2H 8JB (7379 0198/www.cafepasta. co.uk). Covent Garden or Leicester Square tube. **Meals served** noon-11.30pm Mon-Sat; noon-10.30pm Sun. **Average** ££. **Map** p272. Pizza & pasta

First-time diners may be surprised at the conviction with which this pasta-oriented arm of the Pizza Express franchise emulates a smart European restaurant, and that's as true of its interior – from the candle-strewn fireplace and artful light fittings to the gleaming bar and chunky wooden tables – as it is of the food itself. A starter of bruschetta came loaded with sun-dried tomatoes, red onion and shredded fresh basil; a roasted portobello mushroom pizza was effortlessly light and generous of topping; and an enormous portion of chicken and spinach risotto made up in creamy consistency what it lacked in subtlety of flavour. The location

can mean tourists aplenty, but it's an otherwise decent location for an affordable first date.

Food for Thought

31 Neal Street, WC2H 9PR (7836 9072). Covent Garden tube. **Meals served** noon-8.30pm Mon-Sat. **Lunch served** noon-5pm Sun. **Average** £. **Unlicensed**. **Corkage** no charge. **No credit cards**. **Map** p272. Vegetarian

So popular is this Covent Garden stalwart that lunchtimes often see a patient queue snaking up the stairway leading to it. Everything from the conversational efficiency of staff to the cosy seating and wobbly wooden tables lends a community feel, and the daily-changing menu is top-notch. We enjoyed a creamy moussaka packed with green lentils, and a sprightly rocket, broccoli and red pepper salad. Quiche of the day was pleasingly full of spinach but had rather too much cheese on top. Raspberry and almond scrunch, the most popular dessert, is pure decadence: cream, fresh fruit and a crunchy oat base. The ground floor offers the same cut-above vegetarian menu to take away for busy office folk on the move.

Kulu Kulu

51-53 Shelton Street, WC2H 9HE (7240 5687). Covent Garden tube. **Lunch served** noon-2.30pm Mon-Fri; noon-3.30pm Sat. **Dinner served** 5-10pm Mon-Sat. **Average** ££. **Map** p272. Japanese

This small, functional sushi bar satisfies local lunchbreakers on a daily basis. It's certainly not the most visually arresting of restaurants – decoration of its unintentionally retro wooden interior is limited to little more than a poster showing various sushi creations in glorious technicolour – but that doesn't put off the crowds that muscle around the door awaiting takeaways, or sqeeze themselves awkwardly into negligible spaces at the conveyor. Service was non-existent on our visit, so it was cheeky to ask for gratuities on the card machine. Still, we loved the crisp salmon-skin hand-rolls and deep-fried aubergine with ginger and soy sauce, and found chunky prawn tempura full of flavour and deeply satisfying.

Paul

29 Bedford Street, WC2E 9ED (7836 5321/www.paul-uk.com). Covent Garden tube. **Meals served** 7.30am-9pm Mon-Thur; 7.30am-10pm Fri; 9am-10pm Sat; 9am-8.30pm Sun. **Average** ££. **Map** p273. Café

There's something almost obscene about the speed with which branches of this French bakery have spread across the city, yet it just takes a visit to the Covent Garden flagship (launched a century after the first Paul opened its doors in tiny Croix, near Lille) to remind us of its

appeal. The shop sells an array of freshly made baguettes – the sesame and camembert creation is inspired – alongside pastries, fruit tarts and boxed salads for eaters-on-the-go. Further back is the dining area, which we love for its old-fashioned continental charm, where staff serve hot food such as quiches, soups, savoury crêpes and omelettes. They can be harried and forgetful during lunchtimes, so best go for a relaxing breakfast or afternoon tea.

Rock & Sole Plaice

47 Endell Street, WC2H 9AJ (7836 3785). Covent Garden tube. **Meals served** 10am-10.30pm Mon-Sat; 11am-10pm Sun. **Average** ££. **Map** p272. Fish & chips

This Covent Garden fixture – now run by a friendly Greek family – has been serving fish and chips to tourists and locals since 1874. The walls are covered in West End theatre posters and the vibe is busy:

Clerkenwell Kitchen. See p34.

Sophie's
STEAKHOUSE & BAR

NOW OPEN IN COVENT GARDEN

OPEN FROM MIDDAY TO LATE

all tables on the ground floor are frequently taken (remember to check if there are seats available in the basement dining room), and the outside benches are popular in summer. We've occasionally felt that the fish could be fresher, but it comes perfectly fried in well-seasoned, crunchy batter and is served with fantastic chunky chips. There's a small selection of starters including calamares, houmous and chilli king prawn rolls, while the likes of saveloys, chicken nuggets and pies await those not seeking a traditional fish supper.

Silva's

220 Shaftesbury Avenue, WC2H 8EB (7240 0028). Tottenham Court Road tube. **Meals served** 7am-7pm Mon-Fri; 8am-4pm Sat. **Average** £. **Set breakfast** (all day) £5 incl tea or coffee. **No credit cards**. **Map** p272. Café

The loathing with which many view London's immutable army of sandwich chains could easily be tempered with a trip to Silva's, with queues out the door testifying to its dominion over the hearts of local office workers and theatre types come lunchtime. The community feel is bolstered by the effortless banter between customers, most of them on first-name terms, and Silva's seen-it-all Cockney-Italian hostess, who patrols the caff-style pews and hands out wisecracks alongside plates of all-day breakfast, pasta, salads and grilled meats. Those in a hurry settle for toasted ciabattas with superior fillings (basil with mozzarella, crayfish, parma ham), washed down with a freshly squeezed juice or a Lavazza coffee with clarity and potency to put the chains to shame.

★ Wahaca NEW

66 Chandos Place, WC2N 4HG (7240 1883/www.wahaca.co.uk). Covent Garden or Leicester Square

tube. **Meals served** noon-11pm Mon-Sat; noon-10.30pm Sun. **Average** ££. **Set meal** £9.90 per person (minimum 2). **Map** p273. Mexican

Few affordable restaurants have opened in London recently to so much awed murmuring (if not critical acclaim per se) as this Tex-Mex canteen from Thomasina Miers, erstwhile winner of BBC series *MasterChef*. Get past the peak-time queues and you'll find a warehouse-style interior that's a bold mix of block colours, exposed brickwork and arty stone seating inlaid with lights, the whole thing so carefully branded (they even have their own newsletter) that world domination could well be on the horizon. We enjoyed a tapas-style selection of street snacks, including three melt-in-the-mouth pork tacos and two chicken taquitos served with tomato salsa and tangy Lancashire cheese. Quesadillas with mushrooms, cheese and huitlacoche – a fungus that grows on corn, and a Mexican delicacy – are ideal for vegetarians.

World Food Café

1st floor, 14 Neal's Yard, WC2H 9DP (7379 0298/www.worldfood cafenealsyard.co.uk). Covent Garden tube. **Meals served** 11.30am-4.30pm Mon-Fri; 11.30am-5pm Sat. **Average** ££. **Unlicensed** no alcohol allowed. **Map** p272. Vegetarian

The corporate plunder of Covent Garden's bohemian heart may continue apace, but this long-standing meatless mecca in the hippy HQ of Neal's Yard retains a homespun feel reminiscent of the protest days. Staff assemble platters in the middle of the first floor as though they were catering a church fête, and tend to be either harried or distracted when the place gets packed at lunchtimes. Appealing options from around the globe include a Turkish meze plate with

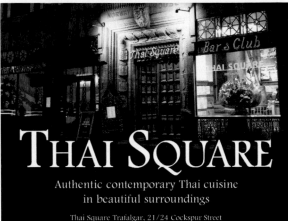

aubergines, tabouleh and pitta bread; Mexican tortilla with refried beans and guacamole; and West African sweet potato stew. The cakes are also consistently first-class. Eat at the counter or nab a window-side table to eye up passers-by in the bustling courtyard below.

Zizzi

20 Bow Street, WC2E 7AW (7836 6101/www.zizzi.co.uk). **Meals served** noon-11.30pm Mon-Sat; noon-11pm Sun. **Average** ££. **Map** p272. Pizza & pasta

A sense of warmth greets you at this Covent Garden branch of Zizzi. Perhaps it's the massive wood-fired oven; maybe it's the body heat generated by pre-theatre diners crammed into closely packed tables. It's probably not the brusque service, but then that's not why people flock to this more refined sister of the ASK chain. It's more to do with the food: simple Italian dishes to suit most taste buds, at a price that won't break the bank. An antipasti platter was a predictable but pleasant mix of the likes of prosciutto, olives, buffalo mozzarella and red onion foccaccia. We also enjoyed our pizzas, a generously topped diavolo with pepperoni and hot peppers, and an indulgent dolcelatte smothered with roast artichokes, sun-dried tomatoes and creamy gorgonzola cheese.

Meal deals

Le Deuxième *65A Long Acre, WC2E 9JH (7379 0033/www.le deuxieme.com).* Set meal (noon-3pm, 5-7.30pm, 10pm-midnight) £13.50 2 courses, £16.50 3 courses. **Map** p272. International
Med Kitchen *24 Cambridge Circus, WC2H 8AA (7240 4748/ www.medkitchen.co.uk).* Set lunch (noon-7pm daily) £13.50 2 courses. **Map** p272. Mediterranan
Med Kitchen *50-51 St Martin's Lane, WC2N 4EA (7836 8289/*

www.medkitchen.co.uk). Set lunch (noon-5pm Mon-Fri) £13.50 2 courses. **Map** p273. Mediterranan
Mela *152-156 Shaftesbury Avenue, WC2H 8HL (7836 8635/www.mela restaurant.co.uk).* Set lunch £2.95-£5.95 1 course. Set meal (5-7pm, 10-11pm) £10.95 3 courses. **Map** p272. Indian
Mon Plaisir *21 Monmouth Street, WC2H 9DD (7836 7243/www.mon plaisir.co.uk).* Set meal (5.45-7pm Mon-Sat; after 10pm Mon-Thur) £13.50 2 courses, £15.50 3 courses. **Map** p272. French

In the area

Café Pasta *2-4 Garrick Street, WC2E 9BH (7497 2779).* **Map** p273.
Canela *33 Earlham Street, WC2H 9LS (7240 6926).* **Map** p272.
Carluccio's Caffè *2A Garrick Street, WC2E 9BH (7836 0990).* **Map** p273.
Gourmet Burger Kitchen *13-14 Maiden Lane, WC2E 7NE (7240 9617).* **Map** p273.
Hamburger Union *4-6 Garrick Street, WC2E 9BH (7379 0412).* **Map** p273.
Just Falafs *27B Covent Garden Piazza, WC2E 8RD (7240 3838).* **Map** p273.
Masala Zone *48 Floral Street, WC2E 9DA (7379 0101).* **Map** p272.
Nando's *66-68 Chandos Place, WC2N 4HG (7836 4719).* **Map** p273.
Pâtisserie Valerie *15 Bedford Street, WC2E 9HE (7379 6428).* **Map** p273.
Pizza Express *9 Bow Street, WC2E 7AH (7240 3443).* **Map** p272.
Real Greek *60-62 Long Acre, WC2E 9JE (7240 2292).* **Map** p272.
Sofra *36 Tavistock Street, WC2E 7PB (7240 3773).* **Map** p272.
Strada *6 Great Queen Street, WC2B 5DH (7405 6293).* **Map** p272.
Wagamama *1 Tavistock Street, WC2E 7PG (7836 3330).* **Map** p273.

Patogh. See p49.

Edgware Road

Abu Ali
*136-138 George Street, W1H 5LD
(7724 6338). Edgware Road or
Marble Arch tube.* **Meals served**
9am-11pm daily. **Average ££.**
No credit cards. Map p276.
Lebanese
Luxuries aren't a priority at this dog-
eared Lebanese café: those smoking
shishas out front are warmed by
electric fan heaters instead of lamps
and drink tea brewed from bags
rather than leaves, while the interior
is like a Middle Eastern greasy
spoon – the Formica tables even
boast red and brown sauce
dispensers. For all this, few local
establishments have such a homely
feel: nary a customer arrives or
leaves without first sharing a joke
and a smoke with Ali the owner,
who seems happiest stoking coals
for the pipes on a makeshift burner
set on the pavement. The food is
excellent: creamy houmous was a
pleasure to mop up with a pile of
warm pitta; a main of shish taouk
(chicken kebab with garlic sauce)
was tender and pleasantly pungent,
another of minced lamb kofte juicy
and generous. Abu Ali is a book that
shouldn't be judged by its rather
battered front cover.

Al-Dar
*61-63 Edgware Road, W2 2HZ
(7402 2541). Marble Arch tube.*
Meals served 10am-1am daily.
Average ££. Set meze £9.50-
£10.50. **Map** p276. Lebanese

It can sometimes feel as though there's little more than tradition maintaining the prominence of this longstanding Edgware Road institution: its functional interior is largely devoid of decoration, let alone personality, and there's none of the familial warmth that characterises other Lebanese restaurants in the area – staff are efficient rather than empathic. That said, we've eaten well here in the past: an extensive variety of kebabs are cooked to order behind the gleaming grill station, and the leather-bound menus list a decent range of dishes to suit every occasion – from breakfasts of eggs with minced lamb to Lebanese pizzas topped with minced lamb, peppers and pine kernels. Prices aren't the lowest locally, but be sure to choose carefully and you can still feast for a tenner.

★ Mandalay

444 Edgware Road, W2 1EG (7258 3696/www.mandalayway.com). Edgware Road tube. **Lunch served** noon-2.30pm, **dinner served** 6-10.30pm Mon-Sat. **Average** ££. **Map** p276. Burmese
This tiny eaterie – constituting just ten wipe-down tables crammed together in simple surroundings – is an unexpected treat. Fans of both Indian and Chinese food will be happy, as Burmese cooking fuses them together with the hot-sweet-sour flavours of South-east Asia: think chilli, coconut, cumin, turmeric, dried shrimps and lemongrass. Don't be daunted by the menu of unfamiliar dishes – Mandalay's charming owners will happily guide you through. To start, try tangles of beansprouts deep-fried in batter and served with silky tamarind sauce. A main course of spiced spinach with potatoes was full of flavour; another of cumin-spiked meatballs in a savoury tomato sauce was fabulous.

Don't leave without trying the fabulous banana fritters, crisp on the outside, melting within.

Melur NEW

175A Edgware Road, W2 1ET (7706 8083/www.melur.co.uk). Edgware Road or Marble Arch tube. **Meals served** noon-11pm daily. **Average** ££. **Map** p276. Malaysian
Melur is a pleasing mix of bronze tiled flooring, redwood tables, brown leather seats and a glass-fronted bar, where expats, students and office workers gather for cheap, cheerful Malaysian eats. Tofu sumbat (deep-fried bean curd served with sliced cucumber and bean sprouts) was a snappy match for its zesty peanut sauce. Sambal udang (stir-fried prawns with a chilli condiment) was deliciously piquant. But mee goreng mamak, a stir-fried noodle dish with a tomato undertone, was let down by overcooked chicken. We finished with bubur cha cha, a typical Malaysian dessert of sweet potato, yam and sago pearls with coconut milk. The drinks list features cocktails, wine and Tiger beer, and service is fleet-footed and cheerful.

Meya Meya

13 Bell Street, NW1 5BY (7723 8983). Edgware Road tube. **Meals served** 9am-11pm daily. **Average** £. **Unlicensed. Corkage** £5. **Map** p276. Egyptian
Lord only knows how many people have slogged up Edgware Road to Meya Meya, only to then stand aghast at its sanitised takeaway interior before turning and shuffling off back down the street. Pity them for not knowing that the restaurant proper actually lies down a pokey flight of stairs, and that it's here where those in the know dine on the Egyptian fiteers (stuffed filo pastry envelopes most closely resembling a pizza) for which Meya Meya is best known: the Cairo fiteer, for example,

contains a hearty helping of smoked beef (basturma) alongside tomatoes, peppers and olives. Those willing to explore the menu will find plenty of alternatives to fiteer, including Egyptian staples such as fuul and falafel – the former well seasoned, the latter crunchy on the outside, authentically green and fluffy within. It might not look like much, but Meya Meya is full of surprises.

★ Patogh

8 Crawford Place, W1H 5NE (7262 4015). Edgware Road tube. **Meals served** 12.30-11pm daily. **Average ££. Unlicensed. Corkage** no charge. **No credit cards. Map** p276. Iranian

Patogh forsakes the forced orientalism of many Middle Eastern restaurants in favour of almost bare mud-coloured walls. Its crew of paper-hat-wearing, Farsi-speaking staff weave effortlessly between a handful of shared tables spread over two tiny floors. The menu includes workmanlike starters of masto khiar (yoghurt, cucumber and mint dip), masto musir (yoghurt with shallots) and houmous, along with freshly baked Iranian bread. Mains are served, like the starters, on functional metal plates, and consist of lamb and chicken kebabs – both tender and delicious, although the latter could have done with longer in the traditional lemon and saffron marinade – either accompanied with buttered rice or wrapped in bread. You could well be in a café in Tehran's central bazaar, were it not for the bottles of BYO booze.

Ranoush Juice Bar

43 Edgware Road, W2 2JR (7723 5929/www.maroush.com). Marble Arch tube. **Meals served** 8am-3am daily. **Average ££. No credit cards. Map** p276. Lebanese

Ranoush, part of the successful Maroush empire, has been squeezing juices and churning out

shawarmas for decades. Behind the busy counter, a modest selection of meze dishes is displayed. Dishes such as falafel can also be wrapped in shami bread – along with pickles and garlicky tahini sauce – to take away; alternatively, you can order your food 'on a plate' and eat at one of the café tables, or while propping up the counter. It may have been fast, but everything was carefully garnished and well presented on our visit. Batata hara (spiced potatoes) contained large chunks of pepper and slices of garlic the size of 1p coins; falafel were crunchy and spicy; tabouleh arrived a little coarsely chopped, but with a lively citrus zing. A great place to call in, both by day or night.

Meal deals

Arturo *23 Connaught Street, W2 2AY (7706 3388/www.arturo restaurant.co.uk).* Set meal £13.95 2 courses. **Map** p276. Italian

In the area

ASK *17-20 Kendal Street, W2 2AE (7724 4637).* **Map** p276.

Euston

Chutneys NEW

124 Drummond Street, NW1 2PA (7388 0604). Euston Square or Warren Street tube/Euston tube/ rail. **Meals served** noon-11pm Mon-Sat; noon-10pm Sun. **Average ££. Set buffet** £6.95. **Set thali** £6.95-£15.95. **Map** p266. Indian

Five minutes north of Euston station, Drummond Street is an unexpected slice of the subcontinent, dotted with Indian sweet emporiums and well-stocked grocers' shops and restaurants, with none of Brick Lane's touts or tourists. Though Chutney's tinted windows and plain exterior look less than promising, inside it's far more inviting: a cosy, convivial dining room painted in rich reds and ochres. The main draw is the all-vegetarian buffet, served every lunchtime and all day on Sunday: vats of saag aloo, delicately-spiced tofu curry and creamy lentil dahl jostle for space with own-made chutneys and chilli-spiked veg of every description, from chickpeas and red cabbage to gleaming baby aubergines. Save space for dessert; we recommend the sweetly sticky semolina pudding, fragrant with cinnamon and cardamom.

Diwana Bhel Poori House

121-123 Drummond Street, NW1 2HL (7387 5556). Euston Square or Warren Street tube/Euston tube/rail. **Meals served** noon-11pm daily. **Average** ££. **Set buffet** (noon-2.30pm) £6.95 (4-7s half-price; under-4s free). **Set thali** £7.95-£8.95. **Unlicensed**. **Corkage** no charge. **Map** p266. Indian

Diwana has been a Drummond Street fixture for time out of mind, drawing families from across the capital with its upbeat atmosphere and menu of south Indian vegetarian street food. The bright interior is functional at best – its wooden panelling, pine tables and dog-eared, laminated menus more reminiscent of a mountain-top canteen than a reputable urban restaurant – but that only further emphasises the quality of the cooking. Bhel poori is the big draw, small plates of savoury snacks (including puffed pooris, samosas, dhals and chutneys), suitable as starters or, ordered in large enough quantities, a meal in themselves. Those seeking more substantial feeding can opt for a crispy filled dosa or a vegetarian thali mixing rice with a variety of vegetable curries; there's also a hearty lunch buffet for those less easily satisfied. Staff aren't exactly renowned for dispensing pleasantries, but service is efficient.

Greens & Beans NEW

131 Drummond Street, NW1 2HL (7380 0857/www.greensandbeans. biz). Euston Square or Warren Street tube/Euston tube/rail. **Meals served** 9am-4pm Mon-Fri. **Average** ££. **Set buffet** (noon-3.30pm) £6.50. **Map** p266. Vegetarian

Drummond Street is best known for its vegetarian Indian diners, making this more modern European eaterie stand out. The ground floor's popular takeaway buffet serves salads and hot dishes, while the basement café feels bright thanks to clean white walls, wooden tables and – on our recent visit – a chipper Australian waitress. Smoothies were thick and divine, but the main courses proved disappointing: nut roast was bland and perched on watery potatoes; a plateful of delicious sprouts with tasteless tomatoes needing more dressing. Happily, pizza was excellent: topped with creamy feta, spinach and thick, flavoursome tomato sauce. G&B is a great place for breakfast; the menu includes millet or quinoa porridge, gluten-free muesli, scrambled eggs, veggie sausages, and wheat or barley grass concoctions.

Pasta Plus

62 Eversholt Street, NW1 1DA (7383 4943/www.pastaplus.co.uk). Euston Square tube/Euston tube/rail. **Lunch served** noon-2.30pm Mon-Fri. **Dinner served** 5.30-10.30pm Mon-Sat. **Average** ££. **Map** p266. Pizza & pasta

Its location on a road known for saunas and strip clubs might make one wonder what the 'Plus' implies, but this family-run Italian offers only decent, good-value food and swift service. A conservatory area lets in plenty of natural light, and the warm welcome is strengthened by complimentary bruschetta. A wide range of main courses includes fish, meat and pasta dishes (all with own-made pasta), but notably no pizza. Spaghetti pescatore arrived piled high with clams, mussels, king prawns and crab claws, and was thoroughly tasty; crab ravioli had a generous amount of crab meat, but the pasta pockets were thick and unpleasantly chewy. The various desserts aren't really worth saving room for – which is lucky, as portions are seriously large.

Peyton & Byrne NEW

Wellcome Collection, 183 Euston Road, NW1 2BE (7611 2142/ www.peytonandbyrne.com). Euston Square tube/Euston tube/rail. **Open** 10am-6pm Mon-Wed, Fri, Sat; 10am-10pm Thur; 11am-6pm Sun. **Lunch served** noon-3pm daily. **Average** ££. **Map** p266. Café

A justifiably popular café that attracts local office workers as well as visitors to the Wellcome Collection, Peyton & Byrne's chic, colourful interior is spot-on, but keeping floors and tables clean and turned over at peak times is a challenge. The counter holds a spectacular array of artful cakes (cupcakes, juicy wedges of pear and almond tart, multi-layered victoria sponge slices), plus a good range of savoury food (salads, pâtés, sausage rolls and pies). For more substantial fare, order the likes of Herdwick lamb cutlets, or spiced tuna burger with chilli and mango chutney. A roasted vegetable skewer, lacking the advertised spelt salad, was below the standard we've come to expect here, but normal service was resumed with a robust, gluten-free chocolate and almond cake.

In the area

Paul *Colonnade, Euston Station, NW1 2RT (7388 9382).* **Map** p266.
Pizza Express *Clifton House, 93-99 Euston Road, NW1 2RA (7383 7102).* **Map** p267.
Prezzo *161 Euston Road, NW1 2BD (7387 5587).* **Map** p266.

Rasa Express *327 Euston Road, NW1 3AD (7387 8974).* **Map** p266.

Fitzrovia

★ Benito's Hat NEW

56 Goode Street, W1T 4NB (7637 3732/www.benitos-hat.com). Goodge Street tube. **Meals served** 11.30am-10pm Mon-Wed, Sun; 11.30am-11pm Thur-Sat. **Average** £. **Map** p266. Mexican

London's Tex-Mex eateries are currently ten a peso, and while there's only one Benito's Hat, the branded interior looks ripe for replication – no doubt something owner Ben Fordham, a former City lawyer, has considered. Lime and orange walls overlook functional wooden tables, with cactus pots sitting precariously among the condiments. The fast-moving production line serves some of the best burritos in town. We plumped for one loaded with slow-cooked pork, and loved the soft, floury tortilla, the freshness of the fiery salsa brava (made several times daily) and the black beans, which were authentically flavoured with avocado leaves. Chicken, steak and vegetable options are also available, as are suitably merciless margaritas.

El Burrito NEW

5 Charlotte Place, W1T 1SF (7580 5048). Goodge Street tube. **Lunch served** 11am-4pm Mon-Fri. **Average** £. **Map** p266. Mexican

El Burrito is currently doing battle with Benito's Hat (*see above*) for control of the area's lunchtime hordes; its prices are slightly lower, but whether its tacos, burritos and quesadillas are better remains open to debate. A queue snakes out of the door at peak times, and most customers choose to take their food away with them – not surprising, given the rather uninspiring interior (the small room at the rear, largely undecorated save a handful of functional tables and chairs, is an unappealing place to eat). Burritos are the main draw; they're filling, juicy and fresh-tasting, though go easy on the potent hot sauce. Our one complaint? Being charged 50p for guacamole or pico de gallo salsa seems a little unfair.

Hamburger Union

64 Tottenham Court Road, W1T 2ET (7636 0011/www.hamburger union.com). Goodge Street or Tottenham Court Road tube. **Meals served** 11.30am-10.30pm Mon-Sat; 11.30am-8pm Sun. **Average ££.** **Map** p266. Burgers

With its canteen feel and retro-modern trappings, Hamburger Union's rapidly expanding chain isn't as fancy a looker as some of its competitors in the gourmet burger world. Despite great claims for the provenance of its grass-reared beef, this fast-food feel is carried over to the burgers. Bacon cheeseburger was flaccid and tasteless (not least the bacon, which was practically translucent), but there are some imaginative alternatives, including a flavoursome paprika-packed chorizo sandwich, or another version with citrus-marinated halloumi cheese. Milkshakes come in ice-cold metal tubs alongside Chegworth juices and Fentimans soft drinks. For the diet-conscious, burgers are available bread-free; for everyone else, we heartily recommend a bowl of the golden, fluffy fries, good enough to be ordered on their own.

★ Indian YMCA

41 Fitzroy Square, W1T 6AQ (7387 0411/www.indianymca.org). Great Portland Street or Warren Street tube. **Lunch served** noon-2pm Mon-Fri; 12.30-1.30pm Sat, Sun. **Dinner served** 7-8.30pm daily. **Average £. Unlicensed** no alcohol allowed. **Map** p266. Indian

Its plastic tables and cheerlessly upholstered chairs may sit somewhere between an office canteen and a cheap hotel lobby, but the cafeteria of this longstanding home for Indian students retains a communal atmosphere befitting a YMCA. Grab a tray and point at whatever you like the look of: curries, chutneys and functional fruit desserts are displayed on plates at the open kitchen. Pay at the till (you'll struggle to break a fiver), find a pew and get to know your neighbour. Chicken curry was delicately spiced but heavy on bones, while a dry vegetable curry was pleasingly powerful, the rice fluffy and generously portioned. It's basic in the extreme, but as popular with patrons rattling cutlery as those who eat with their hands.

Istanbul Meze

100 Cleveland Street, W1P 5DP (7387 0785/www.istanbulmeze.co.uk). Great Portland Street or Warren Street tube. **Meals served** noon-11pm Mon-Thur; noon-midnight Fri, Sat. **Dinner served** 5-11pm Sun. **Average ££. Set lunch** £8.90 2 courses. **Set dinner** £11.90 2 courses. **Set meze** £20. **Map** p266. Turkish

Patterned kilim mats decorate the walls at this popular Turkish restaurant, which retains a local feel despite its central location. Quality starters of grilled halloumi cheese and sautéed Albanian liver were impressive, but would have been better mopped up with pide than the basic pittas we were given. A main course of chicken beyti was lightly spiced and beautifully grilled, with a moist centre; rice was typically Turkish and featured slivers of vermicelli. A satisfying et sote casserole was packed with lamb cubes, tomatoes and green peppers. Worth visiting for its atmosphere alone – on our busy Saturday night visit, a party of young Turks sang cheerfully in the background.

Lantana. See p55.

Italiano Coffee Company

*46 Goodge Street, W1T 4LU
(7580 9688). Goodge Street tube.*
Meals served 7am-11pm Mon-Fri;
8am-11pm Sat, Sun. **Average**
£. Map p266. Pizza & pasta

Its shared metal tables, diner style
seating and tricolour branding seem
more American than Italian, and
there can be few more hectic places
to while away a lunch hour – not to
mention a more farcical ordering
procedure. For those unversed:
mumble your name at the frantic
cashier, then hover with the crowds
while equally overworked chefs
prepare your pizza, prematurely
bolting towards the counter as
names that sound like yours are
called out from the tickets (and they
all sound like yours). A handful of
pizzas are on offer, none of them
outstanding: funghi and neptune
pizzas were alike in their shortages
of mushrooms and anchovies
respectively, and while well cooked
and crisp at the edges, both had an
unpleasant film of oil.

★ Lantana NEW

*13 Charlotte Place, W1T 1SN
(7637 3347/www.lantanacafe.co.uk).
Goodge Street tube.* **Meals served**
8am-3pm Mon-Fri; 9am-3pm Sat.
Average ££. Map p266. Café

This Antipodean-style café was
opened in 2008 by chirpy proprietor
Shelagh Ryan, who hails from Down
Under. It's a good-looking place and
quieter than many in the area,
possibly because of the marginally
higher prices. The super salads
(including one featuring smoky
aubergine and another comprising a
crunchy sugarsnap and red cabbage
combo), brilliant cakes and gourmet
breakfast offerings (poached fruit,
corn fritters, ricotta hotcakes) make
Lantana very different to the usual
daytime caffs. The coffee comes
from Monmouth, and the espresso

machine is the coffee connoisseur's
choice: La Marzocco – we just wish
the barista wouldn't keep slamming
filters on the workstation so loudly.
There's not a great deal of space, but
a few seats in the pedestrianised
alley cater to alfresco diners.

Miga NEW

*29 Goodge Street, W1T 2PP
(7636 7688). Goodge Street tube.*
Lunch served noon-4pm Mon-Sat.
Dinner served 6-11pm daily.
Average ££. Map p266. Korean

This site has witnessed a fairly high
turnover of restaurants in recent
years, but this friendly Korean
eaterie is to be welcomed with open
arms. Decor is simple, there are fresh
flowers on each table and staff are
encouraging to anyone showing an
interest in Korean food. It's worth
ordering the namul, a generous plate
of assorted pickled vegetable
accompaniments (spinach, radish,
sesame-fragrant beansprouts), to
start, or to share. Stone pot bibimbap
(rice, vegetables and sliced beef in a
hot bowl) arrived bright and
sizzling, the rice eventually forming
a succulent crust against the heat of
the container. There's always a soup
special for lunch – on our visit a
simple white miso, wakame and
spring onion number – and dessert
might be red bean or green tea ice-
cream, or a fruit plate.

Ooze

*62 Goodge Street, W1T 4NE
(7436 9444/www.ooze.biz). Goodge
Street tube.* **Meals served** noon-
11pm Mon-Sat. **Average** £££.
Map p266. Italian

Runner-up in the Cheap Eats
category of the 2007 Time Out
Eating & Drinking Awards, Ooze is
still thriving. Risotto is the USP,
though there are alternatives: three
juicy tiger prawns with garlic, chilli
and white wine to start, say, or slow-
roast lamb shank with creamed
potatoes to follow. Our two meaty

risottos (ribeye with sweet onions, rocket and red wine, and pancetta with rosemary, borlotti beans and radicchio) were punchily flavoured and filling, although we were equally tempted by the alle vongole variation (featuring clams, white wine, chilli and garlic). Desserts include own-made ice-creams, pannacotta and tiramisu, plus a tart of the day and Italian cheeses. Service is smiley, and there's a nicely priced wine list. Artful lighting makes the place cosier by night.

Pho

3 Great Titchfield Street, W1W 8AX (7436 0111/www.phocafe.co.uk). Oxford Circus tube. **Meals served** noon-10.30pm Mon-Sat. **Average** ££. **Map** p266. Vietnamese

This second branch of Clerkenwell's original Pho is making waves with the Fitzrovian lunchtime crowd. A great deal of this is thanks to its clean-cut, modern interior – the grey, red and white colour scheme is the epitome of minimalist chic – although most are drawn to its menu, which offers a basic round-up of Vietnam's best-known dishes. Pho's eponymous dish of beef noodle soup was, sadly, let down by the broth on our recent visit – it lacked depth, tasting more of carrots than meat and subtle spices – but a dish of fresh summer rolls was faultless, bursting with herbs and juicy prawns. 'Weasel' coffee was also perfectly brewed, rich with sweet condensed milk. Pho offers only a small sampling of authentic Vietnamese cuisine, but it does so with a fair amount of style.

★ Ragam

57 Cleveland Street, W1T 4JN (7636 9098/www.mcdosa.co.uk). Goodge Street tube. **Lunch served** noon-3pm daily. **Dinner served** 6-11.15pm Mon-Thur; 6-11.30pm Fri, Sat; 6-10.30pm Sun. **Average** ££. **Map** p266. Indian

Ooze. See p55.

A tucked away location off the beaten track should mean relative obscurity for this homely South Indian restaurant, but a reputation many competitors would kill for packs it out at lunch and dinner every day. Punters aren't here for the interior, which appears not to have changed in the three decades since the place opened: dog-eared domestic wallpaper and a few ethnic prints constitute decoration, while laminated menus on the community hall-style tables instil a sense of dread in those ignorant of the quality of what's on offer. We started with a chicken and potato dosa so filling and flavourful that we could have ended there too. A main of Keralan mutton curry featured a satisfyingly potent sauce and heaps of tender meat, while a side of spiced aubergine virtually melted in the mouth. Famously friendly service provides another reason to return.

★ Rasa Express

5 Rathbone Street, W1T 1NX (7637 0222/www.rasarestaurants. com). Goodge Street or Tottenham

Court Road tube. **Lunch served** noon-3pm Mon-Fri. **Average** £. **Map** p266. Indian

There's nothing glamorous about eating out of a plastic tray, yet local office workers regard a lunch from Rasa Express with the reverence most reserve for dinner at the Ivy. Meat and vegetarian curry trays are plucked from a heated cabinet inside the front door, with mango lassi in polystyrene cups and plastic cutlery for the taking. Those keen to tuck in immediately do so at linen-clad tables set against walls as pink as the exterior. Chicken biryani was delicately spiced and big on chunks of tender meat, and came with a chapati, a chickpea curry with a surprising chilli kick, a mild mung bean curry, a dry lentil side and a sweet rice pudding – and all for less than a fiver. Rasa Express is a local legend in its own lunchtime.

★ Scandinavian Kitchen NEW

61 Great Titchfield Street, W1W 7PP (7580 7161/www.scandi kitchen.co.uk). Oxford Street tube. **Meals served** 8am-7pm Mon-Fri; 10am-6pm Sat; 10am-4pm Sun. **Average** ££. **Set lunch** £4.95-£7.75. **Map** p266. Scandinavian

Cute knob-handled mugs, curvy plywood chairs and bright red walls make the Scandinavian Kitchen feel approachable rather than Arctic cool. The lively crowd of local office workers is kept entertained by flirty male staff breaking occasionally into song and a self-deprecating sheet of instructions for eating open sandwiches. Choose from, say, chicken and green pepper salad, Danish or Swedish meatballs, Norwegian smoked salmon, roast beef, or three types of herring; there's also hot soup and hot dogs. Tasty Scandinavian treats include Delicato marzipan nibbles and Gevalia filter coffee. Order at the counter, then take your tray over to the tables. All in all, this healthy lunch spot is more fun than most.

Squat & Gobble

69 Charlotte Street, W1T 4RJ (7580 5338/www.squatandgobble. co.uk). Goodge Street or Warren Street tube. **Meals served** 7am-8pm Mon-Fri; 9am-5pm Sat. **Average** ££. **Map** p266. Café

Treading a balanced line between caff-like homeliness, canteen-style effectiveness and bistro funkiness, Squat & Gobble has proved to be a palpable hit amid myriad lunching options on the restaurant super-highway that is Charlotte Street. Whether you go for a sarnie or a jacket, you can choose from basic fodder (fish-finger sandwich, spud with beans, cheese and bacon) or slightly more imaginative fillings (deep-fried brie and cranberry baguette, tarragon chicken filled potato). There are also plentiful breakfasts, salads, soups and mains up for grabs, from fish cakes to falafel. It's not the biggest venue in town – and queues can be a problem at peak times – but staff are warm and welcoming, and takeaways are always an option.

Vapiano NEW

19-21 Great Portland Street, W1W 8QB (7268 0080/www.vapiano international.com). Oxford Circus tube. **Meals served** 11am-11pm Mon-Fri; noon-11pm Sat; noon-10pm Sun. **Average** ££. **Map** p266. Pizza & pasta

Set over two floors on the site of former brewery-bar Mash, this inaugural UK branch of the popular German chain offers floating fireplaces and 'help yourself' basil gardens to combat the fact that it's essentially a fast-food restaurant – albeit one with smart seating and a swanky chip card, handed to you at the door, on which you clock whatever you order from the range of food court-style pizza and pasta bars, eventually paying when you leave. Food is gathered into groups A (very cheap) to D (quite cheap), although we found simple dishes the most successful: a large caprese pizza was crisp in the right places and subtly seasoned, while pasta with crayfish tails and lobster sauce was limp and strangely flavourless.

Yo! Sushi

11-13 Bayley Street, WC1B 3HD (7636 0076/www.yosushi.com). Tottenham Court Road tube. **Meals served** noon-10pm Mon-Sat, 1-6pm Sun. **Average** ££. **Map** p277. Japanese

With its bizarre '70s tiling, dangling disco light fixtures and double-overhead steel archway looming over diners like some sort of teleportation device, the interior of this branch of Yo! Sushi retains a dated futurism akin to something out of *Battlestar Galactica*. No robots, sadly (Yo! Sushi phased them out years ago), although the need for waiting staff is already negligible: water is delivered from taps at the tables, which also have in-built wasabi drawers, and the countless colour-coded sushi dishes zip purposefully along the kaiten conveyor. Sushi was fresh-tasting and pieces were satisfyingly large: barbecued eel inside-out rolls stuffed with crab, avocado and shichimi (Japanese chilli) were pleasantly powerful; tuna nigiri was meltingly tender; and sides of spicy pepper squid and roasted duck gyoza were crisp and delicious. Only salmon sashimi with a rubbery texture disappointed – and the bill, which was higher than expected.

Meal deals

Archipelago *110 Whitfield Street, W1T 5ED (7383 3346).* Set lunch £12.50 per person (minimum 2). **Map** p266. International

Crazy Bear *26-28 Whitfield Street, W1T 2RG (7631 0088/www.crazy beargroup.co.uk).* Dim sum £3.90-£7. **Map** p266. Oriental

Özer *5 Langham Place, W1B 3DG (7323 0505/www.sofra.co.uk).* Set lunch (noon-6pm) £10.95 1 course incl drink; set dinner (6-11pm) £12.95 1 course incl drink; set meze £10.95-£13.95. **Map** p266. Turkish

In the area

Carluccio's Caffè *8 Market Place, W1W 8AG (7636 2228).* **Map** p266.
dim t *32 Charlotte Street, W1T 2NQ (7637 1122).* **Map** p266.
Harry Morgan's *6 Market Place, W1W 8AF (7580 4849).* **Map** p266.
Leon *275 Regent Street, W1B 2HB (7495 1514).* **Map** p266.
Nando's *57-59 Goodge Street, W1T 1TH (7637 0708).* **Map** p266.
Nando's *2 Berners Street, W1T 3LA (7323 9791).* **Map** p266.
Pâtisserie Valerie *24 Torrington Place, WC1E 7HJ (7580 5249).* **Map** p266.
Paul *277-278 Regent Street, W1B 2HD (7491 8957).* **Map** p266.
Peyton & Byrne *Heal's, 196 Tottenham Court Road, W1T 7LQ (7580 3451).* **Map** p266.
Ping Pong *48 Newman Street, W1T 1QQ (7291 3080).* **Map** p266.
Ping Pong *48 Eastcastle Street, W1W 8DX (7079 0550).* **Map** p266.
Pizza Express *7-9 Charlotte Street, W1T 1RB (7580 1110).* **Map** p266.
Pizza Express *4-5 Langham Place, W1B 3DG (7580 3700).* **Map** p266.
Strada *9-10 Market Place, W1W 8AQ (7580 4644).* **Map** p266.
Ultimate Burger *98 Tottenham Court Road, W1T 4TR (7436 5355).* **Map** p266.
Zizzi *33-41 Charlotte Street, W1T 1RR (7436 9440).* **Map** p266.

Holborn

Aki

182 Gray's Inn Road, WC1X 8EW (7837 9281/www.akidemae.com). Chancery Lane tube. **Lunch served**

noon-2.30pm Mon-Fri. **Dinner served** 6-11pm Mon-Fri; 6-10.30pm Sat. **Average £££. Set lunch** £8.50-£17. **Map** p267. Japanese
Its unassuming and rather worn interior belies the standard of Japanese cooking at Aki. The chef's recommendations make a good diving-in point, or there's a selection of skewered foods such as yakitori or kushiage (battered, deep-fried morsels on a stick). The many small dishes are to be enjoyed with the menu's various sakés and shochus: we went for the delicate chazuke, tender raw sea bream on rice, with hot green tea poured over and a punchy steamed head of garlic with miso paste – best enjoyed with shochu. Nikujaga, a warming braised beef dish with konnyaku jelly, had a sweet and savoury flavour. Sautéed shimeji mushrooms were robustly meaty, and deep-fried oysters hot and juicy. A dish of slightly overcooked sardines proved the only minor letdown.

Bar Polski

11 Little Turnstile, WC1V 7DX (7831 9679). Holborn tube. **Meals served** 4-10pm Mon; 12.30-10pm Tue-Fri. **Dinner served** 6-10pm Sat. **Average ££. Map** p267. Polish
We've always loved Bar Polski for its mix of informal bar aesthetics and decent Polish home-style cooking, but on our last visit it resembled a rowdy pub; a large group was braying over thumping music, making it difficult to enjoy the enterprising range of Polish beers (including lesser-known dark brews like Okocim Porter), the pleasure of having a shot of raspberry syrup in our Zywiec or Tyskie, or the well-organised menu of over 60 vodkas. Vibrant barszcz and tender herring salad went down a treat, but greasy fried pierogi and heavy potato pancakes did little more than mop up the booze. Bar

Polski needs to get its cool vibe back, and we sincerely hope it does so sooner rather than later.

Fryer's Delight

19 Theobald's Road, WC1X 8SL (7405 4114). Holborn tube/19, 38, 55 bus. **Meals served** noon-10pm Mon-Sat. **Average ££. Unlicensed. Corkage** no charge. **No credit cards. Map** p267. Fish & chips
Virtually unaltered since opening in 1962, Fryer's Delight is decked out in a variety of retro caff styles (false ceiling, one mirrored wall, booth seating, pink and pale blue Formica). 'The freshest fish available', says the leaping salmon on the cheery sign outside; sure enough, our haddock was dipped in batter and deep-fried in beef dripping to order. Portions are big, but the plates are curiously small; you'll be grateful for the side plate that holds your generous helping of two pickled onions. The 'no-frills' ethos extends to the menu – there's nothing so fancy as mushy peas on offer, only the processed version – but who cares when the basics are done so well?

Meal deals

Terrace *Lincoln's Inn Fields, WC2A 3LJ (7430 1234/www.theterrace. info).* Set meal (noon-3pm, 5.30-7pm) £15.95 2 courses, £17.75 3 courses. **Map** p267. Modern European

In the area

Café Pasta *95-97 High Holborn, WC1V 6LF (7242 4580).* **Map** p267.
Hummus Bros *37-63 Southampton Row, WC1B 4DA (7404 7079).* **Map** p267.
Paul *296-298 High Holborn, WC1V 7JH (7430 0639).* **Map** p267.
Pizza Express *99 High Holborn, WC1V 6LF (7831 5305).* **Map** p267.
Pizza Express *114 Southampton Row, WC1B 5AA (7430 1011).* **Map** p267.
La Porchetta *33 Boswell Street, WC1N 3BP (7242 2434).* **Map** p267.

Scandinavian Kitchen. See p57.

King's Cross

★ Addis

40-42 Caledonian Road, N1 9DT (7278 0679/www.addisrestaurant.co.uk). King's Cross tube/rail/17, 91, 259 bus. **Meals served** noon-midnight Mon-Fri; 1pm-midnight Sat, Sun. **Average** ££. **Map** p267. Ethiopian

With walls the colour of an African sunset and the sounds of uptempo Ethio-pop mingling with the buzz of diners, Addis offers a generous array of meat, fish and vegetarian dishes. Diners sit at either western-style tables or traditional mesobs (tables with near-floor seating). Service is friendly but slow, giving you time for a couple of Batis (Ethiopian beers) between ordering and eating. Charcoal-grilled lamb kebab was delicately spiced and tender, while yetesom beyaynetu (chickpeas, cabbage and carrots, served with fresh injera – spongy flatbread) was perfect for veggies. Take advantage of the weekday lunch offer to try something different, such as the Horn of Africa favourite fuul (fava beans with feta and falafel), or the more adventurous dulet (spiced lamb innards).

Kitchin N1 NEW

8 Caledonia Street, N1 9AA (7713 8777/www.kitchin-n1.com). King's Cross tube/rail. **Lunch served** noon-3pm, **dinner served** 5.30-11pm daily. **Average** ££. **Set buffet** £6.95 lunch, £12.95 dinner. **Map** p267. International

This spacious buffet restaurant has the impersonal feel of enterprises found in mid-range airport hotels and food courts around the world. A set price allows you to fill up as many times as you like from the central food servery, which is stocked with dishes originating from India, South-east Asia and Italy. There's also an extensive salad bar. Offerings were hit and miss on our visit: the bases of the Italian garlic doughballs were burnt black, and the pizzas were unpleasantly stodgy; Singapore noodles were curiously bland, but the Indian chicken and lamb dishes were competently prepared. The desserts consisted of fruit salad, plus the same sponge and cream cake with five different toppings.

Merkato Restaurant

196 Caledonian Road, N1 0SL (7713 8952). Kings Cross tube/rail/17, 91, 259 bus. **Meals served** noon-midnight daily. **Average** ££. **Map** p267. Ethiopian

Named after Addis Ababa's bustling main trading area, this unpretentious restaurant tries to remain loyal to its Ethiopian roots. The simple red and white interior is suffused with the aroma of incense, the walls hung with Amharic tapestries and Ethiopian portraits. It's a venue better suited to dinner than lunch, and the food – served on traditional injera pancake – canvary in quality. Lega tibs (lamb cubes in green pepper and onion) was meltingly tender, but sweetish spices swamped the fish in assa wot (fish curry); we also felt that the ayib begomen (spinach and cottage cheese) was too salty. That said, it's rare to find own-made tej (tangy honey wine) in London, and you can't fault Merkato's prices.

In the area

Carluccio's Caffè *Upper Level, St Pancras International, NW1 2QP (7278 7449).* **Map** p267.
Peyton & Byrne *The Undercroft, St Pancras International, NW1 2QP (no phone).* **Map** p267.
Rasa Maricham *Holiday Inn, 1 King's Cross Road, WC1X 9HX (7833 3900).* **Map** p267.
Yo! Sushi *The Circle, St Pancras International, NW1 2QP (7084 7121).* **Map** p267.

Knightsbridge

In the area

Ottolenghi *13 Motcomb Street, SW1X 8LB (7823 2707).* **Map** p274.
Pâtisserie Valerie *17 Motcomb Street, SW1X 8LB (7245 6161).* **Map** p274.
Pâtisserie Valerie *32-44 Hans Crescent, SW1X 0LZ (7590 0905).* **Map** p274.
Pâtisserie Valerie *215 Brompton Road, SW3 2EJ (7823 9971).* **Map** p274.
Pizza Express *7 Beauchamp Place, SW3 1NQ (7589 2355).* **Map** p274.
Ranoush Juice Bar *22 Brompton Road, SW1X 7QN (7584 6999).* **Map** p274.
Wagamama *Lower ground floor, Harvey Nichols, 109-125 Knightsbridge, SW1X 7RJ (7201 8000).* **Map** p274.
Yo! Sushi *5th floor, Harvey Nichols, 109-125 Knightsbridge, SW1X 7RJ (7201 8641).* **Map** p274.
Yo! Sushi *Harrods 102, 102 Brompton Road, SW3 1JJ (7893 8175).* **Map** p274.

Leicester Square

Gaby's

30 Charing Cross Road, WC2H 0DB (7836 4233). Leicester Square tube. **Meals served** 11am-midnight Mon-Sat; noon-10pm Sun. **Average** ££. **No credit cards**. Map p269.
Jewish
This New York-style Jewish diner prides itself on function before fashion: hence spartan floor tiles, utilitarian plastic seating and closely packed Formica tables, with a long metal counter by the door serving as a hectic base of operations. A starter of chicken livers fried with onions and served with mild mustard arrived almost before it was ordered, only to be replaced – just five minutes later – with a main course of Hungarian goulash that was fine

if a little too fatty. Sandwiches, bagels and pittas occupy a large part of the menu, as do salads from the counter display. Desserts include baklava and a wonderfully crumbly own-made cheesecake. Gaby's attracts a mix of local office workers and old-timers gesticulating with a vehemence that would make real New Yorkers proud.

★ Jindalle NEW

6 Panton Street, SW1Y 4DL (7930 8881). Piccadilly Circus tube. **Meals served** noon-11pm daily. **Average** ££. **Set lunch** £4.50. **Set dinner** (5-9pm) £8.90. **Map** p269. Korean
Jindalle has bare brick walls and exposed chrome ducts that dangle from the ceiling like the vents of a 1950s airship – it's eccentric, but somehow it works. The menu covers what you'd expect in a British Korean restaurant, plus a handful of more exotic specials to appeal to expats. The three-course set lunch is amazing value: Korean miso soup, kimchi and namul, plus rice and a choice of starters and main courses – including barbecue dishes – prepared at your table on the gas grill. We sampled a fluffy tofu pancake, followed by deliciously tender kalbi (beef rib barbecue), grilled on the bone and then chopped into bite-sized morsels. Service doesn't zip along, but you would struggle to find a more satisfying meal for less in the West End.

Saharaween

3 Panton Street, SW1Y 4DL (7930 2777). Piccadilly Circus tube. **Meals served** noon-11.15pm daily. **Average** ££. **Set lunch** £8.95 3 courses. **Set dinner** £14.95 3 courses incl glass of wine. **Map** p269. North African
Its entrance may not be the most enticing, but once you've made it past the bizarre pastiche columns reminiscent of a school panto set, Saharaween offers a small, cosy

dining space replete with the usual souk-style paraphernalia (berber cushions, brass lamps and the like). The menu is short, offering couscous along with a few less common dishes like tagine sfiria (slow-cooked chicken with cinnamon-scented cheese fritters), and sweet lamb mhamar (cooked with plums and apple, and served with toasted almonds). We enjoyed the mixed meze starter; the vegetarian version comes with zaalouk, falafel and rich tomato and pepper stew. Try a bottle of the decent Moroccan pale rosé, Gris de Guerrouane, with its fresh raspberry flavours.

In the area

Pizza Express 26 Panton House, SW1Y 4EN (7930 8044). **Map** p269.
Pizza Express 80-81 St Martin's Lane, WC2N 4AA (7836 8001). **Map** p273.
Prezzo 8 Haymarket, SW1Y 4BP (7839 1129). **Map** p269.
Strada 39 Panton Street, SW1Y 4EA (7930 8535). **Map** p269.
Wagamama 14A Irving Street, WC2H 7AB (7839 2323). **Map** p269.
Woodlands 37 Panton Street, SW1Y 4EA (7839 7258). **Map** p269.
Yo! Sushi St Albans House, 57 Haymarket, SW1Y 4QX (7930 7557). **Map** p269.

Marylebone

Ali Baba

32 Ivor Place, NW1 6DA (7723 7474). Baker Street tube/Marylebone tube/rail. **Meals served** noon-midnight daily. **Average** ££. **Unlicensed**. **Corkage** no charge. **No credit cards**. **Map** p277. Egyptian
Ali Baba functions largely as a takeaway with a restaurant at the back. Its USP is Egyptian food, and you'll find the full repertoire here.

We're big fans of the fuul – fava beans mashed into a coarse paste with lashings of olive oil and plenty of spices – but the koshari (rice and vermicelli with chickpeas) needed more oil and onion. We also tried the grilled lamb and chicken (both well-cooked, tender cubes of meat), and the Egyptian national dish, molokhia, a soupy stew with a distinctive slimy texture served with rice and, here, chunks of lamb – it's an acquired taste, but this was a good, robust version. You'll need to bring your own booze.

Busaba Eathai

8-13 Bird Street, W1U 1BU (7518 8080). Bond Street tube. **Meals served** noon-11pm Mon-Thur; noon-11.30pm Fri, Sat; noon-10pm Sun. **Average** ££. **Map** p277. Thai
The smell of incense greets diners at Busaba Eathai, the designers of which were so obsessed with wood that benches, tables, chopsticks and even menus all shine with the same rich grain motif. The stylish room is populated with chic diners and attractive servers who ask questions like: 'Are you OK with the dried shrimps in the green papaya salad being a bit strong?' All of which makes one suspect that Alan Yau's fast-food canteen was not designed for Thai purists. On the menu, curries and stir-fries sit alongside some enticing juices (mandarin juice with lemongrass, mint and chilli was refreshing). Tom yam noodle soup was a real sinus-clearer, resplendent with chillies and ample greenery, but with only three rather flavourless prawns – which made the £10.90 price tag seem a bit steep.

Eat & Two Veg

50 Marylebone High Street, W1U 5HN (7258 8595/www.eatandtwo veg.com). Baker Street tube. **Meals served** 9am-11pm Mon-Sat; 10am-10pm Sun. **Average** ££. **Map** p277. Vegetarian

A lunch less ordinary

Fernandez & Wells

Debating the relative merits of the capital's pre-packaged sandwiches serves as a diverting form of water-cooler Top Trumps for bored office workers: Marks & Spencer beats Sainsbury's, obviously, after which common sense dictates that Pret a Manger beats Marks (if only for those ham and egg bloomers), and Eat beats Pret (because it's not owned by McDonald's). But in a city so often at the mercy of grim weather, the prospect of a cold lunch can often seem as attractive as no lunch at all.

Thank heavens, then, for those pitstops offering hot takeaway meals in central London. Chief among those distributing warmth in the lunch hour is diminutive continental-style café **Fernandez & Wells**, where sublime sandwiches are complemented by a range of wholesome soups and stews (both changing daily), and even the option of a gloopy cheese raclette (and not a ski lift in sight). Equally comforting takeouts can be had from **Fuzzy's Grub**, which appeases even the most hard-nosed businessman's nostalgia for his mum's Sunday lunch with containers packed with the likes of topside of beef, leg of lamb and loin of pork with all the trimmings (the crackling runs out quickly). There are also homely pies (chicken, steak and mushroom, cottage) and bangers, both served with heaped mounds of fluffy mash.

Similarly meat-motivated is Fitzrovia's **Blackfoot Butchers**, a charmingly old-fashioned enterprise constructing hearty heated sandwiches with cuts from daily roasted joints, plus a range of seasonal soups (roast butternut squash with bacon, say). Those seeking a more exciting lunch can also plump for a Spanish-style tortilla featuring the likes of own-cured chorizo, or jamón fresh from the carving block.

For a meat feast with dietary plus-points, **Boulevard Deli** in Covent Garden proffers pleasingly blackened sides of spit-roast chickens with salad (plus roast tatties for those not counting the carbs), while **UP Box** has a weekly-changing list of globally inspired 'urban picnics' in compartmentalised cardboard boxes: hot options include the likes of provençal beef stew with mustard mash and braised carrots (French), or free-range chicken tagine with saffron rice and a chickpea and spinach side (Moroccan). Both come with dessert.

For more hot lunches with a Mediterranean flavour, visit **Joy Food** in Soho, which plies hungry punters with generous portions of such body-friendly fodder as grilled chermoula-marinated chicken with couscous, or Moroccan meatballs with rice and veg. **Brindisa**, Exmouth Market's Spanish deli from the renowned tapas chain (*see p162*), offers artisanal soups (lentil and chestnut) and stews (chorizo and chickpea), the contents so flavoursome they could have come from a restaurant, plus posh bread for dunking.

Alternatively, for an Indian or Chinese takeaway with a difference, pick up either a vegetarian lunch tray from **Sagar** (two curries, rice, salad, raitha and a chapati), or a noodle dish composed from a three-step menu (choose your noodles, then ingredients, then sauce) while you wait at **Wok to Walk**.

Finally, **Mellatti** raises two fingers to the notion of pizza as a culinary lowest common denominator, serving squared-off slices that any Roman kitchen would be proud of – loaded with imaginative toppings (potato and fontina cheese, for example) and served in foil bags to retain the heat – as well as decent pasta and risotto dishes.

The plastic squeak of a sandwich packet being opened will never sound quite the same again.

Blackfoot Butchers
14 Charlotte Place, W1T 1SW (7580 5096). **Map** p266.
Boulevard Deli *36 Wellington Street, WC2E 7BD (7836 6789).* **Map** p272.
Brindisa *32 Exmouth Market, EC1R 4QE (7713 1666/www. brindisa.com).* **Map** p270.
Fernandez & Wells
43 Lexington Street, W1F 9AL (7734 1546/www.fernandezand wells.com). **Map** p268.
Fuzzy's Grub *6 Crown Passage, SW1Y 6PP (7925 2791/www. fuzzysgrub.com).* **Map** p274.
Joy Food *11 Berwick Street, W1F 0PL (7287 2939).* **Map** p268.
Malletti *174-176 Clerkenwell Road, EC1R 5DD (7713 8665).* **Map** p270.
Sagar *17A Percy Street, W1T 1DU (7631 3319).* **Map** p266.
UP Box *7 Ludgate Circus, EC4M 7LF (8968 7514/ www.up-box.co.uk).* **Map** p270.
Wok to Walk *4 Brewer Street, W1F OSB (7287 8464/www.wok towalk.com).* **Map** p268.

Garden Café

With a massive skylight lending daytime brightness to bare brick walls and exposed steel pipes, this is a cheerful if occasionally noisy place to eat. Red vinyl booths, an open-plan kitchen and 1950s automobile adverts bring a distinct feel of the American diner, which also extends to the menu. Many main courses feature meat substitutes: burgers, schnitzels, sausages. An adequate starter of fried halloumi with tomato and chilli relish arrived at the same time as the mains, and so wasn't finished. The protein-substitute schnitzel was certainly delicious, but needed a bit more of its delectable white wine and watercress sauce. 'Marylebone hotpot' was warming, with nuggets of soya protein, beans and a nicely rich red wine sauce mopped up with good bread. Tofu replaced tuna in the 'not niçoise' salad, which turned out to be a surprisingly successful substitution.

La Fromagerie

2-6 Moxon Street, W1U 4EW (79350341/www.lafromagerie.co.uk). Baker Street or Bond Street tube. **Meals served** 10.30am-7.30pm Mon; 8am-7.30pm Tue-Fri; 9am-7pm Sat; 10am-6pm Sun. **Average** ££. **Map** p277. Café

Patricia Michelson's high-end deli also offers freshly cooked café food, and its rarefied Marylebone location means that communal tables are usually packed with smart shoppers in search of a high-quality breakfast or late lunch. Fromage-o-philes are spoilt with plates of artisanal cheese served with great bread. The daily changing kitchen menu might include salmon and pollock pie nestled beneath clouds of mashed potato, or rich terrines of foie gras, duck or rabbit. Meal-in-one salads also feature. Artichoke, beetroot, red cabbage, walnut and speck was over-complicated and bitter, but fat-speared asparagus, pea, broad bean

and pearl barley was superb. For dessert, try the creamy tarte au citron or the indulgent, dense chocolate brownies, both of which were delicious.

★ Garden Café

Inner Circle, Regent's Park, NW1 4NU (7935 5729/www.thegarden cafe.co.uk). Baker Street or Regents Park tube. **Open** 9am-dusk daily. **Breakfast served** 9-11am, **lunch served** noon-4pm, **dinner served** (summer) 5-8pm daily. **Average** £££. **Set meal** £16.95 2 courses, £19 3 courses. Café

English cottage garden surrounds make this charming café a prime location for afternoon tea or, in summer, an early dinner. The proudly British and occasionally local menu notes some esteemed suppliers, while the wine list favours France and includes a suitably light Provençal rosé for alfresco drinking. Baby gem and parmesan salad was a successful 'caesar with a twist', with croûtons and a warm, creamy cheese goo dolloped over the crisp leaves. Ribeye steak with garlic and herb butter was a fine cut beautifully cooked, accompanied by plentiful (if lukewarm) skin-on fries. Herb roast chicken also impressed, though its accompanying new potatoes were a tad overcooked. Desserts are delightful and include the likes of gooseberry syllabub.

Golden Hind

73 Marylebone Lane, W1U 2PN (7486 3644). Bond Street tube. **Lunch served** noon-3pm Mon-Fri. **Dinner served** 6-10pm Mon-Sat. **Average** ££. **Unlicensed. Corkage** no charge. **Map** p277. Fish & chips

The pastel-hued art deco fryer is these days used to store menus (the cooking's done in a kitchen at the back), but the Golden Hind still oozes local character entirely in keeping with its arterial Marylebone

Lane location. We tucked into firm fillets of haddock in a light batter, fluffy fish cakes spiked with black pepper and parsley, reliably gnarly chips, an elaborately fanned pickled onion and the mandatory white sliced bread and butter, all washed down with a ginger beer. The Greek owners and staff really make a fuss over customers, especially if they're with children. Posher nosh such as prawns and whitebait is available for those hoping to glam it up a little, and you can bring your own wine, but bear in mind that there's a £5 minimum spend for dinners.

Le Pain Quotidien

72-75 Marylebone High Street, W1U 5JW (7486 6154/www.lepain quotidien.com). Baker Street or Bond Street tube. **Meals served** 7am-9pm Mon-Fri; 8am-9pm Sat; 8am-8pm Sun. **Average** ££. **Map** p277. Café
A fast-expanding, rustically styled chain, Le Pain Quotidien was launched nearly two decades ago by Alain Coumount in Brussels. Bread remains the speciality, with sourdough loaves, baguettes and flutes all baked in house. The farmhouse-style communal tables tend to be packed at weekends with bourgeois locals picking at charcuterie platters, forging their way through fresh, inspired salads or sipping fine teas or coffees. Tartines (open-faced sandwiches) are a big draw, and there are plenty of creative toppings from which to choose, but our pork loin and artichoke heart version was pedestrian at best and certainly didn't justify the £8.50 charge. Curiously, the eat-in and takeaway tartine options differ.

★ Paul Rothe & Son

35 Marylebone Lane, W1U 2NN (7935 6783). Bond Street tube. **Meals served** 8am-6pm Mon-Fri; 11.30am-5.30pm Sat. **Average** £. **No credit cards. Map** p277. Café

A combination general store, deli and caff, Paul Rothe & Son – established in 1900 – is English in the best sense of the word: polite, concerned with quality and open to cultural influences. This family enterprise exemplifies old-school hospitality: from the blackboard beckoning in passers-by to the professional shopkeepers, dressed in white coats, who greet customers like old friends. Shelves are packed with homely jams, relishes and biscuits, as well as unexpected items like Krakus Polish pickles. Patrons cover the spectrum from cabbies and tourists to well-heeled Marylebone shoppers. Most come for proper cups of tea and standard sandwiches – from egg salad to kummelkase (a blend of stilton, cream cheese and caraway) – served on rye, granary, wholemeal or white bread.

Strada

31 Marylebone High Street, W1U 4PP (7935 1004/www.strada.co.uk). Baker Street or Bond Street tube. **Meals served** 11.30am-11pm Mon-Sat; 11.30am-10.30pm Sun. **Average** £££. **Set meal** (11.30am-5pm Mon-Fri) £8.50 1 course incl drink. **Map** p277. Pizza & pasta
Strada bills itself as stylish and contemporary, but its menu, like its decor, sits on the safe side: reliable without ever being in any danger of winning awards for innovation. Food is notorious for being a bit hit and miss, but on our visit the Marylebone branch delivered – for the most part. A plate of seafood pasta was generously loaded with juicy prawns, and the tiramisu, refreshingly, didn't taste of the fridge: nor did the tap water, which is presented free to each table without a hint of a frown. A pizza's central sogginess provided the only downside. Tightly packed tables mean that canoodling is generally out of the question, but for group

gatherings Strada remains a perfectly pleasant, if not particularly memorable option.

Tomoe NEW

62 Marylebone Lane, W1U 2PB (7486 2004), Bond Street tube. **Lunch served** noon-2.30pm Tue-Sat. **Dinner served** 6-10.30pm daily. **Average** £££. **Set lunch** £12. **Set dinner** £25. **Map** p277.
Japanese

Tomoe is understated, its decor limited to simple dark wood furniture, a low ceiling decorated with lanterns, wall-hangings of Japanese script and a pictorial sushi poster pasted to one window. Imported newspapers are left on tables, and the mix of Japanese staff and patrons generates a sense of cultural authenticity. All the usual sushi options are available, although we plumped for chirashi, a bowl of rice topped with an assortment of sashimi; thick, glistening and fresh-tasting cuts of raw tuna, salmon, eel and the like. Tempura prawn maki rolls were also delicious, as was a rich and warming miso soup. Quality is decent rather than outstanding, but polite service and reasonable prices make this one to remember if you're in the area.

Woodlands

77 Marylebone Lane, W1U 2PS (7486 3862/www.woodlands restaurant.co.uk). Bond Street tube. **Lunch served** noon-3pm, **dinner served** 6-11pm Mon-Thur. **Meals served** noon-11pm Fri-Sun. **Average** ££. **Set lunch** £7.50. **Set thali** £15.95-£17.95. **Map** p277.
Indian

Woodlands has been a popular destination for more than 25 years, but its dining room feels modern thanks to a mix of twinkling lights, blond wood floor and mirrored walls. The menu, largely based on South Indian vegetarian cooking, also incorporates a few North Indian

stalwarts. Our meal was variable. Rasam, a tart tomato broth spiked with red chillies and fried flecks of ginger, impressed with its peppery kick. Toasted wheat uppama, simmered with crunchy fried lentils, curry leaves and split cashew nuts, was deliciously creamy and delicate, but uthappam, billed as lentil pizza with vegetable toppings, proved unyieldingly dense and overcooked, and a dosa was let down by bland coconut chutney and lacklustre sambar. Service also needs to be more attentive, another hint that Woodlands has let its guard down.

Meal deals

Eat Thai *22 St Christopher's Place, W1U 1NP (7486 0777/ www.eatthai.net).* Set meal (noon-5pm Mon-Fri) £12.95 bento box. **Map** p277. Thai
Garbo's *42 Crawford Street, W1H 1JW (7262 6582).* Set lunch (Mon-Fri) £10.95 2 courses, £11.95 3 courses, £12.95 smörgåsbord. **Map** p276. Swedish
Ishtar *10-12 Crawford Street, W1U 6AZ (7224 2446/www. ishtarrestaurant.com).* Set lunch (noon-4pm) £10.95 2 courses, £12.95 3 courses. **Map** p277. Turkish
Original Tagines *7A Dorset Street, W1U 6QN (7935 1545/ www.originaltagines.com).* Set lunch (Mon-Fri) £11.50 2 courses. **Map** p277. Moroccan
Phoenix Palace *5 Glentworth Street, NW1 5PG (7486 3515).* Dim sum £2-£3.80. **Map** p277. Chinese
Royal China *24-26 Baker Street, W1U 3BZ (7487 4688/www.royal chinagroup.co.uk).* Dim sum £2.65-£4. **Map** p277. Chinese

In the area

ASK *56-60 Wigmore Street, W1U 2RZ (7224 3484).* **Map** p277.
ASK *197 Baker Street, NW1 6UY (7486 6027).* **Map** p277.

Carluccio's Caffè *St Christopher's Place, W1U 1AY (7935 5927).* Map p277.

Fine Burger Company *50 James Street, W1U 1HB (7224 1890).* Map p277.

Fresco *31 Paddington Street, W1U 4HD (7486 6112).* Map p277.

Fresco *34 Margaret Street, W1G 0JE (7493 3838).* Map p266.

Giraffe *6-8 Blandford Street, W1H 3HA (7935 2333).* Map p277.

Gourmet Burger Kitchen *102 Baker Street, W1U 6TL (7486 8516).* Map p277.

Nando's *113 Baker Street, W1U 6RS (3075 1044).* Map p277.

Pâtisserie Valerie *York House, 15 Great Cumberland Place, W1H 7AS (7724 8542).* Map p266.

Pâtisserie Valerie *105 Marylebone High Street, W1U 4RS (7935 6240).* Map p277.

Paul *115 Marylebone High Street, W1U 4SB (7224 5615).* Map p277.

Ping Pong *29A James Street, W1U 1DZ (7034 3100).* Map p277.

Ping Pong *10 Paddington Street, W1U 5QL (7009 9600).* Map p277.

Pizza Express *13-14 Thayer Street, W1U 3JS (7935 2167).* Map p277.

Pizza Express *21-22 Barrett Street, St Christopher's Place, W1U 1BF (7629 1001).* Map p277.

Pizza Express *133 Baker Street, W1U 6SF (7486 0888).* Map p277.

Pizza Paradiso *9 St Christopher's Place, W1U 1NE (7486 3196).* Map p277.

Prezzo *7-9 Great Cumberland Place, W1H 7LU (7723 7172).* Map p266.

Real Greek *56 Paddington Street, W1U 4HY (7486 0466).* Map p277.

Sofra *1 St Christopher's Place, W1U 1LT (7224 4080).* Map p277.

Square Pie *Selfridges, 400 Oxford Street, W1A 1AB (7318 2460).* Map p277.

Tootsies Grill *35 James Street, W1U 1EA (7486 1611).* Map p277.

Wagamama *101A Wigmore Street, W1U 1QR (7409 0111).* Map p277.

Yo! Sushi *15 Woodstock Street, W1C 2AQ (7629 0051).* Map p277.

Yo! Sushi *Selfridges, 400 Oxford Street, W1A 1AB (7318 3944).* Map p277.

Zizzi *35-38 Paddington Street, W1U 4HQ (7224 1450).* Map p277.

Zizzi *110-116 Wigmore Street, W1U 3RS (7935 2336).* Map p277.

Mayfair

Prezzo

17 Hertford Street, W1J 7RS (7499 4690/www.prezzoplc.co.uk). Green Park or Hyde Park Corner tube. **Meals served** noon-11.30pm Mon-Sat; noon-11pm Sun. **Average** ££. Map p274. Pizza & pasta

The Mayfair branch of this pizza chain looks more like an upmarket English pub than an Italian restaurant – all dark panelled wood and moody lighting, with tables thoughtfully spaced for trysting couples and map-toting tourists. Unfortunately the food isn't especially Italian either: while a silky mozzarella, tomato and basil starter raised our hopes, these quickly sank along with the dough of an undercooked and meagrely topped pizza. The pasta dishes tend to be better, and cheaper, but the dish was delivered to the table with more of a slam than a smile. With a few tweaks, Prezzo could challenge the big boys, but for now this branch has little more than a salubrious setting and some pleasingly low prices to recommend it.

Rocket

4-6 Lancashire Court, off New Bond Street, W1Y 9AD (7629 2889/www.rocketrestaurants. co.uk). Bond Street or Oxford Circus tube. **Bar Open** noon-11pm, **meals served** noon-6pm Mon-Sat. *Restaurant* **Lunch served** noon-3pm, **dinner served** 6-11pm Mon-Sat. **Average** £££. Pizza & pasta

Smartly secluded Lancashire Court provides a peaceful location for

Rocket, the first-floor restaurant of which specialises in creative pizzas (such as goat's cheese and honey with herbs, pine nuts and tomatoes), as well as a few more modern international dishes. Alternatively, find a perch in the ground-floor bar area, which on warm days extends into a lovely courtyard and offers a lunch menu that includes shared platters and large salads. Hearty sandwiches come with thick-cut, well-seasoned fries, although a chicken, mustard and coriander burger was unfortunately paired with a rather stale, supermarket-style white bun. Gravadlax with cucumber and lemon crème fraîche on wholemeal bread was far livelier, but the fish in a fish and chip salad with rocket was almost tasteless without tartare sauce.

★ Tibits `NEW`

12-14 Heddon Street, W1B 4DA (7758 4110/www.tibits.ch). Oxford Circus tube. **Meals served** 8am-11.30pm Mon-Sat; 8.30am-10.30pm Sun. **Average ££. Map** p269. Vegetarian

This vegetarian buffet restaurant forsakes the hessian and macramé so beloved of many meat-free enterprises in favour of velvety fabrics from Designers Guild. The warm dishes, salads and dips on the central island are compiled from an international larder, and all the bakery and dairy products are organic. We loved a salad of dried french beans with walnuts and coriander, creamy yet lumpy tahina, and a zingy quinoa pilaff. Fill your plate and then take it to the coffee shop-style counter for weighing and payment – and to order drinks, whether that be peppermint tea with cornflower petals, freshly squeezed juice, a coffee or a champagne cocktail. Service seemed overly enthusiastic on our visit, but this is a delightful addition to the area.

Meal deals

Momo *25 Heddon Street, W1B 4BH (7434 4040/www.momoresto.com).* Set lunch £14 2 courses, £18 3 courses. Set meze £11.50-£14.50. **Map** p269. Moroccan

Princess Garden *8-10 North Audley Street, W1K 6ZD (7493 3223/www.princessgardenof mayfair.com).* Set lunch £12.50 per person (minimum 2). Dim sum £2.50-£3.80. **Map** p277. Chinese

Sofra *18 Shepherd Street, W1Y 7HU (7493 3320/www.sofra.co.uk).* Set lunch £10.95 1 course incl drink. Set dinner £12.95 1 course incl drink. **Map** p274. Turkish

Sotheby's Café *Sotheby's, 34-35 New Bond Street, W1A 2AA (7293 5077).* Set tea (3-4.45pm Mon-Fri) £5.75. **Map** p268. Café

In the area

ASK *121-125 Park Street, W1K 7JA (7495 7760).* **Map** p277.

Carluccio's Caffè *Fenwick, 63 New Bond Street, W1A 3BS (7629 0699).*

Itsu *1 Hanover Square, W1S 1HA (7491 9799).*

Napket *6 Brook Street, W1S 1BB (7495 8562).*

Napket *5 Vigo Street, W1S 3HD (7734 4387).* **Map** p269.

Pizza Express *23 Bruton Place, W1J 6ND (7495 1411).* **Map** p268.

Prezzo *15 North Audley Street, W1K 6WZ (7493 4990).* **Map** p277.

Rasa W1 *6 Dering Street, W1S 1AD (7629 1346).* **Map** p277.

Strada *15-16 New Burlington Street, W1S 3BJ (7287 5967).* **Map** p268.

Paddington

Satay House

13 Sale Place, W2 1PX (7723 6763/www.satay-house.co.uk). Edgware Road tube/Paddington tube/rail. **Lunch served** noon-3pm, **dinner served** 6-11pm daily.

Average £££. Set meal £15.50-£26.50 per person (minimum 2).
Map p276. Malaysian

Satay House attracts a happy mix of expats, locals and fans of Malaysian food, and the ground-floor room and sleek basement space were almost full on our Thursday evening visit. Buttery squares of roti canai came with chunky dalca (lentil and veg curry); satay chicken skewers were imbued with a lovely lemongrass scent, although they tasted like they'd been grilled for too long. We had no complaints about the luscious begedil (spiced lamb and potato cutlets), or the juicy, generously portioned pineapple curry. The scent of curry leaves also wafted from a plate of tender sotong berempah (stir-fried squid with peppers). A dessert of banana fritters – tender on the inside, crisp without – came with maple syrup and chocolate ice-cream.

In the area

Fresco 93 Praed Street, W2 1NT (7402 0006). Map p276.
Yo! Sushi The Lawn, Paddington Station, W2 1HB (7706 8388).
Zizzi 17 Sheldon Square, W2 6EP (7286 4770).

Piccadilly

Miso

66 Haymarket, SW1Y 4RF (7930 4800/www.misonoodlebar.co.uk). Piccadilly Circus tube. **Meals served** 11.30am-11pm Mon-Sat; 11.30am-10pm Sun. **Average** ££. **Set meal** £10.95-£11.95 bento box. **Map** p269. Oriental

The communal seating in Miso's canteen-style interior is as reminiscent of Wagamama as its menu of wok-fried, soup- or sauce-based noodle dishes, although fewer customers mean less chance of queuing and more of lingering over the post-prandial green tea refills.

We've previously enjoyed efficient, focused service, but on our last visit found staff swift to the point of being perfunctory. Food was equally hit and miss: pork, prawn and Chinese mushroom dumplings were grease-free and generously filled, while a dish combining strips of beef with red pepper and onion in a black pepper sauce was robustly flavoured. Less successful was roast duck with ginger and spring onions, which was pitifully short on meat, and soggy banana fritters with too-soft ice-cream. Still, Miso isn't a bad option for quick refuelling, and its prices are good value.

In the area

Ed's Easy Diner Trocadero, 19 Rupert Street, W1V 7HN (7287 1951). Map p269.
Pâtisserie Valerie 162 Piccadilly, W1J 9EF (7491 1717). Map p269.
Prezzo 8 Haymarket, SW1Y 4BP (7839 1129). Map p269.
Wagamama 8 Norris Street, SW1Y 4RJ (7321 2755). Map p269.
Yo! Sushi Trocadero, 19 Rupert Street, W1D 7DH (7434 2724). Map p269.

Pimlico

Jenny Lo's Tea House

14 Eccleston Street, SW1W 9LT (7259 0399). Victoria tube/rail.
Lunch served noon-3pm Mon-Fri.
Dinner served 6-10pm Mon-Sat.
Average ££. **No credit cards**.
Map p275. Chinese

Victoria's hungry backpackers, confused tourists and time-poor commuters would be more than happy to discover a café like this in their midst. Hidden on quiet Eccleston Street, Jenny Lo's could easily be dismissed as just another too-arty-for-its-own-good boutique gallery – its loud, colourfully painted window obscures the workings of the busy eaterie within. A mainly

Satay House. See p71.

cha cha moon

查查月亮

**Chinese
noodle bar**

**15–21 Ganton Street
London W1F 9BN
(0)20 7792 0088**

**2nd Floor, Whiteleys
151 Queensway
London W2 4YN
(0)20 7792 0088**

www.chachamoon.com

Chinese menu included some surprises, such as Vietnamese cold noodles and seafood laksa; the latter was rich with coconut milk and contained generous amounts of prawns, squid and mussels, but lacked depth of flavour. Better was a satisfying one-plate meal of slow-cooked belly pork on rice. A warm, welcoming atmosphere prevails, and service is just the right side of attentive. A worthwhile find.

In the area
Pizza Express *25 Millbank, SW1P 4QP (7976 6214).* **Map** p287.
Pizza Express *46 Moreton Street, SW1V 2PB (7592 9488).* **Map** p275.

Soho

Amato
14 Old Compton Street, W1D 4TH (7734 5733/www.amato.co.uk). Leicester Square, Piccadilly Circus or Tottenham Court Road tube. **Meals served** 8am-10pm Mon-Sat; 10am-8pm Sun. **Average** ££. **Map** p268. Café
This old-school Italian caff is brimming with character, making it an ideal spot for breaking up Soho shopping sprees with coffee and cake. Dark wood furniture lends a homely feel, and colourful art deco posters adorn the walls. The main draw is the astonishing array of sweet delights filling one long, L-shaped display cabinet, although the hot dishes are equally worth stopping off for. Piping-hot smoked salmon fettuccine came in a seriously substantial portion, with fresh pasta and an artery-clogging amount of cream (our only complaint). For dessert, we couldn't fault the millefoglie, a creamy treat featuring paper-thin layers of flakey puff pastry, but given the café's proudly Italian heritage, we thought the cappuccino could have been better prepared.

Beatroot
92 Berwick Street, W1F 0QD (7437 8591/www.beatroot.org.uk). Oxford Circus, Piccadilly Circus or Tottenham Court Road tube. **Meals served** 9.15am-9pm Mon-Sat. **Average** £. **No credit cards**. **Map** p268. Vegetarian
Beatroot has been providing Sohoites with reliable, healthy and meat-free eating for over a decade. Cheerful staff dole out generous portions of hot dishes and salads from behind the counter. Grab your choice as a takeaway, or eat it at one of a handful of acid-green and orange wooden tables. Salads burst with interesting veg and include red-cabbage coleslaw with fresh dill, a seasonal celeriac and radish number, and greek salad with feta. Ten hot dishes on our visit included chunky moussaka, lentil shepherd's pie, a gingery tofu stir-fry and sausage rolls (the latter a bit burnt). A raspberry and coconut flapjack was soft and lip-smackingly sweet, but short on fruit.

★ Breakfast Club
33 D'Arblay Street, W1F 8EU (7434 2571/www.thebreakfastclubsoho.com). Oxford Circus or Tottenham Court Road tube. **Meals served** 8am-6pm Mon-Fri; 9.30am-5pm Sat. **Average** ££. **Map** p268. Café
There are few more affable temples to nostalgia than this cluttered café, its brick walls covered with '80s memorabilia – from record sleeves of celebrated movie soundtracks (*Back To The Future*, *St Elmo's Fire*) to a T-shirt bearing the surnames of the original *Breakfast Club* actors. Finding a weathered wooden table on which to perch isn't easy at lunchtime, but it's the best way to fully appreciate the similarly sigh-inducing range of comfort food. Breakfasts take centre stage: from a full English and a US variation featuring maple syrup pancakes, to

a Latin American breakfast burrito. But there are also jacket potatoes with toppings less ordinary (goat's cheese, guacamole, grilled chicken), chunky sandwiches (such as the amusingly titled 'When Haloumi Met Salad') and freshly made smoothies galore. A uniquely loveable place, and a characterful alternative to the area's countless sandwich chains.

Café at Foyles

Foyles, 113-119 Charing Cross Road, WC2H 0EB (7440 3207/ www.foyles.co.uk). Leicester Square, Piccadilly Circus or Tottenham Court Road tube. **Meals served** 7am-8.30pm Mon-Sat; 10am-5.30pm Sun. **Average** £. **Map** p268. Café
It's all change at the Foyles cafe. Ray's Jazz has moved upstairs, leaving this perennially popular second-floor lunch spot with double the space in which to scatter mismatched wooden chairs, tables and a handful of leather sofas. All of which means you're more likely to find a seat at which to savour the sandwiches, artisanal quiches or own-made soups; there are also cakes galore, many of them suitable for vegans, and the range of teas and coffees is second to none. Yet there's no denying the fact that – ongoing live jazz performances and the occasional decorative record sleeve notwithstanding – the loss of all that vinyl has turned what once felt like a culturally edgy meeting place into a pretty conventional café.

Canela NEW

1 Newburgh Street, W1F 7RB (7494 9980/www.canelacafe.com). Oxford Circus tube. **Meals served** 9.30am-10.30pm Mon-Wed; 9.30am-11.30pm Thur, Fri; 10.30am-11.30pm Sat; noon-8pm Sun. **Average** ££. **Map** p268. Café

Canela

Set in a cute, black-fronted corner building a stone's throw from Carnaby Street, Canela ('cinnamon' in Portuguese) has a smart interior, artfully lit with vintage chandeliers and belying its eminently affordable menu – although the limited number of tables forced us to eat in a comparatively soulless basement space. The menu features classic Brazilian and Portuguese dishes, including pão de queijo (warm cheese buns), coxinha (a cone-shaped confection of battered chicken, onion and herbs) and bacalhau (salt-cod, served here with potatoes). Lighter Mediterranean flavours appear in quiches, salads and dishes like vegetable lasagne. Puds include the likes of banana cinnamon cake and classic custard tarts. A good bet for an intimate evening meal, although a separate takeaway menu caters to those seeking sustenance on the move.

Cha Cha Moon NEW

15-21 Ganton Street, W1F 9BN (7297 9800). Oxford Circus tube. **Meals served** noon-11pm Mon-Thur; noon-11.30pm Fri, Sat; noon-10.30pm Sun. **Average** ££. **Map** p268. Chinese

This recent venture from Alan Yau is in a similar vein to previous success stories Wagamama (*see p24*) and Busaba Eathai (*see p63*): accessible prices, communal tables and a no-booking policy aimed at on-the-go customers. Noodles are the thing here, inspired by Hong Kong's mein dong (noodle stalls) but with influences from across China, Malaysia and Singapore. Wun tun noodle soup didn't impress, the pastry wrappers far from delicate and the chicken filling stodgy. Roast duck noodle soup was better, the stock exuding 'umami' flavour and the scent of red wolfberries, with fresh and pleasingly al dente

2 Course Lunch £6.90
2 Course Dinner £9.90
www.bistro1.co.uk   info@bistro1.co.uk

"With its exceptionally good food, friendly staff and its vibrant atmosphere, Bistro1 is a dining experience not to be missed. Based on a Mediterranean influence, our menu includes extravagant; meat, chicken, fish and vegetarian dishes, accompanied by a rich selection of world wines.

Our wine menu was brought together considering London's cosmopolitan nature and the different cultural perspectives this city offers to us. Hence, dining at Bistro1 means you know a little bit more about another culture...

33 Southampton
Street Covent
Garden, London,
WC2E 7HE
T: 020 7379 7585

75 Beak Street,
Soho,
London,
W1R 3LF
T: 020 7287 1840

27 Frith Street,
Soho,
London,
W1D 5LE
T: 020 7734 6204

28 Brewer
Street, Soho
London,
W1F 0SR
T: 020 7734 0179

noodles. Dishes as diverse as Sichuan dumplings, zhajiang mian (a dry noodle and pork dish from northern China) and Shanghainese fen pi (cold noodles with jasmine tea-smoked chicken) are also available.

★ Chowki

2-3 Denman Street, W1D 7HA (7439 1330/www.chowki.com). Piccadilly Circus tube. **Meals served** noon-11.30pm Mon-Sat; noon-10.30pm Sun. **Average** ££. **Map** p269. Indian

Chowki's format is alluring: a fairly priced, monthly changing menu of authentic regional cooking (on our visit Lucknow, Goa and the Northwest Frontier), providing three starters and mains plus a dessert. With its soundtrack of chilled beats, communal seating at long wooden tables and low-lit interior, it's ideal for a cheap dinner with chums. A well-judged Goan starter of tender coils of just-cooked squid came coated with a zesty tomato and carom-seed masala and superfluous coriander relish. The Northwest Frontier provided our lamb kofta: flavour-packed meatballs peeping from a pond of yoghurt curry, served with chickpea curry, naan and rice: high marks to all. Within chapati-flinging distance of Piccadilly Circus, Chowki is a undeniable winner.

Ed's Easy Diner

12 Moor Street, W1V 5LH (7434 4439/www.edseasydiner.co.uk). Leicester Square or Tottenham Court Road tube. **Meals served** noon-midnight daily. **Average** ££. **Map** p268. Burgers

From the super-efficient staff and retro counter-top jukeboxes to the famously frills-free menu, this ersatz American-style diner has remained largely unchanged since it opened on this site over two decades ago. The decor feels pretty gauche these days, although it's a good indication of the food: our burgers seemed flavourless compared to those of the countless artisanal burger chains now operating in the capital; fries were ordinary, and onion rings tasted as if they'd been dropped in a puddle. OK, so the butterscotch malts are fine, but how wrong can you go with ice-cream, malted milk powder and butterscotch sauce? That said, Ed's remains as much a Soho fixture as Bar Italia and the seedy Sunset Strip, so they must be doing something right.

Hummus Bros

88 Wardour Street, W1F 0TJ (7734 1311/www.hbros.co.uk). Oxford Circus or Tottenham Court Road tube. **Meals served** 11am-10pm Mon-Wed; 11am-11pm Thur, Fri; noon-11pm Sat; noon-10pm Sun. **Average** £. **Map** p268. Café

The simple and successful formula at this fantastic café and takeaway is to use first-rate houmous as a base for a selection of toppings, which are then scooped up with warm, fluffy pitta bread. Choose from fresh-tasting guacamole, salad, stewed mushrooms, slow-cooked beef and fava beans, or daily specials such as Thai green chicken curry, then add extras such as feta, jalapeños or toasted pine nuts. There are also side dishes along the lines of barbecued aubergine, tabouleh and grilled vegetables. The concept works because the food is nutritious, good value and – best of all – delicious. Finish off with a brownie, baklava or malabi (a milk-based dessert with date honey). Staff are helpful, and there's free Wi-Fi, but the place can become hectic at peak times.

★ Imli

167-169 Wardour Street, W1F 8WR (7287 4243/www.imli.co.uk). Oxford Circus or Tottenham Court Road tube. **Meals served** noon-11pm daily. **Average** ££. **Set lunch** £5.95-£7.95 1 course. **Map** p268. Indian

Imli is a pioneer when it comes to modern Indian cuisine, offering an innovative range of Indian tapas amid vibrant surroundings, its deep orange and pale green walls are brightened by colourful photos of Indian folk and foodstuffs. Standard dishes are rendered well – witness the gingery tang and tender meat of Goan pork; the comforting dhal; the smoky aubergine masala – but the unusual options are even better. Seared slices of masala grilled beef came served atop mild cumin and turmeric mash, and accompanied by a coriander and avocado dip; Imli risotto featured crunchy spiced veg over a creamy mix of mushrooms and arborio rice. Three dishes amount to a substantial two-course meal – great value given the quality.

Just Falafs

155 Wardour Street, W1F 8WG (7734 1914/www.justfalafs.com). Oxford Circus or Tottenham Court Road tube. **Meals served** 10am-10pm Mon-Fri; noon-10pm Sat. **Average** ££. **Map** p268. Café
While the wrap still reigns supreme in this attractive timber-decked refectory, there's more than just falafel on offer. Scrumptiously light Dorset lamb meatballs, for example, are rolled up with red cabbage, spinach, tomato sauce, yoghurt and cucumber, while smoked organic chicken is complemented by roast sweet potato, spinach, and tahini garlic sauce. Order your own combo or opt for one of the well-judged suggestions. The perfectly filling 'regular' size (with two falafels) costs £4.50, with virtuous ingredients such as bean sprouts tempered by lush sauces – although the heavenly aubergine sauce is probably a long way from being low-cal. There's the usual range of espresso-style coffees, soft drinks and bottled smoothies. This Soho outlet is open late and charges a premium to eat in.

Kati Roll Company NEW

24 Poland Street, W1F 8QL (7287 4787/www.katirollcompany.com). Oxford Circus or Tottenham Court Road tube. **Meals served** noon-11.30pm Mon-Thur, Sun; 12.30pm-12.30am Fri, Sat. **Average** £. **No credit cards. Map** p268. Indian
The kati (pronounced 'karti') is as popular in India's colonial-style clubs as it is on its rural railway platforms. While a paratha (flaky flatbread) sizzles on a hot griddle, it's topped with beaten egg that sets to a thin omelette. Garlicky chicken tikka, tangy stir-fried beef, mini lamb patties, paneer or spicy potatoes are put in the middle; add a flurry of red onion slices and a dollop of herby chutney, and the whole lot is then wrapped into a tidy roll. The cooks make everything from scratch using distinctive marinades and fresh, own-ground masalas. We found service abrupt and unhelpful, but food of this quality deserves to get noticed.

★ Maoz Vegetarian

43 Old Compton Street, W1D 6HG (7851 1586/www.maozveg.com). Leicester Square or Tottenham Court Road tube. **Meals served** 11am-1am Mon-Thur; 11am-2am Fri, Sat; 11am-midnight Sun. **Average** £. **Set meal** £4.20-£4.90. **No credit cards. Map** p268. Vegetarian
Now a Soho stalwart, Dutch-company Maoz is also an expanding chain with franchises in places as far-flung as Perth and Florida. It's no surprise that the concept has been a success: its formula of falafel-filled pitta (white or wholemeal) and serve-your-own toppings (shredded purple cabbage, tabouleh, pickled green chillis) is as fast as it is affordable, and as simple as it is nourishing. Opt for the plain falafel for £3.30, or falafel with houmous, fried aubergine or feta for an additional 50p. Belgian-style chips

Cha Cha Moon. See p77.

and salad boxes are also available/ There are a few cramped tables, but this is really a takeaway joint. Late opening hours see the place packed with post-pub punters determined to avoid the dread clutches of the dodgy döner.

Mexicali NEW

26 Berwick Street, W1F 8RG (7434 0518/www.eatmexicali.com). Oxford Circus or Tottenham Court Road tube. **Meals served** 11am-11pm Mon-Sat. **Average £. No credit cards. Map** p268. Mexican
Forget frills, forget thrills; Mexicali is a burrito dispenser for those who want first-rate Mexican street food without trendy branding or artfully ironic interior design. Functionality rules the roost: from the assembly line at which staff take orders and shout numbers (in between toasting tortillas and wrestling burritos into shape at speeds that defy belief), to the communal tables in the drab rear room, its bare walls the same shade of beige as the environmentally friendly card containers food is served in. Our burrito was superb, an enormous but not overly heavy construction of crumbling pork carnitas, the cola and spice marinade distinguishable beneath a fresh and fiery own-made salsa. We came, we ate, we left. And so should you.

Mildred's

45 Lexington Street, W1F 9AN (7494 1634/www.mildreds.co.uk). Oxford Circus or Piccadilly Circus tube. **Meals served** noon-11pm Mon-Sat. **Average ££. Map** p268. Vegetarian
Bookings aren't taken, and you may need to wait at the bar of this gastropub-style vegetarian spot – an often cramped and clamorous place. The harried servers can be a little indifferent and difficult to attract, but bright lighting, modern canvases and young, chic customers lend a lively vibe. The eclectic menu is generally decent – our 'light meal' featured verdant spinach, thick, nicely textured slices of halloumi,

and flavoursome cherry tomatoes. Mixed mushroom and ale pie was too tart (too much balsamic), but its light puff pastry was pleasantly sprinkled with poppy seeds. Mushy peas were spot-on and chips grease-free. Plum tarte tatin with cinnamon ice-cream made for a lush finish.

Mother Mash NEW

26 Ganton Street, W1F 7QZ (7494 9644/www.mothermash.co.uk). Oxford Circus tube. Meals served 8.30am-10pm Mon-Fri; noon-10pm Sat; noon-5pm Sun. Average ££. Map p268. British

It's not built for comfort – the high wooden bench seating demands you place your feet on a bar beneath the table – but comfort food is served in big, soothing spoonfuls. Choose your mash, choose your pie or sausages, choose your gravy. Deciding on mash isn't easy: horseradish, crème fraîche and lemon, and chopped green olive versions are all available. Cheesy mustard mash and champ were good accompaniments to a chicken, leek and ham pie with onion gravy; veg included grilled french beans wrapped in bacon, and mushy or garden peas. London Pride is the only British beer, Fentimans soft drinks strike a nostalgic note, and the short wine list is appealing. Puds are delicious and small enough to squeeze in after a main.

Mr Jerk

187 Wardour Street, W1F 8ZB (7437 7770/www.mrjerk.co.uk). Oxford Circus or Tottenham Court Road tube. Meals served noon-11pm Mon-Sat; noon-8pm Sun. Average ££. Map p268. Caribbean

When its business partners split in 2006, Mr Jerk was renamed Jerk City and the original Mr Jerk rocked up next door. Although the two Caribbean menus are virtually identical, this spacious venue has a large dining area and a separate

rum-stocked bar. We kicked off with mutton soup, packed with hefty chunks of meat on the bone. Keen to try another of the one-pot wonders, we opted for the traditional Jamaican stew of oxtail and butter beans, which tasted wonderfully of real stock. Starchy side dishes (fried plantain, rice and peas, macaroni cheese) help you through the gravy-rich main courses, but be warned that the macaroni comes flecked with spicy peppers. If you can't manage dessert, finish with a creamy soursop punch.

★ Myung Ga

1 Kingly Street, W1B 5PA (7734 8220/www.myungga.co.uk). Oxford Circus or Piccadilly Circus tube. Lunch served noon-3pm Mon-Sat. Dinner served 5.30-10.30pm Mon-Sat; 4.30-10.30pm Sun. Average £££. Set lunch £9.50-£12.50. Map p268. Korean

We like Myung Ga. It could be the laid-back, post-work, pre-theatre vibe, or the zippy service provided by young, enthusiastic waiting staff. Our starter, kimchi and a basket of fried goonmandu (beef dumplings), arrived at the table within seconds, rapidly followed by an enjoyable beef sirloin barbecue – cooked at the table and served with a sesame oil, salt and pepper dip – and a sizzling platter of dak bulgogi (spicy chicken barbecue), prepared in the kitchen to avoid overloading the extractor fans. The menu includes soups, stews and hotpots, but most come for the grills: four or five cuts of beef, pork or chicken will satisfy even the most heavyweight hungers. Myung Ga is justifiably popular, so book ahead for dinner or face a long wait.

Nara

9 D'Arblay Street, W1F 8DR (7287 2224). Oxford Circus or Tottenham Court Road tube. Lunch served noon-3.30pm Mon-Sat. Dinner served 5.30-11pm daily. Average

££. **Set lunch** £6.50. **Set dinner**
£7.50. **Map** p268. Korean
The wooden barbecue tables that
line Nara's narrow dining room are
full most lunchtimes, so come early
or call ahead. In the evenings, most
people order à la carte, but the
service can be erratic. The tolsot
bibimbap – rice, beef, vegetables
and chilli sauce – is put together at
the table in a hot stone bowl that
cooks the rice into a delicious
caramelised crust. It's one of half a
dozen dishes that are part of the
excellent-value set lunch, which
includes Korean miso soup, kimchi
and several types of namul. The
sogogee dop bap was a full-
flavoured stir-fry of beef and
vegetables in a bulgogi-style sauce,
served with an earthenware cup of
fragrant green tea. Decent Japanese
food is also available.

★ Nordic Bakery NEW
*14 Golden Square, W1F 9JF
(3230 1077/www.nordicbakery.
com). Piccadilly Circus tube.* **Meals
served** 8am-8pm Mon-Fri; 11am-
7pm Sat; 11am-6pm Sun. **Average**
£. **Map** p268. Scandinavian
Its simple monochrome signage and
location on media-savvy Golden
Square hint that Nordic Bakery is a
haven of über-stylish Scandinavian
cool. Baskets, tea towels, denim
aprons and a nature-inspired wall
rug stop the hip warehouse-style
interior from feeling too sparse, and
for warmth you can always rely on
the charming staff and fat, tactile
mugs of steaming coffee. Fresh and
wholesome food at the counter
include cute rye rolls filled with
salmon tartar or pickled herring,
though the karelian pies – hand-
shaped rye pastry filled with rice
and topped with egg butter, a
Finnish favourite – should be tried
at least once. Desserts include own-
made cinnamon buns and a wide
range of Scandinavian cakes.

Papaya NEW
*14 St Anne's Court, W1F 0BD
(7734 8994). Tottenham Court
Road tube.* **Meals served** 10.30am-
6.30pm Mon-Fri. **Average** £.
No credit cards. Map p268. Thai
With Thai curries among the
nation's favourite comfort foods, it's
small wonder that this functional
dispenser of Asian culinary hugs
takes such a battering at lunchtimes.
There are other dishes available –
pad Thai noodles and chicken with
cashew nuts – but it's the cardboard
boxes of green curry that keep
punters coming back. They're
creamy but have a surprising chilli
kick, and are packed with tender
chicken and chunky vegetables
(courgettes, red and green peppers,
shredded ginger and lemon grass
stems). Packets of prepared sushi
are also available alongside prawn
crackers and sides (soups, satay,
pork and prawn dumplings), and
there are a few simple seats by the
window for those hoping to delay
their return to the office.

Pâtisserie Valerie
*44 Old Compton Street, W1D
4TY (7437 3466/www.patisserie-
valerie.co.uk). Leicester Square,
Piccadilly Circus or Tottenham Court
Road tube.* **Meals served** 7.30am-
8.30pm Mon, Tue; 7.30am-9pm Wed-
Fri; 8am-9pm Sat; 9.30am-7pm Sun.
Average ££. **Map** p268. Café
The original Soho branch of the
steadily expanding chain retains its
historic decor of rustic wall murals
and simple Formica tables topped
with flowers and folded menus. The
ground floor feels rather hemmed in;
head upstairs to the lighter, airier
first floor for a window table handy
for people-watching. The corner
counter features a gleaming display
cabinet crammed with colourful
confectionary – from gaudily iced
celebration cakes to marzipan
animals for little ones. The menu

offers a simple selection of soups, omelettes, pastas, salads and quiches; the quiche has never disappointed, with delicious pastry and plenty of fresh ingredients. All-day breakfasts run from a full English or eggs benedict to brioche french toast with maple syrup.

★ Princi NEW

135 Wardour Street, W1F 0UF (7478 8888/www.princi.co.uk). Leicester Square or Tottenham Court Road tube. **Meals served** 10am-midnight Mon-Sat; 11am-11pm Sun. **Average ££. Map** p268. Italian

Alan Yau's latest London venture is this affordable Italian bakery-café, created in conjunction with Rocco Princi, sometimes called 'the Armani of bread'. The interior is dominated by a huge water feature that at best evokes a spa, at worst an expensive urinal, while extensive use of soothing limestone makes the modernist interior feel cosy. Best of all are the prices: custard-filled cannoncini are not 80p each, but 80p for three; same with the cookies. If our dish of chicken cacciatora was typical, it was almost enough to feed two – especially once you factored in the slices of bread included in the smart paper bags that hold both napkin and bamboo cutlery. Get a side dish such as potato gratin, polenta or zucchine fritte and you have a feast. The problem is getting your meal from the various counters before it turns cold: we waited so long for coffee that by the time we sat down our lasagne was tepid.

Stockpot

18 Old Compton Street, W1D 4TN (7287 1066). Leicester Square or Tottenham Court Road tube. **Meals served** 9am-11.30pm Mon, Tue; 9am-midnight Wed-Sat; noon-11.30pm Sun. **Average £.** **Set meal** £5.85-£6.50 2 courses. **No credit cards. Map** p268. Café

An old, old favourite, Stockpot never changes and we wouldn't have it any other way. The spartan but comfortable ground floor has booth seating at the back and tables for two at the front – those by the window allow you to watch the strutting Old Compton Street peacocks – while the basement is more functional and less popular. The one-sheet menu offers such delights as gammon with pineapple and other forgotten standards of British mass dining. Little costs over £5, and you can get two courses and a small beaker of red wine for less than a tenner. Omelettes, grills and pasta dishes are your best bets. Keep it simple, enjoy the atmosphere and line the stomach for a night of Soho-based roistering.

Ten Ten Tei

56 Brewer Street, W1R 3PJ (7287 1738). Piccadilly Circus tube. **Lunch served** noon-2.30pm Mon-Fri; noon-3.45pm Sat. **Dinner served** 5-10pm Mon-Sat. **Average ££.** **Set lunch** £6.50-£12. **Set dinner** £14.80-£18.80. **Map** p268. Japanese

There's a gloriously thrown together feel to the boxy interior of this reliable Soho stalwart, its smattering of wooden tables topped with mismatched tea cups and faded plastic soy saucers. The cafeteria vibe was bolstered on our last visit by an unfortunate line in radio-friendly R&B seeping from the stereo. Set lunches offer everything from tempura to teriyaki beef or chicken, all served with vegetables, rice and miso soup, while a kaleidoscopic array of hand-rolled sushi is available alongside a comprehensive list of à la carte options. We plumped for chirashi, a generously heaped bowl of steamed rice topped with a colourful assortment of raw fish – tuna, eel, shrimp and salmon roe – that was disarmingly fresh and delicious.

Maoz Vegetarian. See p80.

Meal deals

Arbutus *63-64 Frith Street, W1D 3JW (7734 4545/www.arbutus restaurant.co.uk).* Set lunch £15.50 3 courses. Set dinner £17.50 3 courses. **Map** p268. Modern European

Azzi *47 Poland Street, W1F 7NB (7287 0997/www.azzikorea.co.uk).* Set lunch £7-£10 3 courses. **Map** p268. Korean

Jin *16 Bateman Street, W1D 3AH (7734 0908).* Set lunch £7.50 1 course. **Map** p268. Korean

Patara *15 Greek Street, W1D 4DP (7437 1071).* Set lunch £12.50-£15.50 2 courses. **Map** p268. Thai

Pierre Victoire *5 Dean Street, W1V 5RN (7287 4582).* Set lunch £7.90 2 courses. Set dinner (4-7pm) £9.90 2 courses. **Map** p268. Brasserie

Red Fort *77 Dean Street, W1D 3SH (7437 2115).* Set lunch £12 2 courses. **Map** p268. Indian

In the area

Bistro 1 *75 Beak Street, W1F 9SS (7287 1840).* **Map** p268.

Bistro 1 *28 Brewer Street, W1F 0SR (7734 0179).* **Map** p268.

Bistro 1 *27 Frith Street, W1D 5LE (7734 6204).* **Map** p268.

Busaba Eathai *106-110 Wardour Street, W1F 0TR (7255 8686).* **Map** p268.

Diner *18 Ganton Street, W1F 7BU (7287 8962).* **Map** p268.

Gourmet Burger Kitchen *15 Frith Street, W1D 4RE (7494 9533).* **Map** p268.

Hamburger Union 22-25 Dean Street, W1D 3RY (7437 6004). Map p268.

Itsu 103 Wardour Street, W1F 0UQ (7479 4790). **Map** p268.

Konditor & Cook Curzon Soho, 99 Shaftesbury Avenue, W1D 5DY (7292 1684). **Map** p268.

Kulu Kulu 76 Brewer Street, W1F 9TX (7734 7316). **Map** p269.

Masala Zone 9 Marshall Street, W1F 7ER (7287 9966). **Map** p268.

Nando's 10 Frith Street, W1D 3JF (7494 0932). **Map** p268.

Paul 49 Old Compton Street, W1D 6HL (7287 6261). **Map** p268.

Ping Pong 45 Great Marlborough Street, W1F 7JL (7851 6969). **Map** p268.

Pizza Express 6 Upper James Street, Golden Square, W1F 9DG (7437 4550). **Map** p268.

Pizza Express 20 Greek Street, W1D 4DU (7734 7430). **Map** p268.

Pizza Express Jazz Club 10 Dean Street, W1D 3RW (7437 9595). **Map** p268.

Wagamama 10A Lexington Street, W1F 0LD (7292 0990). **Map** p268.

Yo! Sushi 52 Poland Street, W1V 3DF (7287 0443). **Map** p268.

South Kensington

Bugis Street Brasserie NEW

Millennium Gloucester Hotel & Conference Centre, 4-18 Harrington Gardens, SW7 4LH (7373 6030/ www.millenniumhotels.co.uk). South Kensington tube. **Meals served** noon-10.30pm daily. **Average** £££. **Set lunch** (noon-4pm) £6.50-£8.50 2-3 courses. **Set meal** £15.50 per person (minimum 2). **Map** p278. Malaysian

Bugis Street was a Singapore tourist nightspot renowned for its parade of transsexual women. This hotel brasserie, with tourists the only diners on our visit, more closely resembles a Singaporean coffee shop, with gold ceiling fans, marble-topped tables, bird cages and muzak. The menu has a Chinese and Singaporean slant, but dishes weren't impressive: chicken satay, not chargrilled but pan-fried and then skewered, was poor; stir-fried king prawns with tamarind sauce were bland. Better was the seafood ho fun, featuring fresh seafood and reasonable flat rice noodles. Our sago dessert seemed to be made with brown rather than palm sugar, and the service was occasionally as inattentive as the kitchen. A less than overwhelming experience.

★ Daquise

20 Thurloe Street, SW7 2LT (7589 6117). South Kensington tube. **Meals served** noon-11pm daily. **Average** £££. **Map** p278. Polish

This cherished café has clocked up more than 50 years of purveying no-nonsense Polish home cooking to students, tourists, old Polish émigrés and new young arrivals. The place has a cosy feel thanks to motherly waiting staff, Formica tables, leatherette banquettes and a straightforward menu. Starters shine: vibrant, beetrooty barszcz with tender uszka; puffy, light and nutty buckwheat blini with smoked salmon or herring and tart apple. To follow, indulge in Russian zrazy (stuffed mincemeat roll) with fluffy kazsa gryczana (baked buckwheat), a creamy mushroom sauce plus a side of beetroot with horseradish. Meals are ideally accompanied by Polish beer and rounded off with vodka (reliable old standards include Zywiec, Zubrówka and Wisniówka). Heroic appetites sample desserts such as traditional sweet cheese pancakes and cheesecakes.

dim t

154-156 Gloucester Road, SW7 4TD (7370 0070/www.dimt.co.uk). Gloucester Road tube. **Meals served** noon-10.30pm daily. **Average** ££. **Map** p278. Oriental

While the dim t chain borrows from old-style Chinese restaurants – slightly tongue in cheek, you'll be offered prawn crackers to start and fortune cookies to finish – it also provides a modern take with its slick good looks and accessible pan-Asian menu. Everyone will find something that tempts, whether it's one of the old favourites (Singapore noodles, Thai green curry) or the wide range of dim sum served in stacked bamboo baskets: prawn and lemongrass dumplings, say, or roasted pork steamed buns. Stir-fried broccoli had a generous kick of garlic, and Shanghai lemon chicken came crisply coated in breadcrumbs. Uptempo dance music and trendy young diners on our last visit made dim t feel like a pre-club pitstop. Dishes are well constructed and the price is right, even if you get the feeling that food quality and service were afterthoughts.

Jakob's

20 Gloucester Road, SW7 4RB (7581 9292). Gloucester Road tube.
Meals served 8am-11pm daily.
Average ££. **Map** p278. Armenian
Jakob's greets diners with a heaped counter of fresh and colourful dishes – roasted vegetable medleys, own-made quiches and the likes of poached salmon fillets. Takeaways are popular with Kensington locals looking for an easy dinner, while those venturing further in will find a number of candlelit tables in a room decorated with Armenian knick-knacks, and with a snug terracotta warmth that makes diners feel immediately at home. Meals are chosen at the main counter and then microwaved – any one dish costs £10.50 when combined with two vegetable sides. The house red from a limited wine list was delicious (if rather expensive at £4 for a small glass) and service was friendly without being fawning.

Spago

6 Glendower Place, SW7 3DP (7225 2407). South Kensington tube.
Meals served noon-11.30pm daily.
Average ££. **Map** p278. Italian
Decorated in warm rust colours and made homely with candles in the evening, this cosy neighbourhood Italian is ideal for comforting lunches or casual dinners. Pizzas are the main draw, pared-down versions of which appear in the starter section of the menu: a garlic and herb version was pleasantly charred, and crunchy and chewy in all the right places. We loved the crespoline (a satisfying spinach and ricotta-filled crêpe), but were disappointed by a lukewarm sausage and saffron risotto. The handful of lone diners present on our visit suggested that Spago is as popular with local workers grabbing a bite on the journey home as it is with families. One annoyance: the incongruous mid '90s Europop playing on a loop had us clamouring for the door instead of dessert.

Meal deals

Awana 85 Sloane Avenue, SW3 3DX (7584 8880/www.awana.co.uk). Set meal (lunch, 6-7pm) £12.50 2 courses, £15 3 courses. **Map** p278. Malaysian
Ognisko 55 Exhibition Road, Prince's Gate, SW7 2PN (7589 4635/www.ognisko.com). Set meal £12 3 courses. **Map** p278. Polish
Pasha 1 Gloucester Road, SW7 4PP (7589 7969/www.pasha-restaurant.co.uk). Set lunch £6 4 dishes, £8-£15 6 dishes. **Map** p278. Moroccan

In the area

ASK 24 Gloucester Arcade, Gloucester Road, SW7 4SF (7835 0840). **Map** p278.
Byron Hamburgers 75 Gloucester Road, SW7 4SS (7244 0700). **Map** p278.

Carluccio's Caffè *1 Old Brompton Road, SW7 3HZ (7581 8101).* **Map** p278.
Kulu Kulu *39 Thurloe Place, SW7 2HP (7589 2225).* **Map** p278.
Nando's *117 Gloucester Road, SW7 4ST (7373 4446).* **Map** p278.
Paul *122 Brompton Road, SW3 1JD (7581 6034).* **Map** p278.
Paul *73 Gloucester Road, SW7 4SS (7373 1232).* **Map** p278.
Paul *47 Thurloe Street, SW7 2LQ (7581 6034).* **Map** p278.

Strand

India Club

2nd floor, Strand Continental Hotel, 143 Strand, WC2R 1JA (7836 0650). Covent Garden, Embankment or Temple tube/Charing Cross tube/ rail. **Lunch served** noon-2.30pm, **dinner served** 6-10.50pm daily. **Average ££. Set meal** £12-£16 per person (minimum 2). **Unlicensed. Corkage** no charge. **No credit cards. Map** p273.
Indian

This canteen-cum-social club with a 1970s interior evidently doesn't feel it needs a makeover. At 8pm on a Thursday night it was packing in the punters – City gents, high-street workers and students. With no concessions to comfort or aesthetics, its winning formula is cheap Indian food, and has been for decades. The restaurant is unlicensed but the small downstairs bar enables you to cash-and-carry bottles of beer to your classroom-style table. Hot lamb madras was simple, straightforward and filling; chicken korma featured tender meat, though the sauce could have been creamier. Portions were generous, but staff were less than attentive, which negated the homely feel for which the place is famous. We were also rather disappointed by our dry naan. Basic the India Club may be, but that shouldn't mean slacking on simple details.

Meal deals

Smollensky's on the Strand
105 Strand, WC2R 0AA (7497 2101/www.smollenskys.com).
Set lunch £4.95 1 course, £7.50 2 courses. Set meal (5-7pm) £10.95 2 courses, £12.95 3 courses.
Map p273. North American

In the area
Leon *73-75 Strand, WC2R 0DE (7240 1717).* **Map** p273.
Pizza Express *147 Strand, WC2R 1JA (7836 7716).* **Map** p273.
Pizza Express *450 Strand, WC2R 0RG (7930 8205).* **Map** p273.
Prezzo *Grand Buildings, 31-32 Northumberland Avenue, WC2N 5BW (7930 4288).* **Map** p273.

Victoria

ASK
160-162 Victoria Street, SW1E 5LB (7630 8228/www.askcentral.co.uk). Victoria tube/rail. **Meals served** noon-11.30pm Mon-Sat; noon-11pm Sun. **Average ££. Map** p274.
Pizza & pasta

It's hard not to compare ASK with its sister chain Zizzi (*see p45*), and wonder exactly what separates them. Similar pizzas, an array of pastas and some safe salads make the quest difficult on face value, but it's the surroundings where ASK stands out. Many of its restaurants are situated in prime positions or in restored listed buildings, and the interiors are artfully decorated. The Victoria branch is impressive, with a swirling staircase and a clean, uncluttered feel lending a relaxing ambience. We've had mixed experiences at ASK, but on our last visit we found seafood ravioli fresh and flavoursome, while a 'vesuvio' pizza was satisfyingly hot thanks to a combination of spiced pepperoni, fresh red chillis and a crisp, chilli flake-infused base. Service was quick and attentive.

Seafresh Fish Restaurant

*80-81 Wilton Road, SW1V 1DL
(7828 0747). Victoria tube/rail/
24 bus.* **Lunch served** noon-3pm,
dinner served 5-10.30pm Mon-Fri
Meals served noon-10.30pm Sat.
Average ££. Set lunch £11.50
2 courses incl tea or coffee.
Map p275. Fish & chips

Light streams through the large
front window on to the clean,
unfussy interior of pine panelling
and leather banquette seating at
Seafresh. It's been around for
donkey's years, but is still dishing
up top-notch fish suppers. A starter
of tangy taramasalata with pitta
bread was thick enough to hold a
spoon upright; light, fluffy cod fillet
had no excess grease in its crispy
batter, nor did the chips (which were
delicious with a large dollop of
tartare sauce). The homely, creamy
fisherman's pie was substantial
enough to satisfy the hungriest sea-
dog's appetite. Dover sole, king
prawns and seafood platters are
available for those with cash to
splash, while the takeaway next
door caters to budget eaters.

★ Sekara

*3 Lower Grosvenor Place, SW1W
0EJ (7834 0722/www.sekara.co.uk).
Victoria tube/rail.* **Lunch served**
noon-3pm daily. **Dinner served**
6-10pm Mon-Sat. **Average ££.**
Set lunch (Mon-Fri) £4.50-£7.95
1 course. **Set buffet** (Sun) £12.
Map p274. Sri Lankan

It's not much to look at (dated photos
of Sri Lankan bigwigs and large
framed paintings recall the owners'
heritage), but it's the cooking that
does the talking here. Expats and
well-travelled diners come for
homely, authentic and keenly priced
island dishes. Vadai (deep-fried
lentil patties) were pleasingly
crunchy with bursts of crisp curry
leaves and toasted cumin, but main

Vincent Rooms. See p92.

Central

courses were the real stars: chicken lamprais, a rich biryani, had gorgeous, bold flavours absorbed from cardamom-infused meat stock; glistening rice was studded with chicken pieces and accompanied by a russet-hued curry made from a raunchy caramelised onion masala. Only the slow service detracted from our enjoyment of a superb meal.

Tiles

36 Buckingham Palace Road, SW1W 0RE (7834 7761/www.tiles winebar.co.uk). Victoria tube/rail. **Lunch served** noon-2.30pm, **dinner served** 5.30-10pm Mon-Fri. **Average £££. Set meal** (dinner) £15 2 courses incl glass of wine. **Map** p274. International

Tiles sits incongrously on a busy road a stone's throw from the traffic hullabaloo of Victoria station. Its large glass windows successfully exclude the cacophony and one can dine in quiet amid the attractive tile-work. We would recommend the 'supper club', a two-course meal with a glass of wine, for diners striving to save without skimping on quality. A tasty carrot, coriander and ginger soup was hearty, while the saltiness of grilled halloumi combined well with pink grapefruit in a pine-nut sprinkled salad. Chargrilled tuna steak with puy lentils was expertly cooked and generous of portion. The 'famous fish cakes' were more fish-flavoured potato than fish, but were almost redeemed by a huge mound of flavoursome, hand-cut chips. A handy spot during train delays.

Meal deals

Kazan *93-94 Wilton Road, SW1V 1DW (7233 7100/www.kazan-restaurant.com).* Set meal (noon-6.30pm) £9.99 per person (minimum 2). **Map** p275. Turkish

In the area

dim t *56-62 Wilton Road, SW1V 1DE (7834 0507).* **Map** p275.

Nando's *107-108 Wilton Road, SW1V 1DZ (7976 5719).* **Map** p275.
Nando's *17 Cardinal Walk, Cardinal Place, SW1E 5JE (7828 0158).* **Map** p275.
Pizza Express *85 Victoria Street, SW1H 0HW (7222 5270).* **Map** p274.
Prezzo *4 Victoria Buildings, 22 Terminus Place, SW1V 1JR (7233 9099).* **Map** p274.
Wagamama *Roof garden level, Cardinal Place, SW1E 5JE (7828 0561).* **Map** p274.
Yo! Sushi *Main concourse, Victoria Station, SW1V 1JT (3262 0050).* **Map** p274.
Zizzi *15 Cardinal Walk, Cardinal Place, SW1E 5JE (7821 0402).* **Map** p274.

Westminster

★ Vincent Rooms

Westminster Kingsway College, Vincent Square, SW1P 2PD (7802 8391/www.westking.ac.uk). St James's Park tube/Victoria tube/rail. **Lunch served** noon-1pm Mon-Fri. **Dinner served** 6-7pm Tue, Thur. Closed 2 wks Apr, July-Sept, 2 wks Jan-Dec. **Average £££.** **Map** p275. International

Its hard not to love the Vincent Rooms, where training waiters and chefs practise their trade and diners get to sample quality food for a fraction of the price they'd pay elsewhere. In the brasserie you may get baked duck egg and spiced tomato with cannellini beans, fennel and lemon pot-roasted pork loin, or passion-fruit crème brûlée. In the Escoffier Room it's a three-course set menu (£22.50) bookended by exquisite canapés and coffee, or tea with petits fours. After starters of seared scallops, and rabbit loin, and mains of john dory with cockle and clam fricassee, and chicken bordelaise, we were duly impressed. Downsides are that the rooms have the vibe of a school hall and the wine list is too short.

Acton

North China

*305 Uxbridge Road, W3 9QU
(8992 9183/www.northchina.co.uk).
Acton Town tube/207 bus.* **Lunch
served** noon-2.30pm, **dinner
served** 6-11pm daily. **Average**
££. **Set meal** £14.50-£22.50 per
person (minimum 2). Chinese
You're unlikely to come across the
wheat-based cuisine of northern
China until you visit this simple
restaurant in Acton – and to be
honest, you might not even come
across it here, so keen are staff to
push the standard Anglo-Canto
dishes offered by the regular menu.
Ask repeatedly for the northern
Chinese list if necessary. Dishes
worth ordering include the boiled
dumplings (ten hearty pork and
ginger-filled parcels) dipped in
vinegar. Cold glass-noodle salad
with shredded chicken offered
interesting contrasts of texture, the
gloopy noodles paired with poached
chicken breast and crunchy
cucumber sticks. The house special
soup noodle, however, was
something of a disappointment, a
peppery yet bland hot-and-sour
stock that didn't pass muster.

Bayswater

Fresco

*25 Westbourne Grove, W2 4UA
(7221 2355/www.frescojuices.co.uk).
Bayswater or Royal Oak tube.* **Meals
served** 8am-11pm daily. **Average**
££. **Set meze** £11.95. **Map** p280.
Lebanese
There's something inspiring about
the health drive of this juice-bar-
cum-Lebanese takeaway and caff,
where fruit fills the front window
and is displayed in framed pictures
on the seaside-yellow walls. The
juice menu is extensive, from
'energisers' involving the likes of
broccoli and beets to 'milky way'
milkshakes, such as the silky
banana and strawberry version with
honey that we tried on a recent visit.
Meze dishes sit in bowls behind the
counter – staff will microwave three
for £4.50 (you can order individually
too). We chose a delicate baba
ganoush with pomegranate seeds,
and a wonderfully full-flavoured
fuul; only a bland batata hara
(potatoes with chilli and coriander)
wasn't up to scratch. Houmous and
falafel pittas are a lunchtime
takeaway favourite.

Kiasu NEW

*48 Queensway, W2 3RY (7727
8810/www.kiasu.co.uk). Bayswater
or Queensway tube.* **Meals served**
noon-11pm daily. **Average** ££.
Set meal (noon-3pm) £8.90
2 courses. **Map** p281. Malaysian
We've had mixed experiences at
Kiasu since it won our Best Cheap
Eats award in 2007, but it remains
popular – we found the place (the
walls painted in confident tones of
blue and grey) packed with mostly
South-east Asian customers. Kueh
pai tee got the meal off to an
excellent start with crisp pastry
cups and distinct flavours of prawn,
bamboo shoot and coriander,
although the acar salad was too
watery. Kangkong belacan (water
spinach with shrimp paste) came
swamped in sauce, though we
appreciated its fragrant aromas,
while soft-shell crabs were sweetly
succulent and served with feather-
light mantou (Chinese buns). Glass
mugs of sweet teh tarik, a blend of
tea and condensed milk, helped
soothe the chilli heat of the dishes.

Ping Pong

*74-76 Westbourne Grove, W2
5SH (7313 9832/www.pingpong
dimsum.com). Bayswater tube.*
Dim sum served noon-11pm
Mon-Wed; noon-midnight Thur-Sat;
noon-10.30pm Sun. **Average** £££.

Set lunch (noon-5pm) £10.99-£11.99. Set meal (Sun) £17.50. Map p280. Chinese

The omnipresence of this rapidly expanding chain makes it a convenient choice, if not a culturally convincing one. No Chinese diners were in attendance on our recent visit to this spacious branch – decked out with geometric screens, functional wooden tables and unforgiving stools – something that could be explained by the food itself. We enjoyed the spectacle of the flowering amaranth tea, which 'bloomed' in our glass, but char siu bau was terrible, the interior of the dry bun containing a smudge of indecipherable stew instead of the expected barbecued pork. The seaweed, rice and duck wraps, of Japanese ancestry, were almost inedibly dry. Only the fried oysters and the Valrhona chocolate bun dessert (filled with plentiful chocolate sauce) passed muster. An underwhelming experience, but Ping Pong manages to reel in the punters all the same.

Urban Turban NEW

98 Westbourne Grove, W2 5RU (7243 4200/www.urbanturban. uk.com). Baywater or Notting Hill Gate tube. **Lunch served** noon-3.30pm, **dinner served** 6-11pm Mon-Sat. **Meals served** 1-10pm Sun. **Average** ££. **Set thali** £5.50-£6. **Set lunch** £9.95. **Map** p280. Indian

This trendy lounge bar is filled with low-slung banquettes, high bar stools and silken cushions, and themed around Indian tapas and cool cocktails. When we made our reservation, staff demanded to know how long we'd have to vacate the table; we've had warmer welcomes at motorway service stations. Nor are we convinced by the cooking; out of five choices, only seared 'gunpowder' prawns were noteworthy for their juicy freshness

and lemony flavour. Tandoori chicken was served with what tasted depressingly like spicy cream of tomato soup. Even the samosas were let down by a pasty, ground-mince filling. The menu indicates that dishes are served as they are prepared: shame that our five orders arrived, like London buses, all at once.

Meal deals

L'Accento *16 Garway Road, W2 4NH (7243 2201).* Set meal £17.50 2 courses. **Map** p280. Italian

Al Waha *75 Westbourne Grove, W2 4UL (7229 0806/www.waha-uk.com).* Set lunch £12.50 platter. **Map** p280. Lebanese

Royal China *13 Queensway, W2 4QJ (7221 2535/www.royal chinagroup.co.uk).* Dim sum (noon-5pm Mon-Sat; 11am-5pm Sun) £2.65-£4.20. **Map** p281. Chinese

In the area

Alounak Kebab *44 Westbourne Grove, W2 5SH (7229 0416).* **Map** p280.

ASK *41-43 Spring Street, W2 1JA (7706 0707).*

ASK *Whiteleys Shopping Centre, Queensway, W2 4SB (7792 1977).* **Map** p280.

Carluccio's Caffè *Westbourne Corner, 108 Westbourne Grove, W2 5RU (7243 8164).* **Map** p280.

Fresco *2nd floor, Whiteleys Shopping Centre, Queensway, W2 4YN (7243 4084).* **Map** p280.

Gourmet Burger Kitchen *50 Westbourne Grove, W2 5SH (7243 4344).* **Map** p280.

Nando's *63 Westbourne Grove, W2 4UA (7313 9506).* **Map** p280.

Pâtisserie Valerie *174-176 Queensway, W2 6LY (7243 9069).* **Map** p280.

Yo! Sushi *Whiteleys Shopping Centre, Queensway, W2 4YN (7727 9392).* **Map** p281.

West

Ground

West

Chiswick

★ Ground NEW

217-221 Chiswick High Road, W4 2DW (8747 9113/www.ground restaurants.com). Turnham Green tube. **Meals served** noon-11pm Mon-Fri; 11am-11pm Sat; 11am-10pm Sun. **Average** ££. Burgers
Those distressed by the growing number of gourmet burger chains snaking their way across London will find sanctuary in this Chiswick independent, more stylish and spacious than the herd thanks to opulent lighting, loft-style exposed brickwork and olive-green leather booths. All the burgers – blue cheese, New York deli, Hawaiian – are available with beanburger alternatives, although vegetarians will be less pleased if the bacon's left in, as it was with our order. Meat burgers are ground more coarsely than at most chains, producing a truly beefy bite, and top marks for perfectly seasoned beer-battered onion rings. Ground's

higher prices make it better suited to a big blow-out than a fast-food fix, but it could certainly teach the chains a trick or two.

Turnham Green Thai NEW

57 Turnham Green Terrace, W4 1RP (8994 3839). Turnham Green tube. **Meals served** 7.30am-2.30pm Mon; 7.30am-2.30pm, 6.30-10pm Tue-Sat. **Average** £. **Unlicensed**. **Corkage** £1 per person. **No credit cards**. Thai

Backpackers swear that Thai street food tastes better with a no-frills approach than it does juxtaposed against fancy china plates and freshly starched white tablecloths. As such, this diminutive Turnham Green restaurant – which resembles a greasy spoon and actually morphs into a bacon buttie-serving café by day – ticks all the right boxes for a bona fide taste of Bangkok. Dishes are cheap, tasty and honest, if a little predictable (think spring rolls, pad thai and som tam). In most cases, they're also entirely authentic, an exception being our laab gai, which contained sliced chicken rather than the traditional minced. Beer and wine is BYO only – the newsagent across the road has cottoned on and started stocking Singha.

Meal deals

Devonshire *126 Devonshire Road, W4 2JJ (7592 7962/ www.gordonramsay.com).* Set lunch £13.50 2 courses, £16.50 3 courses. Gastropub
Fish Hook *6-8 Elliott Road, W4 1PE (8742 0766).* Set lunch £12.50 2 courses, £15 3 courses. Fish
Sam's Brasserie & Bar *11 Barley Mow Passage, W4 4PH (8987 0555/www.sams brasserie.co.uk).* Set lunch (Mon-Fri) £12 2 courses, £15 3 courses. Set dinner (6.30-7.30pm daily) £14 2 courses, £17 3 courses. Modern European

In the area

Carluccio's Caffé *342-344 Chiswick High Road, W4 5TA (8995 8073).*
Eco *144 Chiswick High Road, W4 1PU (8747 4822).*
Giraffe *270 Chiswick High Road, W4 1PD (8995 2100).*
Gourmet Burger Kitchen *131 Chiswick High Road, W4 2ED (8995 4548).*
Maison Blanc *26-28 Turnham Green Terrace, W4 1QP (8995 7220).*
Nando's *187-189 Chiswick High Road, W4 2DR (8995 7533).*
Pâtisserie Valerie *319 Chiswick High Road, W4 5TA (8995 0234).*
Pizza Express *252 Chiswick High Road, W4 1PD (8747 0193).*
Strada *156 Chiswick High Road, W4 1PR (8995 0004).*
Tootsies Grill *148 Chiswick High Road, W4 1PS (8747 1869).*
Woodlands *12-14 Chiswick High Road, W4 1TH (8994 9333).*
Zizzi *235 Chiswick High Road, W4 2DL (8747 9400).*

Ealing

Café Grove

65 The Grove, W5 5LL (8810 0364). Ealing Broadway tube/rail. **Meals served** 10.30am-11pm Mon-Sat; 11am-10.30pm Sun. **Average** £. Polish

Café Grove continues to draw a dedicated following from Polish locals, who see it as much as a community centre as a café, not to mention a gallery for aspiring Polish artists. It doesn't hurt that the food is also first rate: the gypsy pancake was beautifully crisp, brimming with a tender goulash filling and topped with a great wallop of crème fraîche; other knockouts include pierogi (boiled dumplings), which come stuffed with either pork and spinach or cream cheese, and a pork hock virtually falling off the bone.

Be sure to book on Friday and Saturday nights, and starve in advance: portions are big enough to draw gasps from the uninitiated.

★ Sushi-Hiro

1 Station Parade, Uxbridge Road, W5 3LD (8896 3175). Ealing Common tube. **Lunch served** 11am-1.30pm, **dinner served** 4.30-9pm Tue-Sun. **Average** ££. **Set meal** £8-£18. **No credit cards.** Japanese

Only somewhere serving food of this quality could get away with such wild eccentricity. The opening hours are peculiar, with no orders taken after 1.30pm or 9pm (we once witnessed Heston Blumenthal being refused service at 1.32pm). The place is tiny, service often slow and there's no wine – just saké, beer and tea. Yet Sushi-Hiro produces some of London's freshest and most deftly handled sushi and sashimi (there's no noodles, tempura or teppanyaki). Every piece of tuna glistens; every scallop astounds with its sweetness; every sliver of sea bream thrills with its clarity of flavour; and every grain of rice feels as if it's been gently pampered into position. As for everything else about this place – well, we did warn you.

In the area
Carluccio's Caffé *5-6 The Green, W5 5DA (8566 4458).*
Gourmet Burger Kitchen *35 Haven Green, W5 2NX (8998 0392).*
Nando's *1-2 Station Buildings, Uxbridge Road, W5 3NU (8992 2290).*
Pizza Express *23 Bond Street, W5 5AS (8567 7690).*
La Siesta *11 Bond Street, W5 5AP (8810 0505).* Branch of Jamón Jamón.

Hammersmith

Knaypa NEW
268 King Street, W6 0SP (8563 2887/www.theknaypa.co.uk). Hammersmith tube. **Meals**

served noon-10.30pm Mon-Thur, Sun; noon-11pm Fri, Sat. **Average** ££. **Map** p282. Polish

Interior-designed to within an inch of its life, Knaypa clashes a rippled purple plastic ceiling with coloured mirrors, spotlights and shocking red leather chairs; piped dance music lends the feel of a half-deserted disco (the wood furniture and soft lighting of the basement provide a calm alternative). Food is authentic in the extreme. We were brought rich, creamy smalec (seasoned pork fat to be eaten with rye bread) while we waited for our starters of fried smoked cheese with chutneys, and dill-spiked gravadlax. Both seemed oversalted even by Polish standards, although a main of stuffed rabbit leg with creamy mashed potatoes and sage sauce was expertly prepared, and less of a shock to the British palate.

★ Mahdi NEW
217 King Street, W6 9JT (8563 7007). Hammersmith or Ravenscourt Park tube. **Meals served** noon-11pm daily. **Average** £. **Set lunch** (noon-6pm Mon-Fri) £4.50-£5.90 1 course. **Unlicensed** no alcohol allowed. **Map** p282. Iranian

It may not be the homeliest of restaurants – brick walls arching like the inside of a kiln, waiters unduly serious and tables crammed together – but Mahdi is crowned king when it comes to unnecessarily large portions of lovingly prepared, artfully presented Iranian food. Starters supplement the usual repertoire with rarities like ash-e reshteh, a smoky bean and noodle soup thickened with whey. Marinated chicken and lamb kebabs are succulent, super-sized and served with perfectly fluffy rice, but you'd be foolish not to experiment with more traditional dishes like baghali polo ba mahiche: rice with dill and broad beans accompanied by a melt-in-the-mouth lamb shank. It's all so delicious you'll be happy to tuck into the leftovers later that same evening.

★ Los Molinos

127 Shepherd's Bush Road, W6 7LP (7603 2229/www.losmolinosuk.com). Hammersmith tube. **Lunch served** noon-3pm Mon-Fri. **Dinner served** 6-10.45pm Mon-Sat. **Average £££.** **Map** p282. Spanish

With its warm welcome and orange walls decked in a lifetime of accumulated knick-knacks, entering Los Molinos can feel more akin to visiting the home of an eccentric relative than a restaurant. But a restaurant it is, and a fine one: every tapa we ordered was a success in terms of both presentation and taste. Each ingredient could be discerned and savoured in a super-fresh bowl of gazpacho; soupy fabada came packed with tasty morsels of bacon, chorizo and black pudding; shellfish and other goodies were crammed into a creamy, saffron-spiked paella; and a special of steaming mussels excelled in its chunky, garlic and parsley-flecked tomato sauce. This local haunt is worth revisiting time and again.

Polanka

258 King Street, W6 0SP (8741 8268/www.polanka-rest.com). Ravenscourt Park tube. **Meals served** noon-9.30pm Mon-Sat; noon-7.30pm Sun. **Average £££.** **Unlicensed. Corkage** £3 wine, £6 spirits. **Map** p282. Polish

A small Polish grocery shop fronts this deli-restaurant, itself a humble hotchpotch of pine and wicker lampshades, dried flowers and the occasional eye-catching decoration (a boar skin pegged to one wall, a mannequin in traditional dress peering out from an alcove). A starter of barszcz was blood-coloured and rich with beef stock, but mains were disappointing. Pork schnitzel 'Polanka' came with rivers of pale melted cheese, mash that tasted more of butter than potato, and sliced raw tomato. A gelatinous white wine and mushroom sauce overwhelmed the carp it came with, making us enviously eye a rich, creamy bigos served in a bread cob. Service is sweet and attentive, although the '80s soft rock on the stereo can be distracting.

★ Sagar

157 King Street, W6 9JT (8741 8563). Hammersmith tube. **Lunch served** noon-2.45pm Mon-Fri. **Dinner served** 5.30-10.45pm Mon-Thur; 5.30-11.30pm Fri. **Meals served** noon-11.30pm Sat; noon-10.45pm Sun. **Average £££.** **Set thali** £9.95-£12.45. **Map** p282. Indian

This original branch of Sagar remains one of few restaurants in London to serve Udupi vegetarian dishes from Karnataka. The blonde wood interior is embellished with

elegant brass figurines (illuminated at night), and the place is often as busy at lunchtime as it is in the evening. Puffy, spongy idlis soaked up our freshly made sambar and fiery coconut chutney, while uthappam was just the right side of searingly hot, and was made livelier still with a topping of fresh tomato. A cooling contrast came from the vegetable kootu (spinach cooked with yoghurt and coconut). The dosas are also excellent, with delicately spiced fillings from potato to paneer, and prices are among the cheapest you'll find for Indian food of this quality.

Shilpa NEW

206 King Street, W6 0RA (8741 3127/www.shilparestaurant. co.uk). Hammersmith tube. **Lunch served** noon-3pm daily. **Dinner served** 6-11pm Mon-Wed, Sun; 6pm-midnight Thur-Sat. **Average** £. **Set lunch** £4.99 (vegetarian), £5.99 (non-vegetarian). **Map** p282. Indian

There's nothing special about Shilpa's interior – its bright lilac walls, starched white tablecloths and plasma-screen Bollywood movies lending an air of unassuming modernity – but the fiery Keralite food is another matter. Dense and crunchy vadai (lentil fritters with a creamy coconut chutney) were a lovely way to start the meal; a large bowl of rasam broth was also top-notch: rich and warming with a sour hit of tamarind and fresh coriander. To follow, king fish curry with green chillies and coconut milk was a little overcooked, but the masala dosa brought things back on track, the spiced potatoes encased in a perfectly light and crisp pancake. Service is sweet and the set lunches under a fiver are a bargain.

Tosa NEW

332 King Street, W6 0RR (8748 0002). Ravenscourt Park or Stamford Brook tube. **Lunch served** 12.30-2.30pm, **dinner**

Sushi-Hiro. See p99.

served 6-11pm daily. **Average**
££. **Map** p282. Japanese
Sushi lovers will find plenty here to
sate their appetites – silky salmon,
buttery tuna, and sweet, sticky eel
emerging from a hidden kitchen –
but Tosa's true selling point is its
smouldering grill, on to which a
robata chef tosses meaty skewers
from the refrigerated cabinet many
mistake for a sushi counter upon
arrival. Don't miss the asparamaki
(thinly sliced belly pork wrapped
around asparagus spears), the
beefy, lightly chewy ox-tongue, and
the crisp and sticky chicken wings.
Salt-grilling is also done well,
turning mackerel into a crisp and
smoky delight. Tosa is not fancy,
but with an Asahi beer in your
hand and the smell of barbecue in
the air, we can think of many worse
places to spend the evening.

Meal deals

Queen's Arms *171 Greyhound
Road, W6 8NL (7386 5078).*
Set lunch (12.30-3pm Mon-Fri)
£10 2 courses, £14 3 courses.
Map p282. Gastropub

In the area
Pizza Express *158 Fulham
Palace Road, W6 9ER (8563 2064).*
Map p282.

Holland Park

Maison Blanc
*102 Holland Park Avenue, W11
4UA (7221 2494/www.maison
blanc.co.uk). Holland Park tube.*
Meals served 8am-7pm Mon-
Sat; 8.30am-6.30pm Sun. **Average**
££. **Map** p281. Café
The French refer to window
shopping as *lèche vitrine* (window
licking), and it's easy to see why
after ducking under the brightly
coloured awning at Maison Blanc
and peering at the luxurious cakes
on display. This smart stretch of

pavement is now overflowing with
cross-channel imports, including
outposts of Paul and Pâtisserie
Valerie, and on a summer's day it
feels more like boulevard St-
Germain than Holland Park
Avenue. Inside all is *authentique*,
with handsomely crafted tartes au
pommes, quiches lorraine and
decadent mini gateaux, plus an
excellent selection of breads. A few
high stools and a narrow counter
cater to those eating in, while
neighbouring Holland Park is a
picnicker's paradise.

In the area
Pâtisserie Valerie *94 Holland
Park Avenue, W11 3RB (7985
0890).* **Map** p281.
Paul *82A Holland Park Avenue,
W11 3RB (7727 3797).* **Map** p281.
Tootsies Grill *120 Holland Park
Avenue, W11 4UA (7229 8567).*
Map p281.

Kensington

★ Byron
Hamburgers NEW
*222 Kensington High Street,
W8 7RG (7361 1717/www.byron
hamburgers.com). High Street
Kensington tube.* **Meals served**
noon-11pm Mon-Thur; noon-11.30pm
Fri; 10am-11.30pm Sat; 10am-11pm
Sun. **Average** ££. **Map** p278.
Burgers
It may look like your average
burger, but delve beneath the bun
and you'll find a pattie ground from
21 day-aged rump, chuck and
brisket cuts of grass-fed Aberdeen
Angus cows. It's a winning recipe
that makes for a burger with real
bite, one reason the owners have
forsaken novelty constructions and
stuck with the classic 6oz, the
cheeseburger (topped with the likes
of monterey jack or cashel blue),
and the Byron special with dry-cure
bacon and mature cheddar. There's

also a roast portobello mushroom burger with goat's cheese and roasted red peppers for veggies. Nor is the design overdone: the place is sleek and stylish, with pastel-coloured seating, minimal light fittings and a tasteful modern mural across one wall.

Stick & Bowl

31 Kensington High Street, W8 5NP (7937 2778). High Street Kensington tube. **Meals served** 11.30am-11pm daily. **Average** £. **No credit cards. Map** p278. Oriental

Trade is justifiably roaring at this informal Chinese diner, where the ridiculously cheap prices and belt-busting portions stand in stark contrast to most of the surrounding gastro palaces. Office workers, students and shoppers flood the place at lunchtime, most grabbing takeaways and heading out, although some choose to perch on bar stools and eat at the narrow Formica tables. Portions are enormous, while prices are quite the opposite, although it tends to be worth shelling out a few extra pennies for a quality dish such as prawns in black bean sauce, packed with fresh seafood. Cheaper dishes can be rather hit and miss: our beef with ginger and spring onion, for example, was disappointingly let down by tough meat.

Meal deals

11 Abingdon Road *11 Abingdon Road, W8 6AH (7937 0120/ www.abingdonroad.co.uk).* Set lunch (Mon-Sat) £15.50 2 courses. **Map** p278. Modern European
Med Kitchen *3-5 Campden Hill Road, W8 7DU (7938 1830/www.medkitchen.co.uk).* Set lunch (noon-5.30pm Mon-Fri) £13.50 2 courses. **Map** p278. Mediterranean
Med Kitchen *127-129 Kensington Church Street, W8 7LP (7727 8142/ www.medkitchen.co.uk).* Set lunch

(noon-5pm Mon-Fri) £13.50 2 courses. **Map** p281. Mediterranean
Randa *23 Kensington Church Street, W8 4LF (7937 5363).* Set lunch (noon-5pm Mon-Fri) £16 lunch box. **Map** p278. Lebanese
Whits *21 Abingdon Road, W8 6AH (7938 1122/www.whits.co.uk).* Set lunch (Tue-Fri) £15.50 2 courses. **Map** p278. Modern European

In the area

Al-Dar *221 Kensington High Street, W8 6FG (7938 1547).* **Map** p278.
Café Pasta *229-231 Kensington High Street, W8 6SA (7937 6314).* **Map** p278.
Feng Sushi *24 Kensington Church Street, W8 4EP (7937 7927).* **Map** p278.
Giraffe *7 Kensington High Street, W8 5NP (7938 1221).* **Map** p278.
Ottolenghi *1 Holland Street, W8 4NA (7937 0003).* **Map** p278.
Le Pain Quotidien *9 Young Street, W8 5EH (7486 6154).* **Map** p278.
Pâtisserie Valerie *27 Kensington Church Street, W8 4LL (7937 9574).* **Map** p278.
Pizza Express *35 Earl's Court Road, W8 6ED (7937 0761).* **Map** p278.
Prezzo *35A Kensington High Street, W8 5BA (7937 2800).* **Map** p278.
Ranoush Juice Bar *86 Kensington High Street, W8 4SG (7938 2234).* **Map** p278.
Strada *29 Kensington High Street, W8 5NP (7938 4648).* **Map** p278.
Wagamama *26-28 Kensington High Street, W8 4PF (7376 1717).* **Map** p278.

Ladbroke Grove

Armadillo Café

11 Bramley Road, W10 6SZ (7727 9799/www.armadillocafe.co.uk). Latimer Road tube. **Meals served**

West

Tosa.
See p101.

8am-4.30pm Mon-Fri. **Average** £.
Unlicensed no alcohol allowed.
No credit cards. **Map** p282.
Café
The Armadeli that once supplied
the diminutive Armadillo Café with
organic ingredients for its
sandwiches and salads has now
been replaced by a dry-cleaner, but
this local institution keeps on
trucking, fuelling and fuelled by
workers from the Heart FM offices
next door. Sadly, the salads are now
pre-packaged, but a range of made-
to-order panini include innovative
concoctions like brie, bacon and
walnut, while a handful of hot daily
specials cover the likes of curry,
lasagne or chilli con carne, plus
some interesting vegetarian
alternatives. Orange juice is freshly
squeezed and the fresh coffee
remains some of the best in the
area: strong and supremely smooth.
There is extra seating downstairs
and colourful metal tables outside
in the summer months.

Books for Cooks

*4 Blenheim Crescent, W11 1NN
(7221 1992/www.booksforcooks.
com). Ladbroke Grove tube.* **Open**
10am-6pm, **lunch served** noon-
1.30pm Tue-Sat. **Average** £. **Set
lunch** £5 2 courses, £7 3 courses.
Map p280. Café
The well-earned popularity of this
café – a tiny skylit 'test kitchen' in
the back of the renowned bookshop
– has become something of a
burden: we turned up 15 minutes
before noon kick-off, but were met
by the smug faces of those who had
staked out the dozen or so seats
much earlier. Lunch includes a
three-course set menu (using
recipes from the shop's cookery
books) for just £7. On our most
recent visit, dishes gave a nod to
Latin America, including a Mexican
green salad with corn relish and
chilli peanut dressing, and a sweet
ancho chilli and garlic roast
chicken with green rice. Luckily,
we still had room to sample the

delicious cakes: chocolate, whisky and apple, or berries and peaches.

Café Garcia

246 Portobello Road, W11 1LL (7221 6119/www.cafegarcia.co.uk). Ladbroke Grove tube. **Meals served** 9am-5pm daily. **Average** £. **Map** p280. Spanish

A simultaneously convivial and calming atmosphere makes Café Garcia as suitable for bands of shoppers seeking a coffee break from bustling Portobello Road as for lone diners looking for a filling lunch. And it really is a café in the traditional sense, its decor limited to a few sepia photos and some Spanish collectibles behind the counter. On our visit a selection of empanadas and tortillas was on display in the glass-fronted counter along with paella, fabada and other cooked dishes, all ready to be plated and popped in the microwave; plump boquerones and salads were also available. Neighbouring store R Garcia's deli has a tempting array of Spanish meats and cheeses that's not to be missed.

Café Oporto

62A Golborne Road, W10 5PS (8968 8839). Ladbroke Grove or Westbourne Park tube/23, 52 bus. **Meals served** 8am-7pm daily. **Average** £. **No credit cards.** **Map** p280. Portuguese

Like the football teams from Portugal's two biggest cities, pastelarias Lisboa (*see p106*) and Oporto are forever in head-to-head competition. Located on opposite sides of Golborne Road, they sell pretty much the same things at the same prices, so you might as well go for your preference of city or football team – it works for the locals who treat Oporto as an extension of their home, and this despite the borderline vintage feel of its tired furniture and faded photos. The warm savoury pastéis are divine; we gorged ourselves on fillings of chicken and cheese, and salty bacalhau. The coffee came strong and honestly priced, and the pastéis de nata (custard tarts) were wonderfully creamy and eggy.

Galicia

323 Portobello Road, W10 5SY (8969 3539). Ladbroke Grove tube. **Lunch served** noon-3pm Tue-Sun. **Dinner served** 7-11.30pm Tue-Sat; 7-10pm Sun. **Average** ££. **Set lunch** (Tue-Sat) £8.50 3 courses; (Sun) £9.50 3 courses. **Map** p280. Spanish

With its gruff but amenable staff and menu of regional and national dishes – including meat and seafood tapas – Galicia manages to attract a loyal crowd despite a tucked-away location at the quiet end of Portobello Road. We opted for mains of veal in sherry sauce and a tomato-based Galician chicken stew, which arrived with a huge silver platter of simply cooked seasonal vegetables and chips. A quick inspection of the puddings tempted us into ordering a rich caramel flan and a slice of tarta santiago, the latter doused in a generous slug of almond liqueur. With a lively atmosphere, simple decor and solid, dependable cooking, Galicia is as well suited to an informal night with friends as it is to a more intimate tête-à-tête.

George's Portobello Fish Bar

329 Portobello Road, W10 5SA (8969 7895). Ladbroke Grove tube. **Meals served** 11am-11.45pm Mon-Fri; 11am-9pm Sat; noon-9.30pm Sun. **Average** £. **Unlicensed.** **Corkage** no charge. **No credit cards.** **Map** p280. Fish & chips

Jamie Oliver isn't the only one to love George's, a local landmark since 1961 that still pulls in punters of all ages (last time we visited, the Chelsea FC youth team was lining up outside for a post-training feed).

It's a cramped but cheerful space more akin to an American diner than a traditional English chippie. Cod, skate and haddock all come fresh from Billingsgate and are battered to perfection, although we felt our anaemic looking thick-cut chips could have done with a minute or two more in the fryer. The sweet and meltingly textured mushy peas would please even the most discerning palate, but purists may pale at the range of less traditional treats on offer – from spare ribs to döner kebabs.

Lisboa Pâtisserie NEW

57 Golborne Road, W10 5NR
(8968 5242). Ladbroke Grove or
Westbourne Park tube/23, 52 bus.
Meals served 7.30am-7.30pm daily.
Average £. **Map** p280. Portuguese
Its location amid London's second largest Portuguese community means that oversubscription to the Lisboa is a lingering issue – it's not unusual to see punters waiting in the painfully slow queue for nothing more than a quality bica (espresso). Nevertheless, if you want to experience an authentic pastelaria then it's worth hanging around. Take the edge off your coffee with one of the renowned cakes or pastries (some made from recipes dating back to the Middle Ages). Pastéis de nata (custard tarts) remain the favourite with their delicate flaky pastry and rich, gooey centres, and there are always plenty of coconut- and orange-flecked treats being piled into takeaway boxes, no doubt to provide a sweet end to a long Portuguese dinner.

Moroccan Tagine

95 Golborne Road, W10 5NL
(8968 8055). Ladbroke Grove
or Westbourne Park tube/23 bus.
Meals served 11am-11pm daily.
Average ££. **Unlicensed**
no alcohol allowed. **Map** p280.
North African

The cheerful democracy found in Moroccan dining is in full swing at this popular café, where both members of the trendy Portobello Road set and tourists mingle amid scatter cushions and dine to lilting Maghrebi music. The food, sadly, is less harmonious. Starters lacked zing: beetroot salad consisted of undressed cubes of beet on iceberg lettuce, while zaalouk (aubergine dip) was bitter, and falafels dry and flavourless. A light, fluffy mound of couscous partially made up for these lapses, but lamb tagine with artichokes and peas lacked the subtle spicing of the best Moroccan food. It's a shame that food standards have slipped here as this is a nice, casual spot that many people regard with affection.

Santo NEW

299 Portobello Road, W10 5TD
(8968 4590/www.santovillage.
com). Ladbroke Grove tube.
Meals served noon-11pm Tue-Fri; 10am-11pm Sat; 10am-10pm Sun. **Average** £££. **Map** p280.
Mexican
Walls illustrated with agave plants and dinky wood and metal chairs nicely evoke modern Mexico at this café, restaurant and margarita bar. The day menu proffers a good range of the usual quesadillas and burritos, plus tortas (sourdough sandwiches) and bowls of rice and black beans with your choice of toppings – chile colorado (free range pork with chile ancho and chile guajillo stew), say, or grilled prawns. The Mexican waiting staff were friendly and swift to correct the kitchen's confusion over our order, but we were amazed to find all the chefs were Asian. Chilli-fuelled breakfasts are available at weekends, and dishes are posher and pricier in the evening. The margaritas are modest in size, but punchy and delicious.

Meal deals

Essenza *210 Kensington Park Road, W11 1NR (7792 1066/ www.essenza.co.uk).* Set lunch (12.30 6.30pm Mon-Fri) £12 2 courses. **Map** p280. Italian
Mediterraneo *37 Kensington Park Road, W11 2EU (7792 3131/ www.mediterraneo-restaurant.co.uk).* Set lunch (12.30-3pm Mon-Fri) £12.50 2 courses incl coffee. **Map** p280. Italian

In the area

S&M Café *268 Portobello Road, W10 5TY (8968 8898).* **Map** p280.

Maida Vale

★ Red Pepper

8 Formosa Street, W9 1EE (7266 2708). Warwick Avenue tube. **Dinner served** 6.30-11pm Mon-Fri. **Meals served** 11am-11pm Sat; 11am-10.30pm Sun. **Average** £££. **Map** p283. Pizza & pasta

This neighbourhood Italian's extraordinary popularity means that service is of the no-nonsense kind, even on week nights (our polite request to move tables was dismissed with a cursory shake of the head from the higher powers), and dishes arrive with unfailing alacrity. But what fine dishes they are: enticing own-made pastas (fresh artichoke and king prawn ravioli, say, or pappardelle with organic chicken livers and sage), daily-changing specials and enormous thin-crust pizzas. Everything we sampled was exemplary: from a piping-hot pizza parmigiana laden with mozzarella and aubergine, to a plate of perfectly grilled squid, sea bream and luscious king prawns. Regulars rhapsodise about the tiramisu, but the delicious dark chocolate tart (intense in flavour but light in texture) gets our vote every time.

West

Red Pepper

Notting Hill

Costas Fish Restaurant

18 Hillgate Street, W8 7SR (7727 4310). Notting Hill Gate tube. **Lunch served** noon-2.30pm, **dinner served** 5.30-10.30pm Tue-Sat. **Average** £. **No credit cards. Map** p281. Fish & chips

A no-nonsense chippie that was battering cods almost 20 years before Hugh Grant spilled his orange juice over Julia Roberts, and a reliable antidote to the flood of Notting Hill flummery ever since. It might look like a common-or-garden takeaway, but beyond the fryer you'll find a simple dining room furnished with caff-style tables and red leatherette banquettes. The menu's Hellenic accent was evidenced by our starter of oniony taramasalata with toasted pitta (easily enough for two); even more pleasing were mains of meaty rock salmon and delicate lemon sole, as

were the golden brown chips and bowlful of mushy peas. Local families, ravenous toddlers in tow, were tucking in with abandon – and not a media darling in sight.

Nyonya

2A Kensington Park Road, W11 3BU (7243 1800/www.nyonya. co.uk). Notting Hill Gate tube. **Lunch served** 11.30am-2.45pm, **dinner served** 6-10.30pm Mon-Fri. **Meals served** 11.30am-10.30pm Sat, Sun. **Average** ££. **Set lunch** (Mon-Fri) £9 2 courses. **Map** p281. Malaysian

There may be little glamour to its two floors of Formica benches and plain tables, but Nyonya (which means 'Straits Chinese lady') is a fair rendition of the kopi tiams (coffee shops) of the Straits. The Khoo family used to run a respected Peranakan restaurant in Singapore, and their best dishes set the benchmark for this cuisine: penang-style char kway teow is the real deal, pungent and garlicky, while

Taqueria

traditional sour and spicy flavours show up best in a curry tumis of sea bream and okra, laced with tamarind. Daughter Purdey is an expert on kueh (vividly coloured cakes), and the tasting plate is worth exploring, particularly kueh tai tai (purple glutinous rice with sweet coconut jam).

★ Taqueria

139-143 Westbourne Grove, W11 2RS (7229 4734/www.coolchile taqueria.co.uk). Notting Hill Gate tube. **Meals served** noon-11pm Mon-Thur; noon-11.30pm Fri; 10am-11.30pm Sat; noon-10.30pm Sun. **Average** ££. **Map** p280.
Mexican

London's swelling affection for Mexican street food has a friend in Taqueria, with its real-deal tortilla-making machine from Guadalajara and menu exploring masa (maize dough) in many forms – flattened into tortillas for tacos, fried crisp for tostadas and shaped into thick patties for griddled sopes. Masks, movie posters and gorgeous staff make Taqueria easy on the eye as well as the taste buds, and there's a commendable list of tequilas, Mexican beers and aguas frescas. As for the tacos, chicken tinga (with fabulous chipotle sauce) was too liquid, and the garlic prawns could have coped with more garlic. In contrast, the crumbly chorizo sopes were impeccable, and the zingy sea bass ceviche tasted as if it came straight from the ocean.

In the area

ASK *145 Notting Hill Gate, W11 3LB (7792 9942).* **Map** p281.
Feng Sushi *101 Notting Hill Gate, W11 3JZ (7727 1123).* **Map** p281.
Mexicali *147-149 Notting Hill Gate, W11 3LF (7234 4148).* **Map** p281.
Nando's *58-60 Notting Hill Gate, W11 3HT (7243 1647).* **Map** p281.
Ottolenghi *63 Ledbury Road, W11 2AD (7727 1121).* **Map** p280.
Pizza Express *137 Notting Hill Gate, W11 3GQ (7229 6000).* **Map** p281.
Zizzi *2-6 Notting Hill Gate, W11 3JE (7243 2888).* **Map** p281.

Olympia

Alounak

10 Russell Gardens, W14 8EZ (7603 7645). Kensington (Olympia) tube/rail. **Meals served** noon-midnight daily. **Average** ££. **Unlicensed**. **Corkage** no charge.
Iranian

Once among our favourite Iranians, Alounak seems to have lost its shine. Nothing has changed on the surface: its front room remains a temple to the kind of token handicrafts imported ten-a-penny from Tehran, while the rear is dominated by fish tanks, a central fountain and a menacing chandelier. Yet recent visits have revealed a restaurant

satisfying studenty kebab fans while leaving out those seeking traditional Iranian dishes. Grilled sea bass was small and overcooked, and khoresht-e bamieh (lamb and okra stew) consisted of just two pieces of meat floating in a barely seasoned tomato broth. Coming as it does from a culture that loves to bitch about others' food, Alounak is treading a thin line.

In the area

Pizza Express *Olympia Exhibition Centre, Hammersmith Road, W14 8UX (7602 6677).*

Shepherd's Bush

Abu Zaad

29 Uxbridge Road, W12 8LH (8749 5107/www.abuzaad.co.uk). Shepherd's Bush Market tube. **Meals served** 11am-11pm daily. **Average** £. **Map** p282. Syrian
Authentic, affordable Damascene food is done with flair at Abu Zaad, the culinary centre of the Shepherd's Bush strip known as Little Syria and one of few Levantine restaurants in London not to pose as Lebanese. The harsh lighting and tiled floors may appear charmless at the outset, but there's a back room with painted wall panels and inlaid marble tables for those seeking a more intimate evening. Most dishes are meat-heavy (lamb kebabs and various mince-stuffed vegetables baked in yoghurt), but vegetarians needn't despair: meze outshone mains on our visit, and it's tempting to make a meal of these alone. Highlights included baby aubergines stuffed with chilli-flecked walnuts, and tamarind lentils with pasta cubes and shards of fried bread.

★ Adam's Café

77 Askew Road, W12 9AH (8743 0572). Hammersmith tube then 266 bus. **Dinner served** 7-11pm Mon-

Sat. **Average** ££. **Set dinner** £11.50 1 course incl mint tea or coffee, £14.50 2 courses, £16.95 3 courses. **Licensed. Corkage** (wine only) £3. **Map** p282.
North African
With its inexpensive, excellent food and laid-back atmosphere, it's little wonder that Adam's Café has proved so successful since it was set up over 15 years ago. Amiable staff brought out baby balls of lamb, fiery harissa and spicy pickled vegetables to whet our appetites for the starters that followed. The Tunisian classic brik à l'oeuf (a still-soft egg encased in a brittle fan of ouarka pastry) was perfect, while a generous bowl of harira soup was thick and warming. For mains, we enjoyed a large helping of couscous with cumin-infused meatballs in a satisfyingly rich tomato sauce. The decor may be dated, as is the food presentation (parsley garnishes seem very popular), but we wouldn't change a thing about Adam's.

★ Esarn Kheaw

314 Uxbridge Road, W12 7LJ (8743 8930/www.esarnkheaw. com). Shepherd's Bush Market tube/207, 260, 283 bus. **Lunch served** noon-3pm Mon-Fri. **Dinner served** 6-11pm daily. **Average** ££. **Map** p282. Thai
The praise heaped on Esarn Kheaw may seem out of kilter with its uninspiring interior – its mint-green dining room decorated with false exposed beams and framed photos of the Thai royals – but the food here is authentic in the extreme. You'll find old favourites out in force, but adventurous diners will revel in the opportunity to sample the earthier flavours of offal-heavy north-eastern Thai cuisine. The chef's special chicken was a gloriously rich and pungent medley of vegetables and shredded fowl, while papaya salad was a fiery collage of splintered fruit and

carrot, chilli, garlic, dried prawns and peanuts smothered in lemon juice and fish sauce; it boldly eschewed the insipidly sweet versions of this dish found in lesser Thai restaurants.

Patio

5 Goldhawk Road, W12 8QQ (8743 5194). Goldhawk Road tube. **Lunch served** noon-3pm Mon-Fri. **Dinner served** 6-11.30pm daily. **Average** ££. **Set meal** £16.40 3 courses incl vodka shot. **Map** p282. Polish

The cooking seems less reliable and the service more erratic than ever (our recent visit was complicated by a sweet but uncomprehending and incomprehensible Chinese waitress), but Patio retains a quirky charm akin to the home of a Polish aunt, complete with home cooking, a faded, fin-de-siècle air, piano and velvet drapes. Starters are traditional: potato pancakes, bigos, herrings and smoked salmon blini (a whopping torpedo-shaped affair). Cod in a cloying dill sauce and plain

polish sausage à la zamoyski (grilled with onions, horseradish and mustard) were nothing special, and the accompanying vegetables were slightly tired. Cheesecake was lighter than usual (not typically Polish), but sweet cheese pancakes certainly hit the spot. Patio still appeals, but there's always room for improvement.

Red Sea NEW

382 Uxbridge Road, W12 7LL (8749 6888). Shepherd's Bush Market tube. **Meals served** 11am-11pm Mon-Thur, Sun; 11am-midnight Fri, Sat. **Average** £. **Unlicensed** no alcohol allowed. **Map** p282. Eritrean

With its plastic table covers and eccentric decor depicting Eritrean peasant scenes, the legendary Sanaa skyline and a view of Westminster Bridge, Red Sea feels convincingly like an African transport café. Service is somewhat absent-minded and there's not much explanation for those who don't know their way

Lucky 7.
See p114.

around dishes of the region, but the menu ranges confidently over Horn of Africa and Middle Eastern cuisine. Our choice of awaze tibs (lamb cooked in a spicy tomato sauce), shiro (puréed chickpeas) and a range of vegetarian orthodox 'fasting foods' – spinach, potato and lentils – all up-ended as tradition dictates on a springy bed of injera dough. Note that Red Sea is unlicensed, and you can no longer bring your own alcohol.

Som Tam House

131 Askew Road, W12 9AU (8749 9030/www.somtamhouse.co.uk). Ravenscourt Park or Shepherd's Bush Market tube. **Lunch served** noon-3pm, **dinner served** 6-11pm Mon-Sat. **Average** ££. **Map** p282. Thai

Shuffling in from a harsh autumn evening we recently found ourselves warmed as much by Som Tam's charm as its central heating, staff chatting away cheerfully as they seated us amid the Thai curios and house plants that clutter this small, informal eatery. A platter of mixed starters got us off on the right foot, eschewing the rubbery imitations favoured by many competitors in favour of crisp spring rolls packed with vegetables and some sweetly pungent satay skewers. Mains are also a cut above the normal traffic-light Thai curries: penang beef curry had a dry heat tempered by an expert use of basil and lime, while the yellow chicken curry was wonderfully aromatic and packed with tender meat. A deserved local favourite.

★ Sufi NEW

70 Askew Road, W12 9BJ (8834 4888/www.sufirestaurant.com). Hammersmith tube then 266 bus. **Meals served** noon-11pm daily. **Average** ££. **Set lunch** (noon-5pm Mon-Thur) £5 2 courses. **Map** p282. Iranian

Sufi's kitchen is keen on emulating the motherland in more than just token gestures. So there are starters rarely found in London, including kookoo sabzi, a herb omelette rich with coriander, parsley and dill, and ash-e reshteh, a provincial bean and noodle soup thickened with whey and aromatic as grandmother's own. The mains are similarly convincing, with the range of tender kebabs complemented by superb stews including rich, bitter khoresht-e fesenjan (chicken cooked in walnuts and pomegranate juice), and khoresht-e bademjan (lamb with fried aubergines). Unlike the food, the decor is not especially notable, adorned with the usual mix of Tehran trinkets and Persian ephemera including framed prints of wrinkled bazaaris and a panoramic view of pre-earthquake Bam.

Vine Leaves

71 Uxbridge Road, W12 8NR (8749 0325). Shepherd's Bush Market tube. **Lunch served** noon-3pm, **dinner served** 5pm-midnight Mon-Thur. **Meals served** noon-1am Fri, Sat; noon-11.30pm Sun. **Average** ££. **Set meal** (Mon-Thur, Sun) £10.95 3 courses. **Set mezédes** £9.95 mini, £13.95 mixed, £16.95 fish. **Map** p282. Greek

A simple mix of darkwood furniture and walls decorated with colourful Greek trinkets, Vine Leaves is as popular with local lunch-breakers as it is with parties capitalising on its cheerful vibe and abundance of shareable meze – from an enormous portion of expertly grilled haloumi and piping hot dolmades to basturma (spiced, cured meat). All of which is easy to fill up on in itself, but it's a shame to miss the mains, the lamb kleftiko meltingly tender and alive with the tang of lemon and cinnamon, the beef stifado rich with red wine and wonderfully warming. There's also a varied vegetarian menu, and staff are happy to dispense advice on the compatibility of dishes with various Greek wines on the menu.

In the area

Byron Hamburgers *The Loft, Westfield Shopping Centre, W12 7GF (8743 7755).* **Map** p282.
Gourmet Burger Kitchen *Southern Terrace, Westfield Shopping Centre, W12 7GF (8746 1246).* **Map** p282.
Nando's *The Loft, Westfield Shopping Centre, W12 7GF (8834 4658).* **Map** p282.
Nando's *284-286 Uxbridge Road, W12 7JA (8746 1112).* **Map** p282.
Ooze *The Balcony, Westfield Shopping Centre, W12 7GF (8749 1901).* **Map** p282.
Pho *The Balcony, Westfield Shopping Centre, W12 7GF (7436 0111).* **Map** p282.
Pizza Express *The Loft, Westfield Shopping Centre, W12 7GF (8749 1500).* **Map** p282.
The Real Greek *Southern Terrace, Westfield Shopping Centre, W12 7GF (8743 9168).* **Map** p282.
Square Pie *The Balcony, Westfield Shopping Centre, W12 7GF (8222 6697).* **Map** p282.
Wagamama *Southern Terrace, Westfield Shopping Centre, W12 7GF (8749 9073).* **Map** p282.
Wahaca *Southern Terrace, Westfield Shopping Centre, W12 7GF (8749 4517).* **Map** p282.
Yo! Sushi *The Balcony, Westfield Shopping Centre, W12 7GF (3130 1430).* **Map** p282.

West Kensington

Best Mangal

104 North End Road, W14 9EX (7610 1050/www.bestmangal.com). West Kensington tube. **Meals served** noon-midnight Mon-Thur; noon-1am Fri, Sat. **Average £££.** Turkish

It's reassuring to see so many Turkish diners at Best Mangal – and by 'diners' we mean those in the small restaurant behind the bustling takeaway, seating about 30 at close-set tables covered with thick cloths. Service on our last visit was efficient and remarkably fast. Patlıcan esme (grilled aubergine purée) made an excellent starter: smoky and creamy, served with a basket of pide and piping-hot saç bread that was replenished without us having to ask. To follow, yaprak döner kebab showed the heights to which this maligned dish can aspire, its enormous pile of tender sliced meat accompanied by a large fresh salad containing finely diced red cabbage, carrot and lettuce. Best Mangal's reputation in this strongly Turkish neighbourhood is well deserved.

222 Veggie Vegan

222 North End Road, W14 9NU (7381 2322/www.222veggievegan. com). West Kensington tube/West Brompton tube/rail/28, 391 bus. **Lunch served** noon-3.30pm, **dinner served** 5.30-10.30pm daily. **Average ££.** Set lunch £7.50 buffet. **Map** p279. Vegetarian
This all-you-can-eat lunchtime buffet single-handedly refutes the notion that vegans must, by nature, suffer when it comes to eating out, its dozen or so hot and cold dishes so tasty that even hardened carnivores count themselves among its loyal followers. Aubergine parmigiana was a miracle of rich tomato sauce and creamy tofu – no dairy in sight, yet it was impossible not to go back for seconds. Full-flavoured chickpea curry came with nutty, fluffy wholegrain basmati rice, while the house salad was a riot of crunchy shredded veg. For dessert, carrot and walnut cake was light and moist. Despite the busy North End Road outside, the café is a soothing space, small and bright and furnished with smart blonde wood tables and chairs.

West

In the area
Best Mangal II *66 North End Road, W14 9EP (7602 0212).*

Westbourne Park

Crazy Homies NEW
125 Westbourne Park Road, W2 5QL (7727 6771/www.crazy homieslondon.co.uk). Royal Oak or Westbourne Park tube. **Dinner served** 6.30-11pm Mon-Fri. **Meals served** noon-11.30pm Sat; noon-10pm Sun. **Average £££.** **Map** p280. Mexican

Descending into the kaleidoscopic, neon-lit basement of Crazy Homies –it's brash, buzzy and has beats pumping on the stereo – feels like entering an oversized jukebox. Thus supplying the requisite psychedelic intensity for the reeling mix of tequila, mezcal and chilli about to unfold. It's best to go easy on the oversized starters, which include quesadillas with assorted fillings: 'barrio chorizo', mushroom and spinach, or succulent, caramelised 'melting pork'. Buttery guacamole and sour cream were employed to calm things down as a stealthy chipotle salsa unleashed a fiery chilli kick. For mains, a sirloin steak burrito featured very tender meat, while tacos with a super-smooth pinto bean filling provided a pleasant contrast to yet more peppers. Granted, we've eaten better Mexican food in London, but rarely in such party-hearty surroundings.

Lucky 7
127 Westbourne Park Road, W2 5QL (7727 6771/www.lucky7london. co.uk). Royal Oak or Westbourne Park tube. **Meals served** 10am-10.30pm Mon-Thur; 9am-11pm Fri, Sat; 9am-10.30pm Sun. **Average ££.** **Map** p280. Burgers

Tom Conran's cosy operation is arguably the most convincing of London's quasi-American diners.

It's not the menu, which contains few surprises; nor is it the decor, with six green Naugahyde booths set off by an ersatz tin ceiling, vintage rock posters and a funky Pepsi clock. It's more that Lucky 7 doesn't wear its theming with pomposity – this really feels like a neighbourhood hangout. The breakfast menu (served until 5pm) offers the likes of buttermilk pancakes and huevos rancheros, but we opted for a burger; our 'Kalifornian' came ladled with cheese, bacon (crispy but not frazzled), sour cream, a roasted half-tomato and fabulous guacamole. Fries and shakes are only so-so, but a short list of American beers compensates. You'd want one in your district.

★ Mosob
339 Harrow Road, W9 3RB (7266 2012/www.mosob.co.uk). Westbourne Park tube. **Meals served** 6pm-midnight Mon-Fri; 3pm-midnight Sat, Sun. **Average ££.** **Map** p280. Eritrean

Mosob is bedecked in Afro-chic furnishings and has the friendliest waiters in west London. It is also blessed with the best Eritrean cooking in the capital. We started with some tasty mini-sambusas, golden crisp pastries stuffed with fresh meat and tangy vegetables. Next up, the mains: after some advice, we chose zigni, a beef stew with a nutty flavour, which nicely complemented the sourdough taste of the injera. Bebe'ainetu was a fantastic choice for vegetarians, consisting of taster-sized portions of dishes like alicha (stewed cabbage, potatoes and carrots) and shiro (spicy ground chickpeas). There are no African drinks on the menu, regrettably, but with waiters handing out stunning Asmaran travel guides to study between courses, who's complaining?

Barnes

★ Orange Pekoe NEW

*3 White Hart Lane, SW13 0PX
(8876 6070/www.orangepekoeteas.
com). Barnes Bridge rail/209 bus.*
Meals served 7.30am-5.30pm Mon-
Fri; 9am-5.30pm Sat, Sun. **Average**
££. Café

There are few more tranquil places
to indulge in a life-affirming cup of
tea than this riverside gem (winner
of Time Out's Best Tea Room award
2008), with a following of both
families and seasoned leaf lovers
attracted by its villagey charm,
homely cooking and fabulous range
of teas. The cosy atmosphere
extends from the food counter to the
rustic tables at the back, with wild
flowers in alcoves, teatime trinkets
and blackboard menus adding to the
homespun appeal. At the entrance,
rows of tea caddies are filled with
around 50 varieties, and the
knowledgeable, on-the-ball staff are
happy to advise. Food comes in the
form of big, beautiful cakes, hearty
sandwiches and cold lunch platters,
but it's the cream teas and pots of tea
that keep us coming back.

Meal deals

Depot *Tideway Yard, 125 Mortlake
High Street, SW14 8SN (8878
9462/www.depotbrasserie.co.uk).* Set
lunch (noon-3pm Mon-Fri) £12.50
2 courses, £15.50 3 courses. Brasserie

In the area

ASK *Old Sorting Office, Station
Road, SW13 0LP (8878 9300).*
Pizza Express *14-15 Barnes High
Street, SW13 9LW (8878 1184).*
Strada *375 Lonsdale Road, SW13
9PY (8392 9216).*

Chelsea

Chelsea Bun Diner

*9A Lamont Road, SW10 0HP
(7352 3635). Earl's Court tube then*
328 bus. **Meals served** 7am-6pm
Mon-Sat; 9am-7pm Sun. **Average**
££. **Set lunch** £5.95 2 courses.
Map p275. Café

An unlikely oasis of kitsch, the
Chelsea Bun does a roaring
lunchtime trade with local workers
looking for an unpretentious pig-out
without the risk of being spotted,
thanks to its location off the King's
Road. A cheerful red and yellow
awning waves you into a world of
plastic marble-effect table tops,
vintage advertising hoardings and
pumping pop music. The long menu
is ignored by most in favour of
magnificent all-day breakfasts, piled
high with huge quantities of
scrambled eggs, hash browns, bacon
and sausages on beds of potato
skins or buttered toast. Before you
stagger out, arm yourself with
freshly made muffins and cakes at
the deli counter to help you make it
through the afternoon.

★ Haché

*329-331 Fulham Road, SW10 9QL
(7823 3515/www.hacheburgers.com).
South Kensington tube then 414 bus.*
Meals served noon-10.30pm Mon-
Thur; noon-11.15pm Fri, Sat; noon-
10pm Sun. **Average** ££. **Map** p279.
Burgers

Haché's attention to detail sets it
apart from the swathe of more
slapdash burger chains, and the
burgers themselves are made with
a great deal of love – one reason the
toasted ciabattas are left open is so
that diners can admire before they
devour. Our Spanish burger was
topped with a slice of grilled pepper
and a generous disc of goat's cheese
– squashed down, it made for a
mammoth mouthful and held
together well. Downsides: the thick-
cut chips, while crisp, lacked the
inner fluffiness beloved of finer
fries, while the meat-free 'au naturel
veggie burger' (made with
chickpeas, cumin and coriander)

Orange Pekoe

had more than a hint of the shop-bought frozen variety. Given the quality of everything else here, that's rather frustrating.

Itsu

118 Draycott Avenue, SW3 3AE (7590 2400/www.itsu.com). South Kensington tube. **Meals served** 11am-11pm Mon-Sat; 11am-10pm Sun. **Average** ££. **Set meals** £3.95-£9.95 bento box. **Map** p275.
Oriental

Lesser establishments might have buckled under the weight of an association as unfortunate as the death of Victor Litvinenko, but Itsu presses forward with the well-oiled determination of the motor powering its revolving sushi counter. This branch is so popular that diners they can't seat are dispatched upstairs to a trendy lounge bar with an electronic pager. We were thrilled by melt-on-the-tongue seared beef fillet and full-flavoured duck rolls with hoi sin sauce. Pan-Asian dishes such as chicken and coconut soup – think Thai tom kha gai but with more lime – were also skilfully prepared. Just keep an eye on your output as the bill can mount up quickly. Other branches forsake the conveyor belt to focus on takeaways.

Market Place

Chelsea Farmers' Market, 125 Sydney Street, SW3 6NR (7352 5600). South Kensington tube/ 11, 19, 22, 49 bus. **Meals served** 9am-5pm Mon-Fri; 9am-6pm Sat, Sun. **Average** £££. **Map** p275.
Brasserie

Essentially a small wooden shack set amid the toy town bungalows of Chelsea Farmer's Market, this Gallic brasserie-style eaterie has an appealing large outdoor terrace. Its bamboo awning, white picnic tables, oversized umbrellas and potted palms lend a seaside feel – if you can pretend the cars rushing up the nearby King's Road are waves breaking on a beach. Chargrilled beef or chicken features in most of the burgers, open sandwiches and salads, which always taste exceptionally fresh and tend to be accompanied by zingy salsas and crisp french fries. The management is keen to extend Market Place's seasonal shelf-life with outdoor heaters and a canopy, but we suspect it will probably remain a summertime destination.

Napket NEW

342 King's Road, SW3 5UR (7352 9832/www.napket.com). Sloane Square tube then 11, 19, 22 bus.

Meals served 8am-7pm daily. **Average** £. **Map** p279. Brasserie

A superficially stylish café with the tag line 'snob food' might not immediately suggest itself as a cheap eat, but Napket proves it's possible to dine like a Sloane without spending like one. The cramped interior is all black gloss and space-age perspex, accessorised with iPods on tables and baffling photographs of emaciated models. Seating consists of corner perching and two communal tables in front of a counter laden with sandwiches and salads. The former are decent: from the meal-in-itself club sarnie with roast chicken, ham, bacon and emmental, to the virtuous smoked salmon wholegrain baguette. Our salad was less successful – a sickly avocado and artichoke combo lacking the requisite lemon required to cut through its richness – and the Nutella cake was disappointingly dry. No wonder Napket's customers are so skinny.

Meal deals

Big Easy *332-334 King's Road, SW3 5UR (7352 4071/www.bigeasy. uk.com).* Set lunch (noon-5pm Mon-Fri) £7.95 2 courses. **Map** p279. North American

Bluebird *350 King's Road, SW3 5UU (7559 1000/www.blue bird-restaurant.com).* Set meal £15.50 2 courses, £18.50 3 courses. **Map** p279. Modern European

Jimmy's *386 King's Road, SW3 5UZ (7351 9997/www.jimmys chelsea.com).* Set meal (noon-3pm, 5.30-7pm Mon-Sat) £15 2 courses. **Map** p279. British

In the area

Al-Dar II *74 King's Road, SW3 4TZ (7584 1873).* **Map** p275.

Byron Hamburgers *300 King's Road, SW3 5UH (7352 6040).* **Map** p279.

Chelsea Left Wing Café *Duke of York Square, SW3 4LY (7730 7094).* Branch of Pâtisserie Valerie. **Map** p275.

Lisboa Pâtisserie *6 World's End Place, off King's Road, SW10 0HE (7376 3639).* **Map** p279.

Maison Blanc *11 Elystan Street, SW3 3NT (7584 6913).* **Map** p275.

Mexicali *323 Fulham Road, SW10 9QL (7351 7370).* **Map** p279.

Le Pain Quotidien *201-203 King's Road, SW3 5ED (7486 6154).* **Map** p279.

Paul *134 King's Road, SW3 4XB (7581 9611).* **Map** p275.

Pizza Express *The Pheasantry, 152-154 King's Road, SW3 4UT (7351 5031).* **Map** p279.

Ranoush Juice Bar *338 King's Road, SW3 5UR (7352 0044).* **Map** p279.

Earl's Court

As Greek As It Gets

233 Earl's Court Road, SW5 9AH (7244 7777/www.asgreekasitgets. co.uk). Earl's Court tube. **Lunch served** noon-3pm, **dinner served** 5-11pm Mon-Fri. **Meals served** noon-11pm Sat, Sun. **Average** ££. **Map** p279. Greek

Bar-hoppers, birthday groups and couples on awkward-looking first dates all flock to this contemporary Greek restaurant, where the party vibe across both floors (from the raucous bar seating to the more intimate tables at the back) stops short only of actual plate smashing. In fact, despite an authentic menu – classics such as pasticcio (a baked pasta dish) and moussaká sit alongside the lengthy menu of souvláki and gyros (pitta wraps) – there wasn't a Greek in sight on our visit. Still, we enjoyed expertly grilled pork and chicken souvláki, kritiki saláta (cretan tomato and cheese salad with large croutons) and piping-hot spanakópitta (spinach pie) – all of a far better quality than the sound system's rota of trashy Euro pop.

Kappa `NEW`

*139 Earl's Court Road, SW5 9RH
(7244 9196/www.kapparestaurant.
co.uk). Earl's Court tube.* **Lunch
served** noon-3pm Tue-Sun. **Dinner
served** 6-11pm daily. **Average ££.
Set lunch** £6.50-£12.60 bento box.
Map p278. Japanese

A relative newcomer to Earl's Court's
restaurant row, Kappa is a low-key
place, but has a certain stylishness,
with gold-toned walls, candles and
black tables. The owner is a Korean-
born sushi chef and there's a clear
Korean influence on many dishes
here, such as grilled scallops with
gochujang (a Korean spicy bean
paste). A temaki (cone-shaped hand
roll) containing stir-fried pork belly,
rice and the well-loved Korean
condiment kimchi, may have been
difficult to eat, but was spicy and
savoury nonetheless. Dry-fried pieces
of baby squid, spiced with powdered
chilli, were crisp outside, tender
inside. Nigiri sushi is well-turned-out
too. In all, a cut above average.

Mai Food `NEW`

*7A Kenway Road, SW5 0RP (7835
0100). Earl's Court tube.* **Dinner
served** 6.30-10pm Mon-Sat.
Average ££. Map p278. Japanese

London's love of sushi shows no sign
of diminishing, yet the kushiage
restaurants (literally 'skewer fried') so
popular in Japan are still largely
notable by their absence over here.
Thank heavens, then, for this gem of
an eaterie, where chef Saito whips up
a fairy-light array of food cooked in
panko (Japanese breadcrumbs) and
deep-fried. The kushiage sets are
great value, with a variety of skewers
to entice: our favourites were juicy
scallops paired with leeks, stuffed
lotus roots, and prawns wrapped in
aromatic perilla leaves. The teishoku
set meals are also a smart choice, and
include classic tori kara-age (deep-
fried marinated chicken). All come
with rice and miso soup.

★ Troubadour

*263-267 Old Brompton Road, SW5
9JA (7370 1434/www.troubadour.
co.uk). West Brompton tube/rail.*
Meals served 9am-11pm daily.
Average ££. Map p279. Café

From its vintage tin signs and '50s
coffeehouse kettles to its gothic
doors and abundance of nooks,
crannies and secret rooms, this is a
café as big on personality as it is on
portions. A delightful rear garden
comes into its own in summer,
there's an art gallery upstairs, and
guitars hanging from beams hint at
an impressive musical heritage (Joni
and Jimi are among those to have
graced the basement stage). Diners
will find an unpretentious menu
featuring the likes of steaks and fish
cakes, bangers and burgers, plus
soups, sandwiches and a range of
breakfasts from full English to 'anti
heart attack' (fruit, yoghurt, honey
and toast). The conversational staff
could easily be confused for
customers and the laid-back vibe
draws a genuinely creative crowd.

In the area

Masala Zone *147 Earl's Court
Road, SW5 9RQ (7373 0220).*
Map p278.
Nando's *204 Earl's Court Road,
SW5 9QF (7259 2544).* **Map** p278.
Pizza Express *Ground floor,
Earl's Court Exhibition Centre,
SW5 9TA (7386 5494).* **Map** p279.
Strada *237 Earl's Court Road,
SW5 9AH (7835 1180).* **Map** p279.
Wagamama *180-182 Earl's Court
Road, SW5 9QG (7373 9660).*
Map p278.
Zizzi *194-196 Earl's Court Road,
SW5 9QF (7370 1999).* **Map** p278.

Earlsfield

★ Amaranth

*346-348 Garratt Lane, SW18
4ES (8874 9036). Earlsfield rail/
44, 77, 270 bus.* **Dinner served**

fish!kitchen<

Fish Kitchen offers a modern take on the traditional Fish & Chip Restaurant.
Specialising in the best beer battered Fish & Chips, they also offer the highest quality fish from
their own fishmongers (Jarvis of Kingston upon Thames) cooked to the customers liking.
Also on the special boards are such dishes as Dressed hand picked crab, Lobster & chips,
Scallops wrapped in Pancetta and Home made gravadlax.

Take away orders are welcome.
See website or call your local restaurant for more information

starters!

fish! soup w rouille

Classic fish! prawn cocktail

Jarvis own organic
smoked salmon

Smoked haddock rarebit w
tomato & basil salad

Tempura prawns w sweet
chilli sauce

Seafood salad

fish!kitchen<
Beer battered specials

Haddock w chips

Cod w chips

Plaice w chips

Halibut w chips

*Served w lemon, mushy peas and
tartare sauce.*

fish! cake w chips

*All our fish is freshly cooked, and our
chips freshly cut.*

main courses!

Mussels mariniere or provencal

Classic fish! pie

Swordfish club sandwich

Tuna burger w chips

Grilled squid w spicy
tomato salsa

Grilled Dover sole w new
potatoes & hollandaise sauce

The above is an example of our typical menu. A Selection of wines and beers are available.
In a hurry? Take your meal away in one of our smart boxes.

Service not included. All prices inclusive of VAT. All major credit cards accepted.

Kingston	East Sheen	Borough Market	Enquiries
58 Coombe Road	170 Upper Richmond Road West	Cathedral Street	For general enquiries, press
KT2 7AF	SW14 8AW	SE1 9AL	and recruitment
T: 020 8546 2886	T: 020 8878 1040	T: 020 7407 3803	T: 020 8468 1492
		(Take away only)	

www.fishkitchen.com

6.30-11.30pm Mon-Sat. **Average** ££. **Set dinner** £15 2 courses, £20 3 courses. **Unlicensed**. **Corkage** £2.50 (wine). Thai

Amaranth remains one of the busiest Thai restaurants in south-west London (booking is essential, and table turning after one and a half hours not uncommon), but its popularity is well earned. The quality of ingredients is as high as you would expect from the operation that runs the nearby Amaranth Too Thai supermarket. Even dishes from which one might expect the obvious were surprising in their vividness of colour and flavour: pad thai, in particular, was exemplary, and there was no skimping with the grated green papaya in the som tam. Yet prices remain low; the BYO policy helps keep the bill around £13 per head. Service has been unfailingly polite and sweet on our many visits, even when very busy.

★ Cah Chi

394 Garratt Lane, Earlsfield, SW18 4HP (8946 8811/www.cahchi.com). Earlsfield rail/44, 77, 270 bus. **Lunch served** noon-3pm Sat, Sun. **Dinner served** 6pm-midnight daily. **Average** ££. **Set meal** £18 per person (minimum 2) 3 courses. **No credit cards**. Korean

There's been no diluting of the fierce authenticity that characterised the first Cah Chi when it opened in Raynes Park in 1995. Everything we've sampled here has been sensational: from the pa jeon, a flour pancake with a filling of spring onions and seafood, to the yuk-hoi dol-sot bap – raw beef, rice and pickles served in a sizzling stone bowl, which cooks the food on contact and creates an appealing rice 'crust'. Another classic is bulgogi, thin strips of beef marinated in pear juice, seared in front of you and then rolled in a lettuce leaf with spring onion and the Korean 'miso' called chang. Service is smiling and

enthusiastic, and you can bring your own wine but not beer.

★ Kazans

607-609 Garratt Lane, SW18 4SU (8739 0055/www.kazans. com). Earlsfield rail/44, 77, 270 bus. **Dinner served** 6-11pm Mon-Fri; 5-11pm Sat, Sun. **Average** ££. Turkish

The Turkish families framed in the enlarged 1960s photos that adorn the walls would no doubt approve of the faultlessly authentic food at Kazans (not to be confused with the Kazan chain). We started with a mixed cold meze featuring artichokes, houmous, tarama (cod's roe paste) and shaktuka (a creamy dip of fried aubergine, pepper and yoghurt). All were excellent and enormous in size, although the mains certainly deserve saving space for. Alinazik was a rich, spicy lamb stew with aubergine and yoghurt. From the specials board, a delicious rack of lamb came with gratin potato, rocket and caramelised onions; the only difficulty was cutting through the bones without tipping food off the plate. A great local restaurant.

Fulham

Megan's Deli

571 King's Road, SW6 2EB (7371 7837/www.megansdeli.com). Fulham Broadway tube. **Meals served** 8am-6pm Mon; 8am-10pm Tue-Fri; 9am-10pm Sat; 10am-5pm Sun. **Average** ££. **Map** p279. Café

Megan's sits on a strip of the King's Road devoted to upmarket furniture stores, and dining in the glass-fronted restaurant of this former antiques shop still feels unsettlingly like making an appearance in a lifestyle catalogue. String curtains keep window-shoppers at a distance, while candles in teacups and a crackling hearth create a homely feel in the evenings. Loved for its healthy daytime deli fare – quiches, salads and sandwiches – Megan's recently moved into the dinners market, and so far the results seem rather hit and miss. A starter of scallops with asparagus was beautifully tender, and bruschetta with mushroom sauce moreishly delicious, but mains such as penne arrabiata and fish platter proved plainer and less interesting than we'd expected.

Napulé NEW

585 Fulham Road, SW6 5UA (7381 1122/www.madeinitalygroup. co.uk). Fulham Broadway tube. **Lunch served** noon-3.30pm Sat, Sun. **Dinner served** 6-11.30pm Mon-Sat; 6-10.30pm Sun. **Average** ££. **Map** p279. Pizza & pasta

Far more spacious than it looks from the outside, Napulé's airy, split-level room is a delightful place in which to dine, although it's worth requesting a seat in the rear conservatory when the weather is sunny and the roof gets pulled back. The shared antipasti platter has great ice-breaking potential for first dates: a rustic wooden board covered in old favourites (parma ham, mozzarella, bruschetta) and a few new ones (grilled courgette, aubergine, fennel). Pizza by the metre (compulsory for orders of two or more) was also impressive, baked in the traditional Neapolitan-style in a wood-fired oven, although non-pizza lovers are well catered for with a tempting range of meat, fish and pasta dishes. The basement room is good for groups and parties.

Rossopomodoro

214 Fulham Road, SW10 9NB (7352 7677). South Kensington tube then 14 bus. **Lunch served** noon-3pm, **dinner served** 6.30pm-midnight Mon-Fri. **Meals served** noon-midnight Sat, Sun. **Average** ££. **Set lunch** £6.99-£7.99 1 course incl glass of wine. **Map** p279. Pizza & pasta

Cah Chi. See p121.

Visitors are left in no doubt that tomatoes are the fruit of Rossopomodoro's labours, with tins stacked around the room to create an eye-catching installation of which Andy Warhol would be proud. The bright, modern room, upbeat soundtrack and cheerful staff create a tangible buzz even early in the evening, and the pizza-makers in the open kitchen clearly know their craft, expertly executing everything from a simple napoli to the vesuvius: double-layered and bursting with cheese, salami and, of course, tomatoes. Starters were just as successful: a thoughtful waitress warned us that our Italian-style tortilla would take 20 minutes – it was worth the wait.

Meal deals

Sophie's Steakhouse & Bar
311-313 Fulham Road, SW10 9QH (7352 0088/www.sophiessteakhouse.com). Set meal (noon-6pm Mon-Fri) £12.95 2 courses. Map p279. North American
Sukho 855 Fulham Road, SW6 5HJ (7371 7600). Set lunch (noon-3pm daily) £7.95 1 course, £10.95 2 courses. Thai

In the area

Carluccio's Caffè 236 Fulham Road, SW10 9NB (7376 5960). Map p279.
Feng Sushi 218 Fulham Road, SW10 9NB (7795 1900). Map p279.
Fine Burger Company Fulham Broadway Centre, Fulham Broadway, SW6 1BW (7385 1716). Map p279.
Gourmet Burger Kitchen 49 Fulham Broadway, SW6 1AE (7381 4242). Map p279.
Maison Blanc 303 Fulham Road, SW10 9QH (7795 2663). Map p279.
Nando's Fulham Broadway Centre, Fulham Road, SW6 1BY (7386 8035). Map p279.
Paul 166 Fulham Road, SW10 9PR (7373 0429). Map p279.
Pizza Express 363 Fulham Road, SW10 9TN (7352 5300). Map p279.

Pizza Express 895 Fulham Road, SW6 5HU (7731 3117).
Pizza Express Fulham Broadway Centre, Fulham Road, SW6 1BW (7381 1700). Map p279.
Yo! Sushi Fulham Broadway Centre, Fulham Road, SW6 1BW (7385 6077). Map p279.

Norbury

In the area

Mirch Masala 1416 London Road, Norbury, SW16 4BZ (8679 1828/ 8765 1070).

Parsons Green

Meal deals

Establishment 45-47 Parsons Green Lane, SW6 4HH (7384 2418/ www.theestablishment.com). Set lunch (noon-3pm Mon-Fri) £12 2 courses, £15 3 courses. Modern European

In the area

Strada 175 New King's Road, SW6 4SW (7731 6404).

Putney

Buffet Brazil NEW

26 Putney High Street, SW15 1SL (8780 1750). Putney Bridge tube/Putney rail. **Meals served** 11.30am-11pm daily. **Average** ££. Map p293. Brazilian
Based on the churrascaria de rodizio concept – whereby a carver attends your table and serves an endless succession of grilled meats straight from the skewer – this South American outpost is capable of sating the most voracious of carnivores. Unlimited portions of steak, lamb and poultry, marinated overnight in herbs and spices and then continuously rotated on the grill, plus as many trips to the salad bar as your conscience permits,

come for a bargain-priced £14.95, and can be washed down with an assortment of authentic Brazilian beers. The restaurant is dominated by an attractive bar, behind which caipirinhas and mojitos are mixed. Capacity doubles in summer when the place opens on to the street.

★ Cochin Brasserie NEW

193 Lower Richmond Road, SW15 1HJ (8785 6004/www.cochin brasserie.com). Barnes rail/22, 265, 485 bus. **Meals served** 6-11pm daily. **Average** ££. Indian

Named after a city on the coast of Kerala, Cochin is true to its south-west Indian roots, serving light, zesty curries that are as far from the gloopy, high-street tongue-scorcher as it's possible to get. Coconut is the signature ingredient and seafood the speciality; the Travancore prawn fry (served in Keralan households on special occasions) combines both, with red chillies, ginger and lemon providing a fresh, fruity twist. Vegetarians are also well catered for: we loved the unnakkaya, a Keralan snack of plantains stuffed with aromatic rice. On weekends, Cochin's bright, minimalist interior fills with hordes of locals who know they have one of London's best-kept secrets on their doorstep.

Hudson's

113 Lower Richmond Road, SW15 1EX (8785 4522). Putney rail/ 22, 265, 485 bus. **Meals served** 9.30am-10pm Mon-Sat; 9am-9pm Sun. **Average** ££. **Map** p293. International

With its French bistro-style decor and globetrotting menu – ranging from Moroccan tagine and Thai curry to Mexican fajitas – Hudson's aspires to the cosmopolitan. Bare brick walls, eccentric prints, ceiling fans and a profusion of green paint help set it apart from the average local gastropub, while in summer a stylish outdoor eating area fills with west Londoners looking as sophisticated as possible while enjoying what Hudson's really does best: good, old-fashioned comfort food. Sunday roasts, served inside giant Yorkshire puddings with hearty root vegetables and sage and onion stuffing, are unbeatable, especially when followed with lip-smacking home-made desserts such as chocolate brownies and ice-cream or sticky toffee pudding.

Olé

240 Upper Richmond Road, SW15 6TG (8788 8009/www. olerestaurants.com). East Putney tube/Putney rail. **Meals served** noon-11pm daily. **Average** £££. **Map** p293. Spanish

On a recent visit to Olé we found a keyboard player adding swing to an already swinging atmosphere, but decent amounts of space between tables mean you need never feel overwhelmed. The white and beech setting with splashes of primary colour is smart, with floor-to-ceiling windows along the far wall. From the tapas list, calamares had a delightfully crunchy batter, while the creamy, melt-in-the-mouth texture of oven-baked aubergine with a cheesy tomato sauce elicited an enthusiastic response. Our main course, a colourful paella valenciana, lacked a discernible saffron flavour, but made up for it with generous helpings of seafood and chicken. Staff were efficient, whisking away plates and providing finger bowls, hot towels and drinks as required.

Rasa Penang

315 Putney Bridge Road, SW15 2PP (8789 3165). East Putney or Putney Bridge tube/Putney rail. **Lunch served** noon-2.30pm, **dinner served** 6-11pm daily. **Average** ££. **Set lunch** £8.90 2 courses incl coffee. **Set dinner** £14.50 2 courses incl coffee. **Map** p293. Malaysian

Singing for your supper

There's a reason why the words 'cheap' and 'cheerful' have long been bedfellows when it comes to budget cuisine in the capital. The higher the price of a restaurant, the more often diners can be found seated in nervous silence, hyperventilating in the hope that their £10 smoked salmon starter will have been worth the investment. But a £7 fiorentina? Forget about it. The conversation flows, second bottles of wine are ordered with impunity and the evening unravels towards who-knows-where.

Never is this more the case than with those restaurants that offer live entertainment to aid the digestive process. Experiences vary from gorging on a pizza to an accompaniment of fine jazz (the **Pizza Express Jazz Club** and **Soho Pizzeria**), to being serenaded by opera singers: the Battersea branch of **Little Bay** has them wandering between tables every Thursday, Friday and Saturday evening, while Italian wine/snack bar **Viva Verdi** replaces its piped arias with a flesh-and-blood soprano once a month.

The **Green Note** in Camden complements its innovative vegetarian menu with a programme of performances from blues, world and folk musicians, and diners on the **Battersea Barge** can enjoy comedy and cabaret as they tuck into affordable pub-style grub (and take a stroll on deck when acts tip from colourful to cringe-inducing).

Jazz After Dark, in Soho, does exactly what it says on the tin. There's also upmarket karaoke fun to be had over stone-baked pizzas at **Lucky Voice**, salsa dancing to work off spicy Latin American dinners at **Salsa!**, and – most bizarrely – a raucous backroom venue hosting everything from swing jazz bands to zombie Elvis impersonators at after-hours party palace **Marathon Kebab**.

Bear in mind that some venues have admission prices that vary depending on the act or evening – phone for details.

Battersea Barge *Nine Elms Lane, SW8 5BP (7498 0004/ www.batterseabarge.com).*
Green Note *106 Parkway, NW1 7AN (7485 9899/www.greennote. co.uk).* **Map** p296.
Jazz After Dark *9 Greek Street, W1D 4DQ (7734 0545/www.jazz afterdark.co.uk).* **Map** p268.
Little Bay *228 York Road, SW11 3SJ (7223 4080/www.littlebay.co.uk).* **Map** p284.
Lucky Voice *52 Poland Street, W1F 7NH (7439 3660/www.lucky voice.co.uk).* **Map** p268.
Marathon Kebab *87 Chalk Farm Road, NW1 8AR (7485 3814).* **Map** p296.
Pizza Express Jazz Club *10 Dean Street, W1D 3RW (7439 8722/www.pizzaexpresslive.com).* **Map** p268.
Salsa! *96 Charing Cross Road, WC2H 0JG (7379 3277/www.bar salsa.info).* **Map** p268.
Soho Pizzeria *16-18 Beak Street, W1F 9RD (7434 2480/www.soho pizzeria.co.uk).* **Map** p268.
Viva Verdi *6 Canvey Street, SE1 9AN (7928 6867/www.vivaverdi winebar.com).* **Map** p289.

South West

Venetian blinds, dark wood floors, mirrored walls and fresh orchids lend Rasa Penang an air of opulence that belies its bargain basement prices. The menu may not be revelatory – relying on East Asian staples such as hot and sour soups and black bean, sambal and chilli sauces – but it's executed with flawless proficiency and served by staff with a sense of old-fashioned courtesy. The seafood selection is particularly extensive, with more than ten king prawn dishes and a few exotic choices such as whole crab or lobster in ginger sauce, which must be ordered in advance. This local treasure remains largely undiscovered, yet a better-value meal would be hard to come by.

Meal deals

L'Auberge *22 Upper Richmond Road, SW15 2RX (8874 3593/ www.ardillys.com).* Set dinner (Tue-Sat) £13.50 2 courses. French

Enoteca Turi *28 Putney High Street, SW15 1SQ (8785 4449/www. enotecaturi.com).* Set lunch £14.50 2 courses. **Map** p293. Italian

Marco Polo *6-7 Riverside Quarter, Eastfields Avenue, SW18 1LP (8874 6800).* Set lunch (Mon-Fri) £9.95 1 course, £11.95 2 courses. Italian

Phoenix Bar & Grill *162-164 Lower Richmond Road, SW15 1LY (8780 3131/www.sonnys.co.uk).* Set lunch (Mon-Sat) £13.50 2 courses, £15.50 3 courses. **Map** p293. Modern European

Royal China *3 Chelverton Road, SW15 1RN (8788 0907).* Dim sum (noon-3.30pm daily) £3-£5. **Map** p293. Chinese

In the area

Carluccio's Caffè *Brewhouse Street, Putney Wharf, SW15 2JQ (8789 0591).* **Map** p293.

Gourmet Burger Kitchen *333 Putney Bridge Road, SW15 2PG (8789 1199).* **Map** p293.

Nando's *148 Upper Richmond Road, SW15 2SW (8780 3651).* **Map** p293.

Pizza Express *144 Upper Richmond Road, SW15 2SW (8789 1948).* **Map** p293.

Real Greek *31-33 Putney High Street, SW15 1SP (8788 3270).* **Map** p293.

Rocket Riverside *Brewhouse Street, Putney Wharf, SW15 2NS (8789 7875).* Branch of Rocket. **Map** p293.

Strada *147 Upper Richmond Road, SW15 2TX (8789 6996).* **Map** p293.

Tootsies Grill *30 Brewhouse Street, SW15 2TG (8788 8488).* **Map** p293.

Wagamama *50-54 Putney High Street, SW15 1SQ (8785 3636).* **Map** p293.

Sheen

★ Faanoos NEW

481 Upper Richmond Road West, SW14 7PU (8878 5738). Mortlake rail/33, 337, 493 bus. **Meals served** noon-11pm daily. **Average** ££. Iranian

With its staff on first-name terms with locals and its clay walls matted with straw and embellished with sepia prints of pre-revolutionary

Faanoos

Iran, Faanoos does a good job of emulating the warm familiarity of a bustling Tehran kebab house. Starters were uniformly excellent, from smoky kashk-e bademjan (mashed aubergine with garlic and whey) to salad olivieh (shredded chicken salad) and torsh, a Persian pickle packed with chunky vegetables. Mains were similarly satisfying: a tender chicken kebab was yellowed from a long marination in saffron, lemon and onion, while a stew of ghorm-e sabzi (lamb with dried limes, kidney beans and bitter greens) was heavy on the meat and hearty of portion; both were served with mountains of perfectly fluffy, saffron-tinted rice.

★ Mango & Silk `NEW`
199 Upper Richmond Road West, SW14 8QT (8876 6220/www. mangoandsilk.co.uk). Mortlake rail/ 33, 337, 493 bus. **Lunch served** noon-3pm Sun (by reservation only Sat). **Dinner served** 6-10pm Tue-Thur, Sun; 6-10.30pm Fri, Sat. **Average** ££. Indian
There have been plenty of happy faces people in East Sheen since Udit Sarkhel, long a major influence on Indian food in London, became head chef at Mango & Silk. A beige and white colour scheme and wooden flooring create seemly environs for the menu's tour of India's home kitchens. We began with a special of goan squid balchao, succulent seafood in a vinegary masala, cut with sweet cinnamon and fiery red chillies. Standards were maintained by the mains: malai fish curry delivered perfectly cooked cod in a creamy, coconut-milk broth, while murgh makhani produced tender chicken in a buttery tomato sauce. For a more filling installment try the Sunday buffet for a mere £11.95. This good-value, amiable restaurant is doing the neighbourhood proud.

Wandsworth

Brady's
513 Old York Road, SW18 1TF (8877 9599). Wandsworth Town rail/28, 44 bus. **Lunch served** 12.30-2.30pm Mon-Sat. **Dinner served** 6.30-10pm Mon-Wed, Sat; 6.30-10.30pm Thur, Fri. **Average** ££. **Map** p284. Fish & chips
Brady's mismatched wooden furnishings, mermaids painted on the mirrors and fish-themed decor feel more Westcliff-on-Sea than Wandsworth, and there's a great

deal more than mere battered cod on the hastily scribbled menus, which vary depending on the haul of the day. We sampled punchy potted shrimps as a starter, but half-pints of prawns, calamares, anchovies, sardines and cockles were also available. The lunch special of fun-sized fish, chips and sweet mushy peas for under a fiver is great value; the full-price option with chips as an extra perhaps less so. Own-made honeycomb ice-cream sounded a superb dessert, but the kitchen abruptly closed without us being offered the chance to order any.

Dexter's Grill & Bar
20 Bellevue Road, SW17 7EB (8767 1858). Wandsworth Common rail/319 bus. **Meals served** 11am-11pm Mon-Fri; 10am-11pm Sat; 11am-10.30pm Sun. **Average** ££. **Set lunch** (noon-5pm Mon-Fri) £9.95 2 courses, £12.95 3 courses. **Map** p285. North American
High chair for high chair, burger for burger, there's little to distinguish Dexter's from its corporate sibling, Tootsies (*see right*), but that's not a problem: families with young children can't get enough of one, or the other. Like Tootsies, Dexter's is bright and spacious, with large windows, pine furniture and plenty of space to park the pushchair. Both provide colouring books and crayons, and feature a popular kids' menu (the beef bolognese is blended with five 'hidden' vegetables, and there's strawberry and rhubarb crumble for afters). Adults dine well too: a classic burger of smoked back bacon with melted monterey jack cheese was fresh and perfectly executed. Our only quibble in such a family-friendly establishment is the lack of kids' cutlery.

In the area
Nando's *Southside Shopping Centre, SW18 4TF (8874 1363).*

Pizza Express *539-541 Old York Road, SW18 4TG (8877 9812).* **Map** p284.

Wimbledon

Tootsies Grill
48 High Street, SW19 5AX (8946 4135/www.tootsiesrestaurants.com). Wimbledon tube/rail. **Meals served** 11am-10.30pm Mon-Thur; 11am-11pm Fri; 9am-11pm Sat; 9am-10.30pm Sun. **Average** ££. North American
Tootsies – that bastion of lunching yummy mummies and youngsters – has always taken tots, tantrums and teddies in its stride. Staff are smiley, efficient and happy to help stash buggies and set up high chairs. The chain has drafted in author and children's nutritional expert Annabel Karmel to devise the kiddies' menu of mini burgers, fish and cottage pies, and fruit smoothies disguised as healthy 'milkshakes' (the strawberry version has become an unintentional hit with expectant mums). The adult menu includes filling super-food salads and steak sandwiches, but burgers are its biggest draw; served with crisp, golden fries, an army of sauces and plenty of crowd-pleasing toppings, they arrive juicy and with a nice charcoal tinge, in a toasted sesame seed bun.

In the area
Giraffe *21 High Street, SW19 5DX (8946 0544).*
Gourmet Burger Kitchen *88 The Broadway, SW19 1RH (8540 3300).*
Nando's *1 Russell Road, SW19 1QN (8545 0909).*
Paul *87 High Street, SW19 5EF (8946 6321).*
Pizza Express *84 High Street, SW19 5EG (8946 6027).*
Strada *91 High Street, SW19 5EG (8946 4363).*
Wagamama *46-48 Wimbledon Hill Road, SW19 7PA (8879 7280).*

Balham

Cattle Grid NEW

*1 Balham Station Road, SW12
9SG (8673 9099/www.cattlegrid
restaurant.com). Balham tube/rail.*
Dinner served 5-10pm Mon-Thur.
Meals served noon-10.30pm Fri,
Sat; noon-9pm Sun. **Average £££.**
Map p285. Steaks
This spanking new steak joint cooks
its beef to order, and though the
steaks aren't of the quality you'd
find in more expensive restaurants
– ours was a little tough – they are
excellent value, with a 10oz sirloin
costing just £12, served with chips
and a watercress salad. Sauces cost
extra: most of them 50p, though the
béarnaise adds a whopping £2.
Cattle Grid makes decent burgers
too, with dense, firm beef patties,
and the chips are suitably crisp and
dry. If you'd rather have pork, then
ribs or loin steak are available. The
two floors of this modern, narrow
building seem popular with small
parties, and the proximity to Balham
station caters well to herd instincts.

★ Ciullo's

*31 Balham High Road, SW12 9AL
(8675 3072). Clapham South tube/
Balham tube/rail.* **Dinner served**
6-11pm Mon-Thur; 6-11.30pm Fri,
Sat; 5-10.30pm Sun. **Average ££.**
Map p285. Pizza & pasta
Staff are justifiably proud of this
charming, family-owned ristorante,
which passed the authenticity test
on our last visit when two Tuscan
ladies walked in somewhat warily
off the street and were swept up in a
tide of Italian exclamation and
embraces. OK, so the bright orange
walls, dodgy art and bar lined with
dusty bottles of limoncello is
unlikely to win any style awards,
but the food is fantastic and
shockingly affordable. We loved the
fresh, plump sardine starter, and the
pappardelle in a flavourful ragù of
minced venison and dried porcini
was reliably thin and al dente. Pizzas are
perfectly thin and crisp, and our
Tuscan friends seemed perfectly
content with their grilled tuna too.
Old-fashioned Ciullo's continues to
set the standard in the area.

Cattle Grid

★ Fat Delicatessen `NEW`

7 Chestnut Grove, SW12 8JA (8675 6174/www.fatdelicatessen.co.uk). Balham tube/rail. **Meals served** 8am-8pm Mon-Wed; 8am-10pm Thur, Fri; 9am-10pm Sat; 11am-6pm Sun. **Average** ££. **Map** p285. Mediterranean

If the Fat Deli looks like a shop from the outside, then that's because it is. Inside, shelves loaded with bottles, boxes and packets create the air of an apothecary, but there's also homely seating and hearty eating in the form of both superb tapas and simple Italian dishes. A bottle of Tinta de Toro, olives and pan catalan were the perfect antidote to a rainy night in Balham, and slivers of nutty jamón serrano put most parma in the shade. Meatballs in tomato sauce and patatas bravas were great comfort food before the fabada (an Asturian stew of beans, belly pork, black pudding and chorizo). With most dishes costing between £4 and £8, dining at the Fat Deli will be more ruinous to your waistline than your wallet.

Fine Burger Company

37 Bedford Hill, SW12 9EY (8772 0266/www.fineburger.co.uk). Balham tube/rail. **Meals served** noon-10pm Mon-Wed, Sun; noon-11pm Thur-Sat. **Average** ££. **Map** p285. Burgers

The Flaming Lips on the stereo, album art on the walls and menus like mini newspapers – three indicators that FBC fancies itself as hipper than the opposition. The best innovation is the option to upgrade to a 'combo' with half-portions of two side dishes (skin-on, hand-cut chips and fiery onion rings) for £3. Our 'double red hot' burger was one of the biggest in town, with a hefty slice of beef tomato the size of a Big Mac and pickled jalapeños, though proper chilli rather than salsa would have been preferable. With crayons and toys for the young 'uns, FBC is a fun place to eat cheaply, and more spacious than its rivals – who should be watching with interest.

Munchkin Lane `NEW`

83 Nightingale Lane, SW12 8NX (8772 6800). Clapham South tube/ Wandsworth Common rail. **Meals served** 8am-6pm Mon-Fri; 9am-5pm Sat. **Average** £. Café

It may sound twee in the extreme, but Munchkin Lane isn't so child-friendly that grown-ups need cower in fear. The pram posse tend to flock downstairs to the cheerful play area with CBeebies on screen and a storytelling timetable, leaving the ground-floor café a great place for adults to lunch. The menu includes piles of buttery scrambled eggs served with ham and cheese, crisp salads in big bowls (Greek, chicken caesar), filled bagels, baked potatoes and imaginative pasta dishes. There's usually an own-made cake (moist carrot cake on our last visit), and good, strong coffee. The little ones get babycinos, gingerbread men and nursery stalwarts (macaroni cheese, shepherd's pie, fish pie and veg), all sensibly priced.

Polish White Eagle Club

211 Balham High Road, SW17 7BQ (8672 1723/www.whiteeagleclub.co.uk). Tooting Bec tube/Balham tube/rail/49, 155, 181, 319 bus. **Lunch served** noon-3pm, **dinner served** 6-11pm Mon-Sat. **Meals served** noon-11pm Sun. **Average** ££. **Set lunch** (Mon-Sat) £7 2 courses. **Map** p285. Polish

Few of London's cultural immersions feel as authentic as a trip to this building opposite the Polish Kosciol Chrystusa Krola church; the club's interior remains virtually unaltered since the 1930s. The restaurant at the rear is straight out of a '70s wedding, its menu packed with traditional Polish dishes (soups, stews, potato pancakes), which come in suitably generous portions. We liked the sour zurek soup; a shame the rye bread was stale. Bigos stew was full of sausage, sauerkraut and chunks of pork. Desserts ranged from the decent (pancakes with curd cheese) to the mediocre (baked cheesecake lacking the necessary cheesiness). Service is friendly and Saturday nights feature Polish folk bands and zabawa (dance) classes.

Tagine

1-3 Fernlea Road, SW12 9RT (8675 7604). Balham tube/rail.
Dinner served 5-11pm Mon-Fri.
Meals served noon-11pm Sat, Sun. **Average £££. Unlicensed.**
Corkage no charge. **Map** p285.
North African

With shisha-smoking customers at its alfresco tables, and its North African lounge decor enhanced by a sprawl of Berber cushions, Tagine looks inviting, if a little oddly located, opposite the hulking Bedford pub. Our zaalouk starter, a compote of aubergine seasoned with cumin, lacked bite, and a lamb shank main was disappointing: meat that should have fallen off the bone had to be prised off with ungracious cutlery manoeuvres. Chicken tagine was more successful, its tender chunks of chicken sprinkled with green olives, and we'd have followed the meal with Moroccan mint tea if a large pot hadn't cost an eye-watering £8 – the high price claimed to counter the absence of alcohol sales or a corkage charge at this unlicensed restaurant.

Meal deals

Bar Viva *238 Balham High Road, SW17 7AW (8673 6705).* Set dinner £12.95 2 courses. **Map** p285. International
Harrison's *15-19 Bedford Hill, SW12 9EX (8675 6900/www. harrisonsbalham.com).* Set lunch £12 2 courses. Set dinner (6.30-7.30pm) £14 2 courses. **Map** p285. Brasserie

In the area

Nando's *116-118 Balham High Road, SW12 9AA (8675 6415).*
Map p285.
Pizza Express *47 Bedford Hill, SW12 9EY (8772 3232).* **Map** p285.

Battersea

Ace Fusion NEW

110 St John's Hill, SW11 1SJ (7228 5584/www.acefusion.co.uk). Clapham Junction rail or Wandsworth Town.
Meals served noon-11pm Mon-Thur; noon-11.30pm Fri; 10am-11.30pm Sat; 10am-10pm Sun.
Average ££. Map p284.
Caribbean

Ace is doing a good job of curling Battersea's stiff upper lip into a smile. Its fun, informal menu combines African, Caribbean and English cuisines (hence the name), offering ingredients like plantain and ackee alongside shepherd's pie and bangers and mash. The fusion element comes into play with dishes such as mango-stuffed, breaded and fried chicken, and 'creole cod' served with tomato sauce and okra. Succulent jerk-spiced chicken was accompanied by the West Indian staple of saltfish, and very satisfying it was too, especially chased down with a refreshing rum punch. Yam balls were a little bland, but side dishes and desserts garnered bonus points. The decor has a breezy feel echoed by the laid-back funk on the stereo.

L'Antipasto

511 Battersea Park Road, SW11 3BW (7223 9765). Clapham Junction rail. **Lunch served** noon-2.30pm, **dinner served** 6.30-11.30pm Mon-Fri. **Meals served** noon-11.30pm Sat; noon-11pm Sun. **Average ££. Set meal** (Mon, Thur, Sat, Sun) half-price meals, not incl drinks or dessert.
Map p284. Italian

From the warm, family-friendly atmosphere and excellent service to the understated interior and enticing menu, L'Antipasto has been a deserved local favourite from time immemorial. Top marks to starters of polenta alla triestina (polenta with wild mushrooms in a creamy dolcelatte sauce) and parma ham with figs. For mains, fettuccine with salmon was super-fresh, with a soul-satisfying richness that made spaghetti bella donna (with olives and anchovies in a tomato and caper sauce) seem rather less exciting by comparison. The tartufo nero, a delightfully calorific ice-cream bombe, rounded off a great meal. On Monday, Thursday, Saturday and Sunday the restaurant halves its prices, drawing crowds and creating a convivial atmosphere worthy of a real Italian kitchen.

Banana Tree Canteen

75-79 Battersea Rise, SW11 1HN (7228 2828). Clapham Junction rail. **Lunch served** noon-3pm, **dinner served** 6-11pm Mon-Fri. **Meals served** noon-11pm Sat, Sun. **Average** ££. **Map** p284. Oriental

Banana Tree Canteen owes more than a little to Wagamama (bench seats, shared tables, plain rendered walls and servers in matching casuals). The menu features dishes from across South-east Asia, and diners queue here seven nights a week, a sure sign that staff are doing something right. We started with Indonesian gado gado salad, heavy on iceberg lettuce but redeemed by a zingy peanut dressing. Mains were more inspired: mamak lamb curry was perfect, with rich flavours of coconut, lemongrass and lime leaves, and a Vietnamese pork stew seduced us with aromas of cinnamon and white pepper. Mains can be ordered alone or as part of a set meal with rice, glass-noodle salad, prawn crackers and Thai-style corn fritters.

★ Donna Margherita NEW

183 Lavender Hill, SW11 5TE (7228 2660/www.donna-margherita.com). Clapham Junction rail. **Lunch served** noon-2.30pm Fri. **Dinner served** 6-10.30pm Mon-Thur; 6-11pm Fri. **Meals served** noon-11pm Sat; 12.30-10.30pm Sun. **Average** ££. Pizza & pasta

With its open brickwork, rustic Italian wall mural and decorative strings of garlic, Donna Margherita looks outdated to the point of being accidentally stylish. Perfect pizzas, however, never go out of fashion, and here you'll find some of London's finest puffy-yet-crisp bases as foundations for around 20 combinations of topping – although you may be diverted by the tempting pasta and gnocchi dishes made on the premises. We were impressed by the freshness and cooking of the seafood, both in a starter of herb-crusted, wood-roasted squid, and a garlicky pizza frutta di mare. Own-made desserts such as tiramisu are fine, but not worth saving room for. Staff were friendly, easy-going and in no hurry to see us leave.

Galapagos Bistro-Café NEW

169 Battersea High Street, SW11 3JS (8488 4989/www.galapagos foods.com). Clapham Junction rail. **Meals served** 9.30am-9.30pm Tue-Sat. **Average** ££. **Set meal** £10.50 2 courses, £12.50 3 courses. **Map** p284. Café

Galapagos used to be a delicatessen until the arrival of two supermarket giants forced it to make some changes (presumably taking on board Darwin's theory of natural selection that he developed while exploring the islands of the same name). Post-reinvention it's a pleasant café-restaurant; comfy corner sofas, fresh flowers and shelves stacked with boxes of tea create a living room atmosphere. Complimentary olives and canapés were a thoughtful touch, after which the set dinner menu was short and very sweet: two courses for just £10.50. Main courses of fisherman's pie and merguez with spicy rice were filling and delicious, while Mexican pecan pie was nicely spiced with cinnamon, and chocolate fondant was rich and moist.

Gourmet Burger Kitchen

44 Northcote Road, SW11 1NZ (7228 3309/www.gbkinfo.com). Clapham Junction rail/49, 77, 219, 345 bus. **Meals served** noon-11pm Mon-Fri; 11am-11pm Sat; 11am-10pm Sun. **Average** ££. **Map** p284. Burgers

The burgers are anything but predictable at this well-established chain (now with 29 branches around the capital), where an innovative international menu sees Greek-, Thai- and Jamaican-style burgers alongside a beetrooted Kiwi cousin. All are picture-perfect, housed in freshly baked, sesame seed-topped sourdough buns, with lush lettuce and aged cheddar cheese melting alluringly down the sides. There are new organic products too, such as a wild boar burger (albeit at a pricey £8.95 without chips). Vegetarians have five options, from mushroom and camembert to falafel. However, too much relish (on our visit, customers were pulling apart their burgers and rebuilding), cramped seating and a long wait for tables will have to be addressed if GBK is to stay pre-eminent.

Noiya NEW

62 Lavender Hill, SW11 5RQ (7228 7171). Clapham Junction rail. **Lunch served** noon-2.30pm Mon-Fri; 1-2.30pm Sat. **Dinner served** 6pm-midnight Mon-Thur; 6pm-1am Fri, Sat. **Meals served** 1pm-midnight Sun. **Set lunch** (Mon-Sat) £4.95. **Set meal** (Sun) £6.95. **Average** ££. Indian

In a part of town teeming with identikit curry houses, Noiya manages to stand out from the crowd with its contemporary cream and chocolate interior and innovative list of specials. From the signature column we settled on hydra lamb, succulent chunks of meat stewed with chickpeas in a rich tomato and cumin gravy that soaked right into the nariyal pilau (basmati rice steamed with coconut shavings). Mahi king prawn pickled with lime, mint, mustard seeds, garlic and chillies tasted somewhat defeated by an overdose of ingredients, but the hearty blend of lentils in mildly-spiced muchuri dal more than hit the spot. Service seemed slow due to a lack of staff, but we couldn't fault the restaurant's relaxing ambience.

Meal deals

Le Bouchon Bordelais *5-9 Battersea Rise, SW11 1HG (7738 0307/www.lebouchon. co.uk).* Set meal (noon-3pm, 6-7pm Mon-Fri) £15 3 courses. **Map** p284. French

Cinnamon Cay *87 Lavender Hill, SW11 5QL (7801 0932).* Set dinner (Mon-Sat) £13.95 2 courses. International

Osteria Antica Bologna *23 Northcote Road, SW11 1NG (7978 4771/www.osteria.co.uk).* Set lunch (noon-3pm Mon-Fri; noon-5.30pm Sat, Sun) £12.50 2 courses, £15 3 courses. **Map** p284. Italian

Tom Ilic *123 Queenstown Road, SW8 3RH (7622 0555/www.tom ilic.com).* Set lunch (Wed-Fri) £12.50 2 courses, £14.95 3 courses; (Sun) £16.50 2 courses. Modern European

Who ate all the pies?

Few experiences hark back to the London of yesteryear like dining in a traditional pie and mash shop. The kitchens of these much-loved institutions have been turning out the same dishes since the mid 19th century: mountains of functional mash; minced beef and gravy pies plied with liquor (loosely based on parsley sauce); and eels (either jellied and cold or stewed and warm, although their higher price has led to many stores focusing on pie and mash).

The food may be a mere footnote in Britain's contribution to culinary evolution, but there's no denying the beauty of some of the original buildings – from their art deco-style lettering to the scrubbed tile interiors complete with backless wooden benches, marble-topped tables and vintage cash registers set on gleaming steel counters.

The business was dominated by three families from day one: the Cookes, the Manzes and the Kellys. The Cookes, who are reputed to have come first, created something of a local landmark with their glorious Kingsland High Street shop, which opened in 1910; Grade II listed in 1991, it's now a Chinese restaurant, Shanghai (*see p189*), though the decor remains largely unaltered.

The best of the Manze's shops is its first, opened on Tower Bridge Road in 1902 (though the building is ten years older), and still drawing daily queues that snake patiently down the street.

The Kelly shops, situated on two famous East End roads, are held in similar reverence.

Service tends to be brusque, but the banter between staff and old-faithfuls offers a window into an era typified by the community ties lacking in modern London life. And with a gut-busting lunch costing less than a fiver, this remains the very definition of cheap eats.

WJ Arment *7 & 9 Westmoreland Road, SE17 2AX (7703 4974/ www.armentspieandmash.com).* Map p292.
Clark's *46 Exmouth Market, EC1R 4QE (7837 1974).* Map p270.
F Cooke *150 Hoxton Street, N1 6SH (7729 7718).* **Map** p271.
F Cooke *9 Broadway Market, E8 4PH (7254 6458).*
Harrington's *3 Selkirk Road, SW17 0ER (8672 1877).* Map p285.
G Kelly *414 Bethnal Green Road, E2 0DJ (7739 3603).* Map p294.
G Kelly *600 Roman Road, E3 2RW (8983 3552).*
S&R Kelly *284 Bethnal Green Road, E2 0AG (7739 8676).* Map p294.
Manze's *204 Deptford High Street, SE8 3PR (8692 2375).* Map p290.
L Manze *74 Chapel Market, N1 9ER (7837 5270).* **Map** p299.
L Manze *76 Walthamstow High Street, E17 7LD (8520 2855).*
M Manze *87 Tower Bridge Road, SE1 4TW (7407 2985).* **Map** p289.
M Manze *105 Peckham High Street, SE15 5RS (7277 6181).* Map p292.
M Manze *266 High Street, Sutton, Surrey SM1 1NT (8286 8787).*

South

In the area

Giraffe 27 Battersea Rise, SW11
1HG (7223 0933). **Map** p284.
Little Bay 228 York Road, SW11
3SJ (7223 4080). **Map** p284.
Nando's 1A Northcote Road,
SW11 1NG (7228 6221). **Map** p284.
Pizza Express 230-236 Lavender
Hill, SW11 1LE (7223 5677).
Map p284.
Pizza Express 46-54 Battersea
Bridge Road, SW11 3AG (7924
2774). **Map** p284.
Strada 11-13 Battersea Rise,
SW11 1HG (7801 0794). **Map** p284.

Brixton

★ Asmara

386 Coldharbour Lane, SW9 8LF
(7737 4144). Brixton tube/rail.
Dinner served 5.30pm-midnight
daily. **Average ££. Set meals**
vegetarian £27 per person
(minimum 2) , meat £29 per person
(minimum 2). **Map** p286. Eritrean
Peer beyond Asmara's decidedly
inconspicuous façade and you'll find
an oasis of East African calm with
simple seating and efficient service
underpinning a solid menu of
traditional Eritrean cuisine, all
bolstered by evocative coffee and
incense aromas. The spicy lentil
soup looked tempting, but we
plunged straight into main courses
of zigni (spicy beef stew) and
spinach cooked with chilli and oil,
which we shared with an ample
platter of the finest injera we've yet
sampled in London – barley-hued,
moist and delicately tangy. The
traditional coffee ceremony was a
wonderful pageant; diners are given
freshly roasted beans to savour
before the coffee is served with
warm popcorn. An experience as
richly cultural as it is culinary.

Bamboula

12 Acre Lane, SW2 5SG (7737
6633). Brixton tube/rail. **Meals
served** 11am-11pm Mon-Sat; 1-9pm
Sun. **Average ££. Set lunch** £5.70
1 course incl soft drink. **Map** p286.
Caribbean

Franco Manca. See p138.

The vibe at Bamboula remains as authentically Caribbean as is possible for somewhere overlooking Lambeth Town Hall, but the food has drifted a long way from shore. The batter on our cod fritter was greasy, the filling bland and stodgy; much better was ackee and saltfish with plantain: a fluffy slither of banana wrapped around delicately spiced fish. Mains were hit and miss: curry goat, a Bamboula favourite, remains an excellent choice, but baked tilapia was overpowered by a heavy okra sauce. It's not just that the food feels tired. The credit card machine wasn't working, the Red Stripe had run out and the sole waitress seemed more than ready to go home when she closed up after us.

Coma y Punto

94-95 Granville Arcade, Coldharbour Lane, SW9 8PS (7326 0276). Brixton tube/rail. **Meals served** 9am-6pm Mon, Tue, Thur-Sat; 9am-3pm Wed. **No credit cards**. **Map** p286. Colombian

This favoured daytime haunt of Brixton's Colombian community is loud, lively and welcoming to all, and offers a superb menu of hearty South American dishes made with ingredients sourced from stalls in the covered market it calls home. Mains cover the likes of tender chicken steaks with tangy salsa, and red mullet with a satisfyingly crispy skin. We've seldom been able to resist bandeja paisa, the Colombian equivalent of a full English breakfast: with grilled steak, pork belly, red beans, rice and plantain artfully damming a fried egg, this is the essence of soul food. The occasionally chaotic service is made more comical by confusing exchanges of Spanglish between waiters and first-time diners.

Fiesta Bar NEW

30 Acre Lane, SW2 5SG (7733 4206/www.fiestabar.co.uk). Brixton tube/rail. **Meals served** noon-10pm daily. **Average ££. Map** p286. Spanish

The paint may still have been drying on our inaugural visit to Brixton's latest bar-restaurant (located on the site of the ill-fated Z Bar), but there was nothing unfinished about Fiesta's excellent tapas menu. Most dishes hover tantalisingly around the £5 mark. We loved the combination of own-made salsa with fresh-tasting squid kebabs, while crumbly meat balls in a rich tomato sauce were the epitome of comfort food rendered in miniature. The highlight was a seared Japanese steak skewer, its melting tenderness a testament to the wide range of both influences and ability in the kitchen. Food is served until 10pm and the bar mixes a mean cocktail – yet more reasons for locals to be cheerful. After 10pm every night the Fiesta Bar goes into club mode with live performances from Thursday to Saturday.

★ Franco Manca `NEW`

*4 Market Row, Electric Lane,
SW9 8LD (7738 3021/www.franco
manca.com). Brixton tube/rail.*
Meals served noon-5pm Mon-
Sat. **Average** £. **Map** p286.
Pizza & pasta

The winner of Time Out's Best
Cheap Eats award 2008 may seem
spartan to the point of anonymity –
a handful of café tables and a couple
of shared pews in a market
otherwise characterised by
wandering preachers and West
Indian food stalls – but Franco
Manca is a thinking punter's
pizzeria. Its sourdough is left to rise
20 hours before baking and its
ingredients are largely organic (the
owners flew in a specialist from
Sorrento to train their Somerset
supplier in the art of mozzarella-
making). We plumped for a pizza
mixing organic Brindisi chorizo
with mozzarella, the peppery kick of
the meat contrasting with the
smoothness of Somerset's finest, and
a calzone that paired crumbling
buffalo ricotta with a generous
helping of organic pork. Both were
disarmingly good.

Gallery `NEW`

*256A Brixton Hill, SW2 1HF (8671
8311). Brixton tube/rail/45, 109,
118, 250 bus.* **Dinner served**
7-10pm Thur-Sun. **Average** ££.
Portuguese

There's something decidedly
Prohibition-era about the Gallery –
from its access via a secure door at
the back of a fried chicken takeaway
to the cash-only attitude towards
settling the bill. Inside, colourful tiles
and painted murals create the air of
an Aladdin's cave, with a mezzanine
balcony on which diners can
overlook the musicians who often
perform below. The menu favours
pork, salt cod and seafood dishes.
We started with grilled spatchcock
quail in a Madeira wine sauce that

was mopped up with chunks of
high-quality bread. Next came a
succulent piece of peixe espada
(swordfish): a Madeiran favourite
not to be missed. It was refreshing
to see wines with such low mark-ups
– another reason to visit this
unusual restaurant.

Negril `NEW`

*132 Brixton Hill, SW2 1RS
(8674 8798). Brixton tube/rail/
45, 109, 118, 250 bus.* **Dinner
served** 5-10.30pm Mon-Fri. **Meals
served** 10am-10.30pm Sat, Sun.
Average ££. **Unlicensed.**
Corkage £2.50 per person.
Map p286. Caribbean

Caribbean comfort food is the real
deal at Negril. It's a popular spot in
spite of service that slows to a snail's
pace when the place is heaving, and
the cramped, unadorned interior
(decoration is limited to pages torn
from *Heat* covering the walls of the
lone toilet, which is accessed
through the kitchen). Standards
such as jerk chicken and ackee with
saltfish are best enjoyed with a side
of fried plantain, while tender goat
curry should be mopped up with a
perfectly fluffy roti. A hearty brunch
menu featuring the likes of jerk
chicken sausage is popular among
local party animals repairing the
ravages of the preceding night,
while the quaint roadside garden is
charming in summer. Don't forget to
bring your own beer or wine.

In the area

Nando's *234-244 Stockwell Road,
SW9 9SP (7737 6400).* **Map** p286.

Clapham

Abbevilles Restaurant

*88 Clapham Park Road, SW4 7BX
(7498 2185). Clapham Common
tube/35, 37 bus.* **Meals served**
11.30am-3.30pm Mon-Fri. **Average**
££. **Map** p286. British

South

Lunch-only Abbevilles offers swanky Claphamite cuisine at bargain-basement Brixton prices. Its Gallic-influenced menu lists dishes with one-word titles – 'scallops', 'chicken', 'gammon' – followed by helpful one-line descriptions. A deliciously light cheese and spinach soufflé starter with parmesan cream was perfectly formed and piping hot, while crispy duck in filo pastry had a wonderful home-cooked flavour. The only let-down was a helping of chewy tuna in a fish pie otherwise packed with generous chunks of flaky salmon. We liked the homely interior and the eager-to-please employees, and firmly believe that Abbevilles's pioneering work with the First Step Trust (a charity that assists people with learning disabilities find their feet in the workplace) should earn it far more credit than it currently gets.

Breads Etcetera NEW

127 Clapham High Street, SW4 7SS (7720 3601/www.breadsetcetera. com). Clapham Common or Clapham North tube. **Open** 10am-2pm Mon; 10am-6pm Tue-Thur, Sun; 10am-10pm Fri, Sat. **Average** ££. **Map** p286. Café

Appreciative thirtysomethings filled the café of this artisan bakery on Sunday morning, its interior given the feel of a NYC brunch spot by brick walls, maroon and cream striped textiles and, of course, the flavoursome scent of sourdough. Breads (choose from six-seed, walnut, white, wholemeal, olive and herb, and rye) are made from quality organic ingredients. Novelty is provided by the 'DIY toast' option, with Dualit toasters on tables, while all-day brunches (£7-£8) range from greasy ('cowboy': fried egg in white sourdough, with baked beans, spicy sausage, onion and dry-cured bacon) to healthy ('scandinavian': boiled egg, fish roe, ham, cheese, cucumber,

peppers and tomato). Also available are sandwiches, brownies, Luscombe juices and Monmouth coffee.

Café Sol

54-56 Clapham High Street, SW4 7UL (7498 8558/www.cafesol.net). Clapham Common or Clapham North tube. **Meals served** noon-midnight Mon-Thur, Sun; noon-1am Fri, Sat. **Average** ££. **Set lunch** £6.95 incl drink. **Map** p286. Mexican

Café Sol's popularity seems as much to do with its ability to satisfy hedonists as well as hungry masses – Latin beats shake the rafters and shots scatter the bar once the kitchen closes at midnight – but its multicoloured mosaic interior is still a decent place to dine early. It's best known for serving alligator alongside bar snacks such as nachos, barbecued ribs, chicken wings, quesadillas and potato skins. We went for 'armadillo eggs': stubby, super-hot chillies stuffed with refried beans and melting cheese, tempered (but only slightly) by soured cream. Delectable. Cajun sole dotted with tiny prawns was sound too, while pollo pueblo (a log of tortilla-crumbed chicken oozing with cheese, bacon and cream) was complemented by a fresh tomato sauce.

Café Wanda

153 Clapham High Street, SW4 7SS (7738 8760). Clapham Common tube. **Lunch served** 11am-3pm, **dinner served** 7-11pm Tue-Thur. **Meals served** 11am-11pm Fri-Sun. **Average** ££. **Map** p286. Polish

A recent refurbishment to famously retro Café Wanda appears to have left it stuck in the 1980s instead of the '70s in which it once slumbered. No matter: this longstanding bastion of Polish comfort food remains as popular with true-blooded Poles as it does with punters with a taste for culinary tourism. A starter of borscht was among the richest and heartiest we've tasted, while a moreish main of bigos – a stew of pork sausage, sauerkraut and prunes – more than justified its popularity as the tikka masala of Eastern European eating. Our sweet cheese pancake dessert was also first class, leaving little doubt that Café Wanda will still be here to herald in 1990s interior design somewhere around the year 2020.

Breads Etcetera. See p139.

See p139.

Eco

162 Clapham High Street, SW4 7UG (7978 1108/www.ecorestaurants. com). Clapham Common tube.
Lunch served noon-4pm, **dinner served** 6.30-11pm Mon-Fri. **Meals served** noon-11.30pm Sat; noon-11pm Sun. **Average** ££. **Map** p286.
Pizza & pasta
More than a decade has passed since Eco began plying punters with its fast, affordable Italian fare – and from the look of the 1990s-style interior, it seems little has changed in that time. This isn't the spot for an intimate liaison: tables are crammed too close together, and music is cranked so high that you have to shout to be heard. Pancetta-wrapped asparagus was a fine starter, although another of artichoke and buffalo mozzarella was measly with the artichoke. A main of pasta (choose from penne or spaghetti) came with a tasty truffle-oiled, creamy wine sauce, but was light on the porcini and pancetta. While locals swear by the vast pizzas, we would have preferred our fiorentina with a runnier egg and lighter crust. Arrive early to avoid maximum madness.

★ Macaron

22 The Pavement, SW4 0HY (7498 2636). Clapham Common tube.
Meals served 7.30am-7pm Mon-Fri; 9am-7pm Sat, Sun. **Average** £.
No credit cards. **Map** p286. Café
It wouldn't take a large glass of wine to imagine you'd been teleported to

1930s Paris by this brilliant pâtisserie. There's no signage out front: look for the giant pink ice-cream cone by the front door and a few small tables overlooking the Common. The ceiling is painted blue with fluffy clouds and fat cherubs, and the crockery is old Royal Albert bone china – flowery with gold edging. The drinks menu includes coffees, freshly squeezed juices and Chinese tea (over 20 varieties); our pot of nettle tea came full of fresh leaves. The display of baguettes and sandwiches was tempting, but we opted for a creamy, moist leek tart (for which a side salad would have been appreciated). You'd expect the macaroons to be fabulous here – and you'd be right.

Pepper Tree `NEW`

19 Clapham Common Southside, SW4 7AB (7622 1758). Clapham Common tube. **Lunch served** noon-3pm Mon-Fri. **Dinner served** 6-10.30pm Mon; 6-11pm Tue-Fri. **Meals served** noon-11pm Sat; noon-10.30pm Sun. **Average** ££. **Map** p286. Thai

You'll find none of the pretensions Clapham is known for here. The tightly packed rows of wooden canteen tables offer a spot of elbow tennis with the young and noisy clientele – but it's Thai cuisine, not comfort, that punters flock to Pepper Tree for. To start, we enjoyed plump, nutty vegetable parcels packed with beancurd, mushroom, water chestnut and sweetcorn, while a main of finely chopped chilli beef with green peas was grand of portion and generously spiked with Thai basil. Save room for dessert: mango sorbet is a fine palate-cooler, and yellow beancake is a sweet and tasty variation on traditional rice pudding, complemented perfectly by firm slices of fresh mango. Service isn't as saccharine – don't expect an abundance of smiles.

Meal deals

Gastro *67 Venn Street, SW4 0BD (7627 0222).* Set lunch (noon-3pm Mon-Fri) £9.95 2 courses incl coffee. **Map** p286. French

Newtons *33-35 Abbeville Road, SW4 9LA (8673 0977/www.newtons restaurants.co.uk).* Set lunch (noon-3pm Mon-Sat) £8 2 courses, £10.50 3 courses. **Map** p286. Brasserie

In the area

Nando's *59-63 Clapham High Street, SW4 7TG (7622 1475).* **Map** p286.

Pizza Express *43 Abbeville Road, SW4 9JX (8673 8878).* **Map** p286.

Strada *102-104 Clapham High Street, SW4 7UL (7627 4847).* **Map** p286.

Dexter's Grill *36-38 Abbeville Road, SW4 9NG (8772 6646).* **Map** p286.

Colliers Wood

Suvai Aruvi

96 High Street, SW19 2BT (8543 6266). Colliers Wood tube. **Meals served** 11am-11pm daily. **Average** ££. **Unlicensed** no alcohol allowed. **No credit cards.** **Map** p285.
Sri Lankan

This casual café offers traditional Sri Lankan dishes like string hoppers and kothu roti alongside garden-variety rice-based curries. It's more of a takeaway with strip-lit tables than a restaurant per se (the Tamil satellite TV blaring in the background is authentic, if not atmospheric), and although we've had excellent meals here in the past, we found the food variable on our last visit. Chicken masala dosa, large enough to have fed a small army, was overly spiced and lacking in clarity. Kothu roti, strips of thin roti fried with mutton or vegetables to make a spicy biriani-like dish, is usually a safe bet, as are a range of snacks including Sri Lankan mutton rolls. Note that alcohol is completely off the menu.

Kennington

Adulis NEW

*44-46 Brixton Road, SW9 6BT
(7587 0055/www.adulis.co.uk).
Oval tube.* **Meals served** 5pm-
midnight Mon-Thur; 1pm-midnight
Fri-Sun. **Average** ££. **Map** p287.
Eritrean

Every square inch of this light, airy
restaurant seems to honour its
Eritrean heritage, from the framed
photographs of Eritrea's old Italian
railway to the mounted pair of
simple rubber sandals worn by
rebels during the nation's war of
independence. Daring diners will
find a bracing starter in the form of
goe s'nigh (green chillies stuffed
with onion), while mains include a
classic range of meat stews and
pulses served on soft injera bases, as
well as fish and seafood recipes from
the Red Sea. Adulis also offers kitfo
(beef in ghee butter, either lightly
cooked or raw, according to taste).
There's plenty of Asmara beer to
cool hot mouths and the bar also
serves honey wine and zibib,
Eritrea's version of absinthe.

In the area

Pizza Express *316 Kennington
Road, SE11 4LD (7820 3877).*
Map p287.

Lambeth

★ Garden Café NEW

*The Garden Museum, Lambeth
Palace Road, SE1 7LB (7401 8865/
www.museumgardenhistory.org).
Lambeth North tube/3, 77, 344 bus.*
Meals served 10.30am-4.45pm
Tue-Sun. **Average** ££. **Map** p287.
Vegetarian

Lentil lovers and the vegicurious
should tiptoe through the graveyard
and past the topiaried box hedge
tapestry to this fantastic café,
attached to the Garden Museum.
Located inside the restored church

of St Mary-at-Lambeth, it treats
meat-free eating as a suitably
religious experience. The menu
changes seasonally; on a recent visit
the canteen-style selection included
chunks of pumpkin and halloumi
braised in red wine and marjoram –
delicious, hearty, autumnal fuel.
Mains are bolstered with generous
salads of cracked bulgur wheat
plumped with juicy raisins and
crumbled walnut, and lentil, quinoa
and green leaf salads are also
available. Sit in the walled
Tradescant Garden overlooking the
gravestones or slot into the side
nave of the church, atmospherically
lit by candlelight.

Stockwell

A Toca

*343 Wandsworth Road, SW8
2JH (7627 2919). Stockwell tube/
Wandsworth Road rail/77, 77A
bus.* **Meals served** 9am-midnight
daily. **Average** ££. **Map** p287.
Portuguese

You'd be forgiven for instinctively
patting your pocket for your
passport when entering the bright
interior of A Toca, so evocative is
the competing Portuguese chatter of
its devoted locals, staff and big-
screen televisions. The menu
includes a great deal of seafood,
from tapas-style servings of grilled
sardines to boiled octopus. We loved
signature mains of bacalhau a bras,
a mix of salt cod with egg, onions
and potato, and a Mirandesa-style
sirloin cooked with garlic and olive
oil: both featured strong, salty
flavours that went well with one of
the best-value house reds we've
tasted. Save room for the dessert of
honey and almond ice-cream in a
dainty little pot.

Bar Estrela

*111-115 South Lambeth Road,
SW8 1UZ (7793 1051). Stockwell*

South

tube/Vauxhall tube/rail. **Meals served** 8am-11pm daily. **Average** ££. **Map** p287. Portuguese

For many, going for a drink is an excuse to escape the telly; for devoted Portuguese locals, Bar Estrela's mounted screens are the centre of attention. Regulars stop by to catch the footie or a homeland soap while polishing off a plate of steaming clams, but food is of a high quality despite all eyes being on the box. We warmed up with a bowl of delicious caldo verde (spring cabbage soup), then shared a succulent dourada (gilt-head bream) accompanied by the customary combo of boiled potatoes and salad. Our only disappointment was a painfully fridge-cold bolo de bolacha (rich cake made from crushed biscuits pasted together with condensed milk) that should have tasted of creamy coffee. Still, the success of the rest of the meal means we'll certainly be returning.

O Moinho

355A Wandsworth Road, SW8 2JH (7498 6333/www.moinho.co.uk). Stockwell tube/Wandsworth Road rail/77, 77A bus. **Meals served** 10am-11pm daily. **Average** ££. **Map** p287. Portuguese

O Moinho thumbs its nose at its setting on a grubby stretch of Wandsworth Road with its smart waiters, pristine tablecloths and the kind of elegant wine glasses more usually associated with Sloane Square than Stockwell. The walls are decorated with signed football shirts and other Portuguese paraphernalia, adding charm to an otherwise formal setting. Tables are ready-laid with snacks of olives, bread and fish pâtés – but, as in Portugal, you'll be charged for these. Many customers share mains, as portions are massive: we split a seafood and vegetable skewer featuring huge king prawns, tender squid and sweet peppers. But the smartest move was that of our neighbours, who took the soupy seafood rice, pitched at two people, and stretched it to feed four.

Streatham

Bar 61 NEW

61A Streatham Hill, SW2 4TX (8671 0444/www.bar61.com). Streatham Hill rail. **Meals served** 1-11pm daily. **Average** ££. Spanish

Regulars at this well-established south London institution are greeted by name and invited to eat at the bar. Mellow lighting and soft wood tones lend a sense of convivial familiarity to the raised dining area beyond, where families, friends and dates blend comfortably together. Bar 61's tapas menu features plenty of vegetarian options alongside standards such as chorizo and calamares. We particularly liked the abundance of chunky vegetables in deftly seasoned ratatouille, and found the meat on our pork cutlets almost tender enough to cut itself. Everything we sampled was a fine match for the bold Bordón crianza that staff recommended from an extensive list of Spanish wines. A justifiably popular local spot; book ahead to avoid disappointment.

In the area

Nando's *6-7 High Parade, Streatham High Road, SW16 1ES (8769 0951).*
Pizza Express *34 Streatham High Road, SW16 1DB (8769 0202).*

Tooting

Apollo Banana Leaf NEW

190 Tooting High Street, SW17 0SF (8696 1423). Tooting Broadway tube. **Lunch served** noon-3pm,

dinner served 6-10pm Mon-Wed.
Meals served noon-10.30pm Thur-Sun. **Average** £. **Unlicensed.**
Corkage no charge. **Map** p285.
Sri Lankan

Decor may not be Apollo Banana Leaf's strong point (unless junk art of Sahara scenes and Ikea mirrors are to your taste), but staff are solicitous and smiling, prices low and the Sri Lankan dishes among the best you'll find in London. The tastes of the Tamil north of the island are expressed in meals such as mutton string hopper fry, the rice vermicelli cut into chunks and fried with hot, full-flavoured mutton curry. Pay close heed to the menu's chilli-heat warnings; the squid curry is seriously fiery. The extensive menu also incorporates many South Indian and Sri Lankan dosas, rice dishes and the like. The BYO policy is a bonus.

Dosa n Chutny NEW
68 Tooting High Street, SW17 0RN (8767 9200/www.dosa-chutny.com). Tooting Broadway tube. **Meals served** 10am-10.30pm daily. **Average** £. **Set buffet** (noon-10.30pm) £5.95 daily. **Map** p285.
Indian

Dosa n Chutny is part of Tooting's new wave of South Indian eateries, which seem aimed more at the area's recent Tamil immigrants than its non-Asian diners. The restaurant's bright lighting, orange furniture and droning flat-screen TV may seem harsh, but classic breakfast and snack dishes are beautifully prepared, including crisp dosas and idlis with perfect sponge-like textures. The sambar is rich and sweet, in the Chennai style. Other food, including Sri Lankan string hopper dishes, were less impressive, but at prices this low it's churlish to complain. Sample the masala tea: it's as close to Indian chai as you'll find locally. We've regularly been the only non-Asian

diners present; it's time the rest of Tooting discovered this place.

Kastoori
188 Upper Tooting Road, SW17 7EJ (8767 7027). Tooting Bec or Tooting Broadway tube. **Lunch served** 12.30-2.30pm Wed-Sun. **Dinner served** 6-10.30pm daily. **Average** ££. **Set thali** £8.95-£16.50. **Minimum** £8. **Map** p285.
Indian

Are standards slipping at this long-standing vegetarian favourite? On recent visits we've found the service, once cheerful and efficient, to be indifferent and inattentive. Since neither the room (decorated with a few bas-reliefs of temple dancers) nor the menu has changed for what feels like decades, perhaps it's not surprising staff seem bored. Still, the East African Gujarati dishes remain top-notch. The various bhel poori are tantalising explosions of sour-sweet flavours, although it's the 'Thanki family specials' that are most unusual, using African ingredients such as matoki (plantain) and kasodi (sweetcorn) prepared in Gujarati-style vegetable dishes. It's a shame that so few of those listed are ever available, but the tomato curry is a good alternative, mouth-wateringly spicy and disarmingly sweet.

Kusinang Munti NEW
913 Garratt Lane, SW17 0LT (8672 4363/www.kusinangmunti.co.uk). Tooting Broadway tube. **Meals served** 8am-11pm daily. **Average** £. **Map** p285. Oriental

The bright interior may not be big on atmosphere – the crush of so many plain, functional tables more akin to an office canteen than a café, the large mirrors less than flattering and the view on to Garratt Lane dull at best – but Kusinang Munti is slicker than your average oriental buffet. The Philippines' three centuries of colonial domination

South

Garden Café.
See p142.

have left an intriguing Spanish-Mexican influence on the range of dishes, which include the likes of pork or chicken adobo (stewed in soy sauce, vinegar, garlic and peppercorns), satays, lumpiang (similar to spring rolls) and dinuguan (a savoury pork blood stew). Lunch costs just £5.50, dinner £6.50, and the affable staff organise countless parties and in-house events including karaoke.

Radhakrishna Bhavan

86 Tooting High Street, SW17 0RN (8682 0969/www.mcdosa.co.uk). Tooting Broadway tube. **Lunch served** noon-3pm daily. **Dinner served** 6-11pm Mon-Thur, Sun; 6pm-midnight Fri, Sat. **Average £. Minimum** £5. **Map** p285. Indian
The walls of this established Keralite restaurant are covered with photographic wallpaper depicting coconut-fronded beaches and sunsets; a full kathakali dance costume sits imposingly in one corner; and statues of Krishna and his girlfriend Radha adorn the counter. Food-wise, we recommend sticking to specialities such as avial

(vegetable stew), vellappams (large, frisbee-shaped crumpets) and thorans (vegetable stir-fries that include diced beetroot and grated cabbage). The dosas, idlis and vadai are also fine, but several restaurants in Tooting now do these better, and cheaper. Recently we've found RKB inconsistent – on our last visit, a mango and yoghurt curry (kalan) contained yoghurt that had curdled, giving the dish an unappealing lumpy texture – but there's seldom anything to find fault with.

★ Sree Krishna

192-194 Tooting High Street, SW17 0SF (8672 4250/www.sree krishna.co.uk). Tooting Broadway tube. **Lunch served** noon-3pm daily. **Dinner served** 6-11pm Mon-Thur, Sun; 6pm-midnight Fri, Sat. **Average £. Set lunch** (Mon-Sat) £4.95 3 courses. **Set thali** (noon-3pm Sun) £5.95-£7.95. **Minimum** £9.50 (dinner). **Map** p285. Indian
Established in 1973, Sree Krishna was the first South Indian restaurant in Tooting and it remains one of the finest to this day. The interior might

be reminiscent of a hotel lobby in Ootacamund circa 1965, and the service can be oddly somnambulant, but the kitchen was still on fine form on our visit. Give the bhunas, vindaloos and kormas a swerve and choose instead the 'vegetarian starters', the 'dry vegetables' and the 'chef's specials', all of which are distinctively South Indian. We can especially recommend the appam and meat curry – giant, saucer-like crumpets with spicy lamb – and the beetroot thoran, a stir-fry of diced and spiced purple tubers. The huge, crisp dosas are also standout.

In the area
Mirch Masala *213 Upper Tooting Road, SW17 7TG (8672 7500).* **Map** p285.
Nando's *224-226 Upper Tooting Road, SW17 7EW (8682 2478).* **Map** p285.

Vauxhall

Bonnington Centre Café
11 Vauxhall Grove, SW8 1TD (no phone/www.bonningtoncafe. co.uk). Vauxhall tube/rail. **Lunch served** noon-2pm, **dinner served** 6.30-10.30pm daily. **Average** £. **Unlicensed. Corkage** no charge. **No credit cards**. **Map** p287.
Vegetarian
With its abundance of local art, clutter of rescued furniture and bohemian world music soundtrack, this much loved co-operative café seems a world away from the gloomy officialdom of the nearby MI6 headquarters. Each day sees a different set of chefs taking charge of the small kitchen, which invariably leads to the occasional duff dish, although our most recent lunch of butternut squash soup, vegetarian shepherd's pie and white chocolate tart was healthy and hearty. And, at £9 including coffee,

surely one of the best-value three-course meals the capital has to offer. A BYO policy makes the whole experience even more affordable, and the quirky pleasure gardens opposite are the perfect spot for a romantic post-prandial stroll.

Casa Madeira NEW
46A-46C Albert Embankment, SE1 7TN (7820 1117/www.madeira london.co.uk). Vauxhall tube/rail. **Meals served** 11am-11.30pm daily. **Average** £££. **Map** p287.
Portuguese
Casa Madeira has a spick and span appearance complete with starched tablecloths, uniformed waiters and a smart bar. It opened in 2007 and its Portuguese chef didn't have to come far – he previously worked at the adjoining Madeira Café (which has the same owners). While next door now serves popular fry-ups, toasted sarnies and omelettes, Casa Madeira has become the place for real Portuguese cooking. We opted for house specials on our visit: Portuguese-style beefsteak, and pork stew with clams. The former was cooked to perfection and the latter terrific, even if the pork was on the tough side. Were it not for the regular rumble of trains overhead you could easily drift off and imagine yourself lunching leisurely in a Lisbon suburb.

Hot Stuff
19 Wilcox Road, SW8 2XA (7720 1480/www.eathotstuff.com). Vauxhall tube/rail. **Meals served** noon-10pm Mon-Fri; 3-10pm Sat. **Average** £. **Unlicensed. Corkage** no charge. **Map** p287.
Indian
This BYO restaurant has garnered glowing national reviews for its inventive, authentic cooking and ridiculously low prices, yet it remains an enigmatic place, the bright, modern interior in stark contrast to the unprepossessing

alley down which it's located. We've had great meals here in years gone by, but our last visit was hit and miss. Naan breads were wonderfully soft and flaky, but poppadoms had an unpleasant plastic quality; dahl makani was sublimely smokey, but chicken jalfrezi lacked heat (and this despite the mobile tantalisingly dangling hundreds of chillis above our heads). Perhaps we should have visited between Wednesday and Saturday, when staff lay on their tilapia fish masala, an East African curry that is the stuff of local legend.

Zeitgeist @ The Jolly Gardeners NEW

49-51 Black Prince Road, SE11 6AB (7840 0426/www.zeitgeist-london.com). Lambeth North tube/Vauxhall tube/rail. **Meals served** noon-9.30pm Mon-Fri, Sun; 2-9.30pm Sat. **Average** ££. Map p287. German

The main draw at this revamped Victorian pub near Lambeth Walk is its range of German beers – 30 and counting. Bar snacks include meatballs, dried sausages and wholegrain bread with ham and cheese, while sandwiches, soups and grilled sausages with potato salad are served at lunchtime. Popular dishes from north and south Germany feature on the dinner menu: 'heaven and earth' (cloud-like whipped potatoes with moist black pudding and baked apple) and beef stew with bread dumplings both cost less than a tenner, and there are a variety of schnitzels. Black nightclub-style decor and two widescreen TVs showing football are hardly spirit of the age, but this remains an unexpected and welcome venture in Vauxhall.

In the area

Lisboa Pâtisserie *147 South Lambeth Road, SW8 1XN (7587 1612).* Map p287.

Waterloo

Giraffe

Riverside Level 1, Royal Festival Hall, Belvedere Road, SE1 8XX (7928 2004/www.giraffe.net). Embankment tube/Waterloo tube/rail. **Meals served** 8am-10.45pm Mon-Fri; 9am-10.45pm Sat; 9am-10.30pm Sun. **Average** ££. **Set meal** (5-7pm Mon-Fri) £6.95 2 courses. Map p288. Brasserie

Lunchtimes see Giraffe in full family mode – children are given balloons and babycinos, proper food and plenty of attention – but the chain's enduring popularity makes having to wait for a table almost an inevitability, and the high turnover often results in inadequate clean-ups between sittings. Nonetheless, staff are clearly chosen for their sunny ways and the food is gratifying in terms of both value and taste. Our favourite is the vegetarian meze plate, starring tabouleh, houmous, beetroot, falafel, Tunisian ratatouille and warm pitta. We also sampled a brace of burgers: one Aberdeen Angus and one lamb kofta. Both were juicy and delicious. Salads are all pleasingly imaginative: the 'sunshine powerfood' version bursts with nuts, seeds and edamame beans alongside the usual leaves.

Masters Super Fish

191 Waterloo Road, SE1 8UX (7928 6924). Waterloo tube/rail. **Lunch served** noon-3pm Tue-Sat. **Dinner served** 5.30-10.30pm Mon; 4.30-10.30pm Tue-Thur, Sat; 4.30-11pm Fri. **Average** ££. **Set lunch** £7 1 course incl soft drink, tea or coffee. Map p288. Fish & chips

There's real character to this enduring bastion of 'proper' fish and chips, from its mint-green paintwork and exposed new-brick walls to peach faux-marble tables and signed photos of old-school celebs (Mark Curry and 'Lovejoy' among them).

Fresh fish is bought daily from Billingsgate, portions are huge and there are pleasing complimentary extras (three prawns per customer and a basket of sliced baguette to start; gherkins, pickled onions and condiments to go with the mains). Battered cod was a generous, meaty fillet; plaice, while clearly fresh, was wet and overwhelmed by its cloak of batter. Chips were agreeably fat. If you're opting for a takeaway, order in the entrance area decorated with hundreds of football match tickets.

Pizza Paradiso

61 The Cut, SE1 8LL (7261 1221/www.pizzaparadiso.co.uk). Southwark tube/Waterloo tube/rail. **Meals served** noon-midnight Mon-Sat; noon-11pm Sun. **Average** ££. **Set lunch** (noon-5pm daily) £9.95 2 courses incl glass of wine. **Map** p288. Pizza & pasta
Established in 1934, the Italian eaterie formerly known as Ristorante Olivelli may have gone mainstream with its name – and expanded from a one-off Soho stalwart into a three-restaurant mini-chain – but it still has individuality and charm to knock the socks off most of its chain rivals. This small Southwark branch has the atmosphere of a traditional Italian trattoria and food to match. Appealing seafood and meat mains prove there's more to cheap Italian fare than pizza and pasta, although there are plenty of reliable favourites: the salad niçoise is healthy in more ways than one, while pizzas such as the fiorentina and caprina feature crisp bases and an abundance of fresh toppings.

Meal deals

Baltic *74 Blackfriars Road, SE1 8HA (7928 1111/www.baltic restaurant.co.uk).* Set meal (noon-3pm, 6-7pm Mon-Sat) £11.50 2 courses, £13.50 3 courses;

(noon-10.30pm Sun) £13.50 2 courses incl drink, £15.50 3 courses incl drink. **Map** p288. Polish
Tamesa@oxo *2nd floor, Oxo Tower Wharf, Barge House Street, SE1 9PH (7633 0088/ www.tamesa@oxo.com).* Set meal (12.30-3.30pm, 5.30-7.30pm Mon-Fri) £14.50 2 courses. **Map** p288. Brasserie
Troia *3F Belvedere Road, SE1 7GQ (7633 9309).* Set lunch (noon-4pm) £8.75 2 courses. Set meze £9.95 per person (minimum 2). **Map** p288. Turkish

In the area

EV Restaurant, Bar & Delicatessen *The Arches, 97-99 Isabella Street, SE1 8DA (7620 6191).* Branch of Tas. **Map** p288.
Feng Sushi *Festival Terrace, Royal Festival Hall, Belvedere Road, SE1 8XX (7261 0001).* **Map** p288.
Giraffe *Riverside Level 1, Royal Festival Hall, Belvedere Road, SE1 8XX (7928 2004).* **Map** p288.
Konditor & Cook *22 Cornwall Road, SE1 8TW (7261 0456).* **Map** p288.
Le Pain Quotidien *Upper Festival Walk, Royal Festival Hall, Belvedere Road, SE1 8XX (7486 6154).* **Map** p288.
Ping Pong *Festival Terrace, Royal Festival Hall, Belvedere Road, SE1 8XX (7960 4160).* **Map** p288.
Pizza Express *3 The White House, 9C Belvedere Road, SE1 8YP (7928 4091).* **Map** p288.
Strada *Riverside Level 1, Royal Festival Hall, Belvedere Road, SE1 8XX (7401 9126).* **Map** p288.
Tas *33 The Cut, SE1 8LF (7928 2111).* **Map** p288.
Wagamama *Riverside Level 1, Royal Festival Hall, Belvedere Road, SE1 8XX (7021 0877).* **Map** p288.
Yo! Sushi *County Hall, Belvedere Road, SE1 7GP (7928 8871).* **Map** p288.

SOUTH EAST

Bankside

Pizza Express

Benbow House, 24 New Globe Walk, SE1 9DS (7401 3977/www.pizza express.com). Southwark tube/ London Bridge tube/rail. **Meals served** noon-11pm Mon-Sat; noon-10.30pm Sun. **Average** ££. **Map** p289. Pizza & pasta

This two-floor, glass-fronted branch offers alfresco dining and river views alongside the usual range of aesthetic staples: gleaming tiles, artful lighting and couple-friendly tables bearing flowers so identical that they might have come out of a machine. Service was smiling and attentive despite lunchtime crowds, and the pizzas as good as they should be given the billion-or-so times they've been prepared. Our padana featured generous helpings of goat's cheese and spinach, although a combination of red onion and caramelised onion confit rather confused things flavour-wise; a well-assembled la reine was more successful and featured lashings of smokey prosciutto. Reliable, familiar and pleasant on the eye, if Pizza Express were a partner, it would be perfect marriage material.

★ The Table

83 Southwark Street, SE1 0HX (7401 2760/www.thetablecafe. com). Southwark tube/London Bridge tube/rail. **Meals served** 7.30am-5pm Mon-Fri; 9am-3pm Sat, Sun. **Average** ££. **Map** p289. Café

Good-looking artisanal sandwiches are wrapped and waiting on a stand by the entrance of this innovative café, set on the ground floor of an architectural firm. There's also a salad buffet bearing the likes of greek salad, roasted vegetable couscous and barbecued chicken drumsticks. Diners with time to spare go to the back counter, where staff dispense hot meals from a daily menu that includes a soup of the day (garden pea and mint on our last visit), a tart (roast broccoli and gruyère) and a variety of meat and fish cooked to order – from organic minute steaks to Billingsgate-fresh monkfish. Customers eat at one of the chunky wooden pews, many of them watching passers-by through the big windows.

★ Tate Modern Café: Level 2

2nd floor, Tate Modern, Sumner Street, SE1 9TG (7401 5014/ www.tate.org.uk). Southwark tube/ London Bridge tube/rail. **Breakfast served** 10-11.30am, **lunch served** 11.30am-3pm, **afternoon tea served** 3-5.30pm daily. **Dinner served** 6.30-9.30pm Fri, Sat. **Average** £££. **Map** p289. Brasserie

You don't need to love modern art to enjoy this superb place; indeed, it's popular with everyone from trendy designer types to frazzled families with hungry toddlers. It's wonderfully airy, and, thanks to its three glass walls, has excellent views towards the river. The food is great, from a starter of leeks in vinaigrette topped with an oozing poached egg to a main of pollack on white bean purée with cherry tomatoes and aubergine. The menu has British as well as international flavours; we've seen Shropshire fidget pie filled with bacon and apples alongside an Iberian meat plate. Puddings are sophisticated without being flashy; rhubarb compote and custard was prettily layered in a tumbler. Overall, this is an unpretentious, deftly executed enterprise, deserving of its success.

Tsuru NEW

4 Canvey Street, SE1 8AN (7928 2228/www.tsuru-sushi.co.uk). Southwark tube/London Bridge tube/rail. **Meals served** 11am-6pm

Tate Modern Café: Level 2

Mon-Fri. **Tapas served** 6-9pm
Thur, Fri. **Average** ££. **Map** p288.
Japanese

Tsuru is as neat and appealing as a
bento box, with sushi as fresh as the
staff are friendly. A few red lanterns
and framed prints liven up an
otherwise functional interior – an
atmosphere reinforced by the sight
of businessmen dining at window
pews, chopsticks in one hand and
mobiles in the other – but it still feels
spacious and airy. The open kitchen
turns out sushi made with quality
ingredients: line-caught yellowfin
tuna, Shetland salmon and West
Country chicken. Nigiri and maki
rolls came in a taster box alongside
salad leaves and a smoky, own-
made soy and sesame dressing, and
we loved the authentically sweet
katsu curry with breaded and deep-
fried pork cutlet.

In the area

Real Greek *Riverside House,
2A Southwark Bridge Road, SE1
9HA (7620 0162).* **Map** p289.
Tas Pide *20-22 New Globe Walk,
SE1 9DR (7928 3300).* **Map** p289.

Bermondsey

Arancia

*52 Southwark Park Road, SE16 3RS
(7394 1751/www.arancia-london.
co.uk). Bermondsey tube/Elephant*
& Castle tube/rail then 1, 53 bus.
Lunch served 12.30-2.30pm Thur-
Sun. **Dinner served** 7-11pm Tue-
Sat. **Average** £££. **Set lunch**
£8.50 2 courses, £10.50 3 courses.
Italian

A scuffed splash of orange on a
busy grey road, Arancia's bare
brick alcoves, worn floorboards and
old dials on the walls give it an
antique, boiler room air. The
regularly changing menu is
distinguished by its simplicity and
use of bright, fresh market produce.
Our set lunch began with a superb
bowl of delicate pale green zuppa di
stagione, with peas, fennel, baby
spinach and potatoes served with
garlicky bruschetta and parmesan.
This was followed by richly sauced
linguine with aubergines and
peppers. Crespelle pancakes had a
tempting filling of chard and
fontina cheese, although the stalky
veg rather dominated. Our cooling
prosecco was a fine match for the
meal, and although the coffee was
ineffectual, we left happy.

Blackheath

★ Chapters All
Day Dining NEW

*43-45 Montpelier Vale, SE3 0TJ
(8333 2666/www.chapters
restaurants.com). Blackheath rail.*

Meals served 8am-11pm Mon-Sat; 9am-9.30pm Sun. **Average £££**. **Map** p291. Brasserie

Mod Euro restaurant Chapter Two has been reborn as a brasserie/bar, giving budget diners the chance to gorge themselves in glamorous surroundings. You can pop in for breakfast, just a cuppa or a beer, or a full-blown meal. A gleaming bar runs the length of the airy ground-floor room, and both this and the intimate basement space are overlooked by grand mirrors, bare brick walls and arty light fittings. Main courses punch above their price in terms of both ingredients and presentation: we plumped for lamb tagine, which was sweet, subtly seasoned and packed with tender meat, plus salmon fillet paired with bold roasted peppers and chorizo. A dessert of baked cheesecake was also divine.

Laicram

1 Blackheath Grove, SE3 0DD (8852 4710). Blackheath rail. **Lunch served** noon-2.30pm, **dinner served** 6-11pm Tue-Sun. **Average ££**. **Map** p291. Thai

There's something unashamedly old-fashioned about this popular locals' haunt – from the wooden trellis decorated with plastic ivy to the portraits of the Thai royal family on the walls. Friendly service boosts the community feel, and the food is superb. We loved the kitchen's classic spicy seafood tom yam, with salmon among the generous portion of seafood; equally spicy tom kha gai had a typically aromatic coconut broth to take the edge off the specks of red chilli. A delicious Thai sweet and sour chicken was a less sugary variation of the Chinese restaurant classic, and plump prawns stir-fried with garlic, ginger and soy sauce were just right. For afters, there are dessert trolley goodies and exotic fruit galore.

In the area

Pizza Express *64-66 Tranquil Vale, SE3 0BN (8318 2595).* **Map** p291.
Strada *5 Lee Road, SE3 9RQ (8318 6644).* **Map** p291.

Camberwell

Caravaggio NEW

47 Camberwell Church Street, SE5 8TR (7207 1612). Denmark Hill rail. **Lunch served** noon-3pm, **dinner served** 5-11pm Mon-Fri. **Meals served** noon-11pm Sat; noon-10pm Sun. **Average ££**. **Map** p292. Pizza & pasta

Diners travel here from well outside Camberwell: Caravaggio is fast earning a reputation as a quintessentially friendly, unfussy neighbourhood Italian, an image reinforced by the smiling waiter who ushered us to our seat and the baroque wallpaper dotted with prints of works by the Old Master himself. A starter of aubergine stuffed with mozzarella, tomato and fresh basil was rich and delicious, and main courses revealed an affinity with fresh ingredients and bold flavours, from a wild mushroom ravioli in creamy gorgonzola sauce to a mixed vegetable pasta with capers and tomatoes. Both were so filling that we didn't have room for one of the own-made desserts; our post-prandial espresso, though, would have made Italians proud.

★ La Luna

380 Walworth Road, SE17 2NG (7277 1991/www.lalunapizzeria. com). Bus 12, 35, 40, 45, 68, 68A, 171, 176. **Lunch served** noon-3pm, **dinner served** 6-11pm Tue-Sat. **Meals served** 12.30-10.45pm Sun. **Average ££**. **Set lunch** £5.50 1 course incl coffee. **Set meal** £11.90 3 courses. **Map** p292. Pizza & pasta

Seen from the pavement, La Luna doesn't look especially impressive.

Cross its threshold, however, and you're spirited into an oasis of calm, miles from the noise and gritty greyness of the street outside. The atmosphere is welcoming and cosy, largely because the staff couldn't be friendlier; as for the food, La Luna is renowned for its pizzas, and a giant, authentic-looking pizza oven has pride of place in the middle of the restaurant. We opted for the pizza of the day, a delicious combination of smoked mozzarella, pancetta and sun-dried tomatoes, and an elegant confection of aubergine, courgette and goat's cheese; both exceeded expectations. La Luna definitely remains one of Camberwell's best-kept secrets.

Meal deals

Mozzarella e Pomodoro 21-22 Camberwell Green, SE5 7AA (7277 2020). Set lunch (Mon-Fri) £7.50 2 courses. **Map** p292. Pizza & pasta

In the area

Nando's 88 Denmark Hill, SE5 8RX (7738 3808). **Map** p292.

Catford

In the area

Nando's 74-76 Rushey Green, SE6 4HW (8314 0122).

Charlton

Cattleya at Chu & Cho

52 Charlton Church Lane, SE7 7AB (7642 1014/www.cattleyathaimed. com). Charlton rail. **Meals served** 5-11pm Tue-Thur; noon-11pm Fri-Sun. **Average** ££. International
A short walk from Charlton station gets you to this diminutive establishment no larger than a living room, where daring diners will relish the chance to cross continents in one meal. It was run as a Spanish restaurant for nearly a decade, but the new Thai owners now serve a range of eastern nibbles (prawn toast, fish cakes, satay chicken) alongside standard tapas fodder such as jamon serrano, calamares and boquerones. The Thai mains are good: we opted for a deliciously rich and spicy phed phad cha: sliced duck breast with red peppers, fresh chilli and a sprinkling of Thai basil. Desserts run from the likes of banana fritters to chocolate-dipped churros or fresh mango with sweet rice and coconut cream.

Crystal Palace

Domali

38 Westow Street, SE19 3AH (8768 0096/www.domali.co.uk). Crystal Palace or Gypsy Hill rail. **Meals served** 9.30am-10.30pm daily. **Average** ££. **Set lunch** £6.90-£8.90 1 course incl glass of wine or beer. Vegetarian
Vegetarian cafés used to be austere, faintly forbidding places, but there's nothing remotely spartan about this attractive little eaterie. A cool interior – white walls adorned with original art, stripped wooden floors and squishy leather sofas – and an imaginative and extensive menu ensure that Domali is always busy, especially at weekends, when you can expect to have to wait for a table. Mains include the likes of goat's cheese and sweet potato pie, pan-fried salmon, or red onion and ginger dahl – and there are sandwiches for people who can't hang around. Another big star on the menu is the 'Deal' veggie breakfast, which comes with vegetarian sausages and perfectly poached eggs.

Mediterranea NEW

21 Westow Street, SE19 3RY (8771 7327/www.mediterranea london.com). Crystal Palace or Gypsy Hill rail. **Lunch served**

12.30-2.30pm Tue-Sun. **Dinner served** 6.30-9.30pm Mon; 6.30-10.30pm Tue-Sun. **Average ££.** **Set lunch** (Tue-Sat) £4.90 1 course incl drink, £6.90 2 courses incl drink. Italian

Mediterranea is a little patch of Sardinia in the Crystal Palace triangle. Its lunch menu is a bargain: £4.90 gets you a glass of wine (or soft drink) and a generous main course from a list of dishes like chargrilled calamari, chicken breast, tomato and aubergine pasta, or lamb stew with aromatic rice; pay £6.90 and you can also have a dessert. The marinated meats were succulent and tender, but the sautéed potatoes were too buttery and flaccid. Evening meals are slightly more sophisticated (monkfish, poached figs), and the genial owner lays on regular themed nights that put the culinary spotlight on other parts of the Mediterranean. A pleasant enough family restaurant (the kids loved it), but not worth a long trek.

Spirited Palace

105 Church Road, SE19 2PR (8768 0609). Crystal Palace rail. **Meals served** 5-10pm Mon; 11.30am-10pm Tue-Fri; 2-10pm Sat, Sun. **Average ££. Unlicensed. Corkage** varies. **No credit cards.** Vegetarian

There's a homely, almost domestic feel to Spirited Palace, and it went some way towards alleviating the pokiness of the basement dining room into which we were ushered. There's no menu; you simply get what the waiter brings you, in our case a mixed vegan platter whipped up by the Rastafarian chef. Fortunately, all misgivings were dispelled by the delicious spread: marinated tofu, fresh vegetables in a creamy soya sauce and divine dumplings of curried potatoes and onions. The climax came in the shape of a pineapple crumble with soya ice-cream. The space could be improved, but we can forgive many things after such good food and the enjoyably unconventional way it arrived.

Deptford Project

In the area
Pizza Express *70 Westow Hill, SE19 1SB (8670 1786).*

Deptford

Deptford Project NEW
121-123 Deptford High Street, SE8 4NS (07525 351656/www.the deptfordproject.com). Deptford rail/Deptford Bridge DLR. **Meals served** 9am-7pm Mon-Fri; 9am-6pm Sat; 10am-4pm Sun. **Average** £. **No credit cards. Map** p290. Café
Here's something a little different: a café housed in a 1960s train carriage. Deptford Project is part of a regeneration scheme that includes an arts and crafts market and galleries; a brightly painted table runs the length of it, and cheery decking out front adds to the relaxed, arty vibe. The food is unpretentious and homely: lunch might be a light potato salad with crunchy green leaves, or satisfyingly spicy curry on a bed of turmeric-spiked basmati. If you're here at breakfast or in the afternoon, try the excellent muffins topped with eggs from the café's own free-range chickens. Popular with locals, Goldsmiths students and young families, this is a pleasant spot in which to sit back and recharge.

Dulwich

Au Ciel
1A Carlton Avenue, SE21 7DE (8488 1111/www.auciel.co.uk). North Dulwich rail/37 bus. **Meals served** 8.30am-5.30pm Mon-Sat; 10am-5.30pm Sun. **Average** £. **Map** p292. Café
This long-established pâtisserie-chocolatier is charming: attractive window boxes, prettily displayed cakes, jams and sweetmeats, and an array of handmade chocolates from France and Belgium. The simple menu lines up soups, sandwiches and ice-creams, and the staff are friendly (even doing impromptu

magic for bored children). Hot chocolates are piled high with whipped cream, but the teas show less expertise: the cakes (lemon, carrot, chocolate, scones – no surprises there) proved dry and dense, and the chocolate chip cookies were inedibly heavy (even turned down by a sweet-toothed five-year-old). Long gone are the days when Londoners swooned for anything vaguely French, especially when there's better baking to be had in nearby East Dulwich and Herne Hill.

Pavilion Café
Dulwich Park, SE21 7BQ (8299 1383/www.pavilioncafedulwich. co.uk). West Dulwich rail/P4 bus. **Meals served** *Summer* 8.30am-6pm Mon-Thur; 8.30am-7pm Fri-Sun. *Winter* 8.30am-dusk Mon-Fri; 9am-dusk Sat, Sun. **Average** £. **Map** p292. Café
On a quiet weekday, it's bliss to have breakfast, lunch or tea in this airy, modern café overlooking the lawns and rhododendrons of Dulwich Park. But at noon on a sunny weekend, you can expect to queue for an eternity. The all-day full breakfast is great value, the cakes are own-made, and the specials are always interesting (Moroccan lamb soup with pitta bread on our last visit); you can even get wine here. The food policy is commendably organic and seasonal, and new additions (rum hot chocolate, Baileys latte) regularly appear on the menu. It's a pity that the service is painfully slow, because in every other respect this is pretty much the perfect park caff.

Romeo Jones NEW
80 Dulwich Village, SE21 7AJ (8299 1900/www.romeojones.co.uk). North Dulwich rail. **Meals served** 8am-6pm Mon-Fri; 9am-6pm Sat; 10am-5pm Sun. **Average** ££. **Map** p292. Café
Squeeze through this Italian-slanted delicatessen to the tiny tearoom at the back, where the beaming patron will attend to you. Cakes are made by 'small scale local suppliers' (by which we imagine they mean Dulwich mums at their Agas), and you can taste the love that has gone into them. There are also light snacks such as salads and cold meats, but our top tip is the bagels – warmed, not toasted, and made to order with delicious fillings such as parma ham, cream cheese and nectarine or milano salami, mustard and cornichons. There's limited space inside, so take one away and enjoy it on a stroll along the lanes of nearby Dulwich Park.

In the area
Pizza Express *94 The Village, SE21 7AQ (8693 9333).* **Map** p292.

East Dulwich

★ Blue Mountain Café
18 North Cross Road, SE22 9EU (8299 6953/www.bluemo.co.uk). East Dulwich rail. **Meals served** 9am-5pm daily. **Dinner served** 6.30-10pm Tue-Sat. **Average** ££. **Set breakfast** (9am-5pm) £6.95 incl tea or coffee. **Map** p292. Café
Fashionable well before East Dulwich was, Blue Mountain has expanded its range from caffeine and pastries to full-scale, all-day dining. Groups of media mums and their kids can now sit down to modish dishes such as butternut squash risotto with rocket, or pan-fried steak with steamed veg in a coconut curry sauce. But the place hasn't lost its slightly hippy air: it still has the broken crockery mosaic in its outdoor seating area and the interior remains reassuringly quirky. A light lunch of buttery mushrooms and tofu in a soft baguette was delicious, even if the accompanying salad was a bit limp. The coffee and countless cakes are

as delightful as ever, and service is friendly and efficient.

Gowlett NEW

62 Gowlett Road, SE15 4HY (7635 7048/www.thegowlett.com). East Dulwich or Peckham Rye rail/12, 37, 40, 63, 176, 185, 484 bus. **Lunch served** 12.30-2.30pm, **dinner served** 6.30-10.30pm Mon-Fri. **Meals served** 12.30-10.30pm Sat; 12.30-9pm Sun. **Average** *££*. **Map** p292. Pizza & pasta

The smoking ban has been good for this hip, CAMRA-endorsed pub and pizza place: scents of stone-baked dough and home cooking have replaced wafts of fag ash. There's Adnams on tap alongside a changing line-up of real ales. The pizza menu has a seasonal special (a succulent chorizo, mixed pepper and white onion confection on our visit) plus half a dozen other choices: the bestsellers are the Gowlettini (mozzarella, goat's cheese, pine nuts, rocket and prosciutto – or sun-dried tomatoes for veggies) and the American Hot (spicy salami dripping with chilli oil). 'Lucky 7' night on Thursday starts the weekend early, as local musos drop in to spin records and knock back a bottle of the keenly priced organic wines.

★ Jack's Tea & Coffee House NEW

85 Pellatt Road, SE22 9JD (8693 0011). North Dulwich rail. **Meals served** *Summer* 10am-5pm Mon-Fri; 10am-3pm Sat. *Winter* 10am-4pm Mon-Fri; 10am-3pm Sat. **Average** *£*. **No credit cards. Map** p292. Café

Wander off well-trodden Lordship Lane and you might stumble on this charming, family-run café. Friendly service and hearty fare are what give Jack's its soul (with extra character added by the slightly dishevelled decor and old-fashioned till). The signature Swedish meatball and beetroot mayonnaise sandwich hits the spot every time, the tangy chunks of beetroot cutting through the rich, savoury meatballs, all encased in a wonderfully fresh baguette. Other temptations include own-made chicken liver pâté with toast and cornichons, a watermelon, rocket and prosciutto salad, and Jack's special ice-cream sundae. Seasonal produce is on show in wooden crates in front of the bar; in the spring, a tiny garden patio at the back comes alive with flowers.

Sea Cow

37 Lordship Lane, SE22 8EW (8693 3111/www.theseacow.co.uk). East Dulwich rail/176, 185, 196 bus. **Meals served** noon-11pm Tue-Sat; noon-8.30pm Sun. **Average** *££*. **Map** p292. Fish & chips

This is the epitome of the contemporary fish and chip shop: quietly cool decor (wooden slab tables, steel pendant lamps, putty-coloured walls), friendly service, and fine fish. Expect tender chunks of coley, haddock or cod in crisp, mouth-watering batter, a heap of tiny whitebait, or grilled Thai fish cakes. Everything can be accompanied by dense, chunky chips and freshly cooked mushy peas, and there's also a small but well-priced wine list and decent beers (Adnams and Peroni). In the evening, the Sea Cow switches smoothly from providing family suppers to catering for a more buzzy, urbane throng. The only thing lacking is pudding – a few tubs of ice-cream in the freezer wouldn't go amiss.

Thai Corner Café

44 Northcross Road, SE22 9EU (8299 4041). East Dulwich rail/176, 185, 196 bus. **Lunch served** noon-3pm Tue-Sun. **Dinner served** 6-10.30pm daily. **Average** *££*. **Set dinner** £15 2 courses, £18 3 courses. **Unlicensed. Corkage** 35p-50p (beer), £2 (wine). **No credit cards. Map** p292. Thai

TCC has everything one looks for in a local restaurant: it's lively, cheap, cosy and serves fantastic food. Naturally, it's always packed – not that hard, admittedly, with a space the size of an average living room. The menu abounds with fresh, lip-tingling chilli sensations, from the dipping sauces for the usual range of starters to the fragrant pad cha and more forgiving green curry. Even the chicken satay has an excitingly spicy aftertaste, though everything can be prepared with the chilli taken out (useful if you're with kids). The desserts (oranges and coconuts filled with ice-cream) are bought in, but they're not the reason anyone eats here. Bring your own booze, and some cash – they don't take credit cards.

Meal deals

Franklins *157 Lordship Lane, SE22 8HX (8299 9598/www. franklinsrestaurant.com).* Set lunch (Mon-Fri) £13 2 courses, £16 3 courses. **Map** p292. British
Locale *58-60 East Dulwich Road, SE22 9AX (7732 7575/www.locale restaurants.com).* Set lunch £10 2 courses. **Map** p292. Italian

Elephant & Castle

In the area
Nando's *Metro Centre, 119 Newington Causeway, SE1 6BA (7378 7810).* **Map** p289.

Forest Hill

Yune
25 Dartmouth Road, SE23 3HN (8699 0887/www.yune.co.uk). Forest Hill rail. **Lunch served** noon-3pm Mon-Sat. **Dinner served** 5-11.30pm Mon-Thur; 5pm-midnight Fri, Sat. **Meals served** noon-11pm Sun. **Average** ££. **Set lunch** £5.95 bento box.

Romeo Jones. See p156.

Set buffet (Mon-Thur, Sun) £14.90 per person; (Fri, Sat) £16.90 per person. Oriental
Yune is a Chinese restaurant with a Malaysian-Thai twist, and one that has made a good local name for itself by serving affordable and reliably delicious food. The £14.90 set buffet is a great bargain, and offers diners an excellent snapshot of the restaurant's many strengths: choices might include salmon with ginger and spring onion, delicious crispy aromatic duck, or Sichuan chilli char siu (roast pork), and each dish is cooked from fresh ingredients by head chef Mr Lap, who formerly oversaw the kitchen of the New World restaurant in Chinatown for more than 20 years. The atmosphere at Yune could certainly be improved – the dining area is stark and uninviting – but with food this good and so reasonably priced, why worry?

Gipsy Hill

Mangosteen

*246 Gipsy Road, SE27 9RB
(8670 0333). Gipsy Hill rail/322
bus.* **Lunch served** noon-3pm
Fri-Sun. **Dinner served** 6-11pm
Mon-Sat; 6-10pm Sun. **Average**
££. **Set lunch** £6.95 2 courses.
Set dinner (Mon-Thur) £10
2 courses. Oriental

This compact, congenial restaurant
serves a neat variety of Vietnamese,
Thai and other Asian favourites.
Quality is variable: tom yam soup
was chock-full of fresh prawns, but
the flavour of the bamboo shoots
overwhelmed the watery broth; red
chicken curry was even more
disappointing, its sauce decidedly
insipid. The Vietnamese dishes
proved more gratifying, especially
the cold vegetarian spring rolls
generously stuffed with noodles and
tofu (though hoi sin as a dipping
sauce was a lazy accompaniment).
The staff were warm and
welcoming, but were helpful too
late: before we left, the waiter
remarked that we'd ordered all the
wrong dishes – he would have had
the tamarind chicken, pho noodle
soup and banh xeo pancakes. So
now you know.

Meal deals

Numidie *48 Westow Hill, SE19
1RX (8766 6166/www.numidie.
co.uk).* Set meal (Tue-Thur, Sun)
£13 2 courses. International

Greenwich

Buenos Aires Café & Deli

*86 Royal Hill, SE10 8RT (8488
6764/www.buenosairesltd.com).
Greenwich rail/DLR.* **Meals served**
8am-7pm Mon-Fri; 9am-6pm Sat,
Sun. **Average** £. **Corkage** £2.50
(wine). **Map** p290. Argentinian

Owner Reinaldo Vargas was once a
paparazzo, as testified by the
celebrity shots hung between
framed pictures of his beloved
home city on the walls of his
parrilla (grill) restaurant. Starters of
juicy meat empanadas and grilled
provolone cheese fire the taste buds
without sating them; the steaks,
sourced in Argentina, are huge,
tender and packed with scents of
clover – and Vargas has trained his
Ecuadorean chef to char them like
the best Argentinian parrillero. The
400g (14oz) bife de chorizo had the
classic grassy quality of rump; it's
the gaucho's favourite cut. The
menu also features melt-in-the-
mouth milanesa (breaded calf's
meat) – a skinny cut, but enough for
lunch for two. Chips are chunky
and golden, and desserts are all
made on the premises.

Pavilion Tea House NEW

*Greenwich Park, Blackheath Gate,
SE10 8QY (8858 9695/www.
companyofcooks.com). Blackheath
rail/Greenwich rail/DLR.* **Meals
served** *Summer* 9am-6pm daily.
Winter 9am-4pm daily. **Average**
£. **Map** p291. Café

It was nippy on our visit to this
inviting, hexagonal park café, which
ruled out the terrace tables by the
chestnut trees. Still, indoors it was
bright, clean and busy (expect queues
and marauding children during
weekends). The menu lists several
hearty dishes that are perfect after a
good walk; we plumped for
scrambled eggs with smoked salmon,
a portion big enough for two that was
served on thick, generously buttered
toast. The mixed bean casserole was
warming and boasted a rich tomato
flavour, and the sandwiches were
prodigiously filled. We didn't like the
look of the huge cream scone, so
chose a tasty chocolate cake to
improve the rather indifferent coffee.

Peninsula

Holiday Inn Express, Bugsby's Way, SE10 0GD (8858 2028/www.my chinesefood.co.uk). North Greenwich tube. **Meals served** noon-11pm Mon-Fri; 11am-11.30pm Sat; 11am-11pm Sun. **Dim sum served** noon-5pm Mon-Fri; 11am-5pm Sat, Sun. **Average ££. Set meal** £15-£19 per person (minimum 2) 3 courses. **Map** p291. Chinese

This dim sum destination is very popular with Chinese couples and families, but its 450 seats mean you never have to wait long to sit down. The efficient staff breeze about the room (pale creams and browns, linen-topped tables and stackable chairs) as diners choose from the 70-plus items on the dim sum menu. Steamed tripe with ginger and spring onions was clean and crisp, and prawn har gau were plump and fresh, though steamed for too long. Most dishes – pork-filled siu mai dumplings, bean curd rolls in oyster sauce, a plate of deeply coloured chickens' feet – were competent rather than exciting. Dessert was the best part: silky 'mountain spring water' tofu pudding served with lashings of ginger-scented syrup.

Meal deals

Inside *19 Greenwich South Street, SE10 8NW (8265 5060/www. insiderestaurant.co.uk).* Set lunch £11.95 2 courses. **Map** p290. Modern European

In the area

Nando's *UCI Cinema Complex, Bugsby's Way, SE10 0QJ (8293 3025).*

Pizza Express *4 Church Street, SE10 9BG (8853 2770).* **Map** p291.

Herne Hill

Lombok

17 Half Moon Lane, SE24 9JU (7733 7131). Herne Hill rail/37 bus. **Dinner served** 6-10.30pm Tue-Sun. **Average ££. Map** p292. Oriental

There's something for everyone at Lombok, with its pleasing, colonial-lite ambience and a menu that covers almost every South-east Asian cuisine, from Chinese seafood noodles to Thai green and red curries and Vietnamese lettuce wraps. Ingredients are fresh and well sourced, and it's nice to see more unusual dishes such as gaeng karee (a yellow, mild Thai curry, similar to massaman). Salt and pepper squid was delicious, and Burmese rangoon curry was a real hit, featuring fresh fish cooked in coconut milk flavoured with cumin, lime leaves and star anise. Speciality rices include a flavourful garlic and sweet red pepper combo. For dessert, be sure to sample the Thai-style custard with fresh tropical fruit: it's the perfect conclusion to a mouth-tingling meal.

Olley's NEW

65-69 Norwood Road, SE24 9AA (8671 8259/www.olleys.info). Herne Hill rail/3, 68, 196 bus. **Lunch served** noon-3pm, **dinner served** 5-10.30pm Tue-Sun. **Average ££. Set lunch** £7 1 course. **Map** p292. Fish & chips

Olley's is one of south London's best chippies. The place is famous for the 'specials' named after local celebrities and restaurant critics – the James Nesbitt Experience (haddock, chips and peas), say, or the Guy Dimond Experience (another way to say lemon sole with chips, named after *Time Out* magazine's food editor). Although most customers come for the takeaway counter, the mid-sized restaurant is also popular. The fish (cod and haddock, of course, but also hake, halibut, monkfish, skate and others) comes fried in fabulous batter, grilled, steamed or served with a tomato and herb sauce; the chips are about as good as London can offer; and the mushy peas have more texture than most. Service is friendly and suitably informal.

Ladywell

★ Café Oscars NEW

48 Ladywell Road, SE13 7UX (07590 690825/www.cafe-oscars. com). Ladywell rail. **Meals served** 8am-6pm Mon-Fri; 9am-5pm Sat. **Average** £. **Unlicensed** no alcohol allowed. **No credit cards.** **Map** p290. Café

Oscars is the neighbourhood café of dreams, an inviting space with mismatched furniture and a thoroughly Zen-like garden out back, offering the citizens of Ladywell great coffees, light lunches and bucketloads of welcome. The brew, made from Arabica beans, has an earthy, mellow flavour that had us hooked from day one. Sustenance comes in the form of artisanal sandwiches (made with upper crust bread from Blackheath's Boulangerie Jade), quiches and salads, plus homemade soups, cakes and pastries, and a range of old-fashioned milkshakes blended to order. In keeping with the community feel, the café has recently begun to play host to a plethora of local art, which joins the existing floor-to-ceiling Klimt prints that so dazzle the eye.

★ Mason's Bar & Restaurant NEW

38 Ladywell Road, SE13 7UZ (8314 0314). Ladywell rail. **Lunch served** noon-3pm Mon-Sat; noon-4pm Sun. **Dinner served** 6.30-9.45pm Mon-Sat. **Average** ££. **Set dinner** £11 2 courses, £13 3 courses. **Map** p290. Modern European

Who would have thought that, sandwiched between the culinary deserts of Lewisham and Catford, there could be a restaurant that passes all tests for food, price and service? Well, there is – and Mason's is it. The menu changes weekly, with plenty of surprises such as creamy elderflower and duck liver pâté (albeit served with bog-standard soldiers instead of crusty bread), goat's cheese and courgette terrine, and excellent deep-fried brie. Mains are all served with bowls of fresh veg, and the desserts, if you have room, are comfort classics (banoffee pie is the best). There's Erdinger on draught, plenty of fruity Belgian beers, and the Chilean house wines are marvellous. Sunday lunches also turn out some of the best Yorkshire puds we've sampled in south-east London.

Lewisham

Everest Curry King

24 Loampit Hill, SE13 7SW (8691 2233). Lewisham rail/DLR. **Meals served** 11am-11pm daily. **Average** £. **Set meal** £4.50 1 course incl rice. **Unlicensed** no alcohol allowed. **No credit cards.** **Map** p290. Indian

At first sight, the Everest appears to be another neon blot on the charmless A20 corridor, but enlightened locals beg to differ. What this no-frills café and takeaway lacks in comfort, it makes up for in tasty Sri Lankan and South Indian grub, endorsed by a steady stream of local Asians. Choose from a display of 15 curries, and the staff will give your dishes an unabashed whizz in the microwave. We opted for the rice-and-three: a delicate dahl, a chunky jackfish curry, and an eye-wateringly spicy chickpea stew, all served with a generous helping of Ceylon pittu. 'Best place in Lewisham,' said one local Indophile with an enormous smile on his face. So good you'll barely notice the complete absence of booze.

Meze Mangal

*245 Lewisham Way, SE4 1XF
(8694 8099/www.meze-mangal.
co.uk). St John's rail/Lewisham
rail/DLR.* **Meals served** noon-2am
Mon-Thur; noon-3am Fri, Sat; noon-
1am Sun. **Average** ££. **Set meze**
£12.50-£17.50 per person (minimum
4). **Map** p290. Turkish

Its location in the middle of an
notably dilapidated parade doesn't
seem to have put customers off:
Meze Mangal is usually heaving.
The core of the menu is a standard
set of Turkish grills, but pride of
place goes to the authentic ocakbaşı
grill, which is responsible for the
scorch marks on the floor made by
falling cinders. Meze Mangal also
serves vegetarian dishes, a hearty
moussaka and a range of Turkish
pizzas; we tried a very filling
'sucuklu yumurtali peynirli pide', a
boat-shaped pizza with spicy
sausage, egg, cheese and shredded
salad. A tasty, well-formed beyti
(seasoned minced lamb kebab) was
served with a large salad but no rice
– not a problem, as it turned out,
with so much good pide bread to
keep us going.

Something Fishy

*117-119 Lewisham High Street,
SE13 6AT (8852 7075). Lewisham
rail/DLR.* **Meals served** 9am-
5.30pm Mon-Sat. **Average** £.
No credit cards. **Map** p290.
Fish & chips

You can't have a fish supper at this
bright canteen, with its plastic
seating and wipe-clean tables,
because last orders are at 5.30pm –
earlier still if all the fish has been
eaten. Instead, come at 12.30pm –
that's when the fish is freshest and
there's a high chip turnover to
ensure just-fried crispness. The
chunks of fish are so large their
battered ends hang over the plate;
the flesh is firm and flaky, and the
golden batter pleasantly light. We

can't imagine anyone coming here
for anything other than fish and
chips, but there are saveloys, rather
pasty fish cakes and pies, as well as
the option of steamed fish and mash
for people trying to stay in shape.

In the area

Nando's *16 Lee High Road, SE13
5LQ (8463 0119).* **Map** p291.

London Bridge & Borough

Southwark Cathedral Refectory

*Southwark Cathedral, Montague
Close, SE1 9DA (7407 5740/
www.digbytrout.co.uk). London
Bridge tube/rail.* **Meals served**
9am-5pm daily. **Average** ££.
Map p289. Café

The airy, well-ordered dining room
attached to Southwark Cathedral
fills up with older customers looking
for a civilised lunch. It's run like a
canteen, with friendly servers
dishing up hot, freshly made dishes
(pastas, soups and moreish salmon,
haddock and prawn fish cakes) for
reasonable prices (from about £6.95
for a main meal). The trimmings are
all cooked with loving attention to
detail – such as the roast new
potatoes with shimmering, crackly
skins thrown together with
caramelised shallots. The stone
floor, large vases of lilies and
adjacent courtyard make it a
pleasant space to eat in; it's excellent
for a coffee break too, thanks to a
triumphantly good set of cakes and
biscuits, own-made puffed rice slabs
topped with chocolate, or sticky
marmalade flapjacks.

★ Tapas Brindisa

*18-20 Southwark Street, SE1 1TJ
(7357 8880/www.brindisa.com).
London Bridge tube/rail.* **Breakfast
served** 9-11am Fri, Sat. **Lunch**

served noon-3pm Mon-Thur; noon-4pm Fri, Sat. **Dinner served** 5.30-11pm Mon-Sat. **Average** ££. **Map** p289. Spanish

Tapas Brindisa makes its corner of Borough Market seem like Madrid. Bookings aren't taken, so you're likely to spend at least 30 minutes at the bar admiring the way this former warehouse has taken on a Spanish persona – it's now run by well-regarded Spanish food importer Brindisa, which also has a stall at the market. Dishes are based on prime ingredients, such as mojama (air-dried tuna) with sliced pear and olive oil. Thin, ruby-red Joselito jamón isn't cheap, but the quality was outstanding, and grilled lamb chops served with aïoli and fresh mint salad were tender and gently smoky. The staff do their best to keep smiling, but make it plain there are other people waiting for your table.

Tito's

4-6 London Bridge Street, SE1 9SG (7407 7787/www.titoseateries.com). London Bridge tube/rail. **Lunch served** noon-3pm Mon-Fri. **Dinner served** 5-11pm Tue-Fri. **Meals served** noon-11pm Sat, 11am-9pm Sun. **Average** ££. **Set lunch** (Mon-Fri) £8 3 courses. **Map** p289. Peruvian

Though it has the inglorious feel of a motorway café – all bright lights, blaring television and lone businessmen diners – Tito's is held in affectionate local esteem for its no-nonsense, quick and easy menu and friendly staff. The food is mostly Peruvian in style, which translates as hot, meaty and heavy on the carbs: expect items like papa rellena (a potato patty filled with beef and onions) or papa a la huancaina (sliced potatoes covered in milk and cheese). Cocktails, for people who live up to them, involve a lot of pisco, also known as 'Peruvian firewater', and can be knocked back for a relatively affordable £4 a pop – just keep track of how many you've had.

El Vergel

8 Lant Street, SE1 1QR (7357 0057/ www.elvergel.co.uk). Borough tube. **Meals served** 8.30am-3pm Mon-Fri; 10.30am-3pm Sat. **Average** £. **No credit cards**. **Map** p289. South American

Frequented by an entertaining mix of relaxed professionals, local families and celebrity chefs, El Vergel is small but immensely busy. The daily special is reliably good if you don't feel like the standard tortillas or tacos (all delicious); on our visit it was a chicken and tomato bake topped with a heartening cheese crust and served in a warm clay pot. Other dishes include an earthy lentil soup and wafer-thin steak sandwiches; rounding out El Vergel's multinational menu is a larger than life, ultra-creamy cheesecake that sells out every day. Wine is served in tumblers, most of the tables are communal, and there's an ongoing project to cover the walls with customers' graffiti – almost all of it glowing with praise.

Meal deals

Georgetown *10 London Bridge Street, SE1 9SG (7357 7359/ www.georgetownrestaurants. co.uk).* Set lunch (noon-2.30pm) £10 2 courses, £12.50 3 courses. **Map** p289. Malaysian
Kwan Thai *The Riverfront, Hay's Galleria, Tooley Street, SE1 2HD (7403 7373/www.kwan thairestaurant.co.uk).* Set lunch (11.30am-3pm Mon-Fri) £7.95 2 courses. **Map** p289. Thai

In the area

Feng Sushi *13 Stoney Street, SE1 1AD (7407 8744).* **Map** p289.
fish! kitchen *Cathedral Street, Borough Market, SE1 9AL (7407 3801).* **Map** p289.

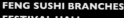

Frizzante@Unicorn Theatre
147 Tooley Street, SE1 2AZ
(7645 0556).
Konditor & Cook *10 Stoney Street,*
SE1 9AD (7407 5100). **Map** p289.
Nando's *215 217 Clink Street,*
SE1 9DG (7357 8662). **Map** p289.
Paul *The Vaults, London Bridge*
Station, Railway Approach, SE1
9SP (7403 7457). **Map** p289.
Pizza Express *4 Borough High*
Street, SE1 9QQ (7407 2995).
Map p289.
Strada *2 More London Place, The*
Riverside, SE1 2JP (7403 8321).
Tas *72 Borough High Street,*
SE1 1XF (7403 7200). **Map** p289.
Tas Café *76 Borough High Street,*
SE1 1LL (7403 8557). **Map** p289.
Wagamama *1 Clink Street, SE1*
9BU (7403 3659). **Map** p289.

New Cross

Thailand
15 Lewisham Way, SE14 6PP (8691
4040). New Cross or New Cross Gate
tube/rail. **Lunch served** 11am-
2.30pm Mon-Fri. **Dinner served**
5-11.30pm daily. **Average** £. **Set**
meal (lunch, 5-7pm) £3.95 2 courses.
Map p290. Thai
Buzzy, no-frills Thailand is much
loved by Goldsmiths students, who
come in droves for its lunchtime
deals. The setting is plain (wooden
tables, plastic flowers, mandalas on
the walls), and the menu has one foot
in the north of Thailand and the
other in Laos. All the staples are here
– red, green, yellow, jungle and
mussaman curries – but it's worth
trying the regional dishes. We
started with bo la lot, tender bundles
of chargrilled beef wrapped in betel
leaves, and a selection of nibbles that
included crisp prawn spring rolls,
properly rubbery fish cake and
tender chicken satay. Laotian duck
breast garnished with sesame paste
hit the spot, as did a subtle laab neau
e-san (hot and sour minced beef
salad from north-east Thailand).

Peckham

★ 805 Bar Restaurant
805 Old Kent Road, SE15 1NX
(7639 0808/www.805restaurant.
com). Elephant & Castle tube/rail
then 53 bus. **Meals served** 2pm-
midnight daily. **Average** ££.
Nigerian
Judge the 805 Bar Restaurant not by
its humble exterior, nor by its simple
white decor; the fact that its two
spacious dining rooms were heaving
with well-to-do Nigerians late on a
Sunday night tells you all you need
to know. Customers come from far
and wide to enjoy the southern
Nigerian staples. The menu lists
favourites like jollof rice, moyin
moyin and egusi (ground melon
seeds served with spinach), and the
signature dish, monika (marinated
grilled fish with chilli sauce). The
asaro (mashed yam pottage cooked
with seasoned tomato and onion) is
gorgeous, as is ewa aganyin (lightly
spiced smoked beans, also
accompanied by fried plantain).
Service comes with a smile, and the
portions are more than generous.

Petitou
63 Choumert Road, SE15 4AR
(7639 2613). Peckham Rye rail.
Meals served 9am-5.30pm Tue-
Sat; 10am-5.30pm Sun. **Average**
£. **Map** p292. Café
Petitou appeared in the leafy
backstreets of Peckham's bohemian
quarter a few years ago, to a chorus
of hallelujahs from locals who had
prayed for a respite from burgers
and fried chicken. Many of the area's
arty types come here regularly,
basking in the informal vibe and
enjoying excellent coffee, nourishing
lunches and a daily menu of delicious
cakes made by hand-picked locals.
Despite increased competition,
Petitou is still the mainstay of the
area's freelance community (not to
mention mums with toddlers),

South East

thanks to its consistent attention to detail, fresh and locally sourced produce (organic where possible), generous portions, fabulous pastries, and fresh juices and assorted teas. We're also big fans of its quietly civilised and mellow atmosphere.

Meal deals

Ganapati *38 Holly Grove, SE15 5DF (7277 2928/www.ganapati restaurant.com).* Set lunch (Tue-Fri) £5.25-£5.95 1 course. **Map** p292. Indian

In the area
Suya Express *43 Peckham High Street, SE15 5EB (7703 7033).* **Map** p292.

Rotherhithe

Café East NEW
Surrey Quays Leisure Centre, 100 Redriff Row, SE16 7LH (www.cafe east.co.uk). Canada Water tube. **Lunch served** 11am-3pm, **dinner served** 5.30-10.30pm Mon-Fri. **Meals served** 11am-10.30pm Sat; noon-10pm Sun. **Average** £. **Unlicensed** no alcohol allowed. Vietnamese

Café East is heaven for fans of pho, many of whom come some distance to get it. The signature pho tai (rare beef noodle soup) – a bowl filled with clear, flavoursome broth with strong notes of roasted onion, cinnamon and star anise – had us hooked from the first slurp. Banh cuon, Vietnam's answer to Chinese cheung fun, was a delicious mix of minced pork, dried shrimp and shiitake mushrooms wrapped in soft flat rice noodles, and topped with fried garlic and beansprouts – a truly hearty starter that could well pass for a meal in itself. The café recently moved from a tiny site in Deptford to new, larger premises in Surrey Quays, which should allow space for its many devotees.

South Norwood

★ Mantanah
2 Orton Building, Portland Road, SE25 4UD (8771 1148). Norwood Junction rail. **Lunch served** noon-3pm Sat, Sun. **Dinner served** 6-11pm Tue-Sun. **Average** ££. **Set dinner** £18 per person (minimum 2) 3 courses. **Set buffet** (lunch Sun) £7.95. Thai

Mantanah creates bold and unmistakably authentic Thai flavours. Our pork dumplings were wonderfully delicate, and rings of deep-fried squid and king prawns were flawlessly light, but the real impact was made by the complex mains. A northern Thailand special made from top-quality chicken had earthy depth and a freshness created by banana blossom, bamboo shoots, a spot of chilli and fresh herbs, and the salad of lemongrass-infused shredded chicken was fiery with more chilli. The menu lists dishes by region, which makes Mantanah a good place in which to try regional specialities. Don't be put off by the drab suburban surroundings or the dining room's lairy yellow walls – the food is excellent, and the service friendly and knowledgeable.

Tower Bridge

Meal deals

Le Pont de la Tour *Butlers Wharf Building, 36D Shad Thames, SE1 2YE (7403 8403/www.lepont delatour.co.uk).* Set meal £13.50 2 courses (bar & grill only). Modern European

In the area
ASK *Spice Quay, 34 Shad Thames, SE1 2YE (7403 4545).* **Pizza Express** *The Cardamom Building, 31 Shad Thames, SE1 2YR (7403 8484).*

EAST

MEAT.

Bethnal Green

★ Gourmet San NEW

*261 Bethnal Green Road, E2 6AH
(7729 8388). Bethnal Green tube/
rail/8 bus.* **Dinner served** 4.30-
11pm daily. **Average £. No credit
cards. Map** p294. Chinese
Gourmet San is most easily
identified by the throng of expectant
diners queuing outside. So what's
the big draw? Part of the answer can
be had looking through the window
– succulent chilli crab and sizzling
fish whizzing between kitchen and
happy diners; the rest of it, in the
form of friendly and efficient service,
comes once you get through the
door. Gourmet San's predominantly
Chinese clientele are keen on the
authentic Szechuan menu, and we
suggest you follow their lead. Don't
ignore the more exotic options:
barbecued rabbit and chicken feet
are both great starters, followed
by deep-fried squid with red radish.
For devoted carnivores, pig trotter is
a house speciality.

Gourmet San

Mai'da NEW

*148-150 Bethnal Green Road,
E2 6DG (7739 2645/www.maida-
restaurant.co.uk). Bethnal Green
tube/rail/8 bus.* **Meals served**
11am-11pm daily. **Average ££.
Unlicensed** no alcohol allowed.
Map p294. Indian
Mai'da has cream walls, mood
lighting, wood furniture, and a
possibly over-ambitious menu that
ropes together North Indian, Parsi,
Pakistani and Indo-Chinese
influences. Starters of lamb chops
and kachay aam ka murgh tikka
(tangy chicken tikka wrapped
around a mango and coriander
filling), were worthy of some of
London's best Indian restaurants,
but the main courses were uneven:
nimbu aur hare dhaniye ka murgh
(chicken curry supposedly flavoured
with lemon and coriander) tasted

like weak soup, and seafood tawa
biriani was bland. Still, our meal was
redeemed by khade masala ka gosht
(lamb flavoured with crushed black
peppercorns, cumin, cardamom,
cloves and bay leaf), and the roomali
roti. Alcohol isn't allowed, so we
suggest you order a sweet lassi.

E Pellicci

*332 Bethnal Green Road, E2
0AG (7739 4873). Bethnal Green
tube/rail/8 bus.* **Meals served**
6.15am-5pm Mon-Sat. **Average £.
Unlicensed. Corkage** no charge.
No credit cards. Map p294. Café
As much social club as caff,
Pellicci's has been warmly
welcoming customers since 1900.
The venerable marquetry-panelled
interior is cramped; sharing tables
is to be expected, nay, relished. An
espresso machine bearing the
Ferrari logo produces coffee and hot
water for mugs of tea; the good-
value cooking includes traditional
English and Italian dishes, sarnies,
classic puds and, most famously, a
roster of glistening fry-ups:
everything from a set vegetarian
breakfast to black pudding. The
staff are endlessly chirpy, and the
chips are rightly renowned – though

East

our bubble could have done with more vegetable bits. Sadly, Nevio Pellicci, king among caff owners, passed away in December 2008, though his legacy lives on.

Wild Cherry

241-245 Globe Road, E2 0JD (8980 6678). Bethnal Green tube/rail/ 8 bus. **Meals served** 10.30am-7pm Tue-Fri; 10.30am-4pm Sat, Sun. **Average** £. **Unlicensed. Corkage** £1. **Map** p294. Vegetarian

Locals love this café, run by members of the London Buddhist Centre, and flock here for weekday lunches and the leisurely Saturday all-day breakfast. It's easy to see why the latter is a draw: puffy American-style pancakes are a strong point, piled with savoury toppings like spinach and mixed mushrooms, or with fruit salad and sweet mascarpone. The vegetarian full English is hugely popular, and includes scrambled eggs or tofu, sausages (a touch tough on our last visit), baked beans, mushrooms and delectably herby tomatoes. Portions are huge and there are free filter coffee refills. Changing artwork decorates the walls, and there's a plant-strewn courtyard for good weather. Staff are amiable and armed with high chairs for little ones.

Meal deals

Bistrotheque *23-27 Wadeson Street, E2 9DR (8983 7900/www. bistrotheque.com).* Set dinner £17.50 3 courses. French

In the area

Nando's *366 Bethnal Green Road, E2 0AH (7729 5783).* **Map** p294.

Bow

Orange Room Café

63 Burdett Road, E3 4TN (8980 7336). Mile End tube. **Meals served** 10am-11.30pm Mon-Sat;

10am-10.30pm Sun. **Average** ££. **Set lunch** £4.95 1 course, £6.50 2 courses incl soft drink. **Set meal** £12.50 per person 2 courses (minimum 2). Lebanese

There has been a change of style at the Orange Room: out with the cosy backpacker aesthetic and (thanks to the smoking ban) slouchy corner for shisha pipes, and in with a clean paint job, canteen tables and hilariously kitsch desert artwork. The food, though, put together in the open kitchen at the top of the single room, remains the same. Classic Brit breakfasts and a nice range of drinks (lassis, date and rosewater cordial, 'fresh' mint tea made from leaves and a teabag) maintain the café vibe, while Lebanese meze (grilled and marinated meats, flatbread and pastries, falafel, houmous and simple herbed salads) give the place a cosmopolitan slant. And when it comes to quality, the execution is only rarely wide of the mark.

Docklands

Carluccio's Caffè

Reuters Plaza, E14 5AJ (7719 1749/ www.carluccios.com). Canary Wharf tube/DLR. **Meals served** 7am-11.30pm Mon-Fri; 9am-11.30pm Sat; 10am-10.30pm Sun. **Average** £££. **Map** p293. Italian

The warmth and clatter, the smell of coffee and baked goods and the shelves of aspirational deli items: these are some of the reasons why suited office folk muster here at lunchtime. The staff are the epitome of Italian cheer, and the food is as appealing as the welcome, from the savoury bread selection with fruity olive oil to the superb cioccolato fondente flavoured with coffee liqueur. Main courses such as sea bass fillets with sautéed potatoes and tomato salsa, penne with courgettes and fried spinach balls, or

East

a huge, business-like salad of roasted vegetables, pesto, olives and mozzarella, make a flavour-filled lunch to linger over, helped along by a bottle of fruity Sicilian fiano from the inexpensive wine list.

★ China Palace NEW

2 Western Gateway, Royal Victoria Dock North, E16 1DR (7474 0808/ www.chinapalaceexcel.com). Custom House DLR. **Meals served** noon-11pm Mon-Thur; noon-11.30pm Fri, Sat; 11am-11pm Sun. **Average £££. Set meal** £16.50-£18.50 per person (minimum 2). Chinese

Formerly known as Superstar, this popular establishment has new management and new chefs – but, thankfully, the food is as good as its predecessor. On a Sunday morning, the venue was abuzz with families and couples enjoying dim sum in a bright and spacious converted warehouse. Nearly all the variants we tried were faultless: scallop cheung fun was delightfully silky and subtle; turnip cake was crisp and rich, with plenty of turnip; and pork and prawn dumplings were intense with the flavour of shiitake mushrooms, belying a dull exterior. The attentive waiting staff noted our desire for dessert after the meal and came back accordingly to take the order; we left feeling well catered for, and highly satisfied.

Mudchute Kitchen NEW

Mudchute Park & Farm, Pier Street, E14 3HP (7515 5901/ www.mudchutekitchen.org). Mudchute DLR. **Meals served** 9am-5pm daily. **Average £.** Café

Mudchute City Farm's café is very much a family zone, with wipe-clean tableclothes and a toy-strewn kiddie corner. You order at the counter, and eat indoors or on one of several outdoor benches next to the stable yard. The changing weekday lunch menu could include lamb stew, farm egg and mayo salad, or fusilli with

garlic shoots, cream and parmesan; the weekend breakfast menu delivers the likes of black pudding with bubble and squeak. A smokehouse has recently been built (staff have already smoked cheeses, geese, ducks, butter, garlic and eggs in it) and a wood-fired oven was added in 2008 – both of which look set to widen the choice of appetising dishes at this lively Docklands farm.

Meal deals

Royal China *30 Westferry Circus, E14 8RR (7719 0888/www.royal chinagroup.co.uk).* Dim sum £2.65-£4. **Map** p293. Chinese

In the area

Itsu *Cabot Place East, E14 4QT (7512 5790).* **Map** p293.
Nando's *Jubilee Place, off Bank Street, E14 4QT (7513 2864).* **Map** p293.
Paul *Jubilee Place, 45 Bank Street, E14 5AB (7719 1755).* **Map** p293.
Paul *Promenade Level, Cabot Place East, E14 5AB (7519 1703).* **Map** p293.
Pizza Express *200 Cabot Place East, E14 4QT (7513 0513).* **Map** p293.
Prezzo *37 Westferry Circus, E14 8RR (7519 1234).* **Map** p293.
Wagamama *Jubilee Place, off Bank Street, E14 5NY (7516 9009).* **Map** p293.
Zizzi *33 Westferry Circus, E14 8RR (7512 9257).* **Map** p293.

Limehouse

Departure NEW

649 Commercial Road, E14 7LW (7702 8802/www.depart.in). Limehouse DLR/rail. **Meals served** 11am-5pm (soup only 5-8pm) Tue-Fri; 10am-5pm Sat. **Average £. No credit cards.** Café

A bright, spacious, semi-industrial conversion of the former Danish Seamen's Mission has created a very pleasant community café and arts centre, the kind of place that sells video tapes and music cassettes (remember them?) and loads of second-hand books. The generously served food (veggie fajitas, pasta or lentil soup on our visit) is organic and own-made; granted, it's heated in a microwave and pretty rudimentary, but it's filling and tasty. For breakfast, you can have muesli with yoghurt, toast or, oddly, merguez sausages. The decor includes a changing array of local art; furniture is schoolroom basic, with some comfy sofas. Have a nose around the lovely screening room and the first-floor terrace.

In the area
La Figa 45 Narrow Street, E14 8DN (7790 0077). Branch of Il Bordello.

Shoreditch

Cantaloupe
35-42 Charlotte Road, EC2A 3PB (7613 4411/www.cantaloupe.co.uk). Old Street tube/rail/135 bus. **Meals served** noon-10.30pm Mon-Sat; noon-9pm Sun. **Average £££**. **Map** p271. International
London's cool, NY-style bar aesthetic (bare brick, battered sofas) all started here, and Cantaloupe is as popular as ever; but because the eating space is only a step away from the drinking area, dining is often a noisy affair. That said, the menu is simple and, in the main, well done. A starter salad of avocado, papaya, palmitos (palm hearts), grapefruit and toasted cashews had a wonderfully tangy lime and chilli dressing; tender, juicy Argentinian steak came with good, chunky chips. The strong Latin wine list has plenty of low-end bottles – though our waitress brought us a more expensive malbec than the one we had chosen, and billed us for it.

Cay Tre
301 Old Street, EC1V 9LA (7729 8662/www.vietnamesekitchen.co.uk). Old Street tube/rail/55, 243 bus. **Lunch served** noon-3pm Mon-Sat. **Dinner served** 5.30-11pm Mon-Thur; 5.30-11.30pm Fri, Sat. **Meals served** noon-10.30pm Sun. **Average £££**. **Set dinner** £19 per person (minimum 2) 2 courses. **Map** p271. Vietnamese
Buzzy and immensely popular with post-workers and pre-clubbers, Cay Tre is a canteen Vietnamese that's a little more upmarket than its Kingsland Road brethren (notice the suave monochrome wallpaper and prices that wiped out our £40 budget). The atmosphere and cheerily efficient service are the same as ever, but the food lacked excitement: the pho (served without herbs to add), crispy dumplings and heaven and earth pork all lacked punch; the Cay Tre salad was a disappointingly church fête-style assemblage of hard-boiled eggs, beetroot and iceberg lettuce. Only the stuffed swimming crab really hit the spot. Beside us, flaming and sizzling cook-at-the-table dishes (Vietnamese longfish, campfire steak) looked a lot more fun – and were wolfed down with relish.

★ Chaat NEW
36 Redchurch Street, E2 7DP (7739 9595/www.chaatlondon.co.uk). Liverpool Street tube/rail then 8, 388 bus. **Dinner served** 6-11pm Tue-Sun. **Average ££**. **Map** p271. Indian
Chaat, which means 'snack food', is a friendly, homely Bangladeshi kitchen just past the northern end of London's most famous curry corridor. It's sparsely decorated but cheerful, and the short menu lists unpretentious comfort food priced between £2.75 and £5.95. We started with aloo and pea 'chops': crunchy mashed potato and pea cutlets, a palliative to the fiery

East

relish made using naga morich (the world's hottest chilli pepper) that rightly carries a warning. Thenga, succulent pieces of bony fish in a tangy mango and tomato gravy, proved to be an excellent choice for a main course once it was ladled on to steamed rice. Some traditional Indian recipes have been slightly tweaked to appeal to a more diverse clientele, but thankfully never stray too far from home.

Frizzante@City Farm

Hackney City Farm, 1A Goldsmith's Row, E2 8QA (7739 2266/www. frizzanteltd.co.uk). Liverpool Street tube/rail then 26, 48 bus/Old Street tube/rail then 55 bus. **Meals served** 10am-4.30pm Tue-Sun. **Average** ££. **Map** p294. Café
City Farm's café is cosy and fittingly rustic: colanders and cheese graters as lampshades, Astroturf seats for kids to play on, and a garden in which you can eat in warmer weather – all this, and a large cast of animals to pet on the farm itself. For breakfast, try the sweet-and-savoury combo of maple syrup-doused waffles with bacon, or a vegetarian plate of farm eggs, roasted tomatoes and hash browns, all chased down with 85p tea. A blackboard menu lists hearty Italian dishes like pappardelle with pheasant ragù, and the children's menu includes pasta with cheese and tomato sauce. Save room for a scoop or two of gelato and you'll leave as content as a calf in clover.

Hanoi Café

98 Kingsland Road, E2 8DP (7729 5610/www.hanoicafe.co.uk). Liverpool Street tube/rail then 67, 149, 242 bus/Old Street tube/rail then 243 bus. **Meals served** noon-11.30pm daily. **Average** £. **Set lunch** (Mon-Fri) £3.80. **Map** p271. Vietnamese
In the words of its owners, Hanoi Café offers 'home-made Vietnamese

Mudchute Kitchen.
See p171.

cuisine in a relaxed atmosphere'. We had plenty of fun with the rustic 'roll your own summer roll' platter, which arrived with circles of rice paper and a bowl of water to soak them in, plus mounds of shredded vegetables, fresh herbs, and vermicelli noodles. Our choice of lime chicken filling, however, was more paltry than poultry – mostly batter. The menu lists pho (noodle soups) and bun (rice noodles), served in massive bowls; Hanoi bun topped with sautéed beef, chicken and king prawns was a satisfying meal in itself, especially when accompanied by strong Vietnamese iced coffee. This may not be the fanciest joint in town, but the food is honest and comforting.

Jones Dairy Café

23 Ezra Street, E2 7RH (7739 5372/www.jonesdairy.co.uk). Liverpool Street tube/rail then 26, 48 bus/Old Street tube/rail then 55 bus. **Meals served** 9am-3pm Fri, Sat; 8am-3pm Sun. **Average** £. **No credit cards. Map** p294. Café

Overhanging ivy and rickety tables announce this very lovely, very small café. You enter through bright green barn doors into something like a welcoming farm kitchen: terracotta tiles, painted brick walls and an elderly stove in the corner, while the open shelves behind the counter are stacked with teapots and mixing bowls. The menu changes weekly, and might include big bowls of asparagus soup or pizzas (baked on site). The own-made lemonade was a dream on a hot day, and the wedge of carrot cake as good as any we've had; on the other hand, the service could have been more helpful. Dishes are available only on Friday and Saturday; on Sunday (when the flower market is on), it's coffee, cakes and bagels only – and a big queue.

Laxeiro

93 Columbia Road, E2 7RG (7729 1147/www.laxeiro.co.uk). Liverpool Street tube/rail then 26, 48 bus/Old Street tube/rail then 55 bus. **Lunch served** noon-3pm, **dinner served** 7-11pm Tue-Sat. **Meals served** 9am-4pm Sun. **Average** ££. **Map** p294. Spanish

A smattering of Alhambra-style tiling, a terracotta colour scheme and the odd potted plant give family-run Laxeiro a cheerful feel. Try the paella with its immense prawns, or the generous tapas, which are perfect for a large group: the authentic tortilla had potato and egg in all the right places, and skinny-cut calamares were far from rubbery. Cochinillo, irresistibly tender suckling pig, came with a gentle tomato and apple sauce, and salty padrón peppers were handled with care. The wine (and sherry) list sticks to Spain, and jugs of sangría are available for sharing. Service can be sketchy, but the staff are usually friendly. Judging by the queues on Sunday, Columbia Road flower market day, Laxeiro is clearly a hit.

Lennie's

6 Calvert Avenue, E2 7JP (7739 3628). Liverpool Street tube/rail then 8, 388 bus. **Meals served** 8am-3.30pm Mon, Tue; 8am-3.30pm, 7.30-10pm Wed-Sat; 9am-2.30pm Sun. **Average** £. **Unlicensed. Corkage** £1. **Map** p271. Café

This bright caff looks out through large windows at the broad flank of St Leonard's church across the street. Plates of prodigiously steaming dishes are delivered promptly from a reheat, along with a mug of strong tea, in portions designed to satisfy local brickies as much as local media bohos. The preparation area consists of a display case for salad and cling-filmed cakes, a counter for big pots of own-made stew, curry, beef pie and lasagne, and a range for frying

East

the breakfast eggs. The staff are obliging but admirably unfussy (cakes arrive with a teaspoon rather than a fork), and the food, although a little sludgy from the microwave, is still tasty and satisfying.

★ Little Georgia NEW

87 Goldsmith's Row, E2 8QR (7739 8154). Liverpool Street tube/rail then 26, 48 bus/Old Street tube/rail then 55 bus. **Meals served** 9am-5pm Mon; 9am-11pm Tue-Sat; 10am-11pm Sun. **Average** ££. **Unlicensed**. **Corkage** no charge. Georgian

The green paintwork, nostalgic photos and soulful Georgian music set the homely tone at Little Georgia. It has no alcohol licence, which, sadly, means no fabulous Georgian wines, but you can bring your own booze for no extra charge. The cooking has risen a notch since our previous visit, and is spicier than at London's other Georgian restaurants. Although khachapuri bread is hard to resist, try lobiani – scrumptious flatbread stuffed with spicy beans and (optional) smoked pork. Garlicky carrot salad was a good foil to the rich beetroot pkhali; add borscht, blini and other delights as meze, or share a hearty main. Chanakhi (lamb, aubergine and potato stew) with pungent red peppers, coriander, and garlic was rich and soothing, though slightly low on the aforementioned lamb.

Loong Kee

134G Kingsland Road, E2 8DY (7729 8344). Liverpool Street tube/rail then 67, 149, 242 bus/ Old Street tube/rail then 243 bus. **Lunch served** noon-3pm Mon-Fri. **Dinner served** 5-11pm Mon-Thur; 5pm-midnight Fri. **Meals served** noon-midnight Sat; noon-11pm Sun. **Average** £. **Unlicensed**. **Corkage** no charge. **No credit cards**. **Map** p271. Vietnamese

Loong Kee is the most northerly of an incredible string of Vietnamese

cafés on Kingsland Road – and one of the finest. Step up off the pavement into the clatter and bustle of typically trendified Shoreditch cheapskates and a smattering of Vietnamese kids, all tucking into Cantonese-style rice or noodle dishes and big bowls of pho. We were disappointed by the bland prawn and beef spring rolls in their typical gelatinous white wrappers, but cheered up by a hearty serving of beef and knotweed canh (hot and sour Vietnamese soup) and by mackerel and pickled vegetables, served steaming in a clay pot. The staff, initially too busy to be anything other than brusque, warmed up once we showed an interest in the food.

Mien Tay NEW

122 Kingsland Road, E2 8DP (7729 3074). Liverpool Street tube/rail then 67, 149, 242 bus/ Old Street tube/rail then 243 bus. **Lunch served** noon-3pm, **dinner served** 5-11pm Mon-Sat. **Meals served** noon-11pm Sun. **Average** ££. **Unlicensed**. **Corkage** no charge. **Map** p271. Vietnamese

What was once a restaurant notable for its north Vietnamese dishes is now one that prides itself on the fresh, sweet flavours of southern Vietnam, a cuisine characterised by its emphasis on seafood and Chinese influences. The stunner of our meal was deep-fried sea bass served whole with slivers of just-ripe mango and lashings of fishy nuoc mam sauce. Almost as good was pho dac biet ('special' pho), which contained superb, irregularly shaped and nicely textured beef balls that had clearly been handmade. Finish with a cup of excellent Vietnamese coffee, a refreshing, smooth brew served with the judicious addition of condensed milk; alternatively, if it's available, try the tra sua tran chau (Vietnamese tapioca pearl tea).

Pinchito Tapas

Pinchito Tapas NEW

*32 Featherstone Street, EC1Y 8QX
(7490 0121/www.pinchito.co.uk).
Old Street tube/rail.* **Tapas served**
10am-11pm Mon-Fri; 5-11pm Sat.
Average £. Map p271. Spanish
Tucked behind Old Street station,
this quiet bar is very Shoreditch, with
exposed brickwork and a chill-out
corner with leather armchairs. It's
named after pincho, the Basque
appetiser of bread piled with various
ingredients, and pinchos galore
welcomed us at the bar counter,
topped with octopus, esqueixada
(salt-cod salad) or chunks of Spanish
omelette – all for a quid each. For
tapas, choose from reliable dishes
such as chickpeas and morcilla, garlic
mushrooms, or octopus and chorizo;
Pinchito also does a late breakfast
menu that includes Spanish fry-ups.
The wine list is exclusively Spanish
and there's a decent selection of
sherries, as well as cocktails, and
although the food isn't remarkable,
enthusiastic staff help give the place
a fun and friendly vibe.

Premises Café/Bistro

*209 Hackney Road, E2 8JL (7684
2230/www.premisesstudios.com).
Liverpool Street tube/rail then 26,
48 bus/Old Street tube/rail then 55
bus.* **Meals served** 8am-11pm Mon,

East

Wed, Thur-Sun; 8am-5.30pm Tue. **Average** ££. **Map** p294. Café

The warm glow emanating from little Premises comes partly from the decor (ethnic instruments, prettily jewelled, multicoloured lampshades, signed photos of the likes of Guillemots, Terry Callier and, er, Charlotte Church), partly the service (quick and winningly relaxed) and partly the contrast (have you seen Hackney Road on a wet Saturday?). Attached to a music studio (hence the pics), the café does Med-slanted bistro fare by night, and fry-ups, sausage 'n' mash, jacket tatties and omelettes by day. Old dears in pearls sip frothy coffee at the back, while sexy young Spaniards nibble each other's ears or roll cigarettes over an Efes and chips in the front. On warmer days, smokers take to a few pavement tables outside.

Que Viet NEW

102 Kingsland Road, E2 8DP (7033 0588). Liverpool Street tube/rail then 67, 149, 242 bus/Old Street tube/rail then 243 bus. **Lunch served** noon-3.30pm, **dinner served** 5-11pm daily. **Average** ££. **Map** p271. Vietnamese

This newcomer is easily the most elegant Vietnamese on the block. The leather-bound menu lists more than 200 dishes: several preparations for frogs' legs, scallops, eels and more, and a mind-boggling number of noodles, soups and stir-fries. Soft-shell crab with lemongrass was stodgy, but the limey rare-beef salad was refreshing. Bun thit nuong (rice noodles with pork and vegetables) scored highly for its juicy grilled pork, but was let down by a watery nuoc cham. You might want to try the tun 'fire pot' (£15-£20 a head), a bubbling vat of broth set at your table, in which you cook pieces of meat, vegetables or seafood. Service seemed a bit rocky, but we'll put that down to opening jitters.

★ Saf

152-154 Curtain Road, EC2A 3AT (7613 0007/www.safrestaurant. co.uk). Old Street tube/rail/55, 243 bus. **Lunch served** noon-3.30pm, **dinner served** 6.30-11pm Mon-Sat. **Average** £££. **Map** p271. Vegetarian

Saf is a bright, strikingly good-looking bar and restaurant filled with fashionable Shoreditch folk. It's part of an international chain, and aims to set new standards for vegan and raw food; indeed, dishes are so pretty it's almost a shame to eat them. Lunch offers a range of wraps, salads, noodles and rice dishes; evenings bring a five-course chef's menu that focuses on local seasonal ingredients. Mains courses include a 'buddha bowl' of rice, green tea-smoked tofu, garlic greens, wakame seaweed and sambal; refined sugar is banned from the desserts (agave syrup is used instead); and 'cheeses' are made from nut milk. The wine list manages to be simultaneously vegan, biodynamic and organic; organic cocktails are available too.

★ Song Que

134 Kingsland Road, E2 8DY (7613 3222). Liverpool Street tube/rail then 67, 149, 242 bus/ Old Street tube/rail then 243 bus. **Lunch served** noon-3pm, **dinner served** 5.30-11pm Mon-Sat. **Meals served** 12.30-11pm Sun. **Average** £. **Map** p271. Vietnamese

Song Que is an efficient, canteen-like operation (be prepared to share tables) that sets the benchmark for Vietnamese cooking in London. The beef pho is the best in town, a superb broth that's rich in spices and served with fresh herbs – ngo gai (saw-leaf herb), rau que (Asian basil) and mint. Bo la lot (minced beef wrapped in betel leaves) came in generous portions, the juicy meat complemented by the chargrilled betel leaves; stir-fried rau muong (morning glory) surprised us with its crisp texture and smoky wok flavours. The only disappointment was dessert, a tepid che bam au (a parfait-like drink of red beans, green jelly, mung beans and coconut milk), but that was easily forgiven after such an impressive meal.

Tay Do Café

65 Kingsland Road, E2 8AG (7729 7223). Liverpool Street tube/rail then 67, 149, 242 bus/ Old Street tube/rail then 243 bus. **Lunch served** 11.30am-3pm, **dinner served** 5-11.30pm daily. **Average** ££. **Set lunch** £4.30. **Unlicensed. Corkage** £1 per person. **Map** p271. Vietnamese

The bus stop and neon sign outside this tiny café do it no favours, but Tay Do's popularity relies on word of mouth. The canteen-style interior fills up quickly at weekends, mostly with locals taking advantage of the BYO policy. Our prawn and pork summer rolls looked lovely but lacked substance; in contrast, we were happy with the banh xeo, with its crisp, turmeric-yellow exterior and filling of juicy chicken and crunchy beansprouts. Caramelised mekong catfish in a clay pot was sizzlingly good too. Service seemed a little careless: we had to open the scorching clay pot ourselves, and when paying, were urged to do so in cash – we learned later that the café does accept credit cards.

Meal deals

Drunken Monkey *222 Shoreditch High Street, E1 6PJ (7392 9606/ www.thedrunkenmonkey.co.uk).* Dim sum (noon-11pm Mon-Fri, Sun; 6pm-midnight Sat) £2.50-£4.50. **Map** p271. Chinese
Hoxton Apprentice *16 Hoxton Square, N1 6NT (7739 6022/ www.hoxtonapprentice.com).* Set lunch (Mon-Fri) £6.95 1 course. **Map** p271. Modern European

In the area

Diner *128-130 Curtain Road, EC2A 3AQ (7729 4452).* **Map** p271.
Miso *45-47 Hoxton Square, N1 6PB (7613 5621).* **Map** p271.
Pizza Express *49-51 Curtain Road, EC2A 3PT (7613 5426).* **Map** p271.
Real Greek *15 Hoxton Market, N1 6HG (7739 8212).* **Map** p271.
Tay Do Restaurant *60-64 Kingsland Road, E2 8DP (7739 0966).* Branch of Tay Do Café. **Map** p271.
Viet Grill *58 Kingsland Road, E2 8DP (7739 6686).* Branch of Cay Tre. **Map** p271.

Spitalfields

Brick Lane Beigel Bake

159 Brick Lane, E1 6SB (7729 0616). Liverpool Street tube/rail/ 8 bus. **Meals served** 24hrs daily. **Average** £. **No credit cards.** **Map** p294. Café

What do we love most about this institution? Perhaps the brilliant moist salt beef, carved as you wait from a slab kept warm in the front window, or the classic smoked salmon and cream cheese, or the bagels (boiled before being baked) these fillings go into. Or could it be the 24-hour opening with hot bread pulled fresh from the ovens all night, or a Brick Lane location that makes this the snack stop of choice for clubbers, imbibers and taxi drivers? Indulge in a piece of New York-style cheesecake or a super-sweet almond slice if you wish (ignore the pastry-heavy sausage rolls), but remember that the bagels are what have kept punters coming back since 1977. A narrow counter caters for eaters-in.

Leon

3 Crispin Place, E1 6DW (7247 4369/www.leonrestaurants.co.uk). Liverpool Street tube/rail. **Meals served** 8am-10pm Mon, Tue; 8am-

10.30pm Wed-Fri; 9am-10pm Sat; 9am-8pm Sun. **Average** ££. **Map** p271. Café

The concept of furnishing the city's time-poor, health-conscious lunch-breakers with a quick-fire menu of Mediterranean superfoods is clearly a hit, but recent visits have suggested that complacency may be undermining Leon's mission. Vegetarian roasted mushroom and plum tomato breakfast baps have been served on unappealingly dry bread, while lunchbox salads have seemed rather small of portion. And a recent sit-down dinner presented a sullen stream of let-downs: from overpoweringly lemony houmous and rubbery sliced chorizo, to a dried-out Devonshire red chilli chicken main, the plate whipped away by over-eager staff while the last mouthful was still being mulled over. A cracking concept the Leon chain may be, but more love and attention is needed.

Maedah Grill NEW

42 Fieldgate Street, E1 1ES (7377 0649/www.maedahgrill.net). Aldgate East tube. **Meals served** noon-11pm daily. **Unlicensed** no alcohol allowed. **Average** ££. **Set meal** £15-£20 3 courses. **Map** p294. Turkish

This interesting new restaurant produces fine Turkish food, but is actually slanted more towards the local Bengali community – which is not to say anyone else is made to feel less welcome. As well as Turkish grills, the menu includes vegetarian dishes, Turkish pizzas and a range of stews. As at many Turkish restaurants, the meat is halal; more unusually, there's a strict no-alcohol policy. The topping on our starter of lahmacun was pleasingly fresh, with pine kernels in the minced lamb; çöp was a generous portion of soft lamb cubes with nicely cooked rice and green salad. The dining room is well

laid out, and there are several private booths for family meals, as well as an unobtrusive takeaway section.

★ Market Coffee House

50-52 Brushfield Street, E1 6AG (7247 4110). Liverpool Street tube/rail. **Meals served** 8am-6pm Mon-Fri; 10am-6.30pm Sat; 9am-6.30pm Sun. **Average** ££. **No credit cards**. **Map** p271. Café

With a creaky, cultured vibe conjuring up New England pioneer-era coffee houses (Ben Franklin wouldn't look out of place amid the dark wooden furniture and wall panels of its lovely late 17th-century building), the Market Coffee House is perfect for history-steeped yet forward-forging Spitalfields. The counter serves the likes of own-made houmous with sourdough bread, crumbly Gloucestershire Old Spot pork pie with tomato chutney and salad, a daily-changing soup (Egyptian lentil on our last visit), and a range of filled bagels and toasted sandwiches. The quality is high enough to ensure a satisfying lunch, with bread from nearby St John, freshly roasted coffee and an interesting range of loose teas to boot, but it's the cosy, old-fashioned vibe that's the real draw.

Rootmaster NEW

Old Truman Brewery car park, off Dray Walk, E1 6QY (07912 389314/www.root-master.co.uk). Aldgate East tube/Liverpool Street tube/rail. **Meals served** 11am-11pm Mon-Sat; 11am-10.30pm Sun. **Average** £. **Map** p294. Vegetarian

Rootmaster is a vegan restaurant set in a (stationary) double-decker bus parked behind Brick Lane. A scattering of outside tables gives diners a space from which to observe the chefs at work in the kitchen, and the top deck has been transformed into a chic diner. Its menu has a Japanese slant, and although tofu is plentiful, there are

East

various other options to maintain interest. Gyoza wraps and a meze platter were tasty starters, and the generously portioned aubergine and edamame stack was so enormous it left no space for the tempura banana dessert. Its friendly staff make Rootmaster a joyful place for a meal, and its unusual setting is prone to wobble amusingly on its springs.

★ Rosa's NEW

*12 Hanbury Street, E1 6QR
(7247 1093/www.rosaslondon.com).
Aldgate East tube/Liverpool Street
tube/rail.* **Lunch served** 11am-3pm,
dinner served 6-11pm Mon-Fri.
Meals served 11am-midnight
Sat; 11am-11pm Sun. **Average**
££. **Map** p294. Thai
Rosa's is a cut above the Thai norm. Although most dishes are familiar, there's a freshness and integrity to the preparation. Take som tam salad: the grated green papaya is often bulked out with carrot or cabbage, but Rosa's version is all papaya, mixed with long beans, cherry tomatoes, chilli, shrimps and cashew nuts. The pad makhuea, meltingly soft chunks of stir-fried aubergine in a yellow bean sauce with chilli and garlic, was stunning, and the accompanying vegetables and garnishes were plentiful. Rosa's has shared tables, so book ahead or turn up early in the evening. It's also a very good-looking place, with architraves cunningly turned into sculptures, attractive lighting, and a second, more spacious dining area in the basement.

Square Pie Company

*105C Commercial Street, E1 6BG
(7375 0327/www.squarepie.com).
Liverpool Street tube/rail.* **Meals
served** 11am-4pm Mon-Sat; 10am-6pm Sun. **Average** £. **Map** p294.
Café
After a year's closure while Spitalfields Market had a facelift, this glowing emporium of pies has been triumphantly reborn; it started life here as a stall back in 2001, and now has several branches across London. The chrome and red interior is fresh yet classic – as are the trademark symmetrical pies, whose fillings run from traditional (steak and Guinness) to quirky (jerk chicken and sweet potato); all are served in funky cardboard boxes.

Saf. See p177.

Our sumptuous chicken pie came with mashed potato and tasty, fresh mushy peas. Monmouth coffee makes the ideal partner for a range of desserts, including home-made Lamingtons and banoffee cake. Square Pie is British to the core and great value to boot: no wonder it has cornered the market.

Story Deli

Old Truman Brewery, 3 Dray Walk, E1 6QL (7247 3137). Aldgate East tube/Liverpool Street tube/rail. **Meals served** noon-10.30pm daily. **Average** ££. **Map** p294.
Pizza & pasta
This cosy little pizzeria has rough-hewn tables, little stools, big wax church candles and a huge plate-glass window through which to gaze at the hectic goings-on of Dray Walk. The blackboard lists pizzas that are that are perfectly thin, crispy from oven-baking and generously topped with the likes of roast chicken and mushroom, prawn and green pepper, or five cheeses; a ham and artichoke pizza featured coppa air-dried ham and came on a board with a mound of rocket. With one exception (a margherita, £9), they all cost £10. Beers include Freedom and Canabia; wine is either £4 or £5 a glass or £14-£20 a bottle. There are fine coffees and teas, plus ice-cream (butterscotch, honey and ginger) for afters.

In the area

Giraffe *Unit 1, Crispin Place, E1 6DW (3116 2000).* **Map** p271.
Pâtisserie Valerie *37 Brushfield Street, E1 6AA (7247 4906).* **Map** p271.
Pizza Express *232 Bishopsgate, EC2M 4QD (7247 2838).* **Map** p271.
Real Greek *6 Horner Square, E1 6EW (7375 1364).* **Map** p271.
S&M Café *48 Brushfield Street, E1 6AG (7247 2252).* **Map** p271.
Strada *88-90 Commercial Street, E1 6LY (7247 4117).* **Map** p271.

Yard *140 Tabernacle Street, EC2A 4SD (7336 7758).* Branch of Café Pasta. **Map** p271.

Stratford

In the area

Nando's *1A Romford Road, E15 4LJ (8221 2148).*
Pizza Express *Theatre Square, Stratford East, E15 1BX (8534 1700).*

Upton Park

Amitas

124 Green Street, E7 8JQ (8472 1839). Upton Park tube then 58, 330 bus. **Meals served** noon-9.30pm Tue-Sun. **Average** ££. **Set thali** £6.50-£8. Indian
Early Sunday evening isn't prime dining time on this bleak street, brightened by sari shops and a clutch of curry houses. A slightly sleeker version of the competition, Amitas is still pretty basic: a well-stocked sweets counter in one half, a relatively spacious and comfortable seating area in the other. A special thali was rather hit and miss for £7.50; we recommend you try something off the specials board instead – one of a range of savoury pooris, perhaps. The lurid ice-cream faluda (with a similar flavour to Turkish Delight and constructed like a sundae) will entertain both children and inner chilren alike. For adults, there's the rarity of a licensed bar with a good range of spirits, beers and wines.

Saravanaa Bhavan

300 High Street North, E12 6SA (8552 4677). East Ham tube. **Meals served** 10am-11pm daily. **Average** £. **Set thali** £7-£8. Indian
Graced with a pair of palm trees made of garish flashing lights,

Saravanaa Bhavan is a bright, busy canteen that serves a mix of South Indian dishes and stir-fries to noisy families and couples of all ages. The central kitchen, separated from diners by glass, is enjoyably theatrical: watch as chefs ladle batter on to a huge hotplate, then peel off another enormous pancake. A masala dosa the width of our table and a barely smaller pair of adai (lentil pancakes) – each served with dips and a minimum of fuss on stainless steel trays – gave us a gutful of tasty vegetarian food for surprisingly little cash. There's a jug of water on each table, but lassis and triveni are also served.

Victoria Park

Fish House NEW

126-128 Lauriston Road, E9 7LH (8533 3327). Mile End tube then 277 bus. **Meals served** noon-10pm daily. **Average** ££. Fish & chips
The Fish House formula of retro-stylish takeaway juxtaposed with table-service restaurant is largely successful. Takeaway customers are assigned two bench tables at which to wait for (or eat) their battered cod, haddock, plaice, rock or scampi and chips. Restaurant customers sit in a slightly clinical space to enjoy the likes of lobster bisque with bread and butter, grilled lemon sole with french fries and garlic butter, and king prawns with aïoli, as well as a range of English puds. We tested the takeaway section; cod and haddock were as fresh as the batter was crispy, and the chips easily met the crunchy-outside-fluffy-inside standard. Italian ice-cream is also available by the scoop.

Namo

178 Victoria Park Road, E9 7HD (8533 0639/www.namo.co.uk). Mile End tube then 277 bus. **Lunch served** noon-3.30pm Fri-Sun.

Dinner served 5.30-11pm Tue-Sun. **Average** ££. Vietnamese
Charming waitresses patter around this modest little café, sister to Huong-Viet in Dalston (*see p186*). The surroundings are mellow if slightly eccentric, with smiling Buddhist statues, red flocked wallpaper and pale blue lanterns; there's also a tiny outdoor patio for warmer weather. The menu is similar to the one at the Dalston restaurant, with several Chinese dishes cropping up alongside more traditional Vietnamese food. The fish cakes were flavourful, with plenty of lemongrass, and we loved the cha ca la vong (monkfish with turmeric and dill). Our favourite, however, was the bun hue (spicy beef noodle soup), which had appropriately tongue-tingling and complex flavours. To drink, there are inexpensive wines from Borough Wines in east London.

★ Pavilion Café NEW

Victoria Park, Crown Gate West, E9 5DU (8980 0030). Bethnal Green tube/rail/Hackney Wick rail/26, 277 bus. **Meals served** *Summer* 8.30am-5pm daily. *Winter* 8.30am-4pm daily. **Average** ££. **No credit cards**. Café
In summer 2007, tea merchant Rob Green and Australian chef Brett Redman transformed this café overlooking Victoria Park's lake. It now serves a menu of organic produce, rare-breed meats and artisanal food to the park's many strollers; pushchairs and toddlers frequently fill the place. Fry-ups are the core of the menu, with moist black pudding and sensational Ginger Pig sausages among the highlights – but try to save room for the cakes (lemon drizzle, brownies and the like). There's award-winning organic earl grey and excellent orange pekoe; coffees are superb, and served with organic milk. The

pair are also committed to greening their business, from cutting waste to sourcing line-caught, unendangered species of fish from Brighton.

Wapping

Il Bordello

81 Wapping High Street, E1W 2YN (7481 9950). Tower Hill tube/DLR then 100 bus. **Lunch served** noon-3pm Mon-Fri. **Dinner served** 6-11pm Mon-Sat. **Meals served** 1-10.30pm Sun. **Average £££.** **Map** p294. Pizza & pasta
This neighbourhood Italian joint is chaotic, but in a way that's cheerful and exciting. Copper panelling and large Lempicka prints adorn the sophisticated interior, and the menu is similarly classy: an impressive range of fresh fish, seafood and good cuts of meat, as well as the expected pizza and pasta options. We went for two pasta dishes, the tagliatelle special with scallops, monkfish and langoustines, and the orecchiette with broccoli, anchovies and chilli. At first, we were transfixed by the electric cheese grater, but our focus soon turned to the enormous portions of wonderfully aromatic food we were served. The pasta tasted fresh, and the combination of flavours was excellent. Should you still have room for dessert, we thoroughly recommend the bold, boozy tiramisu.

In the area

Ping Pong *Tower Bridge House, St Katharine Dock, E1W 1BA (7680 7850).* **Map** p294.
Pizza Express *78-80 Wapping Lane, E1W 2RT (7481 8436).* **Map** p294.

Whitechapel

★ Lahore Kebab House

2 Umberston Street, E1 1PY (7488 2551/www.lahore-kebabhouse.com). Aldgate East or Whitechapel tube. **Meals served** noon-midnight daily. **Average ££.** **Unlicensed.** **Corkage** no charge. **Map** p294. Indian
Over 40 years old, Lahore Kebab House has never had it so good. As noisy and boisterous as a school canteen, it appeals to both families and office workers. The gleaming open kitchen turns out hearty, earthy fare: plenty of smoky grills,

East

Tayyabs. See p184.

onion-ginger-garlic masalas, and hot, buttery bread; weekends bring specials such as trotter curry or haleem (unusually made with chicken rather than lamb, and simmered with cracked wheat). Dhal gosht (lentils cooked with browned lamb in a fried onion masala) was tender and robustly flavoured with garlic and ginger, a marvellous match for tandoori roti. Vegetarians are also well catered for, and we loved the homely spin on paneer curry flecked with peas.

Mirch Masala

111-113 Commercial Road, E1 1RD (7377 0155/www.mirchmasala restaurant.co.uk). Aldgate East tube/15 bus. **Meals served** noon-midnight daily. **Average ££.** **Unlicensed. Corkage** no charge. **Map** p294. Indian

Were it not for the accommodating staff, Mirch Masala's explanation-free menu could be lost on curry lovers unable to distinguish a masala karella daal burji from a deigi saag gosht. The atmosphere is buzzy thanks to a crammed dining room, and the food is a treat of artfully spiced authenticity, free of the violent artificial colours beloved of nearby Brick Lane. Lamb and chicken served on the bone offer something different from the usual curry house fare. The finely ground lamb of shammi kebab was laced with just the right amount of fresh chilli; karahi ginger chicken, served with a mound of shredded ginger, was delicious. No wonder the first branch (Norbury) has spawned siblings here and in Tooting, Southall, Croydon and Ilford.

Nando's

9-25 Mile End Road, E1 4TW (7791 2720/www.nandos.com). Stepney Green or Whitechapel tube. **Meals served** noon-11pm Mon-Sat; noon-10pm Sun. **Average ££. Map** p294. Portuguese

Dishes do come quickly here, but the addition of Mediterranean decor, real crockery, wooden tables and floor-staff puts Nando's a notch above standard fast-food outlets. The chain's success has been secured by succulent Portuguese peri peri (chilli-spiced) chicken, which is served to your spice specification: lemon and herb, medium, hot, or extra hot. Prices vary according to the number of side dishes, and popular choices of peri peri chips and spicy rice keep palates pulsating. The new dish of portobello mushroom with halloumi cheese and chilli jam in a bun or pitta is a tasty vegetarian option. We found staff at this branch friendly and attentive, and despite an incredibly high turnover, the place was kept clean and tidy.

★ Tayyabs

83 Fieldgate Street, E1 1JU (7247 9543/www.tayyabs.co.uk). Aldgate East or Whitechapel tube. **Meals served** noon-11.30pm daily. **Average ££. Unlicensed. Corkage** no charge. **Map** p294. Indian

This canteen is the East End equivalent of the caffs favoured by truckers in South Asia. It has been open since the 1970s, and although the interior has been refurbished and extended, it's still a challenge to bag a table: on most nights, a serpentine queue of City types and young couples winds out of the door. The food is big and bold: deliciously sticky nihari made with lamb shanks simmered in cardamom and clove-scented broth was melt-in-the-mouth tender; dhals are great too, especially a gem of grainy white urad lentils sharpened with lime juice and crowned with a tangle of crisp-fried onions. Yes, the place is crowded and noisy, but service is swift, and the food is usually good.

East

Chingford

In the area
Pizza Express *45-47 Old Church Road, E4 6SJ (8529 7866).*

Dalston

Faulkner's
424-426 Kingsland Road, E8 4AA (7254 6152/www.faulkners.uk.com). Dalston Kingsland rail/67, 76, 149, 242, 243 bus. **Lunch served** noon-2.30pm Mon-Fri. **Dinner served** 5-10pm Mon-Thur; 4.30-10pm Fri. **Meals served** 11.30am-10pm Sat; noon-9pm Sun. **Average** £££. **Set meal** £15.90-£19.90 4 courses (minimum 2). **Map** p295.
Fish & chips
This legendary chippie seems to be attempting a return to its roots under its most recent Turkish owners, largely ignoring the area's youthful middle class in favour of pleasing its original fan base of old-school East Enders. Decorations include net curtains, photos of London past, a fish tank and white linen tablecloths with fake tulips in vases, while the formal service is rather incongruous for a fish and chip restaurant. On the plus side, our huge portion of haddock was bright white, perfectly flaky and covered with crisp, tasty batter. Less impressive were the soft, pale, thick-cut chips. The mushy peas were flavoursome if alarmingly bright green. Traditional English desserts are available for those who still have room after the generous mains.

Huong-Viet
An Viet House, 12-14 Englefield Road, N1 4LS (7249 0877). Dalston Kingsland rail/67, 149, 236, 242, 243 bus. **Lunch served** noon-3.30pm, **dinner served** 5.30-11pm Mon-Sat. **Average** £. **Set lunch** £7 2 courses. **Map** p295.
Vietnamese

There's something feverish about the way this once modest restaurant now flaunts the successes of recent years, plastering positive reviews over walls and menus and sneakily handing out nomination forms for 'restaurant of the year' as 'comment cards'. In the past we'd have signed without a shrug, but on our most recent visit we were presented with a greasy banh xeo (rice flour and coconut milk pancake) and a beef pho that arrived without any of its accompanying herbs and bean sprouts. We moved on and saw glimpses of former glories. Tender chargrilled squid with lemongrass and chilli was fragrant and delectable, while cari ga (chicken curry) tasted of the pleasant sweetness of Vietnamese curry powder. Still a fine restaurant, but one that may be losing its focus.

Istanbul Işkembecisi
9 Stoke Newington Road, N16 8BH (7254 7291/www.istanbul iskembecisi.co.uk). Dalston Kingsland rail/76, 149, 243 bus. **Meals served** noon-5am daily. **Average** ££. **Set lunch** (noon-5pm) £7 2 courses. **Set dinner** (after 5pm) £11.50 2 courses; £16 2 courses incl glass of wine; £18.50 3 courses incl glass of wine. **Map** p295. Turkish
In 1998, this spot won Best Budget Meal in Time Out's Eating & Drinking Awards. Just over ten years later, it's not even in the top four or five best budget meals within a 100-yard radius. Still, that's more a reflection of the fierce competition from other Turkish joints nearby than anything else; the food here is still pretty decent. The bustling canteen atmosphere that defines many Dalston grills is absent: the food is served on white tablecloths, and the grill is out of sight at the back of the long, grey room. But with the exception of tripe soup, a house speciality, the fare is familiar:

19 Numara Bos Cirrik.
See p189.

solid meze, sad salads and, of course, an abundance of grilled meats.

★ Mangal Ocakbaşı

10 Arcola Street, E8 2DJ (7275 8981/www.mangal1.com). Dalston Kingsland rail/67, 76, 149, 243 bus. **Meals served** noon-midnight daily. **Average ££. Unlicensed. Corkage** no charge. **No credit cards. Map** p295. Turkish

Grills take precedence over frills at this hugely popular haunt: diners are asked to choose from the list of kebabs above the counter before taking their seats, the tiled walls are decorated with kilim mats and the classroom-style tables have plain wooden tops and metal legs. But the hallowed status of Mangal's grills is well deserved. A long lamb beyti hung off the edges of our plate and came with chopped leaf salad and bread (both thick pide and fine saç bread), while fresh herbs and spices could be seen and tasted in the minced lamb after it had been sliced. More and more houmous-style starters are available, but don't expect the chefs to stray too far from the grill. Nor should they.

Mangal II

4 Stoke Newington Road, N16 8BH (7254 7888/www.mangal2.com). Dalston Kingsland rail/76, 149, 243 bus. **Meals served** noon-1am daily. **Average ££. Set meal** £16.25 3 courses (minimum 2). **No credit cards. Map** p295. Turkish

On a strip with Turkish restaurants to spare, nightly crowds and a bustling atmosphere remain proof that Mangal II is doing something right. The walls are bright pink and decorated with framed prints; white tablecloths are covered with practical blue covers. Our starter of filo pastry parcels was slightly overcooked, but we were perfectly content with the meltingly tender böbrek (lambs' kidneys). Next, the plump quails that make up bıldırcın were accompanied by a well-constructed mixed salad, while iskender's sauce was an unusually dark brown, and (in a pleasing modification to the traditional recipe) contained mushrooms and other vegetables. To finish, ignore the ubiquitous baklava and sample the tulumba – pastry with cream, pistachios and syrup.

North East

Make the most of London life

★ 19 Numara Bos Cirrik

*34 Stoke Newington Road, N16 7XJ
(7249 0400). Dalston Kingsland
rail/76, 149, 243 bus.* **Meals
served** noon-midnight daily.
**Average ££. Unlicensed.
Corkage** £5. **Map** p295. Turkish
There's much to love about this
wonderful grill restaurant, its small
interior decorated with reliefs
depicting ancient Mediterranean
empires and packed with dedicated
fans. Izgara soğan (grilled onion
with pomegranate sauce) is served
as a complimentary starter and
remains a house speciality; a plate of
onion with chilli also appeared soon
after we arrived, as did a salad.
There's a perfectly decent range of
meze available in addition to these
dishes, should you be ravenous, but
it's the outstanding adana kebab
with fresh spices, sumac and cumin,
which proves what all the fuss is
about. Various branches have
popped up thanks to the spectacular
success of this, the original and, in
our opinion, still the best.

Shanghai

*41 Kingsland High Street, E8 2JS
(7254 2878). Dalston Kingsland
rail/38, 67, 76, 149, 243 bus.*
Meals served noon-11pm,
dim sum served noon-5pm daily.
Average ££. Set meal £13.80-
£22.80 per person (minimum 2).
Map p295. Chinese
The original green and blue tiles,
wrought-metal framed mirrors and
dark wooden booths of this former
eel and pie shop suit its current
incarnation well, exuding the worn
glamour of a Wong Kar-Wai film –
we half expected the staff to be
wearing cheongsams. We were
delighted to discover a traditional
dish of 'lion heads' (minced pork
balls with baby pak choi and bean
curd sheets), but the meatballs were
too dense and over-salty. 'Shanghai
Lady', an interesting name for a rice
dish mixed with diced vegetables,
was unlike anything we've tried in
Shanghai itself, but was enjoyable,
with plenty of crunchy greens in the
soy-flavoured rice. If you're after
something other than common-or-
garden-variety Cantonese cooking,
Shanghai is worth a try.

Sömine

*131 Kingsland High Street, E8 2PB
(7254 7384). Dalston Kingsland
rail/76, 149, 243 bus.* **Meals
served** 24hrs daily. **Average £.
Unlicensed. Corkage** no charge.
No credit cards. Map p295.
Turkish
Unlike most Turkish eateries in this
neck of the woods, this basic canteen
doesn't specialise in grilled meat.
Instead, diners get to choose from
four or five meaty stews that tempt
the passing foot traffic on Kingsland
Road. A subtle culinary enterprise
it certainly is not: with a few
exceptions – such as the excellent
stuffed pepper concoction that
occasionally makes an appearance –
most of the dishes qualify as dull-
but-hearty refuelling food that's far
from ideal on a warm summer
afternoon but fine for a chill winter's
night. The bread, which you'll see
being pounded into shape if you
pass the place at 10am, isn't that
great, but the rice puddings are
dangerously moreish.

Suya Obalende

*523 Kingsland Road, E8 4AR (7275
0171). Dalston Kingsland rail/38,
67, 76, 149 bus.* **Meals served**
noon-midnight Mon-Thur, Sun;
noon-1am Fri, Sat. **Average ££.
Set buffet** (Sun) £9.95. **Map** p295.
Nigerian
This popular Naija chop shop
('Nigerian fast-food outlet') is
affectionately known as the 'African
McDonald's' – a largely innocuous
reference to the price and speed with
which food is served (lightning fast

by Africa's generally more relaxed standards), and not the quality. Specialising in suya (charcoal-grilled seasoned meat or fish), the menu includes other west African favourites from gizzards (popular offal in Africa) to the more adventurous crocodile. Chicken suya was tender and plentiful, although the yams in the asaro (yam and sweet potato porridge) could have been softer. The hand-washing point is a great idea, as is the cheeky 'plate tax', a £2.50 surcharge – donated to charity – for those not clearing their plate during the Sunday buffet.

In the area
Nando's *148 Kingsland High Street, E8 2NS (7923 3555).* **Map** p295.

Hackney

Anatolia Ocakbaşı
253 Mare Street, E8 3NS (8986 2223). Hackney Central rail/26, 48, 55, 253, 277, D6 bus. **Meals served** 11am-midnight daily. **Average** ££. Turkish

Most of the Turkish restaurants in Hackney are found along a short stretch of road in Dalston, but Anatolia has kept the red and white flag flying on Mare Street for years. Supplementing its eat-in trade with a popular takeaway counter, the rather undistinguished dining room is bigger than it first appears from the street, but service remains pleasingly swift. The menu offers few surprises, but you'll still need to choose with care. Mixed meze, for instance, proved a more appetising appetiser than lentil soup. And while a rather curious 'roll shish' (lamb encasing cheese and onion, though we tasted little of either) was pretty unappealing, the mixed kebab offered pound upon pound of charcoal-grilled meaty perfection.

Green Papaya

Cilicia
1 Broadway Market, E8 4PH (7249 8799). Liverpool Street tube/rail then 26, 48 or 55 bus/London Fields rail. **Meals served** 11am-11pm Mon-Fri; 10am-11.30pm Sat; 10am-11pm Sun. **Average** ££. **Set lunch** (11am-5pm) £7.95 2 courses. Turkish

It's hard to miss the blinding orange interior of this, one of few family-friendly eating options along Broadway Market. Middle Eastern musical instruments, hookahs and light fixtures sculpted from gourds deck the walls, while summer sees the conservatory opening on to the rear verandah for alfresco dining away from the relentless hubbub of Saturday traders. The Mediterranean menu doesn't stray far from its Turkish roots: a hot meze starter combined the familiar trio of falafel, houmous and tsatsiki with chunks of juicy halloumi and delectably light mücver (courgette and feta fritters). Tender grilled meats and stuffed aubergines made for simple but satisfying main courses, and the restaurant's friendly, unpretentious vibe was bolstered by its relaxed and efficient staff.

L'Eau à la Bouche

35-37 Broadway Market, E8 4PH
(7923 0600/www.labouche.co.uk).
Liverpool Street tube/rail then 26,
48 or 55 bus/London Fields rail.
Meals served 8.30am-7pm Mon-
Fri; 8.30am-5pm Sat; 9.30am-4pm
Sun. **Average** £. Café

This bijou French deli has been a
foodie hotspot since its arrival on
Broadway Market in 2004. Its
popularity mean you'll struggle to
bag a seat on weekends, but elbow
past the lunchtime rush and you'll
find a gourmet array of artisan
cheeses and pastries. The amusingly
snooty French staff may be aloof,
but they serve some of the best
coffee and snacks in the area.
Quiches are a safe bet, always
crumbly and light, while the
vegetable pastilla (a Moroccan-style
pie) makes for a more hearty lunch.
Save room for desserts along the
lines of fruit crumble tart or pear
flan, and in fair weather grab a table
outside and enjoy the eclectic mix of
Hackney characters drifting by.

L'Epicerie @ 56 NEW

56 Chatsworth Road, E5 0LS
(7503 8172/www.lepicerie56.com).
Homerton rail. **Meals served**
8.30am-7.30pm Mon-Fri; 8.30am-
5.30pm Sat, Sun. **Average** ££. Café
Gentrification has been slow to
arrive in this part of the world, but
Homerton's Chatsworth Road has
been given a definite lift by the
arrival of this delightful little
operation. It's chiefly a deli, stocked
with excellent French cheeses,
tempting meats, a broad and well-
chosen variety of dry goods (some
from France, others from elsewhere
in Europe) and, unexpectedly, a fine
range of wines. But it's also got a few
seats both inside and out, where
locals peruse the *Guardian* while
munching on a variety of tasty
treats: Moroccan wraps, impressive
quiches, freshly baked breads, rich

coffees and some knockout desserts,
including a sensational clafoutis.
You'd certainly want one of these in
your neighbourhood.

★ Green Papaya

191 Mare Street, E8 3QE (8985
5486). London Fields rail/48, 55,
253, 277, D6 bus. **Dinner served**
5-11pm Tue-Sun. **Average** ££.
Vietnamese

It's refreshing to see a Vietnamese
restaurant that proudly highlights
its specials, with dishes of the day
cheerfully splashed across a
blackboard behind the bar. A
delightful salad of thinly shredded
banana flowers with coriander and
a powerful salty-sour dressing set
the pace for the rest of the meal. The
pho ga (chicken noodle soup) here is
sublime – a more delicate dish than
its cousin pho bo (beef noodle soup)
– and we were impressed by the
(rarely seen) smoked tofu. Staff were
amicable and knowledgeable,
explaining the provenance of the
dried 'Vietnamese olives' in a dish of
braised pork belly. Its lonely Mare
Street location means that this joint
isn't as lively as its Shoreditch
counterparts, but we rate highly
both food and atmosphere.

★ LMNT

316 Queensbridge Road, E8 3NH
(7249 6727/www.lmnt.co.uk).
Dalston Kingsland rail/236 bus.
Meals served noon-11pm Mon-
Sat; noon-10.30pm Sun. **Average**
££. **Map** p295. Modern European
Dining at LMNT is an eccentric
experience from the outset – from
tables set in enormous amphorae
and others in tiny galleries to the
decor of drapes, candles and walls
covered in Egyptian hieroglyphs.
The Mediterranean-tinged menu
produced a delicious starter of
grilled portobello mushroom, and a
puy lentil salad with feta so plentiful
we had to leave some to save room.
Breast of duck was beautifully

That Place on the Corner. See p195.

presented and served in wonderfully rich gravy, but the medium-to-well-done ribeye we'd requested was slightly overcooked and a little gristly. On top of that, celeriac remoulade was watery and the fondant potato tasted less than fresh – but it seems churlish to complain when prices are so low and service so swift and helpful.

Lock 7 NEW

129 Pritchard's Road, E2 9AP (7739 3042/www.lock-7.com). Cambridge Heath rail. **Meals served** 8am-6pm Tue-Sun. **Average** £. Café
Part café, part bicycle repair shop, this newcomer's dual identity allows diners to munch on toasted cinnamon bagels while their gears are tuned. The formula is popular with bike-loving locals, and those without wheels of their own can hire a yellow tandem for the day (£20), so as not to feel left out. Even non-cyclists have to admit that Lock 7's canalside location is a pleasant breakfast spot, where bowlfuls of muesli with yoghurt, fruit and honey can be chased with scrambled eggs

and tempting pastries. Lunchtime options change weekly, but quiches and toasted sandwiches appear regularly on the blackboard menu. Lock 7 is quirky and informal, with the gentle clinking of spanners lending a friendly community feel.

Tre Viet

251 Mare Street, E8 3NS (8533 7390). Hackney Central rail/26, 48, 55, 253, 277, D6 bus. **Meals served** 11.30am-11pm Mon-Thur, Sun; 11.30am-11.30pm Fri, Sat. **Average** ££. **Unlicensed. Corkage** no charge. Vietnamese
This veteran café does a brisk trade every single night with Vietnamese families and office workers, many bringing their own alcohol. The menu seems endless, listing the usual suspects alongside such rarities as goat in lemongrass and chilli. We sampled canh chua ca bong lau, a sweet and sour catfish soup chock-full of fish and pineapple, and flavoured with tamarind and the rarely seen taro stem. Fried frogs' legs are usually a wise choice, but on this occasion the crisp batter was somewhat let down

by an overpowering flavour of butter – still, we liked the simplicity of the accompanying onions and Vietnamese coriander. Tre Viet excels in using rare and interesting ingredients, though which dishes include them isn't always apparent from the menu.

★ La Vie en Rose NEW

2 Broadway Market, E8 4QG (7249 9070/www.lavieenrosehackney. co.uk). Liverpool Street tube/rail then 26, 48, 55 bus/London Fields rail. **Meals served** 10am-10pm Mon-Fri; 10am-10.30pm Sat, Sun. **Average** £££. French

Erstwhile home to the relocated Little Georgia (*see p175*), this rose of a restaurant holds prime position at the southern end of Broadway Market. Vast windows flood the spacious interior with daylight, while candlelit tables create a more intimate mood at night under the eye (or rather nipple) of the scantily clad chambermaid painted on the wall. Though lurking at the pricier end of the budget category, the food is fantastic: confit of duck virtually melted off the bone and was served

with a portion of gratin dauphinois fit for the Dauphin himself, while a rump of lamb with wild mushrooms was similarly succulent. Lime crème brûlée proved a zingy finale to the meal. Staff were friendly and accommodating throughout.

Leytonstone

Mudra NEW

715 Leytonstone High Road, E11 4RD (8539 1700). Leytonstone tube/Leytonstone High Road rail/66, 257 bus. **Lunch served** noon-3pm, **dinner served** 5.30-11pm Mon, Wed-Sun. **Average** ££. Indian
Leytonstone isn't exactly foodie central, which makes this new Indian eaterie glitter like a jewel on a threadbare sari. Its interior is smartly designed: sleek and dramatic in gold and black, with blond wood floors; even the obligatory Indian art is more stylish than kitsch. For starters, too-dry vadas (deep-fried lentil patties) were partly redeemed by a lip-smacking coconut chutney, while chicken 65 (deep-fried, diced and spiced

boneless pieces) was moist and moreish. A main of Malabar chicken curry was fragrant and fruity, but a vegetarian option of avial (a Keralan dish made with gourd, yam, banana and pumpkin) was as frustratingly splintery as it was flavourful. Black pepper ice-cream made for a sophisticated finale.

★ Singburi

593 Leytonstone High Road, E11 4PA (8281 4801/www.singburi. co.uk). Leytonstone tube/Leytonstone High Road rail/66, 257 bus. **Dinner served** 6-11pm Tue-Sat; 6-10pm Sun. **Average** £. **Unlicensed**. **Corkage** no charge. **No credit cards**. Thai

Hidden away on a less than salubrious stretch of Leytonstone, this family-run café may not look like much – think strip lights, potted plants and veneer panelling – but it is cosy, with friendly staff, kitsch Thai trinkets and, on our most recent visit, a soothing Billie Holiday soundtrack. The Thai home cooking is similarly soulful: tom kha gai (chicken in coconut milk) was thick, comforting and full of zesty goodness, while gang keow wan (green curry) was subtly flavoured using authentic ingredients such as pea aubergines. Goong sarong (deep-fried prawns in pastry) were less memorable, but the moist and moreish pad thai was virtually perfect. No wonder the place was humming with locals on a dreary Wednesday night.

Newington Green

Beyti

113 Green Lanes, N16 9DA (7704 3165). Manor House tube then 141, 341 bus/73 bus. **Meals served** noon-midnight daily. **Average** ££. **Unlicensed**. **Corkage** (over 1 bottle) £2 per bottle. **No credit cards**. Map p295. Turkish

A short distance from the Turkish dining hubs of Stoke Newington High Street and Harringay's Green Lanes, Beyti remains a great neighbourhood Turkish with a jovial evening atmosphere and a comfortingly kitsch interior mixing traditional Turkish lamps with old-fashioned landscape paintings. On one side, a busy ocakbaşı grill keeps the place toasty as well as filling it with delicious smells. After starters of flavoursome imam bayıldı (aubergine stuffed with tomatoes, onions and garlic) and some delicious own-made houmous, we enjoyed a classic lamb shish kebab – nothing surprising, but solid, standard stuff all the same. Beyti's famously upbeat vibe leads to weekend evening crowds; expect to wait for a table at peak times.

Fifty Six

56 Newington Green, N16 9PX (7359 6377/www.fifty-six.co.uk). Canonbury or Dalston Kingsland rail/73, 141, 341 bus. **Dinner served** 5.30-11.30pm Mon-Fri. **Meals served** noon-11.30pm Sat, Sun. **Average** £££. **Map** p295. Modern European

Small and friendly, with a bustling, comfortable atmosphere and the understated look of a French bistro, Fifty Six is a solid neighbourhood restaurant slap bang in the centre of Newington Green. It's as popular with chattering groups as it is with lone customers popping in for a solitary snack; service is friendly and the food impressively reliable. For starters, asparagus arrived on a dainty polenta cake accompanied by a zingy salsa, while a breadcrumb-coated potato and leek parcel was pleasingly light and fluffy. The delicate notes of artichoke were somewhat lost amid the more powerful flavours of a cheesy spinach cannelloni main, but the dish was satisfyingly creamy and tasty – and an enormous portion. The wine list is good value, another bonus. Our only quibble was the rash of costly side dishes on an otherwise affordable menu.

★ Sariyer Balik

56 Green Lanes, N16 9NH (7275 7681). Canonbury rail/73, 141, 236, 341 bus. **Meals served** 5pm-1am daily. **Average** ££. **No credit cards**. **Map** p295. Turkish
Sariyer Balik's sign might be bigger and its interior a little brighter – the walls now decorated with a clutter of oars, nautical paintings and an exquisite wooden fish relief – but the recent refit has done nothing to change the essential character of this fish specialist. A mixed hot starter included fried squid marinated in vodka, battered mussels in beer, and prawns in spicy tomato sauce (all also available separately). Sea bass melted in the mouth, while steamed anchovies with shards of carrot, onion and potato were also excellent. The restaurant's reliance on which fish can be sourced on any given day means that not everything on the menu is always available, but we've yet to encounter a duff dish.

Abi Ruchi

That Place on the Corner NEW

1-3 Green Lanes, N16 9BS (7704 0079/www.thatplaceonthecorner. co.uk). Canonbury rail/73, 141, 236, 341 bus. **Meals served** 10.30am-7pm Mon-Thur; 10.30am-8pm Fri; 10.30am-2.30pm Sat; 10.30am-3pm Sun. **Average** ££. **Map** p295. Café
That Place manages to be bubbly enough for kids yet adult enough for their sophisticated N16 parents (for whom the very mention of a chicken nugget raises a sneer). Playroom paraphernalia is laid out at one end, with huge windows emphasising the glorious spaciousness. The menu sticks to the tried-and-trusted pasta, panini and big breakfast formula, while children choose from the likes of own-made shepherd's pie, spag bol, and plaice or chicken goujons. Coffee is of a high standard, and cakes are sourced from a local bakery. Staff were overseeing a party at the playful end of the café when we visited, but we received unflustered, efficient attention. The café also runs daily activities for kids, including face-painting, arts and crafts and 'caterpillar music'.

Stoke Newington

Abi Ruchi

42 Stoke Newington Church Street, N16 0LU (7923 4564/www.abiruchi. com). Stoke Newington rail/73, 393, 476 bus. **Lunch served** noon-3pm Mon-Sat. **Dinner served** 6-11pm Mon-Thur; 6-11.45pm Fri, Sat. **Meals served** 1-10.15pm Sun. **Average** £. **Set lunch** £4.50-£5.50 1 course; £5.95-£7.50 2 courses. **Map** p295. Indian
Abi Ruchi cuts no corners when it comes to bringing subtle Keralan cuisine to the capital. All the details are handled properly: from the popadoms (accompanied by small bowls of artfully spiced dips) to the breads (spongy, slightly sweet

nadan dosa) and vegetable sides (gorgeously garlicky spinach fried with onions). We enjoyed a starter of steamed squid stuffed with puréed vegetables flavoured with coconut and herbs – an unusual mix of taste and texture – and a chicken malabar main in a rich tomato sauce, warmly spiced with curry leaves and carrying the delicate fragrance of coconut. The restaurant's lilac interior adds to the serenity of the place, as does the sweet and attentive service.

Il Bacio

61 Stoke Newington Church Street, N16 0AR (7249 3833). Stoke Newington rail/73, 393, 476 bus. **Dinner served** 6-11.15pm Mon-Fri. **Meals served** noon-11.15pm Sat, Sun. **Average** ££. **Map** p295. Pizza & pasta

The unforced amiability of this neighbourhood pizzeria starts with smiles and back-patting from staff welcoming customers like old friends and continues with the complimentary herbed olives and baskets of paper-thin Sardinian bread. On warmer days, waiters open the French doors and put tables on the pavement – treating passers-by to the likes of Dean Martin's 'That's Amore'. The menu has a list of standard Italian pizzas and pastas as well as Sardinian home-style specials such as slow-cooked lamb. We avoided the chip-topped pizza, instead choosing goat's cheese and parma ham versions; both were very salty, but our water jug was topped up throughout. Desserts include Sardinian favourite sebadas (sweet ravioli) and a heavenly tiramisu.

★ Blue Legume

101 Stoke Newington Church Street, N16 0UD (7923 1303). Stoke Newington rail/73, 393, 476 bus. **Meals served** 9.30am-11pm Mon-Sat; 9.30am-6.30pm Sun. **Average** ££. **Map** p295. Café

Blue Legume is best known for its sterling brunches – from sticky, maple syrup-drizzled waffles with fruit and yoghurt to mushrooms on toast with crème fraîche. In the evening it morphs from a sunny café into a low-key neighbourhood bistro, with candles flickering on the mosaic tables, mellow jazz playing in the background and a menu encompassing everything from seafood tagliatelle and tapas to own-made burgers. Friendly waiters deliver giant plates of food: we barely made a dent in a heaped dish of spicy, saffron-infused paella, while a rack of lamb (slightly fatty but perfectly pink) came with a mountain of fluffy mashed potato and plump mushrooms covered in Madeira sauce. This ambitious café is a genuine local asset.

Bodrum Café & Bar

61 Stoke Newington High Street, N16 8EL (7254 6464). Stoke Newington rail/73, 76, 149, 243 bus. **Meals served** 9am-10pm daily. **Average** £. **Set lunch** £6.95 2 courses incl soft drink. **Map** p295. Turkish

One of a collection of neighbourhood cafés on Stoke Newington High Street, Bodrum is a homely spot with canary-yellow walls and flyers advertising local events. It packs in the punters for filling weekend breakfasts – both English and Turkish versions are available – as well as lunchtime omelettes, burgers and the like. By evening, the menu turns Turkish, with a wide range of grills alongside dishes like iskender (meat baked with tomato sauce and yoghurt, and served on bread). We chose köfte, a generous portion of minced lamb seasoned with herbs, which arrived with a diminutive scoop of rice and braised vegetables in place of the traditional salad. Yet more proof, perhaps, of Bodrum's dual nationality.

The great gastropub swindle

Charles Lamb

The rise of the gastropub has been one of the most successful – and noticeable – phenomenons to hit the London dining scene in the past 15 years. The formula is often as well worn as the floorboards: artfully mismatched wooden tables and chairs, flickering candles, reclaimed antiques of dubious origin. Not everyone is a fan of the gastropub: old steamers, for example, forced to watch as their beloved local is given the Llewelyn-Bowen treatment before being reopened with a waiting list for tables.

With the smoking ban dragging the pub trade ever further into the doldrums, it's widely agreed that businesses have to up their game in the kitchen if they want to pull in the punters. Yet somewhere along the line it seems that something went wrong with the idea of the gastropub.

In 1991, when Michael Belben and David Eyre began serving Mediterranean dishes from the **Eagle** in Farringdon (still going strong), they were aiming to provide a laid-back local pub with decent, democratically priced food. Nowadays, many so-called gastropubs are just swanky restaurants that happen to be located in boozers – many don't even serve proper beer, and hardly any come close enough to our criteria for cheap eating to be listed in this guide.

Below are the handful of notable exceptions, and we salute them for staying true to their principles. Here's hoping the current financial crisis results in a few of their peers following suit.

Charles Lamb *16 Elia Street, N1 8DE (7837 5040/www.thecharles lambpub.com).* **Map** p299.
Cumberland Arms *29 North End Road, W14 8SZ (7371 6806/www.thecumberlandarms pub.co.uk).*
Eagle *159 Farringdon Road, EC1R 3AL (7837 1353).* **Map** p270.
Freemasons *2 Wandsworth Common Northside, SW18 2SS (7326 8580/www.freemasons pub.com).* **Map** p284.
Herne Tavern *2 Forest Hill Road, SE22 0RR (8299 9521/ www.theherne.net).*
Norfolk Arms *28 Leigh Street WC1H 9EP (7388 3937/www. norfolkarms.co.uk).* **Map** p267.
Old Nun's Head *15 Nunhead Green, SE15 3QQ (7639 4007/ www.oldnunshead.com).*
Perry Hill *78-80 Perry Hill, SE6 4EY (8699 5076/www. theperryhill.co.uk).*

Café Z Bar

58 Stoke Newington High Street, N16 7PB (7275 7523/www.zcafebar. com). Stoke Newington rail/73, 76, 149, 243 bus. **Meals served** 7am-10pm daily. **Average ££. Set meal £5.95-£8.90 2 courses. No credit cards. Map** p295. Turkish

'One neither desires coffee nor a coffeehouse. One desires to talk with others, coffee is merely an excuse.' So proclaims the Turkish proverb that adorns the wall of this homely café-cum-restaurant. With its unassuming bare wooden tables, local art and scattering of flyers, it's certainly a cosy place for a lazy chat. The meze are standard but good value, the muhamara (a spicy, nutty dip of finely chopped walnuts and green peppers with onion and cinnamon) being particularly tasty. Mains of coban kavurma (diced lamb and chicken stir-fried with peppers, onion, mushrooms and Turkish herbs), and mixed kebabs (chicken shish, lamb shish and meatballs with rice) got the job done, as did the easy-drinking house red.

Fishery NEW

90 Stoke Newington High Street, N16 7NY (7249 6444). Stoke Newington rail/73, 76, 149, 243 bus. **Meals served** noon-10pm Mon-Thur; noon-10.30pm Fri, Sat; noon-9pm Sun. **Average ££. No credit cards. Map** p295. Fish & chips

They were having a tough night at the Fishery; it was busier than expected, as our unfailingly helpful waitress confided. No scallops left for the Arbroath smokie kedgeree, no crayfish left for the dover sole, and a distinct note of asperity from the chef in the open kitchen at the back. That said, this offshoot of the nearby Fishery fishmonger shines in its black and white tiles. There's a wet counter, fryers for the popular takeaway, and canteen tables at

which to sample the palatable house white along with fillets battered or grilled. Tilapia and chips was better than a sole buried in garlic butter and clams or the too-vinegary pickled samphire, but stick to the staples and you'll eat well.

Itto

226 Stoke Newington High Street, N16 7HU (7275 8827/www.itto london.co.uk). Stoke Newington rail/67, 73, 76, 149, 243 bus. **Meals served** noon-11pm daily. **Average £. Map** p295. Oriental

Situated at the quiet end of the high street and plain in appearance (bare lilac walls, wooden stools, undressed tables), Itto nevertheless offers interesting food at affordable prices along with friendly, attentive service. The menu dances around Asia, giving diners the chance to follow up the likes of Japanese tempura with Singapore fried rice, or dry-marinated Chinese ribs with a Thai green curry. Vietnamese beef pho was our favourite: thick noodles, vegetables and thin slices of meat in a heady broth, with rounds of chilli, Thai basil and a wedge of lime on the side allowing customers to adjust the flavour to their liking. Less exciting were stir-fries in thick, sweet sauces reminiscent of Anglo-Chinese takeaways.

Lemon Monkey NEW

188 Stoke Newington High Street, N16 7JD (7241 4454/www.lemon-monkey.co.uk). Stoke Newington rail/67, 73, 76, 149, 243 bus. **Meals served** 8.30am-6pm Mon-Wed; 9am-9pm Thur-Sat; 10am-9pm Sun. **Average £. Map** p295. Café

One of a number of café-delis to have sprouted locally in recent years, Lemon Monkey stocks a decent selection of wines, cheeses and assorted high-end groceries, many organic or Fairtrade, and all enticingly displayed in the spacious, sophisticated interior. An informal

Fishery

peppering of tables and chairs caters to café customers. Eat-in food takes the form of superior sandwiches – we loved the smoked mackerel with capers on thinly sliced rye bread – along with a selection of good-looking salads and cakes, including a superb apricot tart. Seating is spread over two levels; the raised section at the back is a great place to retreat for a mid-afternoon coffee and a perusal of the papers.

Rasa

55 Stoke Newington Church Street, N16 0AR (7249 0344/www.rasa restaurants.com). Stoke Newington rail/73, 393, 476 bus. **Lunch served** noon-3pm Sat, Sun. **Dinner served** 6-10.45pm Mon-Thur, Sun; 6-11.30pm Fri, Sat. **Average** ££. **Set meal** £16 4 courses. **Map** p295. Indian

This original branch of the Rasa chain may not have quite the buzz it opened with in 1997 – wowing critics and locals alike with the vegetarian home cooking of the Keralan Nair caste – but the food remains excellent. Cabbage thoran is still a surprise, a delicate stir-fry singing with the flavours of popped mustard seeds and cumin, the subtle aroma of curry leaves and the texture of shredded coconut. Moru kachiathu is another signature dish, turmeric-stained yoghurt bathing large chunks of orange mango and making for a sweetly spicy dish that tastes as exotic as it looks. The appam pancakes on our recent visit were disappointingly scorched on the outside, but own-made pickles were so magnificent that we quickly forgave this sloppy detail.

Tea Rooms NEW

155 Stoke Newington Church Street, N16 0UH (7923 1870). Stoke Newington rail/73, 393, 476 bus. **Meals served** 11am-6pm Mon, Wed-Fri; 11am-6.30pm Sat, Sun. **Average** £. **Set tea** (Mon, Sat, Sun) £10. **No credit cards. Map** p295. Café

This charming café might be mistaken for a traditional country tearoom were it not for the flyers for local events, contemporary sofa and collection of retro tea and coffee sets. Otherwise the place is tinged with a sepia-tinted sense of rustic nostalgia, from the embroidered tablecloths to the collection of cakes on stands at the round counter, where everything from carrot cake and banana bread to creamy roulades is on display. There are cheese scones as well as sweet ones and a selection of savoury pastries, plus delightful hampers for picnic hunters. A set tea with sandwiches, cream scones and a choice of cakes will set you back £10 on Mondays, Saturdays and Sundays.

North East

Testi

*38 Stoke Newington High Street,
N16 7PL (7249 7151). Stoke
Newington rail/73, 76, 149, 243
bus.* **Meals served** noon-1am
Mon-Thur, Sun; noon-2am Fri,
Sat. **Average** ££. **Map** p295.
Turkish

The name of this popular local is
derived from the Turkish for jug,
but marinated lamb's testicles *are* on
the menu, along with much
ocakbaşı-grilled offal. The walls are
painted a moody orange and
decorated with a mix of European
and Middle Eastern trinkets. The
mixed meze starter was superb,
featuring enormous chunks of
grilled halloumi, fresh-tasting dolma
and rich, creamy houmous, plus a
basket of warm bread to mop it up.
All of which was a meal in itself, and
perhaps should have been: köfte
kebab was dry and over-seasoned.
But we enjoyed the trinity of side
dishes: tomato and onion salad, a
fierce onion and chilli concoction
and, best of all, chargrilled onions in
pomegranate juice.

In the area

Il Bacio Express *90 Stoke
Newington Church Street, N16
0AD (7249 2344).* **Map** p295.
Rasa Travancore *56 Stoke
Newington Church Street, N16
0NB (7249 1340).* Branch of Rasa.
Map p295.

Walthamstow

La Cafeteria

*841 Forest Road, E17 4AT
(8527 1926). Walthamstow
Central tube/rail then 212 or 275
bus.* **Meals served** 7.30am-4.30pm
Mon-Wed; 7.30am-10pm Thur-Sat.
Average ££. **No credit cards**.
Café

It looks like a café, sounds like a café
and serves food in café-sized
portions, but the globetrotting menu

at La Cafeteria is more inventive
than most local lunch spots, and the
food of a much higher quality. It also
now opens Thursday to Sunday
evenings, thanks to public demand.
Dishes skirt the shores of the
Mediterranean, covering inventive
pastas (penne with bacon, spinach,
olives and sun-dried tomatoes, for
instance), elaborate salads and
hearty, healthy couscous options
before landing back on home turf
with bangers, burgers and reliably
belt-busting breakfasts. Local office
workers tend to nip in for one of a
range of top-notch baguettes or
toasted sandwiches, while a variety
of papers and magazines encourage
those with time on their hands to
linger a while; the atmosphere is
family friendly throughout.

Wanstead

Nam An

*157 High Street, E11 2RL (8532
2845). Wanstead tube.* **Lunch
served** noon-2.30pm Wed-Sun.
Dinner served 6-11.30pm daily.
Average ££. Vietnamese

A rickshaw in the vestibule,
towering clumps of artificial bamboo
and a pond teeming with koi carp are
just a few of the decorative nods to
the east at this friendly Vietnamese
eaterie. We opted for sizzling beef,
which was both melt-in-the-mouth
tender and well suited to its
sprightly, chilli-infused sauce; paired
with a special of fried prawn rice
it also made for an interesting take
on surf and turf. Other dishes were
less exciting: crispy duck was
disappointingly dry, while sweet and
sour pork had a glutinous texture
and an unpleasant pre-packaged
flavour. For all that, Nam An's
extensive range of dishes, relaxing
atmosphere and amiable service
make this a good option for those
within rickshaw-riding distance.

North East

Archway

Archgate

5 Junction Road, N19 5QT (7272 2575). Archway tube. **Meals served** 10am-midnight daily. **Average ££. Set dinner** £11.95-£16.95 per person (minimum 2) 2-3 courses. **No credit cards**. **Map** p298. Turkish

This Archway favourite serves hangover-curing brunch fare, salads, sandwiches and burgers, and decent mezedes and kebabs testify to its Turkish heart. A narrow seating area spans the length of a service counter packed with desserts (including traditional rice pudding) before opening up to reveal a slightly more spacious area at the back. Our lunchtime visit found the place peppered with office workers and OAPs tucking into wraps, salads and chips to a background of Smooth FM and friendly waitress banter. Evenings see the atmosphere factor upped a notch with groups of friends devouring well-executed grills and Mediterranean specials. Not a destination venue by any stretch of the imagination, but a local restaurant to be proud of.

Charuwan

110 Junction Road, N19 5LB (7263 1410). Archway or Tufnell Park tube. **Lunch served** noon-3pm Mon-Fri. **Dinner served** 6-11pm daily. **Average ££. Set dinner** £18-£20 per person (minimum 2) 3 courses. **Map** p298. Thai

With its main room laden with ethnic trinkets beneath a suspended Lanna-style ceiling, Charuwan has a more glamorous interior than most of London's Thai restaurants. The cooking won't win awards for innovation, but it's reliable, good value and short on disappointments. Classic Thai fish cakes were spot on and served with a well-balanced sweet-sour chilli sauce; a salad of warm grilled pork and spring onions had a punchy, hot and tangy dressing. A very good mussaman

La Voute

lamb had a complex, spicy peanut sauce, although Thai-style fried fish with chilli sauce was a weak link, the dressing saccharine and unsubtle. Still, with prices that make it easy to return time and again, this kind of blip is easily overlooked.

★ La Voute NEW

10 Archway Close, Archway Road, N19 3TD (7281 7314). Archway tube. **Meals served** 8am-4pm daily. **Average** ££. **Unlicensed** no alcohol allowed. **Map** p298. French
Located in the very heart of Archway, this bright, comfortable, daytime-only spot brings some much-needed café class to N19's burgeoning foodie population. At the front is an elegant counter displaying éclairs, croissants and cheesecake; further back, an appealing garden offers potential weekend lolling and sunny workday escapes. Salads and soups of the day (such as spicy tomato) are available to take away, as are coffees. Mint and lemon tisane was full of fresh,

verdant leaves and brought by warmly welcoming staff. Breakfasts offer halloumi and lamb sausages as well as the expected eggs; a range of inventive Med-style sandwiches (goat's cheese, fresh pear and strawberry jam, for example), served with a fresh green salad, will satisfy at lunchtime.

Camden Town & Chalk Farm

Asakusa

265 Eversholt Street, NW1 1BA (7388 8533/8399). Camden Town or Mornington Crescent tube. **Dinner served** 6-11.30pm Mon-Fri; 6-11pm Sat. **Average** ££. **Set dinner** £5.60-£10.80. **Map** p296. Japanese
Few things testify to the quality of a restaurant's cooking as a combination of 'squat-chic' decor and near-nightly queues out the door. Asakusa's menu makes few concessions to readability, though

staff are happy to help decipher the staggering range of authentic dishes. Mixed tempura (fat prawns and assorted veg) was hot and crisp, while sushi (juicy eel maki) and sashimi (yellowtail) were of a high standard. Small dishes are difficult to resist: beef tataki didn't deliver the tenderest meat in town, but had plenty of flavour and was nicely presented. Buta kakuni, a slow-cooked pork belly dish, was rich and warming with an appetisingly sweet undertone. Book ahead if you want a ground-floor table; otherwise, it's down to the basement.

Bento Café NEW

9 Parkway, NW1 7PG (7482 3990/ www.bentocafe.co.uk). Camden Town tube. **Meals served** noon-10.30pm Mon-Thur, Sun; noon-11pm Fri, Sat. **Average** ££. **Set lunch** £5.90 bento box. **Map** p296. Japanese
Its position beside Camden's Jazz Café makes Bento popular with smoky bohemians filling up before a show, but you'll find all walks of life packing the place out nightly. The interior is decorated with bamboo shoots, lanterns and vintage Japanese weapons, and there's something decidedly Zen-like about the layout of dark wood tables. Sushi is hand-rolled behind a central counter – a Kyoto starter platter tasted fresh, although was a little prone to falling apart – and mains are artfully presented: the seafood grill was an elaborate bundle of scallops, seared prawns and squid held together by a banana leaf and a stem of pickled ginger. Pork and prawn dumplings were golden brown, grease free and packed with piping hot, powerfully flavoured meat.

Bintang

93 Kentish Town Road, NW1 8NY (7813 3393). Camden Town tube/ Kentish Town tube/rail. **Dinner served** 5.30-11.30pm Mon-Thur,
Sun; 5.30-11.45pm Fri, Sat. **Average** £. **Set meals** (5.30-7.30pm Mon-Thur; 5.30-11.30pm Sun) £8.99 3 courses. **Unlicensed**. **Corkage** £2 wine, 50p beer. **Map** p296. Oriental
Immune to the vagaries of fashion and the march of inflation, Bintang hasn't changed its kitsch interior – or its prices – in years. Sandwiched in a run-down row of shops, its tiny dining room is a hospitable jumble of bamboo cladding, tribal masks, lanterns and fairy lights. The pan-Asian menu is equally esoteric, with mains ranging from lemongrass-infused curries to laksa; the star turn is whole baked sea bass for under a tenner. Starters are less inspired, and often deep-fried: prawn toast, pakoras, spring rolls and the like. The modest prices and BYO policy mean the place is often overrun with raucous parties; if the decibels become unbearable, head to the basement or retreat into the garden.

Diner NEW

2 Jamestown Road, NW1 7BY (7485 5223). Camden Town tube. **Meals served** 10am-11pm Mon-Thur; 10am-midnight Fri; 9am-midnight Sat; 9am-11pm Sun. **Average** ££. **Map** p296. Burgers
This faux American diner looks right at home in a part of London already verging on a theme park, its interior a marriage of tastefully tattered red leather booths, metallic napkin dispensers and steer horns hung over the black tiled bar – manned on our visit by an uncanny Tarantino lookalike in a garish Hawaiian shirt. Suitably cute waitresses serve burgers in dinky plastic baskets; a Cajun chicken burger comprised two grilled breasts in a toasted bun, subtly seasoned and well assembled, although the all-beef double decker was a little fatty and tricky to hold together. Shakes are thick and thirst-quenching, the fries crisp and fluffy.

North

All-day American breakfasts and blue-plate specials cater to Camden's wannabe truckers.

Feng Sushi
1 Adelaide Road, NW3 3QE (7483 2929/www.fengsushi.co.uk). Chalk Farm tube. **Lunch served** 11.30am-3.30pm Mon-Fri. **Dinner served** 6-10pm Mon-Wed; 6-11pm Thur, Fri. **Meals served** 11.30am-11pm Sat; noon-10pm Sun. **Average** ££. **Set meal** £8-£15 bento box. **Map** p296. Japanese

Perhaps it's the decor – functional at best, and with a strange preference for tables that are either too high or too small – but we've often found this branch of Feng Sushi curiously quiet, despite exemplary service, superb sushi and a handy proximity to the bustle of Camden market. Purists might baulk at chives and cream cheese on a menu that also features 'Japanese fish and chips', but stick to the classics and you can't go far wrong. Salmon and avocado maki were satisfyingly fat and fresh-tasting, and shiitake tempura was nicely crisp and not too heavy. Special mention should be made of the ingredients: tuna is line-caught and the salmon comes from an organic Loch Duart farm.

Guanabana NEW
85 Kentish Town Road, NW1 8NY (7485 1166/www.guanabana restaurant.com). Camden Town tube. **Lunch served** noon-3pm Wed-Fri. **Dinner served** 5-11.30pm daily. **Meals served** noon-11.30pm Sat, Sun. **Average** ££. **Set meal** (5.30-7.30pm) £9.50 3 courses. **Unlicensed. Corkage** £2 wine, 50p beer. **Map** p296. International

Guanabana is a fun fusion restaurant with a lovely bamboo-ceilinged garden-cum-terrace at the rear. The menu of Argentinian Mexican, Caribbean and Colombian dishes is punctuated with wild cards such as jasmine-perfumed Thai rice,

beer-battered onion rings and coleslaw. Try starters of red jalapeños stuffed with cream cheese, glazed chicken wings, or cassava chips with tomato salsa. Food is often as easy on the eye as it is on the palate: pan-fried bass came as a tower of succulent fillets between layers of crisp greens and a delicious feta cheese mash. Desserts include sweet potato and banana fritters with coconut ice-cream. Bring your own booze, or stick with a fresh fruit mocktail.

Jamón Jamón
38 Parkway, NW1 7AH (7284 0606). Camden Town tube. **Meals served** noon-11.30pm Mon-Thur, Sun; noon-12.30am Fri, Sat. **Average** ££. **Set meal** (noon-5pm Mon-Fri) 2 dishes for the price of 1. **Map** p296. Spanish

Weekend evenings at Jamón Jamón are boisterous affairs: tables are often pushed together to make room for birthday parties, and the sound of laughter can eclipse quiet conversation, which is deeply Spanish if not very conducive to a romantic meal for two. Nor is the interior exactly eye-catching – just 'Jamón Jamón' cast in metal and protruding from the otherwise bare walls at regular intervals – but the tapas, although unimaginative, are deftly executed. Squid in tomato sauce featured generous chunks of tender seafood, a plate of fried whitebait was fresh and enormous, and there was a marked flair even to standards such as patatas bravas and sliced chorizo, the rich meat of the latter matched with roasted red peppers and a red wine sauce. A deserving local favourite.

Marine Ices
8 Haverstock Hill, NW3 2BL (7482 9003/www.marineices.co.uk). Chalk Farm tube. **Lunch served** noon-3pm, **dinner served** 6-11pm Tue-Fri. **Meals served** noon-11pm

Sat; noon-10pm Sun. **Average**
££. **Map** p296. Pizza & pasta
Lovers of all things old-fashioned
get a lift at this retro ice-cream
parlour, where tubs of fresh fruit
sorbet (lemon, papaya) jostle for
space with cones of own-made ice
cream (Caribbean coconut, toffee
crunch). It's a great place for families
and group get-togethers (staff are
happy to serenade customers with
'Happy Birthday'). The happy vibe
can border on noisy, but the food is
good value and tasty. To start,
there's a fine range of antipasti,
including garlicky bruschetta; then
come pizzas, meat (plenty of veal)
and pastas. The family-run business
started in 1928, and the owners are
proud of their history. Pictures of
family members adorn the walls,
next to those of minor celebrities and
their scrawled autographs.

★ Masala Zone

*25 Parkway, NW1 7PG (7267
4422/www.masalazone.com).
Camden Town tube.* **Lunch served**
12.30-3pm, **dinner served** 5.30-
11pm Mon-Fri. **Meals served**
12.30-11pm Sat; 12.30-10.30pm
Sun. **Average** ££. **Set thali**
£7.80-£10.70. **Map** p296. Indian
A buzzy vibe, fair prices and decent
regional and pan-Indian food make
Masala Zone one chain about which
it's justified to wax lyrical. This
Camden branch has an eye-
catching decor that assembles
1930s-style posters, retro artefacts
and colourful lampshades. We
loved a starter of gol guppas –
puffed pastry globes filled with tart
tamarind water spiked with black
salt – and a main course of smoky
lamb korma had tender morsels of
meat in a robust onion masala.
Equally memorable was chicken
lazeez, the meat simmered in a
broth-like curry delicately infused
with floral notes and citrussy
cardamom. The thalis are always a

safe bet, and take the stress out of
ordering; they all include daily
specials of dhal and side dishes.

★ El Parador

*245 Eversholt Street, NW1 1BA
(7387 2789/www.elparadorlondon.
com). Mornington Crescent tube.*
Tapas served noon-3pm, 6-11pm
Mon-Thur; noon-3pm, 6-11.30pm
Fri; 6-11.30pm Sat; 6.30-9.30pm Sun.
Average ££. **Map** p296. Spanish
First impressions don't favour the
visually unremarkable El Parador –
from its forgettable frontage to its
plain decor – but fine ingredients
and excellent cooking bring its
innovative menu to life. From the
selection of 16 vegetable tapas, we
chose inventive roast beetroot with
chestnuts and red onion in a
balsamic reduction, and Calasparra
rice with roasted aubergines, peas
and mint – both were superb
assemblies of flavours and textures.
The servings of fish and meat were
equally impressive: seared scallops
with buttered spinach, and chicken
livers fried in sherry with serrano
ham. It's rare that a family-run diner
like this can be called a destination
restaurant, but El Parador is well
worth a trip across town.

Roundhouse NEW

*Roundhouse, Chalk Farm Road,
NW1 8EH (0870 389 9920/
www.roundhouse.org.uk). Chalk
Farm tube.* **Meals served** 11am-
6pm daily (late openings on gig
days; check website for details).
Average ££. **Map** p296. Brasserie
Free tables may be rarer than hens'
teeth during a pre-performance
dinner scrum, but swing by for a
lazy midweek lunch and you'll find
this a glorious place to while away
the afternoon. Block white walls
lend an angular modernism that is
bolstered by minimalist tables and
chairs – it's a bit like dining in a
three-dimensional modern artwork.
Food is a cut above the average:

North

chicken and lentil stew featured large chunks of meat and a hearty, delicately spiced sauce; venison burger – thick and juicy and served with an intoxicating slab of stilton – was let down only by a rather grim port and cream sauce (served, mercifully, in a separate pot). Desserts (from double-chocolate brownies to apple pie with saffron and anise) are served with either clotted cream or vanilla ice-cream that comes from neighbouring Marine Ices (*see p205*).

★ Teachi NEW

29-31 Parkway, NW1 7PN (7485 9933). Camden Town tube. **Meals/dim sum served** noon-11pm Mon-Sat; noon-10.30pm Sun. **Average** ££. **Set lunch** £6.80 1 course. **Map** p296. Chinese

Teachi's mix of dim sum and bite-sized Chinese delicacies has seldom failed to impress since the restaurant opened in 2007. Flash-fried salt and pepper squid was light and delicious, despite being served in what looked like a wicker dustpan; marinated salmon bellies were tender enough to nearly fall off the sticks they were barbecued on; and an interesting take on duck pancakes offered tasty chunks of meat coated in airy batter and cut into triangles. Our only complaint concerned the atmosphere: decor is pleasant, with a convincing if conventional mix of sculpted rosewood screens, potted bamboo plants and Chinese wall art, but we've seldom dined in a restaurant lit so unnecessarily brightly.

Trojka

101 Regents Park Road, NW1 8UR (7483 3765/www.troyka restaurant.co.uk). Chalk Farm tube. **Meals served** 9am-10.30pm daily. **Average** ££. **Set lunch** (Mon-Fri) £9.95-£11.95 2 courses. **Licensed**. **Corkage** £3 wine, £15 spirits. **Map** p296. Russian

We can't get enough of the easy-going atmosphere at Trojka. Where better to repair for a steaming bowl of borscht after a walk over Primrose Hill on a chilly Sunday afternoon? Service can be hit and miss, but you can pop in for just a coffee, and fellow diners are an intriguing mix of aspiring pop stars and local families. Dark wood furniture, ruby-red walls and a huge Chagall-esque painting of a trojka (a wooden sleigh drawn by three horses) add to the authentic and homely vibe. The food is good too: top marks for the dill-infused herring starter and the light puffy blinis with assorted toppings, including smoked trout or salmon, egg mayonnaise, caviar, and aubergine purée. We can also recommend the succulent roasted duck breast, served with prune sauce. A violinist or accordion player performs on some evenings.

Tupelo Honey NEW

27 Parkway, NW1 7PN (7284 2989/ www.tupelo-honey.co.uk). Camden Town tube. **Meals served** 10am-6pm Mon, Sun; 10am-11pm Tue-Sat. **Average** ££. **Map** p296. Café

This homely café injects a rustic sweetness and sophistication into Camden Town. A glass counter is piled high with delectable own-made cakes and deep dishes of comfort food, and you'll struggle to find better coffee locally. We enjoyed a huge slice of piping-hot chicken and mushroom pie packed with tender meat and chunky vegetables, and a mammoth portion of spinach lasagne; both came with fresh, imaginative salads. You can dine at artfully distressed wooden tables at the rear, the white walls flickering with shadows cast by candles and the roaring open fire, but there are also two other floors, the uppermost with a superbly intimate balcony terrace.

Diner. See p204.

★ Yum Cha NEW

*27-28 Chalk Farm Road, NW1
8AG (7482 2228). Chalk Farm
tube.* **Meals/dim sum served**
noon-11pm Mon-Thur, Sun; noon-
midnight Fri, Sat. **Average ££.**
Map p296. Chinese

Within weeks of Yum Cha's 2008
opening, local families and savvy
Chinese students had laid claim to
the tables at peak dim sum time
(noon-2pm). The facade is less than
shiny, but the interior has handsome
wood detailing and a prominent
golden Buddha. The chefs, hailing
from Hong Kong, ensure that hard-
to-master dishes are executed as
flawlessly as the classics: pan-fried
turnip cake was crisp and golden
brown, and har gau (steamed
shrimp dumplings) had delightfully
tender, elastic skins. Best of all were
the mini egg custard tarts, so unlike
the stodgy, stale variety found in
other establishments. Service was
sweetly attentive, the unobtrusive
tea refills much appreciated. A gem
of a restaurant.

Meal deals

Belgo Noord *72 Chalk Farm Road, NW1 8AN (7267 0718/www.belgo-restaurants.com).* Set lunch £6.50 1 course. **Map** p296. Belgian

In the area

Haché *24 Inverness Street, NW1 7HJ (7485 9100).* **Map** p296.
Lisboa Pâtisserie *4 Plender Street, NW1 0JP (7387 1782).* **Map** p296.
Nam An *14-16 Camden High Street, NW1 0JH (7383 7245).* **Map** p296.
Nando's *57-58 Chalk Farm Road, NW1 8AN (7424 9040).* **Map** p296.
Pizza Express *85 Parkway, NW1 7PP (7267 2600).* **Map** p296.
La Porchetta *74-77 Chalk Farm Road, NW1 8AN (7267 6822).* **Map** p296.
Strada *40-42 Parkway, NW1 7AH (7428 9653).* **Map** p296.
Wagamama *11 Jamestown Road, NW1 7BW (7428 0800).* **Map** p296.

Crouch End

La Bota

31 Broadway Parade, Tottenham Lane, N8 9DB (8340 3082/www.labota.co.uk). Finsbury Park tube/rail then 91, W7 bus. **Lunch served** noon-2.30pm Mon-Fri; noon-3pm Sat. **Dinner served** 6-11pm Mon-Thur; 6-11.30pm Fri, Sat. **Meals served** noon-11pm Sun. **Average** ££. Spanish

A blackboard full of promising specials complements an already extensive menu at this justifiably popular Spanish local. Padrón peppers, lightly blackened and salted, stimulated the taste buds for the meal to come. Calamares fritos in a light batter were cooked and seasoned to perfection, requiring nothing more than a sprinkling of lemon juice; and the rabbit stew was hearty and well prepared. The place was packed with a lively mix of families, friends and couples, all enjoying themselves amid the low-key decor of wooden tables, pale walls, posters, prints and Spanish knick-knacks. Stools at the bar cater to passers-by who fancy a light bite and a bottle of beer.

Satay Malaysia

10 Crouch End Hill, N8 8AA (8340 3286). Finsbury Park tube/rail then W7 bus. **Dinner served** 6-10.45pm Mon-Thur, Sun; 6-11.45pm Fri, Sat. **Average** ££. **Set dinner** £12-£14 per person (minimum 2). **No credit cards.** Malaysian

On one level, it's easy to see why this Chinese-Malay restaurant has become a staple of the Crouch End dining scene. The service is attentive but tactfully so, portions are hearty, and the selection of dishes is wide-ranging enough to please the fussiest of diners, with a decent range of set menus. Unfortunately, the food itself can be less than reliable. A recent meal opened with a desert-dry mixed satay starter, stumbled on through a main course of sambal prawns without any discernible flavour, and ended on a low note with a rubbery coconut pancake. The one outstanding dish was a tender and tasty beef curry – which proves that the kitchen is capable of better.

Meal deals

Les Associés *172 Park Road, N8 8JT (8348 8944/www.lesassocies.co.uk).* Set dinner (Mon-Fri) £12 2 courses, £15 3 courses. French
Bistro Aix *54 Topsfield Parade, Tottenham Lane, N8 8PT (8340 6346/www.bistroaix.co.uk).* Set dinner (Mon-Thur, Sun) £15 3 courses. French

Finchley

Burger Bar NEW

110 Regent's Park Road, N3 3JG (8371 1555). Finchley Central tube.

Masala Zone. See p207.

Meals served noon-midnight Mon-Thur; noon-11pm Sun. **Average** ££. **No credit cards.** Jewish

This kosher diner looks the part, with framed photos of 1960s America hanging above plain tables, and dark wooden benches outside. Portions are huge: 300g (11oz) of juicy beef burger in a bun filled with extras such as aubergine, fried egg, sweet potato or beetroot. Wraps (which come in pairs) are thin and chargrilled, with a filling of, perhaps, sliced minute steak or chicken anointed with sweet chilli sauce. The piles of chips are enormous. Veggies can have a portobello mushroom burger with a side salad of mixed leaves with avocado, red onions and pine nuts; children get chicken wings or nuggets, or a small burger and faux milkshake. Desserts include apple pie and a warm chocolate pud.

★ Khoai Café

362 Ballards Lane, N12 0EE (8445 2039). Woodside Park tube/82, 134 bus. **Lunch served** noon-3.30pm, **dinner served** 5.30-11.30pm daily. **Average** ££. **Set lunch** £5.45 1 course, £7.45 2 courses. Vietnamese

The airy interior of this colourful café (a sibling to the Crouch End original) is sleek and modern, and the food is flawlessly executed, from summer rolls that didn't skimp on prawns to fragrant minced beef rolled in betel leaves and chargrilled. The southern-style hu tiu (a Chinese/South-east Asian noodle soup made with pork broth) contained chicken, prawn, grilled fish cake and chives, and was delicate and soothing. Bun tom cang nuong goi xoai was the highlight: fat, butterflied tiger prawns fresh from the grill, topped with slivers of juicy mango and served with vermicelli noodles, crunchy carrot and cucumber, plus Vietnamese herbs and a piquant

nuoc cham sauce. It's a shame that desserts are bought in, as in all other respects this is a winner.

Orli

108 Regents Park Road, N3 3JG (8371 9222). Finchley Central tube. **Meals served** 8am-11pm Mon-Thur, Sun; 8am-4pm Fri. **Average** ££. **Unlicensed** no alcohol allowed. Jewish

The decor is unremarkable: plain dark tables and chairs, photos of the USA, unsubtle lighting. What brings in the punters is the all-day menu: omelettes, borekas (filled filo parcels) and danish pastries for breakfast, through to full evening dinners. In between there's freshly squeezed orange juice, coffees and an inviting selection of cakes. The cooking is at its best when simple: grilled salmon or sea bass (rather than the fish in cream sauce), or deep bowls of gutsy soup with fresh challah rolls. A 'bebe' starter salad featured creamy houmous with pickles and hard-boiled egg. The staff were amiable, agreeing to turn down the music and apologising for not having a ripe avocado.

Meal deals

Ottomans *118 Ballards Lane, N3 2DN (8349 9968).* Set lunch £5.95 2 courses. Turkish

In the area

ASK *Great North Leisure Park, Chaplin Square, N12 0GL (8446 0970).*
Nando's *Great North Leisure Park, Chaplin Square, N12 0GL (8492 8465).*
Zizzi *202-208 Regent's Park Road, N3 3HP (8371 6777).*

Finsbury Park

Los Guaduales

53 Stroud Green Road, N4 3EF (7561 1929). Finsbury Park tube/

rail. **Lunch served** noon-3pm, **dinner served** 6-11pm Mon-Fri. **Meals served** noon-11.30pm Sat, Sun. **Average** ££. **Map** p297. Colombian

A rainy January weeknight is never really the best time to gauge a restaurant's atmosphere, but a range of niggling issues soured a recent visit to Los Guaduales: skipping CDs, toilets without soap or hot water, and painfully slow service despite a lack of diners. A shame, as we've previously enjoyed the party vibe at this cheerful Colombian restaurant – pleasantly decked out in bamboo furnishings, framed tapestries of forest scenes and a few ethnic trinkets (pan pipes, pottery) – as much as the food. The latter was hit and miss: a chorizo starter was dried out, although another of garlic prawns was juicy and generous of portion; a main of spicy seafood stew was packed with prawns, squid and the biggest mussels we've ever seen, but our steak (served on a sizzling plate) was unpleasantly fatty. We'll put it down to an off night.

Jai Krishna

161 Stroud Green Road, N4 3PZ (7272 1680). Finsbury Park tube/rail. **Lunch served** noon-2pm, **dinner served** 5.30-11pm Mon-Sat. **Average** £. **Set meal** £6.95 1 course. **Unlicensed**. **Corkage** £1.25 wine, 30p beer. **No credit cards**. **Map** p297. Indian

The mix of polystyrene ceiling tiles and spearmint walls decked with posters of Krishna might not make it into *World of Interiors*, but this homely local's vegetarian cuisine remains a big draw – and there's plenty of it. Despite heeding advice that we were ordering too much, we were still filled up by our starter of patra (alvi leaves rolled in batter, sliced and served with tamarind sauce). Then came a special thali for two, with bhajis, tarka dhal, rice,

chapatis and a choice of two curries (chickpea curry was rich and mildly spicy, spinach panir a little watery). The fact that the ice-cream was nothing to write home about was rather academic: we couldn't have eaten more if we'd wanted to.

Le Rif NEW

172 Seven Sisters Road, N7 7PX (7263 1891). Finsbury Park tube/ rail. **Meals served** 8am-10.30pm Mon-Fri; 10am-10pm Sat, Sun. **Average** £. **Unlicensed** no alcohol allowed. **No credit cards**. **Map** p297. North African

This excellent Moroccan restaurant (appropriately located at the end of Medina Road) won't win any prizes for interior design – it's the standard N7 caff look scattered with trinkets from the souk – but it deserves high praise for its fine food. Staff are happy to steer you to the day's best dishes – on our last visit, fresh and flavoursome houmous served with vegetables and a pile of warm pitta, followed by a generously portioned chicken tagine served in a traditional terracotta pot. But it was lamb tagine that won the day: tender chunks of lamb gently sweetened with honey, prunes and cinnamon, for less than £5. To drink, there are fresh fruit smoothies and sweet mint tea, but no booze.

In the area

Nando's *106 Stroud Green Road, N4 3HB (7263 7447)*. **Map** p297.
La Porchetta *147 Stroud Green Road, N4 3PZ (7281 2892)*. **Map** p297.

Haringay

Antepliler

46 Grand Parade, Green Lanes, N4 1AG (8802 5588). Manor House tube/29 bus. **Meals served** noon-11.30pm daily. **Average** ££. Turkish

On a street famous for its Turkish cafés, Antepliler stays popular by having a more adventurous menu than its neighbours. The cooking is hearty and vigorous, and the diners mostly Turkish. It's a noisy and often hectic place, with a vaguely Ottoman feel: large mirrors, a high ceiling patterned in wood, a line of wall tiles decorated with complex patterns and chairs with unusually low backs. A starter of fıstık lahmacun (minced lamb 'pizza' on pide bread) was rather small, but powerfully flavoured with pistachio (fıstık). A main of soğon kebab – meatballs with grilled unskinned shallots and a pomegranate sauce – was served in a hot metal dish accompanied by fine pide and a side salad. Staff were helpful, but too few for such a busy venue.

La Viña

3 Wightman Road, N4 1RQ (8340 5400/www.la-vina.co.uk). Harringay rail/29, 341 bus. **Meals served** 5pm-midnight Mon-Sat. **Average** ££. Spanish

There's something enticing about the glow from La Viña's large windows on a dark night in north London; inside, kitsch Spanish landscapes and a cheerful crowd of loyal locals enliven plain wood furnishings. The choice of tapas and paella is extensive, if unadventurous. Prawns in garlic and wine were large and juicy, and we enjoyed the moist morcilla (Spanish blood sausage) and fresh grilled sardines, all washed down with a decent house Rioja. There were some off notes: a rubbery bounce to the squid, grit in the spinach and an eye-watering acidity to the dressed artichoke. But overall, this friendly little restaurant delivers a satisfying tapas experience; we eventually left with smiles on our faces and pleasantly full stomachs.

Highbury

Exquisito

167 Blackstock Road, N4 2JS (7359 9529). Arsenal tube/Finsbury Park tube/rail. **Dinner served** 5-11.30pm Mon-Fri. **Meals served** 11am-11.30pm Sat, Sun. **Average** £££. **Map** p297. Mexican

In a refreshing change to the typical Mexican restaurant penchant for putting a Latin twist on everything from drinks to toilet dispensers, Exquisito – set amid the bodegas and betting shops of Blackstock Road – goes no further than a couple of ponchos pinned to the walls and an inner bunting of terracotta tiles. The kitchen's insistence on breaking down culinary borders can have mixed results: duck fajitas would have been better with shredded rather than cubed meat, but pollo relleno (chicken stuffed with chilli and cheese on a bed of spiral fries) was bursting with flavour and built to satisfy a large appetite. Chorizo and garlic bread were delivered with a rustic flourish on wooden plates. A cheerful, charming place.

İznik

19 Highbury Park, N5 1QJ (7354 5697/www.iznik.co.uk). Highbury & Islington tube/rail/4, 19, 236 bus. **Lunch served** noon-3.30pm Mon-Fri; 11am-4pm Sat, Sun. **Dinner served** 6-11pm daily. **Average** ££. **Map** p297. Turkish

The interior is full of fascinating clutter, including a chain mail surcoat and helmet hanging inside the front door. Nor is the food quite what you'd expect: instead of the familiar grills, İznik has built its reputation by concentrating on Ottoman stews and baked dishes. A mixed meze was first rate and included patasea köftesi (lightly textured potato balls), small triangular meat börek with an interesting, dusty pastry texture, houmous, tarator (bread, walnut and garlic dip) and fried courgette patties. After such a pleasing start, we were surprised that the karni yarik (aubergine stuffed with lamb and vegetables) was rather bland, never previously a problem here. Fortunately, the grilled chicken İznik was up to standard, served with a dressed salad of lettuce, olives and pomegranate seeds.

Olive Tree

177A Blackstock Road (entrance on Mount Grove Road), N5 2LL (7503 5466). Arsenal tube/Finsbury Park tube/rail. **Dinner served** 6.30-11pm Tue-Sat. **Average** ££. **Set meze** £9.90 per person (minimum 2). **Map** p297. Greek

What this unassuming Greek taverna lacks in style and (on our midweek visit) customers, it more than makes up for in service. The Tree's ebullient mamma welcomes guests like long-lost relatives, and offers fantastically animated advice on the kitchen's finest mezedes. They don't disappoint: creamy melitzanosalata (aubergine purée) served with fluffy, own-made pitta, and hearty portions of tender lamb souvlaki accompanied by fragrant rice. The vibe was family-friendly, but for a more vivid atmosphere, visit at the weekend (although bear in mind that it's often booked solid for the hour before kick-off at the nearby Emirates Stadium) – or bring a gang and make your own party.

Yildiz

163 Blackstock Road, N4 2JS (7354 3899/www.yildizocakbasi.co.uk). Arsenal tube/Finsbury Park tube/rail. **Meals served** 11am-midnight daily. **Average** ££. **Set lunch** £7.50 2 courses incl soft drink. **Map** p297. Turkish

Set on a little parade just off Finsbury Park's main drag, Yildiz has been redecorated and now has cream walls adorned with small framed pictures and decorative plates. The meze selection is enticing, and a range of side dishes (grilled onion with pomegranate sauce and a terrific salad of sliced gherkin on our visit) accompany the mains, making starters largely unnecessary. Excellent quail was served with rice cooked just-so, and including slivers of vermicelli – a typically Turkish addition. İskender kebab was tender as well as tasty. Vegetarians are offered a choice of five mains served with rice, salad and bread; desserts are limited to baklava and ice-cream. Swift, unobtrusive staff added to our enjoyment.

In the area

Il Bacio Highbury *178-184 Blackstock Road, N5 1HA (7226 3339).* **Map** p297.

Highgate

Al Parco

2 Highgate West Hill, N6 6JS (8340 5900). Tufnell Park tube/Gospel Oak rail. **Meals served** 11am-10pm daily. **Average** ££. Pizza & pasta

Walkers coming off Hampstead Heath could do worse than pop in here for a generously portioned, thin-crust pizza fresh from the oven. Al Parco is a small, unassuming outfit turning a decent trade amid a clutter of books and bendy lamps, and walls dotted with old photos of Italian screen legends. The back section is an odd extension that feels like someone's conservatory, and overlooks a triangle of turf between the Heath and nearby houses. The pizzas are numerous – including a selection helpfully made without tomato sauce – and the likes of lasagne are available for diners looking to break the mould. When not twirling pizzas with

Roundhouse.
See p207.

commendable skill, the staff are polite and personable, if sometimes a little lackadaisical.

Bistro Laz NEW
1 Highgate West Hill, N6 6JS (8342 8355/www.bistrolazcafe.com). Tufnell Park tube/Gospel Oak rail. **Meals served** 7am-11pm daily. **Average** ££. International
This parkside spot may dish up full English breakfasts and classic caff grub of a morning, but come the evening it turns into a thriving local bistro with a menu mixing Turkish and European fare. The pavement tables are popular with couples and families in summer; the interior is cosy, with a model ship hanging from the ceiling, open brickwork and woven fabric banquettes – a little old-fashioned, perhaps, but good enough for a date if you're on a budget. A mixed meze platter featuring superb saksuka, cacik and rich houmous was followed with decent lamb and falafel pitta sandwiches served with salad and fries – all very filling. There's also a list of pasta and burger options.

Café Mozart
17 Swains Lane, N6 6QX (8348 1384). Gospel Oak rail/214, C2, C11, C12 bus. **Meals served** 9am-5pm Mon; 9am-10pm Tue-Sun. **Average** £. **Map** p298. Café
Though it's now run by the same people, Café Mozart is always as busy without quite reaching the same level of easy bonhomie as neighbouring Kalendar (*see p218*). As if to please its musical namesake, the café takes an old-fashioned Austrian approach to decor: rickety wood panels, rustic furniture and an old violin nailed to the wall for good measure. There's also an attractive spread of cakes: large slabs of sachertorte and chocolate slices aplenty are best shared, accompanied by mugs of decent coffee. Tiny tots can get a headstart in the habit of a lifetime with voguish babycinos. For the purist diner, sauerkraut, bratwurst and the like are all well executed, though specials such as tomato crêpes with spinach may be more tempting for those seeking a lighter lunch.

North

★ Kalendar

15A Swains Lane, N6 6QX (8348 8300). Gospel Oak rail/214, C2, C11, C12 bus. **Meals served** 8am-10pm Mon-Fri; 9am-10pm Sat, Sun. **Average** £. **Map** p298. Café

Café society on Swains Lane is ruled by Kalendar, the friendliest of the street's nosh shops and also the most popular: punters will hover expectantly if you're lucky enough to grab a sunny terrace table in the warmer months. Breakfast here is a joy, from artful eggs Benedict and grease-free variations on the full English to chunky cups of coffee made with beans from the Monmouth Coffee Company. Sandwiches are also expertly made – try the grilled halloumi with grated carrot and crunchy lettuce – and the deli counter serves a reliably delicious range of delights, from artisanal cheeses to tempting stacks of cakes bought in from Konditor and Cook.

Pavilion Café NEW

Highgate Woods, Muswell Hill Road, N10 3JN (8444 4777). Highgate tube. **Meals served** *Summer* 9am-9pm daily. *Winter* 9am-4pm daily. **Average** ££. Café

Wisteria and rose bushes provide a bucolic setting for this café in the middle of Highgate Woods. The printed menu, supplemented by a few blackboard specials, has a Mediterranean slant, with bowls of pasta and dishes such as pan-fried salmon on puy lentils. We opted for meze: fresh, warm falafel, grilled chorizo and a dip of butternut squash and hazelnuts (there were plenty more to choose from), all served with warm, spongy pitta bread. Kids have their own menu of goujons, pasta and the like; and the list of sweet things includes wheat-free lemon and polenta cake and chocolate brownie with ice-cream. Organic ingredients are frequently used, and drinkers can enjoy the likes of Pitfield Brewery beers and bottled Westons ciders.

In the area

dim t *1A Hampstead Lane, N6 4RS (8340 8800).*
Pizza Express *30 High Street, N6 5JG (8341 3434).*
Strada *4 South Grove, N6 6BS (8347 8686).*
Zizzi *1 Hampstead Lane, N6 4RS (8347 0090).*

Holloway

★ Tbilisi

91 Holloway Road, N7 8LT (7607 2536). Highbury & Islington tube/rail. **Dinner served** 6.30-11pm daily. **Average** ££. **Map** p297. Georgian

It's a mystery that Tbilisi isn't packed. It has a well-priced menu, stylish red decor and cheerful, chatty service. A mixed platter starter delivered spinach pkhali (a rich, intensely flavoured pâté made with pounded walnuts), beetroot (in a zingy walnut sauce) and fluffy khachapuri (flatbread). Georgian stews make ideal comfort food for chill winter nights; Tbilisi's include chakapuli (lamb in an intense, tarragon-infused plum sauce) and chakhokhbili (a rich chicken and tomato stew flavoured with ajika, a Georgian spice blend). Or, try the renowned chicken tabaka, flattened under a heavy lid, fried and served with walnut or plum sauce. From the good Georgian wines, we chose Kindzmarauli – its sweet blackberry flavours sit well with spicy fare.

Hornsey

Meal deals

Le Bistro *36 High Street, N8 7NX (8340 2116).* Set meal £12.50 2 courses, £14.50 3 courses. French

Islington

★ Afghan Kitchen

*35 Islington Green, N1 8DU
(7359 8019). Angel tube.* **Lunch
served** noon-3.30pm, **dinner
served** 5.30-11pm Tue-Sat.
Average £. No credit cards.
Map p299. Afghan

It's wise to relish the social benefits
of dining elbow to elbow with
complete strangers, as you're
unlikely to get more than a tired
smile from staff on busy weekends
at this popular haunt. Two tiny
floors are embellished with little
more than communal wooden tables
and gregariously fronded pot plants,
and the short menu offers just four
meat and four vegetarian dishes.
Ghorm-e sabzi (lamb and spinach
stew) was as rich and flavoursome
as its Iranian equivalent; lavand-e
murgh (chicken in yoghurt) subtly
combined creamy coolness with a
mild chilli kick. Prices are
ridiculously low (the priciest main is
less than twice that of seeded
Afghani bread), and the operation is
so original and invigorating that
you'll leave feeling culturally sated
as well as stuffed.

Candid Arts Café

*Candid Arts Trust, 3 Torrens
Street, EC1V 1NQ (7837 4237/
www.candidarts.com). Angel tube.*
Meals served noon-10pm Mon-
Sat; noon-5pm Sun. **Average ££.**
Map p299. Café

Despite a forbidding entranceway
illuminated by flickering strip
lighting, the café at this progressive
charity gallery boasts a suitably
bohemian feel – bolstered, on our
visit, by a harmonica tutorial taking
place in an adjacent room, nearby
conversations about Mikhail
Bulgakov, and backgammon being
played at a nearby table. Service
was less attentive than we'd have
liked, but the low-slung sofas and

candlelit surroundings helped create
a warm and welcoming atmosphere.
That said, the café remains a better
place to stop for lunch than dinner,
with a range of cakes, coffees and
teas that outweigh the merits of its
functional mains, including the likes
of roast chicken and grilled salmon
– both served with rice and salad –
and a vegetarian aubergine bake
that we found a tad undercooked.

Gallipoli Again

*120 Upper Street, N1 1QP (7359
1578/www.cafegallipoli.com). Angel
tube.* **Meals served** noon-11pm
Mon-Thur; noon-midnight Fri;
10.30am-midnight Sat; 10.30am-
midnight Sun. **Average ££. Set
lunch** £12.95 3 courses. **Set dinner**
£15.95 3 courses incl coffee. **Set
meze** £8.95 lunch, £10.95 dinner.
Map p299. Turkish

This Upper Street stalwart is a fine
example of a formula that ain't
broke and shouldn't be fixed. On any
night of the week you'll find the
place packed to bursting – there's
seemingly always room for one more
table in the cosy interior – and
buzzing with energy. The kitchen
churns out faultless mezedes
(squeaky halloumi, broad beans
with yoghurt, super fresh tabouleh),
generous kebabs and fine vegetarian
dishes to an appreciative local
crowd. It's not the place for an
intimate dinner á deux (Gallipoli
Bazaar at no.107 is a better bet for
those on dates), as the atmosphere
can border on the intrusively noisy:
flaming shots and dancing on the
tables are considered compulsory
birthday activities here.

Gem

*265 Upper Street, N1 2UQ (7359
0405/www.gemrestaurant.org.uk).
Angel tube/Highbury & Islington
tube/rail.* **Meals served** noon-
midnight Mon-Sat; noon-10.30pm
Sun. **Average ££. Set lunch**
£6.95 3 courses, £8.95 4 courses.

Breakfasts of champions

Breakfasts in London may be traditionally associated with physical rather than financial indulgence, but set your sights (and your budget) a little higher and you could find yourself breakfasting in a restaurant you wouldn't usually be able to afford dinner in.

Chief among such ventures is the **Dorchester Grill Room**, where the likes of smoked haddock kedgeree and eggs Benedict are served beneath a giant mural of a pensive, tartan-clad Scotsman. Equally grand is the cavernous, multi-domed brasserie of the **Wolseley** in Piccadilly, where a designated 'Head of Breakfast' oversees everything from pâtisserie baskets and omelettes Arnold Bennett (rich with cream and smoked haddock) to upmarket variations on the full English.

Those seeking an upper-class English spread without the ceremony will find what they're looking for at **Smiths of Smithfield**, which caters to both hungry commuters and hungover weekend warriors with superior bacon butties on thick crusty bread, and double bacon and fried egg toasties. Equally meaty options appear on the morning menu at **St John Bread & Wine** (Old Spot bacon sandwiches, devilled kidneys on toast), and the **Rivington Bar & Grill**, while the **Botanist** offers a menu of bloody marys – including one spiked with red meat jus – along with grilled kippers, sautéed cepes on toast and, of course, the full works.

Finally, for an international breakfast with real flair, visit the **Providores & Tapa Room**, which offers such oddities as paprika roast potato, feta and edamame tortillas, and banana and pecan-stuffed French toast with bacon. The most important meal of the day? It is now.

Botanist *7 Sloane Square, SW1W 8EE (7730 0077/www. thebotanistonsloanesquare.com).* Breakfast served 8-11.30am Mon-Fri; 9-11.30am Sat, Sun. **Map** p275.
Dorchester Grill Room
The Dorchester, 53 Park Lane, W1A 2HJ (7629 8888/www.the dorchester.com). Breakfast served 7-10.30am Mon-Fri; 8-11am Sat, Sun. **Map** p274.
Providores & Tapa Room
109 Marylebone High Street, W1U 4RX (7935 6175/www.the providores.co.uk). Breakfast served (Tapa Room) 9-11.30am Mon-Fri; 10am-3pm Sat, Sun. **Map** p277.
Rivington Bar & Grill *28-30 Rivington Street, EC2A 3DZ (7729 7053/www.rivingtongrill. co.uk).* Breakfast served 8-11am Mon-Fri. **Map** p271.
St John Bread & Wine
94-96 Commercial Street, E1 6LZ (7251 0848/www.stjohnbread andwine.com). Breakfast served 9-11am Mon-Fri; 10-11am Sat, Sun. **Map** p271.
Smiths of Smithfield
67-77 Charterhouse Street, EC1M 6HJ (7251 7950/www.smithsof smithfield.co.uk). Breakfast served 7am-4.45pm Mon-Fri; 10am-4.45pm Sat; 9.30am-4.15pm Sun. **Map** p270.
Wolseley *160 Piccadilly, W1J 9EB (7499 6996/www.thewolseley. com).* Breakfast served 7-11.30am Mon-Fri; 8-11.30am Sat, Sun. **Map** p269.

Set dinner £9.95 3 courses, £12.95 4 courses. **Map** p299. Kurdish

The decoration at this popular, unpretentious Kurdish restaurant is agricultural, with authentic farm implements suspended from walls and ceiling. Our small portion of complimentary stuffed qatme bread was as outstanding as ever. Starters of moist mücver courgette fritters were tasty, if slightly oily; kısır (salad of chopped parsley, tomatoes, onions and crushed wheat) was good, but lacked the piquant freshness that we've previously relished here. In contrast, a main course of bıldırcın – wonderfully tender and flavoursome grilled quail with a fresh chopped salad – was above reproach. The six vegetarian mains are mostly based on aubergine; the kebab version was enjoyable, if slightly bland. A small portion of honeyed baklava with ice-cream made the ideal finish. The attentive service is to be cherished.

Maghreb

189 Upper Street, N1 1RQ (7226 2305/www.maghrebrestaurant.co.uk). Angel tube/Highbury & Islington tube/rail. **Meals served** 6-11.30pm daily. **Average** ££. **Set dinner** (Mon-Thur, Sun) £10.95 2 courses, £13.95 3 courses. **Map** p299.
North African

The decor of bright yellow walls, red silk lanterns and red and blue upholstery at Maghreb manages to resist cliché, and chef-owner Mohamed Faraji offers some interesting modern variations of traditional Moroccan dishes. Crab and prawn tabouleh had fresh, clean accents of parsley and lemon, but the pièces de resistance were smoky grilled merguez, innovatively served with earthy puy lentils. The sauce in the lamb tagine with prunes wasn't as rich and gloopy as we'd have liked, but was tasty nonetheless; rabbit tagine with raisins and pears was less successful. Desserts include

Moroccan pastries, pancakes and a dark chocolate and pistachio terrine, while the Moroccan wine list features Les Coteaux de l'Atlas: a full-bodied, spicy red that is also the first Moroccan premier cru wine.

Mem & Laz

8 Theberton Street, N1 0QX (7704 9089/www.memlaz.com). Angel tube/Highbury & Islington tube/rail. **Meals served** 11.30am-11.30pm Mon-Thur, Sun; 11.30am-midnight Fri, Sat. **Average** ££. **Set meal** (11.30am-6pm) £6.95 2 courses, £8.95 3 courses. **Map** p299.
Turkish

Mem & Laz's founding father Memet is expanding his property along Theberton Street, and soon the lovely, throbbing sea cabin that is Mem & Laz – hung with coloured lanterns and West End posters – will cover a glorious 400sq ft. There's a pile of hot bread, shot through with sun-dried tomatoes or prunes, before you even pick up the menu. Whole sardines marinated in lemon juice and coriander are an engaging first encounter, and the seafood casserole is a broad sweep across the ocean bed, set in a delicate tomato sauce and served in an iron skillet. Chargrilled chicken breast, served in a thick honey and mustard sauce, tasted more like a buttery korma than anything even vaguely Mediterranean, but was deliciously moreish all the same.

★ Le Mercury

140A Upper Street, N1 1QY (7354 4088/www.lemercury.co.uk). Angel tube/Highbury & Islington tube/rail. **Meals served** noon-1am Mon-Sat; noon-11.30pm Sun. **Average** ££. **Map** p299.
French

Dripping candles cast a cosy light around this delightful French restaurant, frequently packed but with another dining room on the first floor. The menu follows the classic French bistro theme, but there are a few surprise combos thrown in. Starters such as chèvre chaud, moules marinière and foie gras are complemented by less Gallic fare such as deep-fried squid. Mains included a pleasing lamb shank with rosemary jus (the entrecôte grillée was average by comparison), as well as seared mackerel with beetroot, fennel and lime pickle, and roast pork with black pudding. Desserts included the ubiquitous crème brûlée, and roast rhubarb with basil ice-cream. An imaginative and affordable selection of dishes, cooked to a reasonable standard, and with wine from £10.45 per bottle.

★ Ottolenghi NEW

287 Upper Street, N1 2TZ (7288 1454/www.ottolenghi.co.uk). Angel tube/Highbury & Islington tube/rail. **Meals served** 8am-10.30pm Mon-Sat; 9am-7pm Sun. **Average** £££. **Map** p299. Café

Ottolenghi is more than just an inviting bakery. Behind the pastries, cakes and biscuits piled in the window is a prim deli counter heaving with lush salads and an inventive array of cold dishes like french beans with red onions, chervil and hazelnuts, or roasted sweet potatoes with avocado, rocket and pistachios in an orange cumin dressing. For dinner, the menu adds starter-sized hot dishes to mix and match, but the canteen-style central table, slow-footed service and bright white decor are not for special occasions; the place is better suited to sprightly suppers. We loved our combinations of mouth-watering guinea fowl with sweetcorn risotto cake, and well-seasoned roast lamb with spiced aubergine. Unmissable.

S&M Café

4-6 Essex Road, N1 8LN (7359 5361/www.sandmcafe.co.uk). Angel tube. **Meals served** 7.30am-11pm Mon-Fri; 8.30am-

11pm Sat; 8.30am-10.30pm Sun. **Average** ££. **Map** p299. Café

Famously preserved by S&M founder Kevin Finch, the decor of the former Alfredo's café is a mix of periods, with panelling, lairy blue Formica tables and tiny red leather chairs. It's cramped but jovial, and efficient staff handle busy periods well, taking names and honouring tables so customers don't have to queue. The all-day breakfasts are as popular as the eponymous sausage and mash, while the blackboard promotes Sunday lunch-type meals. On our visit the rather thin onion gravy and serving of bubble and squeak were not hot, unlike the wild boar and calvados sausages they accompanied, but we enjoyed the chicken and asparagus bangers partnered by tasty potato, parsnip and turnip mash. Drinks include freshly squeezed orange juice, mugs of cappuccino and a floral-medicinal dandelion and burdock.

Sedir

4 Theberton Street, N1 0QX (7226 5489/www.sedirrestaurant.co.uk). Angel tube/Highbury & Islington tube/rail. **Meals served** 11.30am-11.30pm Mon-Thur, Sun; 11.30am-midnight Fri, Sat. **Average** ££. **Set lunch** (11.30am-5.30pm) £6.95-£7.95 2 courses. **Set meal** £18.95 per person (minimum 2) 3 courses. **Map** p299. Turkish

In good weather, staff put tables on the narrow pavement outside; indoors, the dark red walls are dominated by enormous prints of European paintings of Ottoman bazaars and harems. Sedir's extensive menu has become less exclusively Turkish and more generically Mediterranean, but the core remains Turkish, and the dishes we ordered were first rate. We started with a thickly rolled spinach pancake in a rich tomato sauce, and delicately fried Albanian liver. To follow, sea bass was grilled

in an authentic Turkish manner, yet came with mashed potato, broccoli and runner beans that, while not traditional, went well. An enjoyable dining experience, though it would have been improved by a little more space between tables.

Viet Garden

207 Liverpool Road, N1 1LX (7700 6040/www.vietgarden.co.uk). Angel tube/Highbury & Islington tube/rail. **Lunch served** noon-3.30pm daily. **Dinner served** 5.30-11pm Mon-Thur, Sun; 5.30-11.30pm Fri, Sat. **Average** ££. **Set lunch** (Mon-Fri) £6.50 2 courses. **Map** p299. Vietnamese
White and airy, gently elevated above street level, and with one long window perching you above Islington's back alleys, Viet Garden is a lovely space, but navigating its complex menu can be a game of chance. The Hanoi beef you order may taste of takeaway sweet-and-sour sauce, while your friend, by some lucky stab in the dark, gets the delicate tarragon chicken with a paper-thin breadcrumb coating and a mysterious, aromatic tang. A starter of salt and pepper fish, liberally laced with raw dill, was deliciously dry yet succulent, but battered squid, accompanied by a thimbleful of salt, lined the stomach the way a battered sausage might before a big night out. Still, a risk worth taking at least once.

Zigni House

330 Essex Road, N1 3PB (7226 7418/www.zignihouse.com). Angel tube/38, 56, 73, 341 bus. **Meals served** noon-midnight Mon-Thur, Sun; noon-1.30am Fri, Sat. **Average** ££. **Set buffet** (7-10pm Fri, Sat) £15 incl drink. **Map** p299. Eritrean
There's a childish sense of fun about a restaurant that allows you to eat the tablecloth that the food is served on: the injera pancake upon which Eritrean cooks set out their

La Bota. See p211.

wares becomes hearty stuff once the sauces have got into the grain, and a pleasure to tuck into. Proprietor Tsige Haile is a heroine back home – she wrote the first Eritrean cookbooks – and her restaurant bridges the gap between eaterie and chill-out room with its painted tables and zebra rugs. Our falafel starter seemed strangely meagre, and main courses mingle together, so make sure you choose contrasting stews; zigni derho is fiery, with a jerk chicken edge, while alicha lamb is mellowed by lentils. The weekend buffet offers the best of all worlds.

Meal deals

Fish Shop *360-362 St John Street, EC1V 4NR (7837 1199/www.thefish shop.net). Set lunch £10.50-£13.50 2-3 courses. Set dinner £17 2 courses.* **Map** p299. Fish

Isarn *119 Upper Street, N1 1QP (7424 5153). Set lunch £5.90 3 courses.* **Map** p299. Thai

Med Kitchen *370 St John Street, EC1V 4NN (7278 1199/www.med kitchen.co.uk). Set meal (noon-7pm Mon-Fri) £13.50 2 courses.* **Map** p299. Mediterranean

Med Kitchen *334 Upper Street, N1 0PB (7226 7916/www.medkitchen. co.uk). Set lunch (noon-5pm Mon-Fri) £13.50 2 courses.* **Map** p299. Mediterranean

Sabor *108 Essex Road, N1 8LX (7226 5551/www.sabor.co.uk). Set lunch (Sat, Sun), set dinner (Tue-Thur, Sun) £15 2 courses, £17.50 3 courses.* **Map** p299. Colombian

In the area

ASK *Business Design Centre, 52 Upper Street, N1 0PN (7226 8728).* **Map** p299.

Banana Tree Canteen *412-416 St John Street, EC1V 4NJ (7278 7565).* **Map** p299.

Breakfast Club *31 Camden Passage, N1 8EA (7226 5454).* **Map** p299.

Carluccio's Caffè *305-307 Upper Street, N1 2TU (7359 8167).* **Map** p299.

Fine Burger Company *330 Upper Street, N1 2XQ (7359 3026).* **Map** p299.

Gallipoli Bazaar *107 Upper Street, N1 1QN (7226 5333).* **Map** p299.

Gallipoli Café Bistro *102 Upper Street, N1 1QN (7359 0630).* **Map** p299.

Giraffe *29-31 Essex Road, N1 2SA (7359 5999).* **Map** p299.

Hamburger Union *341 Upper Street, N1 0PB (7359 4436).* **Map** p299.

Miso *67 Upper Street, N1 0NY (7226 2212).* **Map** p299.

Nando's *324 Upper Street, N1 2XQ (7288 0254).* **Map** p299.

Pizza Express *335 Upper Street, N1 0PB (7226 9542).* **Map** p299.

La Porchetta *141 Upper Street, N1 1QY (7288 2488).* **Map** p299.

Sangria *88 Upper Street, N1 0PN (7704 5253). Branch of Jamón Jamón.* **Map** p299.

Strada *105-106 Upper Street, N1 1QN (7226 9742).* **Map** p299.

Wagamama *N1 Centre, 39 Parkfield Street, N1 0PS (7226 2664).* **Map** p299.

Yo! Sushi *N1 Centre, 39 Parkfield Street, N1 0PS (7359 3502).* **Map** p299.

Kentish Town

Mario's Café

6 Kelly Street, NW1 8PH (7284 2066). Camden Town tube/ Kentish Town tube/rail. **Meals served** 7.30am-4pm Mon-Sat. **Average** £. **Unlicensed** no alcohol allowed. **No credit cards.** **Map** p298. Café
This tiny neighbourhood café is generally full to bursting point, but that's part of its charm. Run by the affable Mario (on first-name terms with most of his customers), its tables fill up with regulars squeezed together to peruse the papers,

complain about the football and linger for ages over cups of tea. The menu is a mix of Italian caffè and Brit greasy spoon, with breakfast options ranging from ciabatta with prosciutto and poached egg to classic fry-ups mopped away with enormous hunks of toast. Lunchtimes bring no-nonsense caff-style specials (lamb with roast spuds, say), toasted focaccia and proper home-made pasta; the spinach and ricotta tortellini, handmade by Mario's mum, is simply not to be missed.

Queen of Sheba

12 Fortress Road, NW5 2EU (7284 3947/www.thequeenofsheba. co.uk). Kentish Town tube/rail. **Meals served** 1-11.30pm Mon-Sat; 1-10.30pm Sun. **Average** ££. **Map** p298. Ethiopian

The aroma of incense billows out to greet you as you enter this restaurant, its dark interior a funky clash of ancient and modern, with Amharic crucifixes on walls and a pair of high-booted, Amazonian waitresses – an exotic combination that has won it an enthusiastic western following. The menu features modestly priced classics (spicy stews and puréed pulses served on spongy injera bread), a few in-house inventions, and a range of raw meat dishes (kitfo is the Ethiopian equivalent of steak tartare). With a small kitchen handling what tends to be a heavy flood of orders, this isn't the place for a snappy meal, so get your orders in smartish, order an Ethiopian beer, and slowly savour the experience.

In the area

Nando's *227-229 Kentish Town Road, NW5 2JU (7424 9363).* **Map** p298.
Pizza Express *187 Kentish Town Road, NW1 8PD (7267 0101).* **Map** p298.

Muswell Hill

Feast on the Hill

46 Fortis Green Road, N10 3HN (8444 4957). East Finchley or Highgate tube then 43, 134 bus. **Meals served** 8am-5pm Mon-Sat; 9am-5pm Sun. **Average** ££. Café

Wooden furniture and Jack Vettriano prints make for an innocuous interior at this Muswell Hill institution, which now bears the logo of Feast, the long-associated deli next door. The format remains the same: all-day breakfasts and a short lunch menu served from noon to 5pm, plus a new range of kids' options. Breakfasts include the classics, as well as olive and chorizo frittata with herb salad (a fish pie lunch seemed ordinary by comparison). The drinks list caters to all, with smoothies, teas and coffees, and half a dozen red and white wines available by the glass or bottle. Finish with a tasty fruit crumble or baked cheesecake, and browse through the papers provided.

Sushi 101 NEW

Raglan Hotel, 8-12 Queens Avenue, N10 3NR (8883 6274/www.sushi 101.co.uk). Highgate tube then 43, 134 bus/Finsbury Park tube then W7 bus. **Meals served** 11am-10.30pm daily. **Average** ££. **Set lunch** £6-£7. Japanese

Behind the Victorian features of the Raglan Hotel, Sushi 101 purveys an appetising line in new-style Japanese: mains such as miso-smeared lamb cutlets, and desserts like green tea ice-cream paired with still-hot mango tempura. However, the basics don't always pass muster. Chutoro (medium fatty tuna sashimi) was off-colour and off-flavour on our most recent visit. Fancier items concocted by an ex-Nobu chef work better. Mango and crabmeat maki were satisfyingly

Gem. See p219.

soft, fresh and skilfully constructed. The L-shaped restaurant provides table and counter dining and is smart – though shiny black surfaces, white vinyl cuboid seating and a 1980s pop soundtrack make for an oddly retro experience. The fish tank set into one wall must be a child-pleaser, but couples and groups of business people appear to be the norm at lunchtime.

Toff's

38 Muswell Hill Broadway, N10 3RT (8883 8656). Highgate tube then 43, 134 bus. **Meals served** 11.30am-10pm Mon-Sat. **Average** ££. **Set meal** (11.30am-5pm) £5.95-£7.95 1 course incl tea or coffee. Fish & chips

Toff's has a loyal following, with customers queuing for takeaways as well as downstairs tables. We were shepherded upstairs to a wood-panelled dining room with white paper on the tables and sepia pictures of the fish trade on the walls. The blackboard promotes alternatives to cod, including trout, halibut, squid and scampi. A fish cake starter was

crisply crumbed, the interior a fine paste generously flavoured with parsley; battered haddock and rock were beautifully fresh (matzo and grilled options are options), but the chips were greasy. Honest-to-goodness coleslaw, made in-house, outshone the bright but bland mushy peas. The old-fashioned puddings are huge, and service is effusive and kind. Finish with refreshing mint tea or Greek-style coffee.

Meal deals

Bakko *172-174 Muswell Hill Broadway, N10 3SA (8883 1111/ www.bakko.co.uk).* Set lunch (Mon-Fri) £8.90 3 courses. Turkish

In the area

ASK *43 Muswell Hill Broadway, N10 3AH (8365 2833).*
Fine Burger Company *256 Muswell Hill Broadway, N10 3SH (8815 9292).*
Giraffe *348 Muswell Hill Broadway, N10 1DJ (8883 4463).*
Maison Blanc *61 Muswell Hill Broadway, N10 3HA (8883 7520).*

Pizza Express *290 Muswell Hill Broadway, N10 2QR (8883 5845).*
La Porchetta *256 Muswell Hill Broadway, N10 1DE (8883 1500).*

Palmers Green

Rimini

314 Green Lanes, N13 5TT (8882 8880). Palmers Green rail. **Lunch served** noon-2.30pm Tue-Fri. **Dinner served** 5.30-11pm Tue-Thur; 5.30pm-midnight Fri. **Meals served** 1pm-midnight Sat; 1.30-10pm Sun. **Average** ££. Pizza & pasta

Rimini ticks all the boxes for the attributes a good neighbourhood restaurant should have. Popular, friendly and reliable, it's the sort of place families and couples can return to again and again, safe in the knowledge that the food won't disappoint or the surroundings change. The pizzas are thin, crisp and generous in size, while the range of specials includes the likes of breaded monkfish with prawns. Small touches add to the experience:

starters of chicken liver were appropriately pink on the inside, garlic bread properly pungent, and lemon sorbet sharp and refreshing. The mainly Italian staff are always on the ball and seldom forget a face, and are happy to wash out animal-themed ice-cream bowls for the kids to take home with them.

Southgate

La Paella

9 Broadway, N14 6PS (8882 7868/www.lapaellatapasbar.com). Southgate tube. **Lunch served** noon-3pm, **dinner served** 6-11pm Tue-Sun. **Average** ££. Spanish

La Paella satisfies a huge swathe of local Hispanophiles with its typical Catalan interior and attention to culinary detail – from bread that's part-baked on the premises to a choice of own-made desserts. In between is a good range of tapas including albondigas (meatballs in a spicy tomato sauce) and octopus, though it's the eponymous paella that tends to grace most tables, packed with fresh ingredients and with a heart-warming Mediterranean richness that defies its suburban setting (you're best off calling ahead and ordering half an hour in advance). Add to this a family-friendly midweek vibe and a more raucous party atmosphere on the weekends – sometimes with live music – and it's not hard to see why the place continues to thrive.

In the area
Pizza Express *94 Chaseside, N14 5PH (8886 3300).*

Stamford Hill

Spark Café

White Lodge Mansion, Springfield Park, E5 9EF (8806 0444/

North

www.sparkcafe.co.uk). *Stamford Hill or Stoke Newington rail/253, 254 bus.* **Meals served** *Summer* 10am-6pm daily. *Winter* 10am-4pm daily. **Average £. No credit cards.** Café The Grade-II listed White Lodge Mansion that houses this child-friendly park café is a magnificent building best enjoyed outdoors at the plastic tables in its garden. The café has a homely charm, and attracts legions of families with toddlers and pets in tow. The focus is on healthy food, including freshly prepared hot and cold sandwiches, and delicious meze platters – ours was bursting with a three-bean and chickpea salad, tabouleh and houmous, and the 'Absolute Med' plate brought fresh stuffed vine leaves, falafels and a summery tomato salad. Own-made carrot cake was slightly too sweet, but the banana cake was terrific. Staff are accommodating and mellow: as they say themselves, 'a tranquil atmosphere is conducive to good digestion'.

Tufnell Park

Lalibela
137 Fortess Road, NW5 2HR (7284 0600). Tufnell Park tube/134 bus. **Dinner served** 6pm-midnight daily. **Average ££. Map p298.** Ethiopian
Photos of Emperor Haile Selassie, examples of national costume and wall friezes of the Queen of Sheba story make one of London's oldest Ethiopian restaurants feel rather like an ethnographic museum. Still, Lalibela is a fixture for both Ethiopian expats and Europeans who appreciate the Horn of Africa's traditional cuisine. Awaze tibs (sautéed lamb) and tsom bayentu (a melange of vegetarian food), ritually arranged in small piles on a sourdough base, were fresh, tasty and promptly served – although the injera, made from a mix of grains

rather than the classic, hard-to-locate tef, was less sour than it should be. Food is served on traditional low tables, and diners ordering coffee at the end can luxuriate in the extended Ethiopian ceremony.

Turnpike Lane

Penang Satay House
9 Turnpike Lane, N8 0EP (8340 8707). Turnpike Lane tube/29 bus. **Dinner served** 6-11pm Mon-Thur, Sun; 6pm-midnight Fri, Sat. **Average ££. Set dinner** £12-£14.50 per person (minimum 2) 3 courses. Malaysian
Stuck on an unpromising stretch of Turnpike Lane, and with a rather dated interior, Penang Satay House isn't immediately appetising. But this unpretentious Malaysian restaurant is what budget eating is all about: good grub at great prices. Not a single dish disappointed on our last visit, with orange chicken and melt-in-the-mouth beef rendang among the highlights. Every element of the cooking showed attention to detail, from the mixed fried rice to the piquant peanut sauce, and portions were generous enough to make chomping our way through the £14.50 set menu a pleasurable struggle. Staff were welcoming and efficient; even though the place was busy, we were encouraged to linger over a glass or two of highly drinkable house wine.

Winchmore Hill

In the area
Pizza Express *701 Green Lanes, N21 3RS (8364 2992).*

Wood Green

In the area
Nando's *Hollywood Green, Redvers Road, N22 6EN (8889 2936).*

Belsize Park

Oliver's Village Café

92 Belsize Lane, NW3 5BE (7813 0048). Belsize Park tube. **Meals served** 8am-5pm Mon-Fri; 9am-4pm Sat, Sun. **Average** £. **No credit cards.** Map p300. Café
A short skip from the boutiques of Belsize village, this cosy café does brunches, lunches and afternoon teas in a 1950s-style setting. Windows are lined with pretty flowerpots and cupcakes, the metal counter topped with a marvellous array of sponges; breakfasts range from full English to cinnamon french toast and pain au chocolat served with steaming continental coffee. There's a daily lunch specials board listing tasty soups and dishes such as homity pie and pasta bake, as well as sandwiches, paninis and cakes if you're after a light bite. When the sun is shining, pink-patterned tables and garden chairs offer airy seating in the pleasingly plant-filled courtyard.

★ Zara

11 South End Road, NW3 2PT (7794 5498). Belsize Park tube/ Hampstead Heath rail. **Meals served** noon-11.30pm daily. **Average** £££. Map p300. Turkish
There's a relaxed and cosy feel to Zara, and its food is excellent: this is the kind of spot where you could happily prolong your meal over a leisurely dessert or Turkish coffee. Inside, cushioned benches run along walls decorated with Turkish paintings, patterned tiles and photos; in summer, the glass front opens up and tables are set out on the wide pavement. Mixed meze were served with first-rate pide, and included handsome sigara böreği, beautifully textured egg-shaped falafel, a rich kısır, cacik and houmous. Grilled sea bream with salad was superlative, and külbastı

– yielding, thin fillets of grilled lamb with oregano – equally good, and accompanied by salad and basmati rice. The staff were exceptionally helpful.

In the area

ASK *216 Haverstock Hill, NW3 2AE (7433 3896).* Map p300.
Gourmet Burger Kitchen *200 Haverstock Hill, NW3 2AG (7443 5335).* Map p300.
Pizza Express *194A Haverstock Hill, NW3 2AJ (7794 6777).* Map p300.
Tapeo *177 Haverstock Hill, NW3 4QS (7483 4242).* Branch of Jamón Jamón. Map p300.
Tootsies Grill *196-198 Haverstock Hill, NW3 2AG (7431 3812).* Map p300.

Brent Cross

In the area

Carluccio's Caffè *Brent Cross Shopping Centre, NW4 3FN (8203 6844).*
Wagamama *Brent Cross Shopping Centre, NW4 3FN (8202 2666).*

Golders Green

L'Artista

917 Finchley Road, NW11 7PE (8458 1775). Golders Green tube. **Meals served** noon-midnight daily. **Average** ££. Italian
For over two decades, Golders Green institution L'Artista has been scenting the air around the station with its wafts of fried garlic – and be warned, its famous pizza garlic breads are strictly for confirmed garlic lovers. The menu overflows with decent Italian classics, but L'Artista is at its best with a crisp pizza and a drinkable bottle of red. The portions are extremely generous (you'll struggle to finish three courses), and don't be misled by the photos on the dessert menu:

the tiramisu is own-made and deliciously alcoholic. Every ten minutes or so, the dining experience is enhanced as a train passing overhead rattles the photos of '80s celebrities that adorn the wall. One day Phil Collins will fall.

Beyoglu
1031 Finchley Road, NW11 7ES (8455 4884). Golders Green tube. **Meals served** noon-11pm daily. **Average ££. Set buffet** £10 per person (minimum 2). **Set dinner** £12-£13.75 3 courses incl coffee. Turkish

The grill has been moved away from the door to make the interior more roomy, and Beyoglu has recently introduced a £10 lunch deal: this offers access to a self-service cold meze bar (houmous, kısır, cacik and good pide, plus beetroot and potato salads), followed by a main course and coffee or tea. Chicken shish was excellent – large chunks of meat served with rice and a fresh salad – but although the kaburga ribs tasted good, they were chewy in the centre and scorched on the outside – quite a disappointment, given that on previous visits we've found the kitchen's output to be uniformly good. Still, the service is reliably friendly, which makes dining at Beyoglu an enjoyable affair.

Carmelli
126-128 Golders Green Road, NW11 8HB (8455 2074/www.carmelli. co.uk). Golders Green tube. **Meals served** 6.30am-midnight Mon-Thur; 6.30am-1hr before sabbath Fri; 1hr after sabbath Sat-midnight Sun. **Average £. Unlicensed** no alcohol allowed. **No credit cards.** Jewish

Within London's Jewish community, Carmelli is an enduringly and rightfully popular purveyor of quality food. Quite how they makes their bagels so crispy on the outside yet so soft on the inside has baffled the minds of many rabbinical scholars, but it's probably the main reason why Jews are known to visit the place more frequently than the synagogue. You can't go wrong with a smoked salmon and cream cheese bagel, but you'd also do well to try the borekas (filo pastry with various fillings), or take home a chollah or rye bread. On a Saturday night you'll have to fight your way through a dense throng – and bear in mind that during Passover, the bread is unleavened.

Chopstick NEW
119 Golders Green Road, NW11 8HR (8455 7766). Golders Green tube. **Meals served** noon-midnight Mon-Thur, Sun; 6pm-5am Sat. **Average ££. Set meal** £15.99 3 courses incl soft drink. **No credit cards.** Chinese (kosher)

Chopstick has Chinese staff, red lanterns and – apart from the absence of pork – a menu typical of many Soho noodle bars. Most starters and many of the chicken dishes arrive in batter (though many are immersed in sweet, bright sauces); thinly sliced steak comes in a peppery sauce; and vegetarians will be pleased to find curried and stir-fried veg here, as well as crispy seaweed and edamame (soy beans in their pods). The set menus are popular with hungry teenagers – though parents might want to avoid the potato wedges and caramelised chicken wings, and could well prefer a pot of green tea to the insipid sorbets. Don't miss the delectable chocolate fritters for dessert.

Coby's Café & Flowers
115A Golders Green Road, NW11 8HR (3209 5049). Golders Green tube. **Meals served** noon-midnight Mon-Thur; 8am-1pm Fri; 1hr after sabbath-2am Sat; 10am-midnight Sun. **Average ££. Set breakfast** £6.80 1 course incl soft drink. **Unlicensed** no alcohol allowed. Jewish

A café that doubles up as a florist may sound perfect for a romantic lunch, but Coby's isn't an amorous sort of place: the rattle of tube trains reminds you every five minutes that you're eating beneath a railway arch. The menu is perhaps a little too varied, with Jerusalem toasts and falafels jostling for space next to pasta dishes, crêpes and pizzas; still, order carefully and you'll be pleasantly surprised. The melwach (Yemenite pastry) is baked on the premises and comes with a delicious, fiery sauce. There's no alcohol to wash it down with, but the mango smoothies are freshly made and great value. Keep an eye on the expensive extras, though – we weren't particularly enamoured by the prospect of paying £2 for a Nescafé or £3.60 for oven chips.

Daniel's Bagel Bakery

12-13 Hallswelle Parade, Finchley Road, NW11 0DL (8455 5826). Golders Green tube. **Meals served** 7am-9pm Mon-Wed, Sun; 7am-10pm Thur; 7am-1hr before sabbath Fri. **Average £. No credit cards.** Jewish

Carmelli (*see p231*) may be the most renowned purveyor of bagels in north-west London, but those in the know would argue that the real pinnacle of bagel greatness lies slightly further north, at Daniel's. This place has been a surefire hit for many years, making a variety of seeded loaves, rolls, crumbly croissants encrusted with Marcona almonds, and a nice line in treats for the kids – from mini bagels to 'his and hers' bootee-shaped meringues. It goes without saying that there's a surfeit of smoked salmon; this being the age of globalisation, Daniel's even serves it in sushi form. It's worth trying a loaf of chollah, the Jewish sabbath bread, which is made with egg and could be a softer, savoury cousin of brioche.

Din Café

816 Finchley Road, NW11 6XL (8731 8103/www.dincafe.co.uk). Golders Green tube. **Meals served** 8am-11pm Mon-Thur; 8am-5pm Fri, Sat; 9.30am-11pm Sun. **Average ££. Café**

Temple Fortune isn't the obvious place to seek out Mediterranean café culture, but with the advent of Din Café – an establishment blessed with outdoor seating, a sociable, relaxed atmosphere and simple, well-made food – that state of affairs may well be changing. We were impressed by the Boerewars roll, which was filled with a lightly spiced lamb and beef sausage as dark and rich as venison, and the fresh and chunky fruit salad. The lime green walls might not be to everyone's taste, but it certainly brightens the interior almost as much as the friendly and personable South African owners. They like to change and adapt their menu, so expect new dishes – especially now they've started opening for dinner.

★ Dizengoff's

118 Golders Green Road, NW11 8HB (8458 7003/www.dizengoff kosherrestaurant.co.uk). Golders Green tube. **Meals served** 11am-midnight Mon-Thur, Sun; 11am-1hr before sabbath Fri; 1hr after sabbath-midnight Sat. **Average £££. Jewish**

It's easy to see why Dizengoff's is such a long-standing favourite among its hard-to-please local clientele. Steaming bowls of chicken soup are ferried on to packed tables by hassled but friendly staff, and the whole scene is overlooked by canvas-mounted photographs of Tel Aviv. There's a huge range of dishes on offer, and grilled meats are a house speciality. While the main courses and specials can be a bit pricey, you can make your own value meal here by

Brew House. See p236.

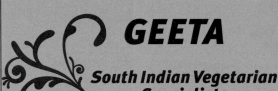

combining several side dishes together – try the chopped liver, vine leaves, houmous and tabouleh. The falafels are perfect: brown and crisp on the outside, yielding to green fluffiness within. Finish off with a fresh mint tea and a sweet and sticky baklava.

Entrecote NEW

102 Golders Green Road, NW11 8HB (8455 3862). Golders Green tube. **Meals served** 10.30am-midnight Mon-Thur, Sun; 7.30pm-3am Sat. **Average** ££. **No credit cards.** Jewish

Entrecote joins a dozen or so other kosher restaurants on Golders Green Road, although its bar-style set-up – with stools, a counter and striking silver, black and red decor – makes it seem more modern than most. The name conjures up images of a juicy French steak, but here beef gets the Jewish treatment: beaten thin, deftly seared and flipped on a grill, then chopped and scooped into freshly made pancakes. The menu is sensibly short: apart from steak there's chicken or chorizo, and side dishes include chunky chips, onion rings, guacamole and salads. It's all good-value, straightforward food, and the production on our visit was smooth and speedy. Try one of the refreshing fruit shakes made with berries, mango or passion fruit.

Kimchee

887 Finchley Road, NW11 8RR (8455 1035). Golders Green tube. **Lunch served** noon-3pm Tue-Fri; noon-4pm Sat, Sun. **Dinner served** 6-11pm Tue-Sun. **Average** ££. **Set lunch** £5.90-£6.90. Korean

Most of the capital's many Korean restaurants are clustered around Soho or New Malden, making Kimchee feel exotically out of place in the middle of Golders Green. It's highly atmospheric too: the dining room is styled like a traditional yeogwan (Korean inn), complete

with attentive waitresses in traditional costume, Korean village scenes on the wallpaper and gas barbecues set into aged wooden tables. The menu is short and predictable, but every dish we tried was well prepared. The house kimchi had real fire, and we enjoyed the smooth yolky flavour of the bibimbap (rice in a hot bowl). Another enjoyable dish was the tangsuyuk, hunks of tender battered beef served in a sweet-and-sour sauce with fresh pineapple, providing a lively counterpoint to the tartness of the kimchi.

Sam's NEW

68-70 Golders Green Road, NW11 8LM (8455 9898/7171). Golders Green tube. **Meals served** noon-10pm daily. **Average** ££. **Set lunch** (noon-4pm) £7.95 2 courses incl tea or coffee. Fish & chips

Sam's restaurant and takeaway stands out on Golders Green Road for its large dimensions, homely atmosphere and fine food. Fish comes fried, grilled or steamed, or in generous, Mediterranean-style dishes such as moist, herby fish kebab with tomato sauce and rice. Chippie staples such as mushy peas are nicely done too. Refreshing salads arrive just before the main courses, making the starters superfluous – and leaving welcome room for dessert. The admirably light lockshen pudding (a Jewish speciality of noodles, eggs and raisins) had a well-judged cinnamon edge sweetly offset by vanilla ice-cream, and the rice pud was creamy and delicious. Staff are kind and gracious, and good with children, and the lunchtime meal deals are a favourite with local pensioners.

Meal deals

Café Japan *626 Finchley Road, NW11 7RR (8455 6854).* Set lunch £8.50 bento box. Japanese

In the area

Pizza Express *94 Golders Green Road, NW11 8HP (8455 9556).*

Hampstead

★ Brew House

Kenwood, Hampstead Lane, NW3 7JR (8341 5384/www.companyof cooks.com). Archway or Golders Green tube then 210 bus. **Meals served** *Apr-Sept* 9am-6pm (9pm on concert nights) daily. *Oct-Mar* 9am-dusk daily. **Average** ££. **Map** p300. Café

Peak times at this much loved Kenwood institution may appear chaotic, but look carefully and you'll see staff working like a well-oiled machine. The daily menu will feature some sort of gourmet sausages served with gravy and roast veg, plus a hot dish (such as lamb shanks) and something quichey; locals frequently opt for the deal on soup with bread, an apple and a piece of cheese. Sweets run from breakfast pastries to papaya and rhubarb fool. Look in the self-serve cabinets for plump sandwiches that put the West End chains to shame – ham with honey and caper mayonnaise, coronation chicken – and come early for the famous cooked breakfasts, which feature those fabulous sausages, lush grilled mushrooms, wonderfully creamy scrambled eggs and wholesome toast.

★ Chaiwalla NEW

4A-5A Perrins Court, NW3 1QS (7435 2151/www.chaiwalla.info). Hampstead tube. **Meals served** 8.30am-8.30pm daily. **Average** £. **Map** p300. Café

Inspired by tea stalls in Kolkata, West Bengal, Neil Sanyal has taken the tradition of serving spiced tea in clay pots and brought it to leafy Hampstead. Modern styling gives Chaiwalla an urban appeal, with low seating, Indian inlay work, and images of Asian street scenes across the walls. Its earthenware tumblers, made in West Bengal, are disposable in India, but customers here are encouraged to take them home. The masala chai scores top marks – spiked with ginger and cinnamon, and with just the right balance of milk. Lunches and sweetmeats are available, but we recommend samosas for the classic Indian afternoon-tea experience. Choose from six generously proportioned varieties – all baked rather than deep-fried – including lovely chicken and paneer samosas with a lively ginger, garlic and chilli spicing.

Jin Kichi NEW

73 Heath Street, NW3 6UG (7794 6158/www.jinkichi.com). Hampstead tube. **Lunch served** 12.30-2pm Sat, Sun. **Dinner served** 6-11pm Tue-Sat; 6-10pm Sun. **Average** ££. **Set lunch** £8.80-£15.90. **Map** p300. Japanese

Jin Kichi is very much a come-as-you-are, neighbourly sort of dinner spot; the premises seem lived in, with charming rice paper lanterns, tables poked in every which way, and an island counter where the chef expertly plies his trade. The menu is vast – from noodles and rice dishes to simmered dishes, grills, sushi and sashimi – and it's all of a decent standard. Highlights included succulent tsukune (grilled chicken balls with yakitori sauce), skewered chicken livers that tasted like a fine pâté, and the best agedashidofu (fried tofu in broth) we've had in London. An inside-out yellowtail and avocado roll was fresh and light. This is Japanese party food: tasty things to nibble with a few drinks.

Louis Pâtisserie

32 Heath Street, NW3 6TE (7435 9908). Hampstead tube. **Meals served** 9am-6pm daily. **Average** £. **Unlicensed** no alcohol allowed. **Map** p300. Café

This Hungarian pâtisserie is a rare gem, a refined tearoom that enfolds you in sepia-toned surroundings as soon as you step through the door. Seated behind the ornate ironwork and chocolate-box displays on comfortable leather benches, you may find elderly folk telling postwar stories or quietly perusing the papers with a cup of tea. As you settle down for the afternoon, you'll be invited to cast your gaze over a mouthwatering platter of cream cakes, with the likes of chestnut slice, strawberry cheesecake, marzipan moon, chocolate swirl and apple pie among its delights, although the prosaic names do nothing to convey the cakes' magnificence. At lunchtime, there's a reliable selection of rolls and croissants. The perfect place for family tea on a Sunday afternoon.

In the area

Carluccio's Caffè *32 Rosslyn Hill, NW3 1NH (7794 2184).* **Map** p300.
dim t *3 Heath Street, NW3 6TP (7435 0024).* **Map** p300.
Giraffe *46 Rosslyn Hill, NW3 1NH (7435 0343).* **Map** p300.
Maison Blanc *76 Hampstead High Street, NW3 1QX (7443 9722).* **Map** p300.
Le Pain Quotidien *1 South End Road, NW3 2PT (7486 6154).* **Map** p300.
Paul *43 Hampstead High Street, NW3 1QG (7794 8657).* **Map** p300.
Ping Pong *83-84 Hampstead High Street, NW3 1RE (7433 0930).* **Map** p300.
Pizza Express *70 Heath Street, NW3 1DN (7433 1600).* **Map** p300.
Woodlands *102 Heath Street, NW3 1DR (7794 3080).* **Map** p300.

Hendon

In the area
L'Artista *17 Central Circus, NW4 3AS (8202 7303).*

Brilliant Kids Café.
See p238.

Kensal Green

★ Brilliant Kids Café

*8 Station Terrace, NW10 5RT
(8964 4120/www.brilliantkids.co.uk).
Kensal Green tube/Kensal Rise rail.*
Meals served 8am-6pm Mon-Fri;
9am-5pm Sat; 10am-4pm Sun.
Average ££. Café
We did bring a kid to Brilliant, but
it's not essential; plenty of sprogless
customers were at the front end,
away from the child-friendly area at
the back of the café. Many come for
the substantial all-day breakfast,
with its thick bacon rashers and
sausages; others know, as we do,
that the daily special hot lunch
(chicken pie, shepherd's pie, curry)
is usually special indeed. In addition,
the pastries are superb (especially
the rough-hewn, individual quiches),
and the salads and fillings for the
fresh bagels and loaves are
imaginative and wonderfully fresh.
Everything chalked up on the board
can be scaled down for kids, and
both the food and the children's
workshops in the studio next door
(£5 per hour) are fantastic value.

Gracelands

*118 College Road, NW10 5HD (8964
9161/www.gracelandscafe.com).
Kensal Green tube.* **Meals served**
8.30am-5pm Mon-Wed; 8.30am-10pm
Thur, Fri; 9am-10pm Sat; 9.30am-
3pm Sun. **Average** ££. Café
Bow-haired toddlers and bouncing
babies smeared with organic sweet
potato greet you at the door of this

Small & Beautiful. See p240.

North West

convivial café, but fear not: the affable women who run Gracelands provide the child-free with a quieter corner, often in the shop next door. Food is made with care and served in big portions; breakfasts include fry-ups, eggs benedict or pastries; lunchtime specials run to the likes of chicken or lentil stew, or lighter choices such as deliciously buttery garlic mushrooms on toast. Quiches (goat's cheese and sweet potato is a popular combination) are served with chunky salads of puy lentils, tomatoes and basil, plus roasted veg. Creative workshops are run in the community rooms.

★ Tong Khanom Thai
833 Harrow Road, NW10 5NH (8964 5373). Kensal Rise tube.

Lunch served noon-3pm Mon-Fri. **Dinner served** 6-10pm Mon-Sat. **Average** £. Thai
The green walls, photo of the Thai king and old refrigerator topped with a laughing Buddha set a homely tone, enhanced by the staff's friendly, casual manner and the simple flavours of the food; there's also live (and loud) traditional music. The menu contains some real gems and is excellent value. Chicken wrapped in pandan leaves was outstanding, the meat infused with lemongrass and steamed to fragrant perfection; we also enjoyed the fresh, flavourful stir-fried morning glory with garlic and chilli. On the night of our visit, one couple came in with a bottle of champagne – and given that most dishes cost under £5, it's tempting to push the boat out just as they did.

Kilburn

Abyssinia
9 Cricklewood Broadway, NW2 3JX (8208 0110). Kilburn tube. **Dinner served** 6pm-midnight Mon-Fri. **Meals served** 2pm-midnight Sat, Sun. **Average** ££. Ethiopian
The Ethiopian diners eating tilapia and listening to the latest sounds from Addis look very happy at Abyssinia, and the friendly welcome and lovely smell of frankincense help you forgive its rather dark, drab decor. After considering such delicacies as kitfo (spicy, raw minced beef) and doro wot (a stew of chicken and hard-boiled eggs), we settled on the assa wot (fish stew), which had a similar texture to mince but lacked the spice for which Ethiopian food is famous. However, the dish worked well with the injera flatbread with which almost all main courses are served. The tej (honey wine, similar to mead) was tasty, but the highlight

of the meal was the Ethiopian coffee, served at the end after an elaborate roasting ceremony.

Kovalam

12 Willesden Lane, NW6 7SR (7625 4761/www.kovalam restaurant.co.uk). Kilburn tube/98 bus. **Lunch served** noon-2.30pm daily. **Dinner served** 6-11pm Mon-Thur, Sun; 6pm-midnight Fri, Sat. **Average** ££. **Set meal** (vegetarian) £18-£35 serves 2-4; (non-vegetarian) £26-£48 serves 2-4. **Map** p283. Indian

A long, thin restaurant with neat tables and white tablecloths, Kovalam looks like a typical curry house. However, the menu has several traditional South Indian delights to savour, especially from Kerala. A succulent king prawn malabar was offset by a smooth, spicy coconut sauce, which begged to be scooped up with handfuls of rice, Kerala-style. An unusual vegetarian option was a light filo parcel mildly spiced and stuffed with spinach and soft pumpkin. Hot and deliciously greasy Kerala porata (flatbread) was the perfect accompaniment to a chunky saag paneer, our one culinary sally into northern India. It was a pity that the seafood department was let down by an overcooked squid masala.

Small & Beautiful

351-353 Kilburn High Road, NW6 2QJ (7328 2637/www.smalland beautifulrestaurant.co.uk). Kilburn tube/Brondesbury rail/16, 32 bus. **Meals served** noon-11.30pm Mon-Sat; noon-10.30pm Sun. **Average** ££. **No credit cards**. **Map** p283. Brasserie

Quirkily and individually decorated (Botticelli posters, organ pipes and a brightly painted ceiling), Small & Beautiful doesn't take itself too seriously. The menu gives customers just enough of a choice without bewildering them, and the prices are

fabulous: come for lunch and you get a hearty three-c ourse meal for under £10 (excluding drinks). The food is variable in quality, but generous: a squid starter impressed with its pleasingly crisp breadcrumb coating, but a main dish of lamb goulash could have done with a bit more flavour. Desserts are dependably pleasant and, like the rest of the menu, nicely priced. Welcoming and comfortably busy most evenings, this is a safe bet for an enjoyable meal that won't leave you out of pocket.

In the area

Little Bay *228 Belsize Road, NW6 4BT (7372 4699)*. **Map** p283.
Nando's *308 Kilburn High Road, NW6 2DG (7372 1507)*. **Map** p283.

Mill Hill

In the area

Pizza Express *92 The Broadway, NW7 3TB (8959 3898)*.

St John's Wood

Harry Morgan's

31 St John's Wood High Street, NW8 7NH (7722 1869/www.harry ms.co.uk). St John's Wood tube. **Meals served** 9am-10.30pm Mon-Fri; 10am-10.30pm Sat, Sun. **Average** ££. **Map** p300. Jewish (non kosher)

The awning tells you what this long-standing restaurant has to offer: salt beef, chopped liver, chicken soup, blintzes, borscht. Inside, the decor is simple and functional, and at the back is a bar – although few people drink alcohol with their hefty portions of Jewish-style food. The menu caters to the lunch-and-shop crowd, with houmous, falafel and salads; fish comes in trendy versions, and even the fried haddock is served hot (unlike the cold fish served in

England since Spanish Jews brought the dish over). Harry's doesn't follow kashrut rules, so patrons can choose dairy desserts after their meat. We found these hit and miss, but the cheesecake and the warm almond tart were genuine treats.

Natural Burger Company NEW

12 Blenheim Terrace, NW8 0EB (7372 9065). St John's Wood tube. **Meals served** noon-11pm Mon-Sat; noon-10.30pm Sun. **Average** ££. **Map** p300. Burgers

The party of supersized Americans chowing down here suggested that Natural Burger Company is doing something right (though said customers may have had problems with the tiny toilet). It's also telling that everyone requested 'no mayo' and 'no relish', as NBC tends to load its burgers with gunk. Fortunately, the toasted ciabatta buns are up to the job, and each burger is pinned smartly upright with two skewers. Vegetarians will be impressed by the whopping vegetable stacks, less so by the fountain of juices that erupted from our too-rare 'natural burger'; also, we'd rather taste blue cheese than 'blue cheese sauce'. Real fruit in the milkshakes is a bonus, though, as is the side option of chicken wings in piri piri sauce.

Meal deals

Royal China Club *68 Queen's Grove, NW8 6ER (7586 4280/ www.royalchinagroup.co.uk).* Dim sum (noon-5pm) £2.30-£5. **Map** p300. Chinese

In the area

Carluccio's Caffè *60 St John's Wood High Street, NW8 7SH (7449 0404).* **Map** p300.
Maison Blanc *37 St John's Wood High Street, NW8 7NG (7586 1982).* **Map** p300.
Pizza Express *39A Abbey Road, NW8 0AA (7624 5577).* **Map** p300.

Swiss Cottage

Camden Arts Centre Café

Corner of Arkwright Road & Finchley Road, NW3 6DG (7472 5516/www.camdenartscentre.org). Finchley Road or Hampstead tube/ Finchley Road & Frognal rail. **Meals served** 10am-5.30pm Tue, Thur-Sun; 10am-8.30pm Wed. **Average** ££. **Map** p300. Café

Light and airy while at the same time being warm and welcoming, the daytime-only Camden Arts Centre Café is an oasis of arty calm that provides a refuge from the incessant traffic of Finchley Road. The menu isn't substantial, but meets most lunch requirements, and the food is usually delicious. We found that our meze plate was let down only by the rather bland houmous; at the pricier end of the spectrum, stuffed pepper was excellent and came with a generous portion of mixed salads. Freshly made sandwiches or paninis and soups of the day offer quicker, lighter options. Decent coffees and cakes, not to mention a selection of board games, provide yet further reasons to visit.

Green Cottage

9 New College Parade, Finchley Road, NW3 5EP (7722 5305). Finchley Road or Swiss Cottage tube. **Meals served** noon-11pm Mon-Sat; noon-10pm Sun. **Average** ££. **Set meal** £16-£29 per person (minimum 2). **Map** p300. Chinese

Friendly Green Cottage has simple, utilitarian decor over two floors, but its menu is far more exciting than that of the average Chinese restaurant. Cantonese food is at its core, and roast meats are a house speciality. We enjoyed a soup of slivered roast duck with fish, bamboo shoots and shiitake mushrooms (and grappled with seafood rolls that fell apart in our chopsticks); a chicken and bean curd hotpot was robustly seasoned with saltfish and ginger. Choi sum in a shrimpy Malaysian sauce was a little chewy, but fried rice with slices of broccoli stem, shreds of delicious dried scallop and wisps of egg white was superb. Many locals have been dining here for years, and we would too if we lived within walking distance.

Meal deals

Eriki *4-6 Northways Parade, Finchley Road, NW3 5EN (7722 0606/www.eriki.co.uk).* Set lunch £12.95 thali. **Map** p300. Indian
Hellenic Restaurant
291 Finchley Road, NW3 6ND (7431 1001). Set lunch £9.95 2 courses. **Map** p300. Greek
Wakaba *122A Finchley Road, NW3 5HT (7443 5609).* Set buffet (lunch) £6.60. **Map** p300. Japanese

In the area

Fine Burger Company *O2 Centre, 255 Finchley Road, NW3 6LU (7433 0700).* **Map** p300.
Mahdi *2 Canfield Gardens, NW6 3BS (7625 4344).* **Map** p300.
Nando's *O2 Centre, 255 Finchley Road, NW3 6LU (7435 4644).* **Map** p300.
Pizza Express *227 Finchley Road, NW3 6LP (7794 5100).* **Map** p300.
Yo! Sushi *O2 Centre, 255 Finchley Road, NW3 6LU (7431 4499).* **Map** p300.

West Hampstead

Czechoslovak Restaurant

74 West End Lane, NW6 2LX (7372 1193/www.czechoslovak-restaurant.co.uk). West Hampstead tube/rail. **Dinner** served 5-10pm Tue-Fri. **Meals served** noon-10pm Sat, Sun. **Average** ££. **No credit cards. Map** p300. Czech

Even early in the week, this relaxed, retro spot buzzes with a diverse crowd cocking a snook at healthy eating: young Czechs and Slovaks, older workmen downing Budvar, and happy diners with no Czech connections whatsoever. Hearty chicken noodle or creamy sour cabbage soups start things off; if you're feeling adventurous, try utopenec v octe (pickled sausage), or bramborák se slaninou (potato pancake with extraordinarily fat bacon). Mains are enormous: you'll feel close to exploding if you finish the fried carp with its huge potato salad, or the crumbly roast lamb in a sea of creamy spinach sauce with knedliky – and you'll need the good Czech beer to wash it all down and make some room for the apricot dumplings in butter.

Elephant Walk NEW

98 West End Lane, NW6 2LU (7328 3308/www.elephantwalk.biz). West Hampstead tube/rail. **Lunch served** noon-3pm Sat; 12.30-4pm Sun. **Dinner served** 5-11pm daily. **Average** ££. **Map** p300. Sri Lankan
If you've been to Sri Lanka before, the scent of cloves and cinnamon emanating from the warm, friendly Elephant Walk will spirit you right back to the teardrop spice island. A traditional egg hopper seemed simply flavoured until zingy coconut sambal kicked in, and a South Indian-inspired masala dosa was a generous portion of delicious crisp pancake stuffed with softly spiced potato. Tender lamb and okra curry had hints of cumin, and a lush pumpkin curry featured large wedges of succulent veg floating in a smooth sauce of coconut and ground spices. A flaccid naan bread brought the average down a little, but sweetened with a salt lassi and presented with a bill under £30, we left singing the place's praises.

Parsian. See p244.

Nautilus NEW

27-29 Fortune Green Road,
NW6 1DT (7435 2532). West
Hampstead tube/rail then 328 bus.
Lunch served 11.30am-2.30pm,
dinner served 4.30-10pm Mon-
Sat. **Average** £££. **Map** p300.
Fish & chips

Nautilus is a pristine, family-run
outfit known for friendly service
and quality cooking, if not for its
decor (though elsewhere the fruit-
illustrated condiment trays would
be fashionably kitsch). The menu
runs from chicken and scampi to
Dover sole, fillets and cutlets, fried
in matzo or grilled. The prices may
seem steep, but the ingredients are
great and portions are gigantic: our

plaice fillet took up most of the
plate. Add a bowl of houmous or
taramasalata to start and you'll
have no room for the ready-made
desserts sourced from DiSotto's.
The carafes of wine are shaped like
vinegar bottles and, unfortunately,
our wine was distinctly on the
vinegary side too. Still, we'll come
back for the warmth of the welcome
and the excellent fried fish.

Sushi Bar Gen

243 West End Lane, NW6 1XN
(7431 4031). West Hampstead
tube/rail. **Lunch served** noon-
2.45pm, **dinner served** 6-10.45pm
daily. **Average** ££. **Set lunch**
£7.30-£8.50 bento box. **Map** p300.
Japanese

Four smiling chefs working behind the counter set the friendly tone at this impressive address. The interior is small and basic, the emphasis here being on dishing out great sushi in double-quick time. Indeed, our line-up of hot miso soup, steaming and salty edamame beans and wonderfully misshapen and undeniably fresh tuna and avocado Californian rolls took only 40 minutes from putting in our order to empty plates. To follow, we shared a bowl containing two enormous and juicy tempura prawns atop a tangle of buckwheat noodles in a warming, sweet-spicy broth. A blackboard lists daily specials (sea bass on our visit). Around us, the tables quickly filled up with West Hampstead's sushi lovers enjoying affordable, quality creations.

In the area
Banana Tree Canteen
237-239 West End Lane, NW6 1XN (7431 7808). **Map** p300.
Gourmet Burger Kitchen
331 West End Lane, NW6 1RS (7794 5455). **Map** p300.
Nando's *252-254 West End Lane, NW6 1LU* (7794 1331). **Map** p300.
Pizza Express *319 West End Lane, NW6 1RN* (7431 8229). **Map** p300.

Whetstone

In the area
ASK *1257 High Road, N20 0EW* (8492 0033).
Pizza Express *1264 High Road, N20 9HH* (8446 8800).

Willesden

★ Little Star
26 Station Parade, NW2 4NH (8830 5221/www.littlestarrestaurant. co.uk). *Willesden Green tube.* **Lunch served** noon-3pm, **dinner served**

6pm-midnight Mon-Sat. **Meals served** noon-11pm Sun. **Average** ££. **Set meal** (Mon-Thur) £6.85 2 courses. International
This popular spot, illuminated only by fairy lights and tea lights, has a cosy atmosphere equally suitable for a romantic dinner or a relaxed meal with friends and family. Although the murals decorating the walls are pure French bistro, the menu has a more eclectically European reach, with some French (we enjoyed an excellent duck confit) alongside German, Italian and Spanish entries. Still, some dishes are hard to place: our steak topped with aubergine, portobello mushroom, feta cheese and chilli was certainly enigmatic, but delicious nonetheless. Portions are large and prices small, and be sure to study the list of specials, which can, oddly enough, be cheaper than the standard fare.

Parsian
228 High Road, NW10 2NX (8830 0772). *Willesden Green tube.* **Meals served** noon-midnight daily. **Average** ££. Iranian
It's hard to keep track of the number of Iranian restaurants opening around Willesden and Kilburn, but this newcomer is definitely one worth remembering. The decor is basic, but we found staff friendlier than at the more famous Iranians in west London – they even asked if we'd like our food kept in the oven when one of our party briefly stepped outside – and the quality was head and shoulders above many of its competitors. We loved the creamy kashk-e bademjan, a thick aubergine and whey dip mopped up with bread hot from the clay oven, and the bogoli polo ba mahiche, a slow-cooked lamb shank falling apart on a mountain of perfectly fluffy Persian rice flavoured with dill and lima beans. A welcome addition to the area.

Emchai

Barnet, Hertfordshire

Emchai

*78 High Street, Barnet, Herts EN5
5SN (8364 9993). High Barnet tube.*
Lunch served noon-2.30pm daily.
Dinner served 6-11pm Mon-Thur;
6pm-midnight Fri, Sat; 5-10pm Sun.
Average ££. **Set meal** £15-£18.50
per person (minimum 2). Oriental
Bright walls, multicoloured lanterns
and fairy lights bring a hint of the
South-east Asian night market to
this bustling joint, and the
fashionably attired young families
and groups of friends give the place
a terrific buzz. The menu visits
various parts of Asia, from 'Assam'
red snapper to Chinese crispy duck
and Singaporean laksa. The latter
was tame, but succulent satay
chicken was tinged with aromatic
lemongrass. Highlights were tender
venison stir-fried with black pepper
sauce, and side dishes of the
greenest gai lan and garlicky
spinach, but a dish of prawns in

honey and oats was foiled by leaden,
overcooked shellfish. There are fresh
juices, beers and a bargain-priced
wine list; desserts include sago
pudding, fritters and ice-creams.

Meal deals

Loch Fyne *12 Hadley Highstone,
Barnet, Herts EN5 4PU (8449
3674/www.loch-fyne.com).* Set
lunch £11 2 courses incl glass
of wine. Fish

Croydon, Surrey

★ Malay House

*60 Lower Addiscombe Road,
Croydon, Surrey CR0 6AA (8666
0266). East Croydon rail then 197,
312, 410 bus.* **Lunch served** noon-
2pm Tue-Thur. **Dinner served**
6-11pm Tue-Sat. **Average** ££.
Unlicensed. Corkage £1 per
person. Malaysian
Judging by the flattering scrawls in
the guestbook at this family-run
restaurant, Malay House is a well-
loved local that has served plenty of
happy customers over the years. We

OUTER LONDON

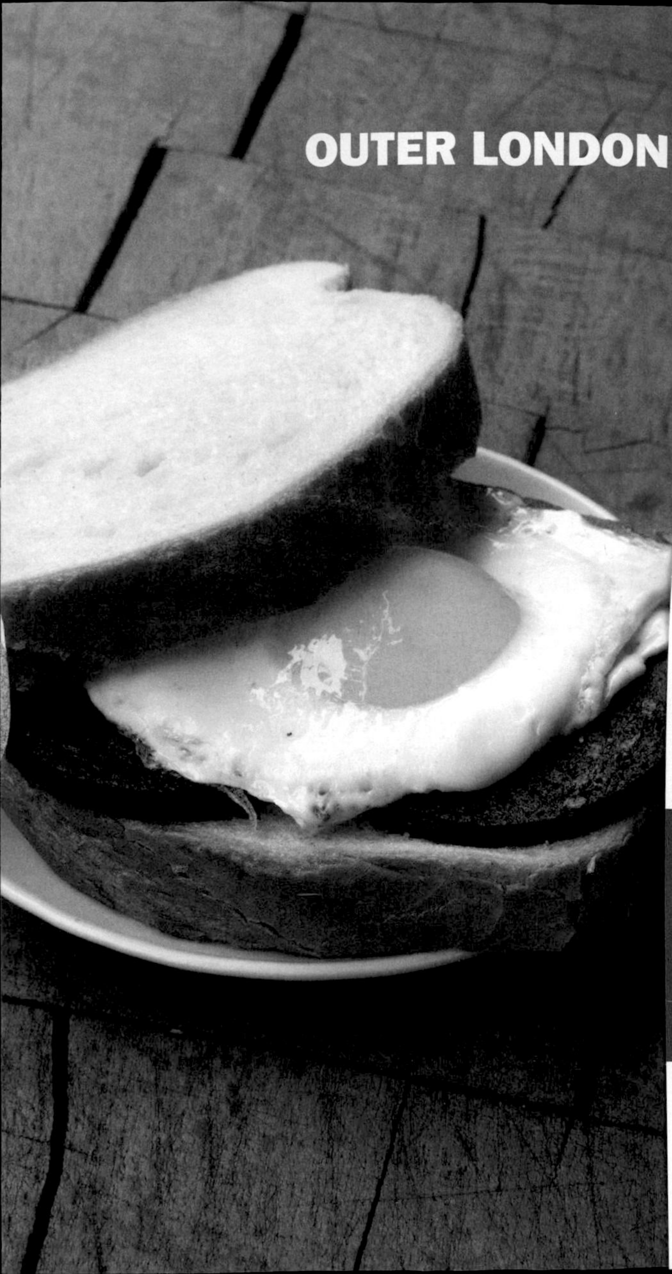

were soon seduced by the whole operation – from the welcoming decor, with warm wood accents and beautiful batik prints, to the broad smiles that came with our food. Chicken and lamb satay were grilled to perfection, with a proper sauce heaving with crushed peanuts; less successful were spicy fish cakes, unpleasantly heavy and with a greasy exterior. Mains, beautifully presented, were agreeably authentic: a rich, coconutty beef rendang was mopped up with fluffy rice, while Penang char kway teow had an impressive smoky wok flavour, and was further improved by the addition of spicy-sweet sambal.

In the area

Little Bay *32 Selsdon Road, Croydon, Surrey CR2 6PB (8649 9544).*

Miso *11-12 Suffolk House, George Street, Croydon, Surrey CR0 1PE (8681 5084).*

Miso *103-105 High Street, Croydon, Surrey CR0 1QG (8681 7688).*

Nando's *Valley Leisure Park, Beddington Farm Road, Croydon, Surrey CR0 4XY (8688 9545).*

Nando's *26 High Street, Croydon, Surrey CR0 1GT (8681 3505).*

Wagamama *4 Park Lane, Croydon, Surrey CR0 1JA (8760 9260).*

Yo! Sushi *House of Fraser, 21 North End Road, Croydon, Surrey CR0 1RQ (8760 0479).*

Zizzi *57-59 Southend, Croydon, Surrey CR0 1BF (8649 8403).*

Eastcote, Middlesex

★ Nauroz

219 Field End Road, Eastcote, Middx HA5 1QZ (8868 0900). Eastcote tube. **Meals served** noon-midnight Tue-Sun. **Average** ££. **Licensed. Corkage** no charge. Indian

Eastcote's best-known community caff is a longstanding magnet for curry aficionados. Succulent kebabs, rustic dhal and full-flavoured curries are served in a brightly lit dining area set with functional furniture. A fish tikka starter delivered juicy cod chunks cooked to perfection and cloaked in a smoky crust of gingery yoghurt; nihari, a meltingly tender lamb stew, scored bonus points for its sticky, spicy stock infused with fennel seeds and sweet cardamom; and slow-cooked butter beans, simmered in tangy tomato masala with peppery fenugreek leaves, were a marvellous match for hot, buttery nan. Service can be erratic, but boisterous Punjabi banter keeps the entertainment factor high. Save space for the dreamy, creamy rice pudding topped with a generous flurry of pistachio nuts.

Edgware, Middlesex

Aviv NEW

87-89 High Street, Edgware, Middx HA8 7DB (8952 2484/www.aviv restaurant.com). Edgware tube. **Lunch served** noon-2.30pm, **dinner served** 5.30-10.30pm Mon-Thur, Sun. **Average** £££. **Set lunch** (noon-2.30pm Mon-Thur) £9.95 2 courses. **Set meal** £16.95-£20.95 3 courses. Jewish

There's little time for culinary contemplation at popular Jewish restaurant Aviv. Inside it's all gleamingly modern, brightly lit and brisk to the point of being brusque – a succession of waiters will have demanded a drinks order before you've even had time to remove your coat. But Aviv is clearly doing something right: it buzzes with a vivacious, older crowd choosing from Israeli hors d'oeuvres and kosher versions of European favourites. A juicy, well-seasoned lamb shashleek was a welcome sequel to a silky, smoky aubergine tahini, although stuffed mushrooms and a matbucha salad featuring cooked red peppers and tomatoes were less inspiring. The list of own-made desserts included a divine, non-dairy banoffee pie with a smothering of rich muscovado caramel, and a pleasingly soft pavlova topped with a handful of fresh strawberries and mango.

B&K Salt Beef Bar

11 Lanson House, Whitchurch Lane, Edgware, Middx HA8 6NL (8952 8204). Edgware tube. **Lunch served** noon-3pm, **dinner served** 5.30-9.15pm Tue-Sun. **Average ££. Unlicensed. Corkage** no charge. Jewish

Class divides persist in the Jewish community, and if St John's Wood is on one end of the scale, this restaurant at the grimy end of Edgware's high street is definitely at the other. From its nondescript frontage, you could easily mistake B&K for a funeral parlour, and the average age of the clientele doesn't exactly lend the place a glamorous look, but the atmosphere inside offers an unbeatable throwback to an old East End Yiddish spirit that is fast disappearing. The food is homely and heartwarming, with chicken soup like mamma used to make, and portions of salt beef so big we needed a doggy bag to take the leftovers home with us. Moribund appearances notwithstanding, it's no wonder people come from miles around to visit the place.

Biazo NEW

307 Hale Lane, Edgware, Middx HA8 7AX (8958 8826/www. biazo.co.uk). Edgware tube. **Meals served** noon-11pm Tue-Fri; 1-11pm Sat; 1-10pm Sun. **Average ££. Set lunch** (1-4pm Sun) £13.99 2 courses. **Unlicensed** no alcohol allowed. Nigerian

If you're new to West African cooking and want to ease yourself into a world of cow foot, snails and chicken gizzards, Biazo – with its stylish Afropean decor and friendly, efficient service – is a good place to start. The extensive menu of mostly Nigerian dishes (with a few from Ghana and Kenya) on our visit included fried yam preceded by a tasty bowl of crunchy, deep-fried chin-chin biscuits, and followed by an elegantly spiced efo egusi (spinach with ground melon seeds), waakye (rice and beans) and an ample portion of stewed tilapia. Die-hard fans of traditional Nigerian cuisine may find the rice not quite moist enough, and the spicing a little too mild. There's no alcohol allowed.

Booba's NEW

151 Hale Lane, Edgware, Middx HA8 9QW (8959 6002). Edgware tube/Mill Hill Broadway rail. **Meals served** noon-10pm Tue-Sun. **Average ££.** Fish & chips

Named after a Yiddish grandma, this plain Turkish and Jewish takeaway and restaurant dips its fish in matzo meal instead of batter before frying, and serves no shellfish. Starters include houmous and taramasalata with warm pitta; mains include eight types of fish, grilled or fried, and served with chips or boiled potatoes and salad. Portions are generous, and our haddock was crisp and flaky, and we enjoyed the chips, but the salad was limp. To wind up the meal, Turkish coffee or cappuccino can be ordered along with own-made apple pie and the sort of ice-cream that recalls childhood seaside holidays. We'll soon be back to try the halibut or trout: at these prices, who wouldn't?

Zan Zi Bar

113 High Street, Edgware, Middx HA8 7DB (8952 2986/www.zanzi barrestaurant.co.uk). Edgware tube. **Lunch served** noon-3pm, **dinner**

served 6-10.30pm Mon-Fri. **Meals served** noon-10.30pm Sat, Sun. **Average ££. Set lunch** (Mon-Fri) £6.95 1 course. Indian

Award-winning service from a courteous young team comes as a much welcome standard at this unpretentious pub and restaurant. Local north Indian families came in droves for Diwali when we visited, sharing sizzling plates of Punjabi classics like on-the-bone chicken tikka and tender reshmi kebabs to a toe-tapping Bollywood soundtrack. We plumped for crispy vegetables in the lightest of batters, followed by a deliciously rich Goan fish curry and a pleasantly piquant sarson ka saag (curried spinach and mustard leaves). The central bar lends an open-plan feel, and a contemporary makeover (cream wood panelling, saffron drapes and pastel colouring) ensures that the venue sits very comfortably in restaurant territory.

In the area

Nando's *137-139 Station Road, Edgware, Middx HA8 9JG (8952 3400).*

Harrow, Middlesex

Blue Ginger

383 Kenton Road, Harrow, Middx HA3 0XS (8909 0100/www.bg restaurant.com). Kenton tube/rail. **Lunch served** noon-3pm Tue-Sat. **Dinner served** 6-11pm Mon-Sat. **Meals served** 1-10.30pm Sun. **Average ££. Set meal** £15 3 courses. Indian

Blue Ginger is clearly popular with Kenton's well-to-do Asian families. Porsches and Mercedes crowd the car park, and flat-screen TVs and black leather couches dot the interior. The menu brilliantly captures Delhi's thriving Punjabi-Chinese food scene, so a meal could

Nauroz. See p247.

Discover the city from your back pocket

Essential for your weekend break,
25 top cities available.

POCKET SIZED
from £6.99

start with either pan-fried masala fish in a delicious ginger, chilli, coriander and peppercorn crust, or masala mogo (deep-fried cassava patties tossed in a distinct sweet and sour sauce). Cultural purists might prefer paneer bhurji (shredded paneer cooked with tomatoes, onions and coriander), or the fish masala, a helping of tilapia fillets in a tomato broth infused with ginger and garlic, and topped with roasted mustard seeds and fresh coriander.

Golden Palace

146-150 Station Road, Harrow, Middx HA1 2RH (8863 2333). Harrow-on-the-Hill tube/rail. **Meals served** noon-11.30pm Mon-Sat; 11am-10.30pm Sun. **Dim sum served** noon-5pm Mon-Sat; 11am-5pm Sun. **Average ££. Set meal** £15-£26.50 per person (minimum 2). Chinese

The dim sum here is famous, but the evening menu is becoming an even better venue to visit. This spacious venue has the obligatory starched white tablecloths and uncomfortable seats, but we couldn't fault the friendly, attentive waitresses, who heard our preferences and returned with a range of dishes they thought we might like. Braised belly pork, wrapped in thin beancurd sheets then deep-fried, was unusual – the beancurd resembled crisp filo pastry, in enjoyable contrast to the meltingly tender (though greasy) pork belly. Charcoal-roast duck was succulent and flavoursome, but lacked the distinctive smoky aroma of this time-consuming technique.

★ Masa

24-26 Headstone Drive, Harrow, Middx HA3 5QH (8861 6213). Harrow & Wealdstone tube/rail. **Meals served** 12.30-11pm daily. **Average ££. Set meal** £19.95 (2 people); £30 (2-3 people); £49.95 (4-5 people). **Unlicensed. Corkage** no charge. Afghan

Masa's exotic decor has burgundy walls, carved wooden furniture and a smart, neon-backlit ceiling dominated by a central chandelier – but there's nothing formal about dining here. Local Afghan families eat with one eye on the big screen, enjoying starters like smoky mirza ghasemi (smoky aubergine with garlic, yoghurt and walnuts) and sabzi bourani (steamed spinach, yoghurt and herbs), with handfuls of flaky nan fresh from the oven. Mains include lamb and chicken kebabs chargrilled in the open kitchen, and a range of curries: chicken karahi was richly flavoursome, with just the right level of chilli kick, while a slightly oversalted lamb sabzi was thick with spinach. Large glasses of dogh (yoghurt drink) were flavoured with fresh mint and chunks of cucumber, and were a cool contrast to the more fiery dishes.

★ Ram's

203 Kenton Road, Harrow, Middx HA3 0HD (8907 2022). Kenton tube/rail. **Lunch served** noon-3pm, **dinner served** 6-11pm daily. **Set meal** £16.50 (unlimited food and soft drinks). Indian

This small café, widely regarded as the jewel in Kenton's crown, is simply furnished with wipe-clean tables and images of Hindu deities, and champions the best of Gujarati vegetarian cooking. We gave top marks to the pani puri (crisp puffed pastry discs filled with diced onion and chickpeas), a perfect match with minted, chilli-speckled tamarind water; pau bhaji (buttery potato mash simmered with onions, tomatoes and peppers) was also first rate. Main courses included a deliciously tart, soupy kadhi (gram flour simmered with yoghurt, mustard seeds and curry leaves). For a taste of sunshine, order a fresh lime soda seasoned with black salt and toasted cumin.

Outer London

Stein's. See p256.

In the area

Nando's *300-302 Station Road, Harrow, Middx HA1 2DX (8427 5581).*
Nando's *309-311 Northolt Road, South Harrow, Middx HA2 8JA (8423 1516).*
Pizza Express *2 College Road, Harrow, Middx HA1 1BE (8427 9195).*
Sakonis *5-8 Dominion Parade, Station Road, Harrow, Middx HA1 2TR (8863 3399).*

Hounslow, Middlesex

In the area

Nando's *1 High Street, Hounslow, Middx TW3 1RH (8570 5881).*
Pizza Express *41-43 High Street, Hounslow, Middx TW3 1RH (8577 8522).*

Ilford, Essex

★ Mandarin Palace

559-561 Cranbrook Road, Gants Hill, Ilford, Essex IG2 6JZ (8550 7661). Gants Hill tube. **Lunch served** noon-4pm, **dinner served** 6.30-11.30pm Mon-Sat. **Meals served** noon-midnight Sun. **Dim sum served** noon-4pm Mon-Sat; noon-5pm Sun. **Average** ££. **Set dinner** £19.50-£39 per person (minimum 2). Chinese

Now more than 30 years' old, this legendary Chinese restaurant on a roundabout near Gants Hill tube is no desolate takeaway. The decor is old-fashioned, but a cheerful buzz rose from a smart, mainly Chinese clientele on our visit. A smiling waitress showed us to a table set with crisp white linen, fresh flowers, peanuts and pickled cabbage. Then came exquisite dumplings (prawn and chive a highlight), and tender baby squid in a gingery curry sauce, plus well-filled oyster and beancurd rolls and coriander-specked fish balls. Grilled water-chestnut paste and sesame prawn rolls were hits too, but the heavy wrapping on cheung fun (steamed rice pasta parcels) disappointed. Everything arrived hot, fresh and fragrant, including scented hand towels that followed the complimentary oranges.

In the area

Nando's *I-Scene, Clements Road, Ilford, Essex IG1 1BP (8514 6012).*

Outer London

Kingston, Surrey

Cammasan

*8 Charter Quay, High Street,
Kingston, Surrey KT1 1NB
(8549 3510/www.cammasan.
co.uk). Kingston rail.* **Lunch served**
noon-3pm, **dinner served** 6-11pm
Mon-Fri. **Meals served** noon-11pm
Sat, Sun. **Average** ££. **Set meal**
£14.90-£20.90 per person (minimum
2). Oriental

Refreshingly low-key and still
commendably independent in a sea
of famous-name chain restaurants
exploiting the wharfside location,
Cammasan is in fact two separate
restaurants. The first-floor dining
room serves high-quality traditional
Chinese food, while the informal
noodle bar downstairs (where we
ate) serves huge portions of dishes
from all over Asia to customers at
communal benchside tables. Chilli
beef noodle soup had a fiery heat
that complemented rather than
drowned the spices, and the beef
was sliced across the grain and
flash-cooked to keep it tender in the
classic mainland Chinese style.
Honey-basted ribs had less of a wow
factor, but were still competently
prepared. You can order grass jelly
and other speciality Asian drinks, as
well as wine and beer.

fish! kitchen

*58 Coombe Road, Kingston, Surrey
KT2 7AF (8546 2886/www.fish
kitchen.com). Norbiton rail/57,
85, 213 bus.* **Meals served** noon-
10pm Tue-Sat. **Average** £££.
Fish & chips

Kingston's fish! kitchen looks like a
shiny-tiled tribute to fish and chip
cafés of the past, but with modern
touches – from swordfish club
sandwiches to the red pepper salsa
served with daily grills. When
owner Tony Allan's adjacent
fishmonger Jarvis is open, choose
from the counter; otherwise, grills

are chalked up on a blackboard. A
fresh tuna steak from the latter was
a success, but a dish of fish and
chips disappointed: the tartare sauce
was insufficiently astringent, and
the beer batter on our otherwise
commendable haddock was thick,
podgy and soft. There was also a
chip problem: we were told that the
potatoes had too high a sugar
content, hence their rather burnt
exteriors and undercooked interiors,
but the friendly young team
knocked them off the bill.

★ Riverside Vegetaria

*64 High Street, Kingston, Surrey
KT1 1HN (8546 0609/www.rsveg.
plus.com). Kingston rail.* **Meals
served** noon-11pm daily. **Average**
££. Vegetarian

This Thames-side terrace restaurant
opened in 1989, but feels a decade or
two older: the carnations and
wooden chairs with colourful tie-on
cushions are delightfully kitsch.
Organic apple wine came quickly
by the glass, and the gorgeous
complimentary garlic bread was
made from a nutty wholemeal loaf.
Stuffed avocado was buried under
iceberg lettuce, cucumber and french
dressing, and a masala dosai (South
Indian pancake stuffed with spiced
potatoes), with a helpful kick of
coconut sambal, was delicious.
When the mains arrived, it was clear
we'd ordered too much: enormous
helpings of a rather retro salad came
with everything; Jamaican stew was
a spicy mix of beans, sweet potato
and coconut milk; red lentil and
avocado kedgeree was equally
flavourful. A wonderful experience.

Terra Mia

*138 London Road, Kingston, Surrey
KT2 6QJ (8546 4888). Kingston
rail.* **Lunch served** noon-2.30pm,
dinner served 6-11.30pm Mon-
Sat (occasional Sun). **Average** ££.
Set lunch (Mon-Fri) £5 1 course.
Pizza & pasta

Although it stands next to a busy junction, there's a relaxed, family feel to Terra Mia, fostered by the dog-eared postcards and football memorabilia scattered around the walls, and by the cheery, child-friendly service from waiters who swap banter in Italian. There's a handful of specials (starters and mains) chalked on the board, but the core of the menu is a solid and fairly priced range of standard pizzas and pastas (choose your own shape), prepared in simple, unpretentious and satisfying fashion. The desserts – mostly based on ice cream – have something of a straight-from-the-freezer air, but overall, eating here is a comforting experience. You'll feel like you're having supper with your Italian in-laws.

Meal deals

Blue Hawaii *2 Richmond Road, Kingston, Surrey KT2 5EB (8549 6989/www.bluehawaii.co.uk).* Set meal £11.95, unlimited barbecue £15 2 courses. Hawaiian

In the area

Byron Hamburgers *4 Jerome Place, Charter Quay, Kingston, Surrey KT1 1HX (8541 4757).*
Carluccio's Caffè *Charter Quay, Kingston, Surrey KT1 1HT (8549 5898).*
Gourmet Burger Kitchen *42-46 High Street, Kingston, Surrey KT1 1HL (8546 1649).*
Nando's *37-38 High Street, Kingston, Surrey KT1 1LQ (8296 9540).*
Paul *3-5 Eden Walk, Kingston, Surrey KT1 1BP (8549 6799).*
Pizza Express *5 The Rotunda, Kingston, Surrey KT1 1QJ (8547 3133).*
Strada *1 The Griffin Centre, Market Place, Kingston, Surrey KT1 1JT (8974 8555).*
Wagamama *16-18 High Street, Kingston, Surrey KT1 1EY (8546 1117).*

Zizzi *43 Market Place, Kingston, Surrey KT1 1JQ (8546 0717).*

New Malden, Surrey

★ Hamgipak

169 High Street, New Malden, Surrey KT3 4BH (8942 9588). New Malden rail. **Meals served** 11am-10pm Mon, Tue, Thur-Sun. **Average** ££. Korean

This may be a tiny, family-run affair, but the attention is in the details – such as the utilitarian blond wood benches and tables with hooks under the chairs to hold bags. Delicious Korean side dishes begin the meal; the kimchi was clearly own-made, and the spiced potato slices were a treat. Most people come for the warming chigae stew, and our soo doo boo version of soft tofu, oysters and an egg in zingy kimchi broth was just the thing for a chilly night. Barbecued short ribs and belly pork came in amazingly large portions. The place was only half full on our weekend visit, but the service was top-notch throughout, with a great deal of kindly Korean hospitality from the owner.

★ Jee Cee Neh

74 Burlington Road, New Malden, Surrey KT3 4NU (8942 0682). New Malden rail. **Lunch served** noon-3pm, **dinner served** 6-11pm Tue-Fri. **Meals served** 11.30am-10.30pm Sat, Sun. **Average** ££. Korean

Jee Cee Neh is upbeat, inviting and sophisticated; the long dining hall is lined with dark wood barbecue tables – packed out with Korean families most lunchtimes – and a modernist mural of green stripes runs along one wall. A bowl of yukkaejang (a rich, chilli-infused broth of shredded beef, egg and green onions, with a kick any mule would be proud of) could easily have fed two. We barely had space for the main course: tender belly pork fried with chilli and ssam jang (fermented bean paste). Enormous jeongol stews, served bubbling at the table, seem the dish of choice for locals. The drinks menu runs to wine, beer, and lemon and cucumber soju (rice wine). Korean barley tea is free.

Palace NEW

183-185 High Street, New Malden, Surrey KT3 4BH (8949 3737). New Malden rail. **Meals served** noon-11pm Mon-Sat. **Average** ££. Korean
Of the roughly half dozen Korean canteens dotted around New Malden High Street, Palace sits at the bottom end of the price spectrum, and the location attracts shoppers looking for a quick bite. Inside, you'll find a relaxed café vibe (the friendly owners have covered the walls with Korean bric-a-brac), and barbecue fare cooked on cute, 1950s-style chrome gas burners. A quick bowl of fish and kimchi chigae (a warming stew of green onions, fermented cabbage leaves, chilli and mackerel, with a smouldering chilli heat) came with six small plates of namul and pickles – the garlic stems in sweet chilli sauce were particularly tasty. Great food, but atmospherically better suited to a quick lunch than a lingering dinner.

You-Me

96 Burlington Road, New Malden, Surrey KT3 4NT (8715 1079). New Malden rail. **Set meal** £17.90-£19.90 per person. Korean
You-Me is small, homely and slightly chaotic, which adds to its charm. Tables covered in pink doily tablecloths are divided by wood and paper screens, and the walls are covered in posters. We like this place as much for its friendliness as its food; the genial owners are keen to explain the rules of Korean dining, and the menu has photos of every dish. We also love the home-made taste of the wangmandu: steamed rice dumplings stuffed with meat and vegetables, a little like Chinese bao buns. Khan pung gi (garlic chicken) was less impressive; the batter was a little stodgy and the flavours muted. Based on past experience, the soups, stews and barbecues tend to be better than the range of fried dishes.

Richmond, Surrey

Chez Lindsay

11 Hill Rise, Richmond, Surrey TW10 6UQ (8948 7473/www.chez lindsay.co.uk). Richmond tube/rail. **Meals served** noon-10.45pm Mon-Sat; noon-9.45pm Sun. **Average** £££. **Set lunch** (noon-3pm Mon-Sat) £14.50 2 courses, £17.50 3 courses. **Set dinner** (after 6pm) £18.50 2 courses, £21.50 3 courses. French
Lindsay Wooton's famously lively restaurant has been serving rustic French fare for years, and is as popular as ever. When it's busy, service can be frustratingly slow, but a sunny atmosphere and view of the Thames do help. Authentic Breton cooking is the thing, but you'll need to order carefully. Seafood dishes are one of the kitchen's strong points, but the top billing has to go to the nutty buckwheat galettes, which come with a huge choice of fillings. Simple ham, cheese and spinach was perfect, especially with a refreshing Brittany cider; more adventurous options include chitterlings, onions and mustard sauce. Pancakes also tend to make the best puddings: a frangipane crêpe was divinely sweet and buttery. Bistro classics were decidedly less memorable: onion soup lacked flavour, and the apple tart failed to excite.

Outer London

Stein's

*55 Richmond Towpath, west
of Richmond Bridge, Richmond,
Surrey TW10 6UX (8948 8189/
www.stein-s.com). Richmond tube/
rail then 20mins walk or 65 bus.*
Meals served *Summer* 11am-
9pm daily. *Winter* noon-6pm Sat,
Sun. **Average** ££. German

This family-friendly Bavarian beer
garden is a stone's throw from
Richmond bridge. Converted from a
ramshackle ice-cream parlour in
2004, it consists of a kiosk with a
sizeable kitchen behind it, and a
clutch of benches beside the river;
there's also a safe, small area where
under-fives can play. The menu is all
German. The Bavarian cheese and
sausage sharing platter was
excellent – three cheeses, seven cold
meats, salad and gherkins, and some
soft bread rolls. Bratkartoffeln
(potatoes sautéed with bacon, onion
and spices) was fine comfort food,
and you can also get some mean
breakfasts and strudel desserts.
German beer flows freely, and the
Almdudler (apple-flavoured herbal
lemonade) is delicious. Order at the
kiosk, then wait for your food.

In the area

ASK *85 Kew Green, Richmond,
Surrey TW9 3AH (8940 3766).*
Carluccio's Caffè *31-35 Kew
Road, Richmond, Surrey TW9 2NQ
(8940 5037).*
Giraffe *30 Hill Street, Richmond,
Surrey TW9 1TW (8332 2646).*
Gourmet Burger Kitchen
*15-17 Hill Rise, Richmond, Surrey
TW10 6UQ (8940 5440).*
Maison Blanc *27B The Quandrant,
Richmond, Surrey TW9 1DN
(8332 7041).*
Nando's *2&4 Hill Rise, Richmond,
Surrey TW10 6UA (8940 8810).*
Paul *13 The Quadrant, Richmond,
Surrey TW9 1BP (8940 5250).*
Pizza Al Rollo *20 Hill Street,
Richmond, Surrey TW9 1TN
(8940 8951). Branch of Café Pasta.*

Strada *26 Hill Street, Richmond,
Surrey TW9 1TW (8940 3141).*
Wagamama *3 Hill Street,
Richmond, Surrey TW9 1SX
(8948 2224).*
Zizzi *4-5 King Street, Richmond,
Surrey TW9 1ND (8332 2809).*

Southall, Middlesex

★ Brilliant NEW

*72-76 Western Road, Southall,
Middx (8574 1928/www.brilliant
restaurant.com). Southall rail.*
Lunch served noon-3pm Tue-
Fri. **Dinner served** 6-11.30pm
Tue-Sun. **Average** ££. Indian

Wafts of incense shroud a Ganesh
figurine by the front door, a screen
belts out Bollywood pop, and the
happy chatter of a full house creates
a chaotic buzz. The food is a
Kenyan/Punjabi take on Indian
cuisine. From the own-made pickles
(including the sharp lemon and
mustard seed creation served in
many Punjabi homes), to soft, thin
roomali (handkerchief) roti, every
dish on our recent visit packed a

Brilliant

punch. Starters included the Kenyan favourite nyama choma (salty, lemony grilled lamb chops with a good hit of chilli). Silky seekh kebabs of ground lamb with fresh green chilli and coriander, and fried tilapia fillets in spicy gram-flour batter, were both superbly tasty, as was a generous main of boneless chicken spiced with cumin.

Madhu's

39 South Road, Southall, Middx UB1 1SW (8574 1897). Southall rail. **Lunch served** 12.30-3pm Mon, Wed-Fri. **Dinner served** 6-11.30pm Mon, Wed-Sun. **Set meal** £17.50-£20 per person (minimum 6) 16 dishes incl tea or coffee. Indian
Gleaming glass panels, glossy black tiles and crisp table linen set the scene for upmarket dining at Southall's smartest restaurant. The dishes are mainly North Indian, but menu specialities such as nyama choma (smoky lamb ribs, much loved for their lemony zing) have an African twist. Deep-fried mini patties of grated paneer, pounded peas and

chopped fenugreek had a tangy tease of peppery flavour that worked well with the sweetness of tamarind chutney, but a main course of chicken curry simmered with slivers of gourd was let down by an oily masala that rather overpowered the fruit. Disappointingly, the very same spice base reappeared in a chickpea curry, and although the breads were excellent, we felt Mahdu's fell short elsewhere – the service, for example, could do with being more confident and less obsequious.

New Asian Tandoori Centre (Roxy)

114-118 The Green, Southall, Middx UB2 4BQ (8574 2597). Southall rail. **Meals served** 8am-11pm Mon-Thur; 8am-midnight Fri-Sun. **Average** ££. Indian
In business for over 30 years, this family-run Southall institution has expanded from takeaway joint to 'tandoori centre'. Beyond the canteen-style takeaway hall, a functional, brightly lit central room has frosted windows, tiled floors and

long communal tables. The largely Punjabi menu, characterised by rich and earthy flavours, includes a few good South Indian dishes. Our pakoras, although a little dense and doughy, were lifted by fresh coriander; the Indian truck driver's favourite, chana dhal, was perfectly thick, buttery and tempered with toasted cumin seeds. The chickpeas in the chana bhatura were fragrant and judiciously spiced, but the accompanying bhatura (deep-fried dough) was deflated and oily. The nan, happily, was sweet, light and flaky. One downside to the dining experience was the service: friendly, but painfully slow.

In the area

Mirch Masala *171-173 The Broadway, Southall, Middx UB1 1LX (8867 9222).*

Sudbury, Middlesex

Five Hot Chillies

875 Harrow Road, Sudbury, Middx HA0 2RH (8908 5900). Sudbury Town or Sudbury Hill tube. **Meals served** *noon-midnight daily.* **Average** *££.* **Unlicensed.** **Corkage** *no charge.* Indian Contrary to its name, Five Hot Chillies offers authentic Punjabi cooking that won't scorch your taste buds. If you can't grab the attention of the friendly but busy waiters, simply place your order at the counter of this clean, no-frills café. We started with juicy lamb kebabs and a zesty plate of chilli paneer. For mains, it's best to choose a dish made in the karahi, an iron wok used to prepare food in Punjabi households. Karahi gosht was scrumptious: tender mutton pieces in a thick tomato, ginger, garlic and chilli sauce (order nan, roti or rice to soak up the oil). Karahi saag paneer – a blend of spinach, cream and shallow-fried paneer – was less

impressive, but the almond kulfi with which we finished our meal was rich and superbly refreshing.

Sutton, Surrey

In the area

Nando's *9-11 High Street, Sutton, Surrey SM1 1DF (8770 0180).*
Pizza Express *4 High Street, Sutton, Surrey SM1 1HN (8643 4725).*
Zizzi *13-15 High Street, Sutton, Surrey SM1 1DF (8661 8778).*

Teddington, Middlesex

In the area

Pizza Express *11 Waldegrave Road, Teddington, Middx TW11 8LA (8943 3553).*

Twickenham, Middlesex

Meal deals

Brula *43 Crown Road, Twickenham, Middx TW1 3EJ (8892 0602/www.brula.co.uk).* Set lunch (Mon-Fri) £15 2 courses. French
Ma Cuisine Le Petit Bistrot *6 Whitton Road, Twickenham, Middx TW1 1BJ (8607 9849/ www.macuisinetw1.co.uk).* Set lunch £12.95 2 courses, £15.50 3 courses. French

In the area

Loch Fyne *175 Hampton Road, Twickenham, Middx TW2 5NG (8255 6222).*
Pizza Express *21 York Street, Twickenham, Middx TW1 3JZ (8891 4126).*
Sagar *27 York Street, Twickenham, Middx TW1 3JZ (8744 3868).*
Zizzi *36 York Street, Twickenham, Middx TW1 3LJ (8538 9024).*

Outer London

Uxbridge, Middlesex

★ Satya

33 Rockingham Road, Uxbridge, Middx UB8 2TZ (01895 274250). Uxbridge tube. **Lunch served** noon-3pm, **dinner served** 6-11pm daily. **Average ££. Set buffet** (noon-3pm Mon-Fri) £6.50. Indian

A shocking fuchsia facade belies the stylish interior (taupe and deep red walls, crisp white tablecloths, soft lighting and wooden floors) of this neighbourhood restaurant. We were warmly greeted by a line of waiters eager to recommend their native Keralan dishes – uthappam, idlis, adai with avial – and the likes of methi bhajia (dense, deep-fried balls made from fenugreek leaves and banana). The house speciality is chicken with fresh ginger, onion and green chilli, perfect with the coconut-flecked rice. Chutneys were fresh and tangy, making ideal partners. The potato filling of the masala dosa could have been less vigorously mashed, ditto the pumpkin cooked with black-eyed beans, but flavours were clean and light, and the food was thoughtfully spiced.

In the area

Nando's *The Chimes Centre, Uxbridge, Middx UB8 1GE (01895 274277).*
Pizza Express *222 High Street, Uxbridge, Middx UB8 1LD (01895 251222).*

Wembley, Middlesex

Karahi King

213 East Lane, Wembley, Middx HA0 3NG (8904 2760). North Wembley tube/245 bus. **Meals served** noon-midnight daily. **Unlicensed. Corkage** no charge. Indian

If you're in the mood for pleasingly greasy, cheap and cheerful Punjabi food, cooked before you in the open kitchen, this is the place for you. To prepare most of its dishes, Karahi King uses the karahi (a wok-like vessel) and lots of oil. There's a wide choice of vegetarian food, such as karahi chana (chickpeas), bhindi (okra) and paneer, but we opted for karahi saag gosht – which turned out to be a rather uninspired green mush of lamb pieces, cardamom shells and spinach. Karahi chicken tikka was better: the onion, garlic, tomato and coriander were fresh, and each bite ended with a tangy burst of lemon. Main courses are huge, so skip the starters – although the chilli bhajia (battered, deep-fried whole chillies) is delicious.

Sakonis

129 Ealing Road, Wembley, Middx HA0 4BP (8903 9601). Alperton tube/183 bus. **Breakfast served** 9-11am Sat, Sun. **Meals served** noon-10pm daily. **Average £. Set buffet** (breakfast) £4.99; (noon-4pm) £7.99; (7-9.30pm) £10.99. Indian

This no-frills flagship branch of the vegetarian chain is popular with locals. Turnover is fast, service efficient but abrupt, and the food keeps punters returning. As well as the popular buffet, a wide menu includes Indo-Chinese, South Indian specialities, and snacks with an East African influence. Pani puri (puffed pastries filled with potatoes and tamarind water) were light and crisp enough to hold the thin, spiced sauce, and crunchy aloo bhajia (potato slices fried in coriander-flecked batter) were delicious. Disappointments included the bhel poori – too sweet and lacking tang – but aloo papadi chat (crushed popadoms, potatoes and spikes of raw onion smothered with sweet yoghurt and herby chutney) was spot-on. Iced lassis were also perfect.

Sanghamam

531-533 High Road, Wembley, Middx HA0 2DJ (8900 0777/ www.sanghamam.co.uk). Wembley Central tube. **Meals served** 8am-11pm daily. **Average £. Set lunch** (11am-4pm) £3.95 3 dishes. **Set thali** £4.95-£6.95. Indian

Sanghamam claims to serve Gujarati, North and South Indian food, and Chinese dishes, but its antecedents are Tamil; most of the customers and all the staff speak rapid Tamil or thick Tamil-accented English, and Tamil songs play in the background. A tomato and onion uthappam (fluffy South Indian pancake of fermented rice and lentil batter) was fresh from the pan, filling and tasty; the accompanying coconut, coriander and turmeric chutneys were full-flavoured too. More variable were the sambars (South Indian vegetable curries): the first was lukewarm and bland, the second surprisingly hot, spicy and delicious. The trappings at Sanghamam may be utilitarian – heavy steel cutlery, laminated menu cards and fast, no-frills service – but it's a safe bet for quick, wholesome, good-value South Indian food.

In the area
Nando's *420-422 High Road, Wembley, Middx HA9 6AH (8795 3564).*

Woodford, Essex

George's [NEW]

164 George Lane, South Woodford E18 1AY (8989 3970/www.georges fishbar.co.uk). South Woodford tube. **Lunch served** noon-2.30pm, **dinner served** 5-10.30pm Tue-Sat. **Average ££.** Fish & chips

George Nicola's fish and chips joint was treated to a swish makeover in 2007 that transformed it from a cheap and cheerful chippie into an enviable local restaurant. At the front you'll find a pristine cooking and takeaway area where cod, squid and the likes are battered and bagged up for customers in a rush; at the back is a romantically lit restaurant serving everything you'd expect from a traditional fish and chips spot, plus a sizeable list of Cypriot meze and souvlaki. A dish of complimentary nibbles (olives, pickles, raw veg) comes while you peruse the menu; portions are generous, and starters like the creamy tahini dip are better shared if you have a hope of cleaning your plates during the main course.

Pizzeria Bel-Sit

439 High Road, Woodford Green, Woodford, Essex IG8 0XE (8504 1164). W13, 20 bus. **Lunch served** noon-2.30pm Tue-Sat, **dinner served** 6-11pm Mon-Sat. **Average ££. No credit cards.** Pizza & pasta

There's a corner of Woodford that will be forever Italy. The decor at this bustling restaurant mixes the Italian passion for *calcio* (football jerseys and scarves adorn the walls) with the Essex passion for celebrity (signed mug shots include one of *EastEnders* actor Steve McFadden). Amazingly, it works, though that's perhaps more to do with the Rimini-born owners and their warm and welcoming staff. The keenly priced and generously portioned food is of a high standard. Starters include the usual garlic breads and sharing plates, and pizzas are the highlights of the mains; the calzone genovese, filled with clams, squid, prawns and mozzarella, was superb. For dessert, profiteroles with white and milk chocolate sauce are an indulgence not to be missed.

In the area
Pizza Express *76 High Road, South Woodford E18 2NA (8924 4488).*

INDEXES & MAPS

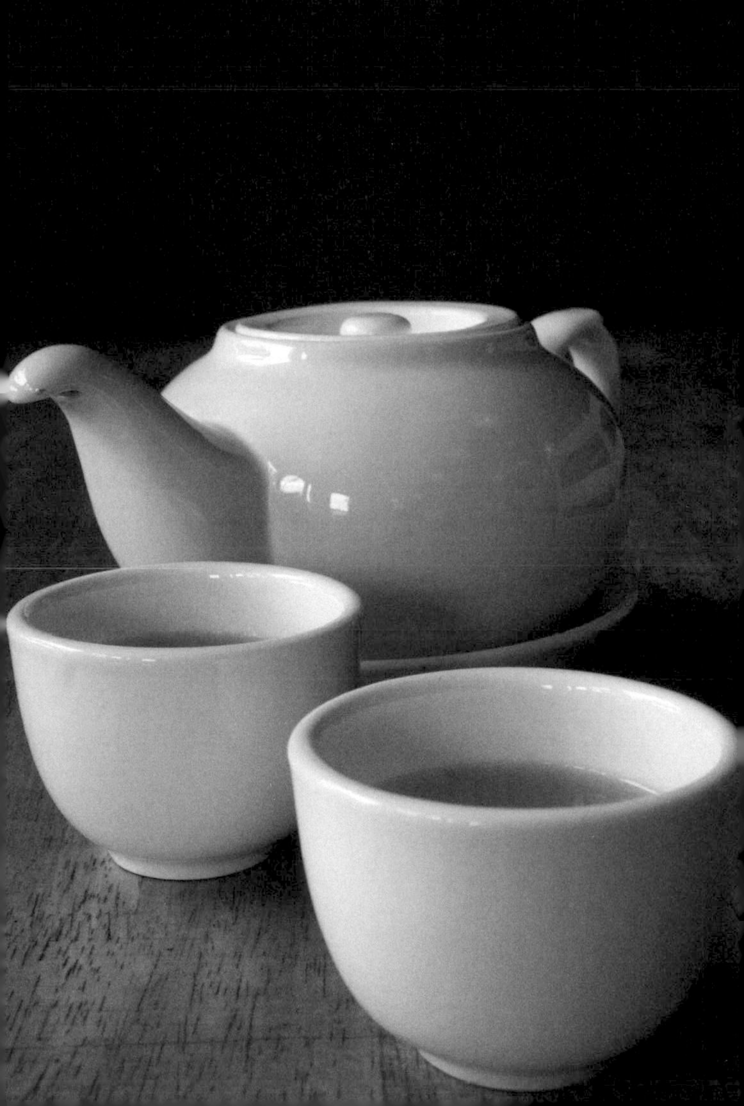

Greater London

MILL HILL   BARNET

STANMORE   EDGWARE   FINCHLEY

NORTH WEST

PINNER   WEALDSTONE   KINGSBURY   HENDON

HARROW   KENTON   GOLDERS GREEN   HAMPSTEAD

OUTER LONDON

See p30U

NORTHOLT   WEMBLEY   CRICKLEWOOD   ST JOHN'S WOOD

See p283

GREENFORD   PERIVALE   WILLESDEN   KILBURN

HARLESDEN   KENSAL RISE   MAIDA VALE   PADDINGTON

See pp264-265

A40(M)

WEST   NOTTING HILL

SOUTHALL   HANWELL   EALING   ACTON   KENSINGTON

M41   **CE**

SHEPHERD'S BUSH

HAMMERSMITH   EARL'S COURT   CHELSEA

HESTON   M4   BRENTFORD   CHISWICK

KEW   See p282   FULHAM

BARNES   PARSONS GREEN

PUTNEY

See p293

HOUNSLOW   RICHMOND UPON THAMES   WANDSWORTH

See p284

TWICKENHAM

SOUTH WEST

HANWORTH

TEDDINGTON   OUTER LONDON   WIMBLEDON

SUNBURY

HAMPTON   KINGSTON UPON THAMES   MERTON

EAST   SHORDTON   NEW   MORDEN

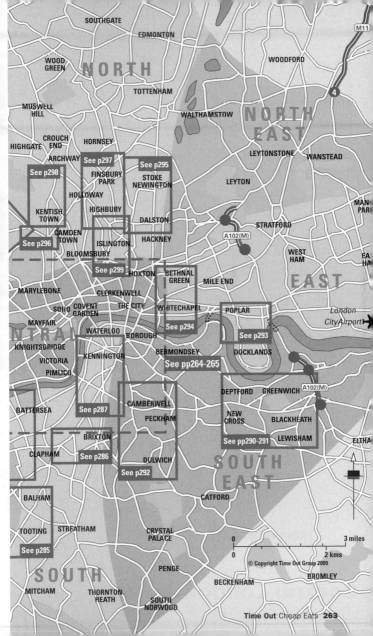

SOUTHGATE

EDMONTON

M11

WOOD
GREEN

NORTH

WOODFORD

4

MUSWELL
HILL

TOTTENHAM

HORNSEY

WALTHAMSTOW

NORTH
EAST

LEYTONSTONE

WANSTEAD

HIGHGATE

CROUCH
END

ARCHWAY

See p297

See p298

FINSBURY
PARK

See p295

STOKE
NEWINGTON

LEYTON

MAN
PARK

HOLLOWAY

HIGHBURY

KENTISH
TOWN

See p296

CAMDEN
TOWN

DALSTON

STRATFORD

A102(M)

ISLINGTON

HACKNEY

WEST
HAM

EA
HA

BLOOMSBURY

See p299

HOXTON

BETHNAL
GREEN

MILE END

EAST

MARYLEBONE

CLERKENWELL

SOHO

COVENT
GARDEN

THE CITY

WHITECHAPEL

POPLAR

London
CityAirport

MAYFAIR

CENTRAL

WATERLOO

See p294

See p293

KNIGHTSBRIDGE

BOROUGH

DOCKLANDS

VICTORIA

KENNINGTON

BERMONDSEY

PIMLICO

See pp264-265

DEPTFORD

GREENWICH

A102(M)

BATTERSEA

See p287

CAMBERWELL

PECKHAM

NEW
CROSS

BLACKHEATH

CLAPHAM

BRIXTON

See p286

DULWICH

See pp290-291

LEWISHAM

ELTHA

See p292

SOUTH
EAST

BALHAM

CATFORD

TOOTING

STREATHAM

See p285

CRYSTAL
PALACE

0   3 miles

0   2 kms

© Copyright Time Out Group 2009

SOUTH

MITCHAM

THORNTON
HEATH

PENGE

SOUTH
NORWOOD

BECKENHAM

BROMLEY

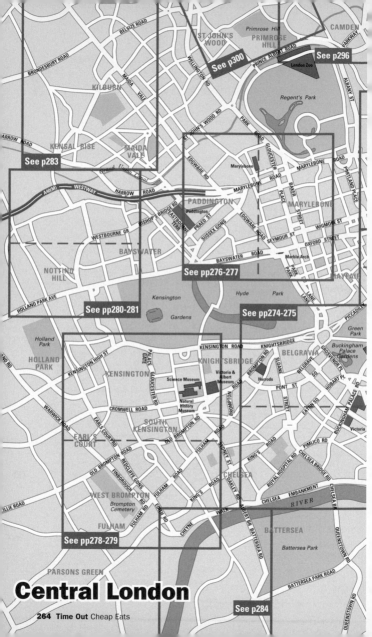

See p300

See p296

See p283

See pp276-277

See pp280-281

See pp274-275

See pp278-279

See p284

Central London

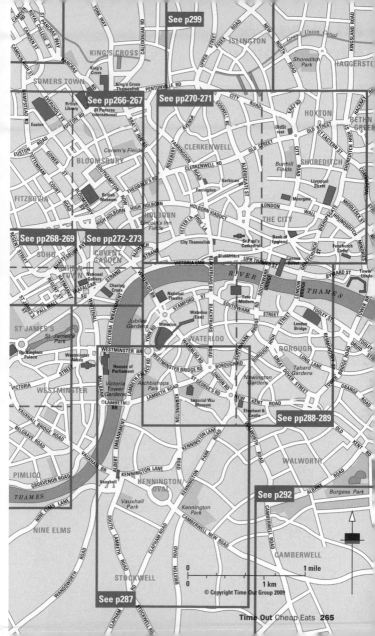

See p299
See pp266-267
See pp270-271
See pp268-269
See pp272-273
See pp288-289
See p292
See p287

© Copyright Time Out Group 2009

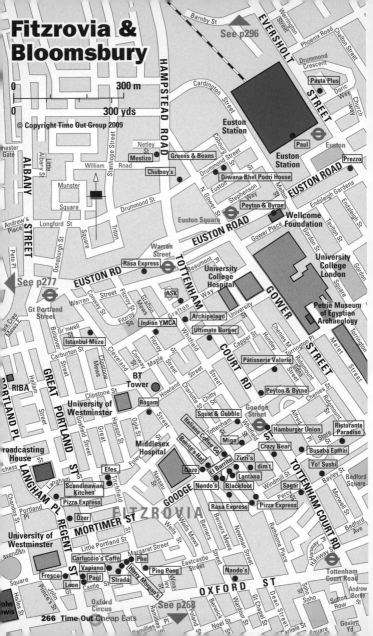

Fitzrovia & Bloomsbury

See p296

0   300 m

300 yds

© Copyright Time Out Group 2009

See p277

See p268

Barnby St

EVERSHOLT STREET

Warrington Crescent

Phoenix Road

Chalton St

Drummond Crescent

Cardington Street

Pasta Plus

Doric Way

Church Way

HAMPSTEAD ROAD

Netley St

Mestizo

William Road

Stanhope Street

Greens & Beans

Chutney's

Drummond Street

Coburg Street

Euston St

N Gower St

Euston Station

Euston Station

Paul

Euston

EUSTON ROAD

Prezzo

Diwana Bhel Poori House

Stephenson Way

Peyton & Byrne

Endsleigh Gardens

Endsleigh St

ALBANY STREET

Little Albany St

Munster Square

Longford St

Drummond St

Triton Street

Euston Square

EUSTON RD

Gower Place

Wellcome Foundation

Taviton St

Gordon St

Andrew's Place

Peto Pl

Osnaburgh St

Warren Street

Rasa Express

EUSTON RD

TOTTENHAM

Gower Place

University College London

Gordon Square

Gt Portland Street

Park Cres Mews E

Warren Street

Conway Street

Fitzroy St

Beaumont

Grafton Way

University College Hospital

University Street

GOWER STREET

Chenies M

Huntley St

Ridgmount

Torrington Pl

Torrington Square

Petrie Museum of Egyptian Archaeology

Malet Street

Torrington

ASK

Grafton Mews

Indian YMCA

Archipelago

Ultimate Burger

Capper St

Pâtisserie Valerie

RIBA

GREAT PORTLAND

Hallam St

Carburton Street

Clipstone Mews

Istanbul Meze

Gr'nwell

Cleveland Street

Maple Street

Conway Street

Whitfield Street

Charlotte St

Chitty St

Goodge Street

Peyton & Byrne

Ridgmount St

Alfred Pl

Chenies St

Ridgmount St

BT Tower

Clipstone St

Howland Street

Ragam

Goodge Street

Squat & Gobble

Tottenham

COURT RD

Hamburger Union

Store St

Ristorante Paradiso

University of Westminster

Gosfield Street

Great Titchfield Street

Hanson St

Ogle St

Foley St

Middlesex Hospital

Nassau

Benito's Hat

Italiano Coffee Co

Miga

Zizzi's

dim't

Crazy Bear

Busaba Eathai

Yo! Sushi

Windmill St

Bayley St

Bedford Square

Broadcasting House

chess

LANGHAM PL REGENT ST

Langham St

Efes

Scandinavian Kitchen

Pizza Express

Özer

Chandos St

Portland St

GOODGE ST

Tichfield St

Ooze

El Burrito

Nando's

Blackfoot

Lantana

Sagar

Percy

Rasa Express

Pizza Express

Morwell St

Bedford Ave

University of Westminster

Cavendish Square

MORTIMER ST

FITZROVIA ST

Wells Mews

Wells St

Berners Mews

Berners Street

Newman Street

Rathbone Place

Tottenham Court Rd

John Lewis

Hanles St

Fresco

Leon

Carluccio's Caffè

Vapiano

Paul

Strada

Pho

Harry Morgan's

Ping Pong

Eastcastle Street

Margaret Street

Little Portland St

Winsley

Nando's

Hanway St

Hanway Pl

Tottenham Court Road

Oxford Circus

OXFORD STREET

Ramillies

Poland St

Berwick

Noel St

Gt Chapel St

Wardour St

Dean St

Soho St

Sutton Row

Andrew Borde St

Goslett Yd

Carlisle St

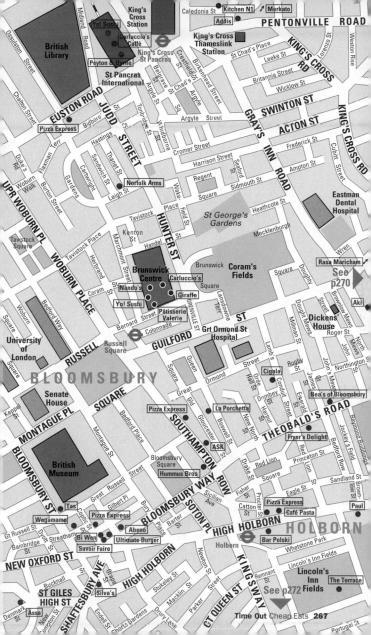

Caledonia St   Kitchen N1   Merkato
Addis
PENTONVILLE ROAD

King's Cross Station
Yo! Sushi
Carluccio's Caffè
King's Cross St Pancras
Peyton & Byrne
St Pancras International
Midland Road

King's Cross Thameslink Station
St Chad's Place
St Chad's St
Leeke St
Britannia Street
Wicklow St

EUSTON ROAD   JUDD   ST
SWINTON ST
ACTON ST

British Library
Ossulston Street
Chalton Street

Pizza Express
Flaxman Terr
Duke's Rd   Woburn Walk
Burton Street
Gardens
Cartwright
Gardens
Sandwich St
Thanet St
Hastings   St
Leigh St
Bidboro St

Birdborough
Argyle Street
Argyle   Square
Cromer Street
Harrison Street
Regent   Square
Sidmouth St
Seaford St
Frederick Street
Ampton St
Cubitt   St

GRAY'S   INN   ROAD
KING'S   CROSS   RD
King's Cross Rise
Weston   St

Norfolk Arms

UPR WOBURN PL
WOBURN   PLACE
Tavistock Square
Tavistock Place
Herbrand   Street
Marchmont   Street
Kenton   St
Handel   St
HUNTER   ST
Wakefield St
St George's Gardens
Heathcote St
Mecklenburgh   Square

Eastman Dental Hospital
Wren   St

Tavistock   Place

Woburn   Square
Bedford Way
University of London
Coram   St
Brunswick   Square
Coram's Fields
Doughty   Street
Millman   St
Roger St

Rasa Maricham
See p270
Aki

Brunswick Centre
Carluccio's
Nando's
Giraffe
Yo! Sushi
Pâtisserie Valerie
Bernard Street
Colonnade
Brunswick   Square
GRENVILLE   ST
Lansdowne   Terr
Guilford   St
Grt Ormond St Hospital
Lamb's   Conduit   Street
Dombey   St
Rugby   St
Emerald   St
Orde   Hall   St
John   St
James   St
Northington   St
North   Mews
Dickens' House
Brownlow   Mews
Doughty   Mews

RUSSELL   SQUARE
Russell Square
GUILFORD   ST
Great   Ormond   Street
Queen   Square
Cigala
Bea's of Bloomsbury

BLOOMSBURY
Senate House
Montague St
Bedford Place
MONTAGUE PL
BLOOMSBURY ST
Keppel St
Montague   Street

THEOBALD'S   ROAD
Fryer's Delight
Raymond   Buildings
Jockey's   Field
Bedford   Row
Princeton   St
Red Lion   Square
Sandland   St
Brown-   low St

Pizza Express
La Porchetta
Gloucester   St
Boswell   St
New North   St
Old   Gloucester   Street

SOUTHAMPTON   ROW
Bloomsbury   Square
ASK
Drake   St
Fisher   St
Eagle   St
Proctor   St
Catton   St
Pizza Express
Paul

British Museum
Great Russell   Street
Gilbert   Pl
Bury   Place
Bloomsbury   Way
SOTON   PL
Sicilian   Ave
Barter   St
HIGH   HOLBORN
Café Pasta
HOLBORN
Whetstone Park

Tas
Wagamama
Pizza Express
Abeno
Bi Won
Ultimate Burger
Savoir Faire
Hummus Bros
Comic   Show
Dyott   Streatham
Streatham   St

Bar Polski
KINGSWAY
See p272
Lincoln's Inn Fields
The Terrace

NEW OXFORD ST
Gt Russell St
Bainbridge St
HIGH   HOLBORN
GT   QUEEN   ST

Bucknall   St
ST GILES HIGH ST
SHAFTESBURY   AVE
Silva's
Stukeley St
Macklin   St
Parker   Street
Remnant   St
Newton   St

Assa
Denmark St
New   Compton   St
Endell   St
Short's   Gardens
Drury   Lane

Portugal   St

Soho & Chinatown

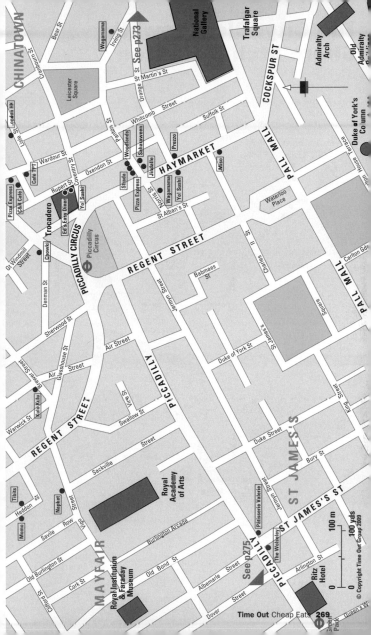

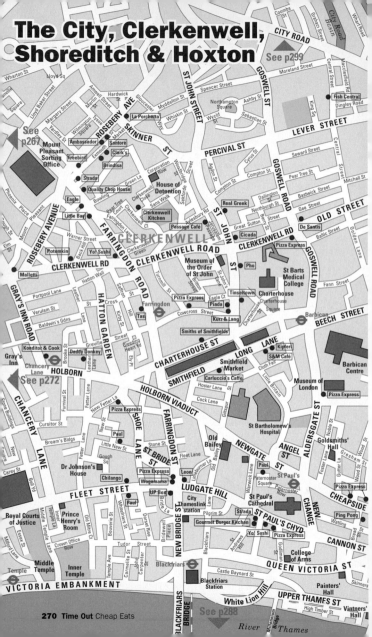

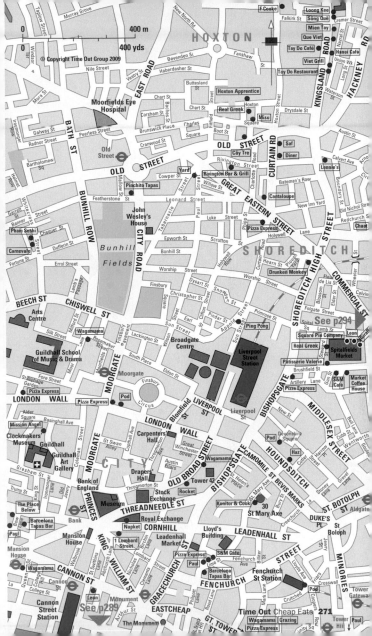

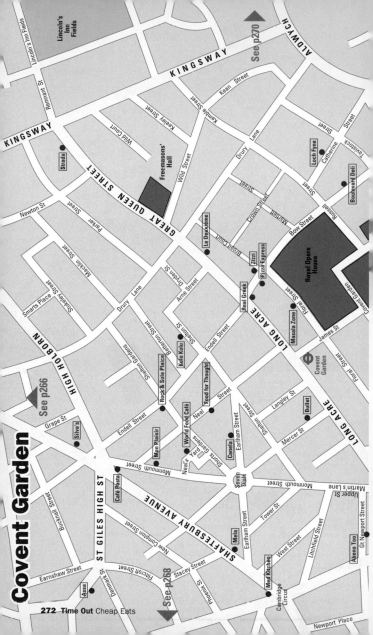

Covent Garden

Lincoln's Inn Fields

KINGSWAY

See p270

KINGSWAY

Remnant St

Lincoln's Inn Fields

KINGSWAY

Keeley Street

Kemble Street

Kean Street

ALDWYCH

Tavistock Street

Catherine Street

Russell Street

Loch Fyne

Boulevard Deli

Wild Court

Freemasons' Hall

Wild Street

Drury Lane

Marquis Street

Crown Street

Bow Street

Newton St

GREAT QUEEN STREET

Parker Street

Macklin Street

Smarts Place

Stukeley Street

Le Deuxième

Broad Court

Zizzi

Pizza Express

Real Greek

Masala Zone

Royal Opera House

Covent Garden

Floral Street

James St

HIGH HOLBORN

See p266

Grape St

Silva's

Drury Lane

Dryden St

Arne Street

Shelton St

Endell Street

LONG ACRE

Floral Street

Stukeley Gardens

Betterton Street

Rock & Sole Plaice

Kulu Kulu

Food for Thought!

Neal Street

Langley St.

Buffet

LONG ACRE

Endell Street

Mon Plaisir

World Food Café

Shorts Gardens

Neal's Yard

Canela

Earlham Street

Shelton Street

Mercer St

Monmouth Street

Upper St Martin's Lane

Grape St

Café Pasta

Seven Dials

Monmouth Street

Gt Newport St

ST GILES HIGH ST

SHAFTESBURY AVENUE

Bucknall Street

New Compton Street

Mela

Earlham Street

Tower St

West Street

Litchfield Street

Abeno Too

Earnshaw Street

Flitcroft Street

Stacey Street

Phoenix St

Maf Kitchen

Cambridge Circus

Newport Place

Denmark St

Assa

See p268

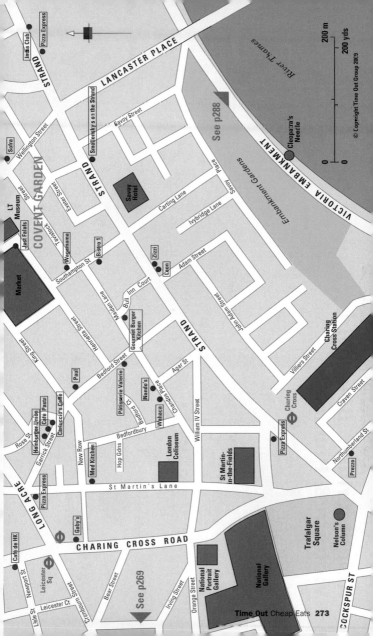

STRAND

Juan Club
Pizza Express

LANCASTER PLACE

River Thames

Wellington Street

COVENT GARDEN

Sofra

Exeter Street

STRAND

Smollensky's on the Strand

Savoy Street

See p288

© Copyright Time Out Group 2009

200 m
200 yds

LT Museum

Tavistock Street

Just Falafs

Wagamama

Bistro 1

Southampton St

Savoy Hotel

Carting Lane

VICTORIA EMBANKMENT

Cleopatra's Needle

Embankment Gardens

Ivybridge Lane

Savoy Place

Market

King Street

James Street

Floral Street

Henrietta Street

Bull Inn Court

Zizzi

Leon

Adam Street

John Adam Street

Charing Cross Station

Maiden Lane

Gourmet Burger Kitchen

Bedford Street

STRAND

Agar St

Villiers Street

Craven Street

Paul

Pâtisserie Valerie

Bedford St

Nando's

Wahaca

Church Street

William IV Street

Charing Cross

Pizza Express

Northumberland St

Rose St

Hamburger Union

Café Pasta

Carluccio's Caffè

Garrick Street

New Row

Bedfordbury

Hop Gdns

London Coliseum

St Martin-in-the-Fields

Prezzo

LONG ACRE

Pizza Express

Med Kitchen

St Martin's Lane

Gaby's

Café de HK

Newport St

Leicester Sq

CHARING CROSS ROAD

Bear Street

Irving Street

Orange Street

National Portrait Gallery

National Gallery

Trafalgar Square

Nelson's Column

Lisle St

Leicester Ct

Cranbourn Street

See p269

COCKSPUR ST

Time Out Cheap Eats **273**

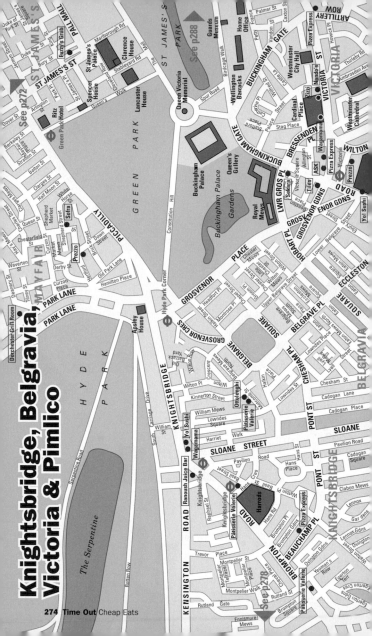

Knightsbridge, Belgravia, Victoria & Pimlico

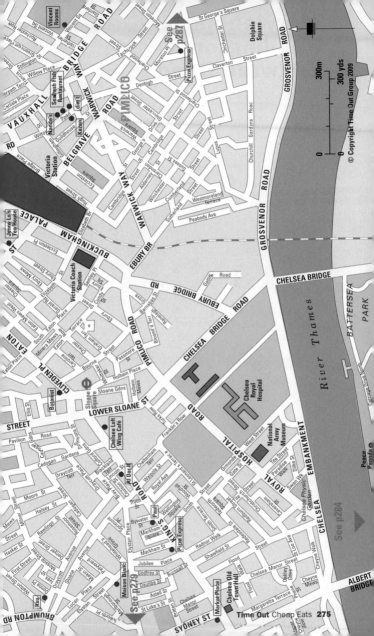

VINCENT ROOMS
Vincent Sq
St George's Square
Dolphin Square

MARYLEBONE ROAD
PIMLICO
VAUXHALL BRIDGE ROAD
WARWICK ROAD
BELGRAVE ROAD
WARWICK WAY
Willow Place
Carlisle Place
Sealish Fish Restaurant
diner
Nando's
Kazan
Victoria Station
Guildhouse
Denbigh Street
Warwick Square
George's Drive
Cambridge Street
Sussex Street
Lupus Street
Moreton Street
Claverton Street
Churchill Gardens Road
Tachbrook Street
Pizza Express
Clarendon St
Gloucester Street
Cambridge St
St George's Drive
Sussex Street
Clarendon Street
Winchester Street
Cumberland Street
Westmoreland Terrace
Peabody Ave
Sutherland Street

GROSVENOR ROAD
See p287

BUCKINGHAM PALACE ROAD
Jenny Lo's Tea House
Eccleston Pl
Eaton Terrace
Elizabeth Bridge
Ebury Bridge Place
Victoria Coach Station
EBURY BR
EBURY BRIDGE ROAD
Gatliff Road

CHELSEA BRIDGE
River Thames
BATTERSEA PARK

EATON
Eaton Mews West
Eaton Place
Cliveden Place
Botanist
LOWER SLOANE ST
Sloane Gdns
Holbein Place
Sloane Square
Chelsea Left Wing Café
At Duck
SLOANE STREET
CHELSEA BRIDGE ROAD
ROYAL HOSPITAL ROAD
Chelsea Royal Hospital
National Army Museum
West Street
Tite Street
Paradise Walk
EMBANKMENT
CHELSEA
Peace Pagoda
See p284

STREET
Pavilion Road
Cadogan Gardens
Draycott Place
Blacklands Terr
Lincoln St
Anderson St
Paul
Bywater St
Markham Square
Pizza Express
KING'S ROAD
Wellington Square
Royal Ave
Walpole St
St Leonard's Terr
Ormonde Gate
Cheltenham Terr
Franklin's Row
Turks Row
Durham Place
Swan Walk
Dilke St
Christchurch Street
Redburn St
Tedworth Square
Radnor Walk
Shawfield St
Flood St
St Loo Ave
Chelsea Manor Street
Oakley Gardens
Cheyne Walk
Cheyne Mews

BRUMPTON RD
Pond Place
Moore St
First Street
Halsey St
Hasker Street
Rawlings St
Denyer Street
Cadogan St
Sloane Avenue
Whitehead's Grove
Anderson St
Maison Blanc
See p279
Markham St
Jubilee Place
Bodley St
Dovehouse St
Astell St
Markham Place
Chelsea Old Town Hall
Chelsea Manor Street
Margaretta Terrace
SYDNEY ST
ALBERT BRIDGE
St Luke's St
Britten St

Time Out Cheap Eats 275

300m
300 yds
© Copyright Time Out Group 2009

Marylebone, Paddington & Edgware Road

Frampton St

Mandalay

EDGWARE RD

Church St

Church St

Carlisle Mews

Adpar St

Hall Place

Broadley Street

Penfold Pl

Paddington Green

Newcastle Pl

Meya Meya

Bell St

Edgware Rd

Lisson Street

Ranston St

Daventry St

Ashmill St

Shroton St

Cosway St

LISSON GROVE

Harewood Avenue

Blandford Sq

Melbury Terr

Balcombe St

Boston Place

Ivor Pl

Marylebone Station

Marylebone

MARYLEBONE

Wyndham St

Enford St

Edgware Rd

CHAPEL ST

Transept St

Harcourt St

Homer St

Seymour Place

Garbo's

Cabbell St

How

Homer Row

Melur

Star St

SUSSEX GDNS

OLD MARYLEBONE RD

Crawford Place

Shouldham St

Molyneux St

Bryanston Pl

See p280

Herbet Road

North Wharf Rd

Paddington Basin

St Mary's Hospital

South Wharf Road

PRAED ST

St Michael's Street

Star Street

Fresco

Satay House

EDGWARE

Patogh

Brendon St

Harrowby St

Brown St

Seymour Pl

Paddington

Norfolk Place

Somers Mews

Norfolk Cres

Cambridge Square

Norfolk

Burwood Pl

Iran Restaurant

Nutford Pl

Stourcliffe St

George St

Yo! Sushi

London Street

Norfolk Square

SUSSEX GARDENS

Radnor Mews

Gloucester

Square

Radnor Place

Hyde Park Cres

Oxford Square

Crescent

Porchester Place

Park West Pl

ROAD (A5)

Abu Ali

Kendal St

Al-Dar

Sussex Place

Clifton Place

Strathearn Pl

Hyde Park Square

ASK

Connaught St

Albion Street

Arturo

St George's Fields

Ranoush Juice Bar

Connaught Square

Seymour Pl

Stanhope Pl

Bathurst Mews

Bathurst Street

Sussex Sq

Stanhope Terr

Brook St

Hyde Park Gdns Mews

Hyde Park Gardens

Clarendon Place

Albion Cl

Albion Street

Hyde Park Street

Lancaster Gate

See p281

BAYSWATER ROAD (A40)

North Carriage Drive (The Ring)

HYDE PARK

0   300 m

0   300 yds

© Copyright Time Out Group 2009

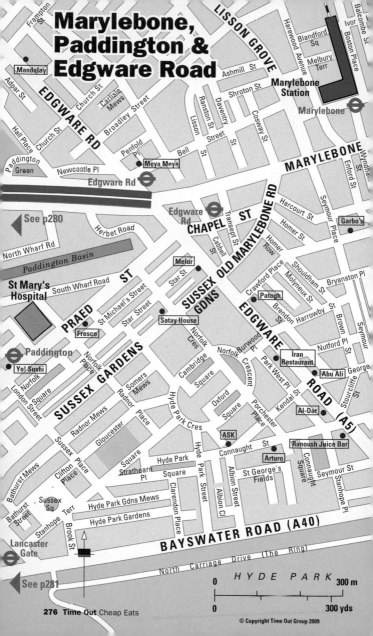

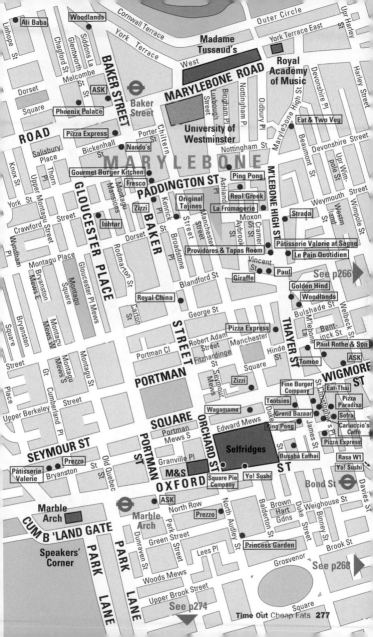

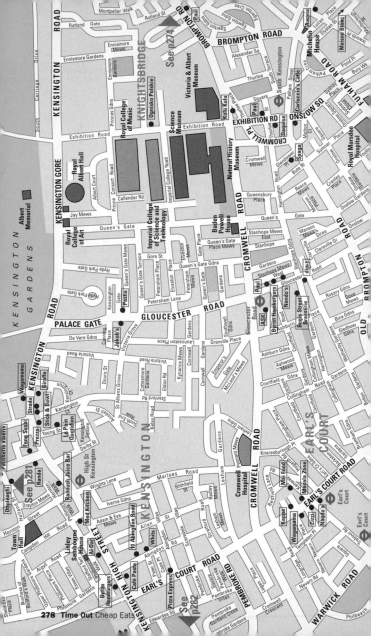

Montpelier Walk
Rutland   Gate
Rutland St
Egerton Cres
Egerton Gdns
Awana
Lucan Place
Elystan Place
Elystan St
BROMPTON ROAD
Paul
Michelin
House
Maison Blanc

Ennismore
Mews
BROMPTON RD
Alexander Sq
South Kensington
Pond Pl
Bury St

Ennismore Gardens
Pelham Street
Carluccio's Caffè

KENSINGTON

Ennismore Gardens Mews

See p274

KNIGHTSBRIDGE

Thurloe Place
South Terrace
Sydney Street
Sydney Place

Princes Gdns

Victoria & Albert Museum

South Kensington
Thurloe Square

Paul
St

Kulu Kulu

Daquise

Carnival Marsden
Hospital

Royal College of Music

Ognisko Polskie

Science Museum

Exhibition Road

EXHIBITION RD

Thurloe St

Pelham St
Melton Ct

CROMWELL PL

Sumner Place

Onslow Sq

Reece
Mews

Cranley
Place

Onslow Gardens

KENSINGTON GORE

Royal Albert Hall

Prince Consort Road

Albert Court

Callendar Rd

Natural History Museum

Imperial College Road

Cromwell
Mews

Queensberry
Place

Bute St
Glendower Pl

Harrington Road

Reece
Mews

Albert Memorial

Jay Mews

Royal College of Art

Queen's Gate

Imperial College of Science and Technology

Gore St
Gate Place

Gate

Baden Powell House

Queen's
Gate Place Mews

Manson
Mews

Clareville Gr

Rosary Gdns

Bina Gdns

Dove
Mews

KENSINGTON GARDENS

Hyde Park Gate

Queen's Gate Terrace

Kensington
Gate

Elvaston
Place

Petersham Place

Queen's Gate Gdns

Stanhope Mews
East

Stanhope

Stanhope Mews
West

CROMWELL

Gloucester
Road

Pasha

Petersham Lane

Queen's Gate

Paul

Stanhope Gdns

Gloucester

Nando's

OLD BROMPTON

Glendower
Gdns

PALACE GATE

De Vere Gdns

Victoria Grove

Jakob's

Canning
Place

GLOUCESTER ROAD

Cornwall
Gardens

Southwell
Gardens

ASK

Byron Hamburgers

Bugis Street
Brasserie

ROAD

Ashburn Gdns

Launceston Place

Cornwall

Grenville Place

Emperor's
Gate

Ashwood
Mews

Collingham
Gardens

Wetherby Gardens

KENSINGTON ROAD

Victoria Road

Douro Place

Cornwall
Gardens

Kynance Mews

McLeod's Mews

Ashburn Gdns

Collingham
Road

Wetherby
Gardens

Cottesmore
Gardens

St Albans Grove

Eldon Rd

Courtfield
Gardens

Collingham
Place

Bramham Gardens

Wagamama

Giraffe

Stanford Rd

Strada

Kensington
Square

Stick & Bowl

Fung Sushi

Prezzo

La Pain Quotidien

Young St

Derry St

Randa

Kensington Church St

Patisserie Valerie

South End Row

South
End

Kensington
Court

Lexham Gdns

Knaresborough Rd
St's Ct Gdns

EARL'S COURT

See p281

Ognisko?

Randa

Randoush Juice Bar

Holland St

Drayton Mews

Med Kitchen

Wrights Lane

Marloes
Road

Lexham Gardens

Mai Food

Masala Zone

Kapar

Earl's Court
Gardens

Earl's
Court

Town Hall

Od Bhajj

Campden Hill Road

Hornton St

Byron Hamburgers

Linley
Sambourne
House

Scarsdale
Villas

Al Fez

Whits

Allen
St

Adam & Eve
Mews

Iverna Gdns

Blithfield
St

Radley
Mews

Radley
St

Cromwell
Hospital

Lexham
Mews

Wagamama

Hogarth Rd

Earl's Court Square

EARL'S COURT ROAD

Trebovir Rd

Zizzi

Nando's

Templeton Pl

Duchess of Bedford's Walk

Sheldrake Place

Aubrey Walk

Phillimore Place

Stafford Terrace

Upper Phillimore Gardens

Phillimore Gardens

Argyll Rd

Essex Villas

KENSINGTON HIGH STREET

Campden Hill

b) Abingdon Road

Abingdon
Road

Stratford Rd

Cope St

Marloes Road

EARL'S COURT ROAD

Café Pasta

Pizza Express

Pembroke Square

Pembroke Rd

Pembroke Villas

Pembroke Gardens Close

Pembroke Gardens

Nevern Rd
Nevern Pl

WARWICK ROAD

Longridge Road
Kenway Rd

Philbeach

Trebovir Rd

See p282

PEMBROKE RD

278 Time Out **Cheap Eats**

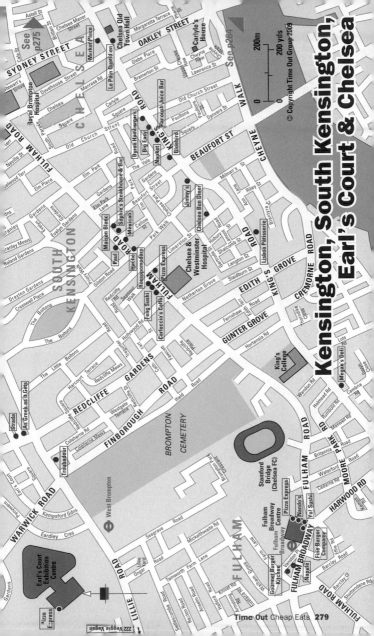

Kensington, South Kensington, Earl's Court & Chelsea

See p275

See p284

© Copyright Time Out Group 2009

200m

200 yds

Astell St
Chelsea Manor Street
Chelsea Old Town Hall
Margaretta Terrace
OAKLEY STREET
Carlyle's House

SYDNEY STREET
Britten St
Market Place
Glebe Place
Cheyne Row
Phene St
Oakley Gdns
Upper Cheyne Row

Royal Brompton Hospital
Dovehouse Street
Manresa Rd
Le Pain Quotidien
Bramerton St
Old Church Street
Lawrence St
CHEYNE WALK

FULHAM ROAD
Carlyle Square
Old Church Street
Carlyle Square
Raroush Juice Bar
Faulkons
Danvers St

Neville's Terr
Elm Park Rd
Elm Place
Byron Hamburgers
Big Easy
Napket
Bluebird
The Vale
BEAUFORT ST
Milman's St
Ashburnham Rd

CHELSEA

SOUTH KENSINGTON

Evelyn Gardens
Elm Park Gardens
Gertrude St
Roland Gardens
Stanley Mews
Sophie's Steakhouse & Bar
Elm Park Lane
Beaufort Street
Park Walk
Jimmy's
Hobury St
Bijou's St
Riley Rd

Drayton Gardens
Maison Blanc
Mexicali
Callow St
Chelsea Bun Diner
Shalcomb St
Langton St
Cresswell Place
Paul
Hache
FULHAM ROAD
Rossopomodoro
Limerston St
Chelsea & Westminster Hospital
Blantyre St
Lisboa Pâtisserie
KING'S GROVE

The Bottons
Redcliffe Rd
Seymour Walk
Pizza Express
EDITH GROVE
Stadburn St
CREMORNE ROAD

The Bottons
Redcliffe
Hollywood Rd
Ifield Rd
Chng Sushi
Carluccio's Caffè
Netherton Grove
Ferndale Ter
GUNTER GROVE

The Little Bottons
Harcourt Terrace
Redcliffe Mews
Cathcart Rd
Fawcett St
Hortensia Rd
King's College
Fulham Rd

Strada
As Greek as it Gets
REDCLIFFE GARDENS
Westgate Terrace
Redcliffe Rd
Ifield
ROAD
Megan's Deli
Holmead Rd
Turnbold Rd
Cambria Rd
Lots Rd

Troubadour
Coleherne Court
Coleherne Mews
FINBOROUGH ROAD
BROMPTON CEMETERY
WARWICK ROAD
West Brompton
Kempsford Gdns
Eardley Cres
Seagrave Road
Mickethwaite Rd
Britannia Rd
FULHAM ROAD
Waterford Rd
HARWOOD RD
Cedarne Rd

Stamford Bridge (Chelsea FC)
Fulham Broadway Centre
Fulham Broadway
Pizza Express
Nando's
Yo! Sushi
MOORE PARK ROAD
Maxwell Rd
Barclay Rd

Earl's Court Exhibition Centre
LILLIE ROAD
FULHAM ROAD
Walham Pl
Vanston Pl
Gourmet Burger Kitchen
Napule
Fine Burger Company
Barclay Rd
Shottendene Rd
FULHAM ROAD

Pizza Express
222 Veggie Vegan
Seagrave Road
Ongar Rd
Lillie Yard
Farm Lane
Tamworth Rd
Anselm Road
Rostrevor Road

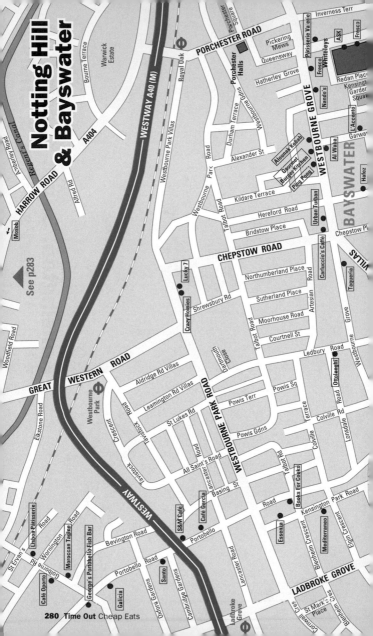

Notting Hill & Bayswater

PORCHESTER ROAD

WESTWAY A40 (M)

GREAT WESTERN ROAD

HARROW ROAD

WESTWAY

BAYSWATER

WESTBOURNE GROVE

VILLAS

LADBROKE GROVE

Anberley Road
Regent's Canal
A404
Bourne Terrace
Warwick Estate
Royal Oak
Alfred Rd
Woodfield Road
Ekistone Road
Westbourne Park Villas
Westbourne Park Road
Porchester Square
Pickering Mews
Queensway
Porchester Halls
Hatherley Grove
Durham Terrace
Westbourne Park
Alexander St
Kildare Terrace
Hereford Road
Bridstow Place
CHEPSTOW ROAD
Northumberland Place
Sutherland Place
Moorhouse Road
Courtnell St
Talbot Road
Westbourne Park Road
Westbourne Crescent
Tavistock
Aldridge Rd Villas
Leamington Rd Villas
St Lukes Rd
All Saint's Road
Lancaster Road
Basing St
Powis Sq
Powis Terr
Powis Gdns
Colville Terrace
Colville Rd
Lonsdale Road
Colville
Ledbury Road
Artesian Road
Westbourne Grove
Chepstow Pl
Chepstow Road
Talbot Road
Shrewsbury Rd
Dartmouth Close
Davistock Crescent
Gornington Road
Bevington Road
Golborne Rd
Portobello Road
Oxford Gardens
Cambridge Gardens
Ladbroke Grove
Lancaster Road
WESTBOURNE PARK ROAD
Talbot Road
Kensington Park Road
Blenheim Crescent
Elgin Crescent
St Mark's Place
Kensington Gardens Square
Redan Place
Inverness Terr
Patisserie Valerie

See p283

Mosob
Whiteleys
ASK
Fresco
Frisco
Nando's
L'Accento
Garwa
Alounak Kebab
Gourmet Burger Kitchen
Ping Pong
Al Waha
Urban Turban
Hafez
Carluccio's Caffe
Taqueria
Lucky 7
Crazy Homies
Ottolenghi
Books for Cooks
Essenza
Mediterraneo
St Ervan's
Lisboa Pâtisserie
Moroccan Tagine
George's Portobello Fish Bar
S&M Café
Café Garcia
Portobello
Santo
Galicia
Café Oporto

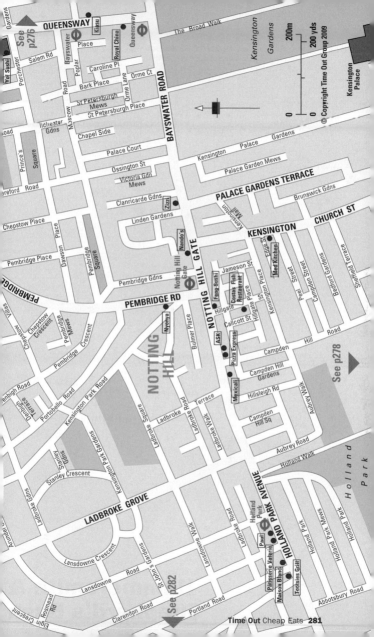

Bryony Road
Australia Road
South Africa Road
Armadillo Café
BBC
Television
Centre
Wood Lane
Ariel Way
WOOD LANE
Byron
Hamburgers
Gourmet Burger
Kitchen
Nando's
Ooze
Pho
Pizza Express
Real Greek
Square Pie
Wagamama
Wahaca
Yo! Sushi
Westfield
Shopping
Centre
Sawley Road
Dunraven Road
Oaklands Grove
Ellerslie Road
Bloemfontein Road
Frithville Gardens
Aycliffe Rd
Wormholt Road
Sedgeford Rd
Thorpebank Road
Galloway Road
Ormiston Grove
Ashchurch Grove
Aldbourne Road
Wood Lane
Pennard Road
Sterne St
Shepherd's
Bush Market
Shepherd's
Bush
UXBRIDGE ROAD
Red Sea
Esarn Kheaw
Nando's
Bulwer St
UXBRIDGE
ROAD
Beckwin Road
Askew Cres
Vespan Rd
Vine Leaves
Abu Zaad
Shepherd's Bush Mkt
Rockley Road
See
p281
Findon Road
St Stephen's
Ave
Godolphin Rd
Thornfield Road
Percy Rd
Boscombe Road
SHEPHERD'S
BUSH
Adam's Café
Minford Gardens
Sufi
Hadyn Park Road
Goodwin Road
Cardross Road
Snowy Road
Scott's Road
Patio
Westwick Gdns
Netherwood Road
Lakeside Rd
Addison Gardens
Blythe Rd
Som Tam House
Westville Rd
Netherwood Gdns
Richmond Way
Ashingdon St
Park Villas
Greenside Road
GOLDHAWK ROAD
Goldhawk
Road
Richford St
Sulgrave Road
Melrose Gdns
Batoum Gdns
Bolingbroke Rd
GOLDHAWK
Ravenscourt Sq
Benbow Road
Coulter Rd
Averill St
Hammersmith
Grove
Lena Gdns
Blythe Rd
Sterndale Rd
Caithness Rd
ROAD
Overstone Road
PADDENSWICK ROAD
Brackenbury Road
Carthew Road
Bradmore Pk Rd
Aldensley Rd
Banim Street
Southerton Road
Los Molinos
SHEPHERD'S BUSH ROAD
Brook Green
Brook Green
See
p278
Ravenscourt Park
GLENTHORPE RD
Hammersmith
Rowan Road
Hamlet Gdns
Ravenscourt Gardens
Tosa
Knaypa
Polanka
Shilpa
KING STREET
HAMMERSMITH RD
BEASDON RD
Hammersmith
St Peter's Square
St Peter's Road
Mahdi
Sagar
KING STREET
Hammersmith
HAMMERSMITH FLYOVER
British Grove
GREAT WEST ROAD
Upper Mall
RD
HAMMERSMITH
Queen Caroline St
Yeldham Road
Biscay Road
St Dunstan's Rd
River Thames
HAMMERSMITH BRIDGE
Chancellor's Road
Winslow Road
Margravine Rd
Pizza
Express
FULHAM PALACE ROAD
Glentham Road
Bridgeview Gdns
River Thames
Colwith Rd
Chiswick Mall
LONSDALE ROAD
Nowell Road
Boileau Road
CASTELNAU
Trinity Gardens
Aspenlea Rd
Greyhound Rd
Nella Rd
Rainville Rd
Horsman Rd
Kingsmere Rd
0   400m
0   400 yds
© Copyright Time Out Group 2009

282 Time Out Cheap Eats

Hammersmith &
Shepherd's Bush

Maida Vale & Kilburn

Loveridge Road
IVERSON RD
W Hampstead Station
West Hampstead
Broadhurst Gdns

0   300m
0   300 yds
© Copyright Time Out Group 2009

Small & Beautiful
Brondesbury Station
KILBURN
Nando's
Netherwood Street
Sheriff Road
Compayne Gdns
Dyne Road
Hemstel Road
Dynham Road
Cotleigh Road
Avenue
Avenue
Gascony
Mossina
Kingsgate
Torbay Road
Callcott Road
Streatley Road
Buckley Road
Kovalam
Iverson Pass
Cranfield Gardens
Greencroft Gardens
SOUTH HAMPSTEAD
Aberdare Gardens
Goldhurst Terrace
See p300
WILLESDEN LANE
QUEX ROAD
WEST END LANE
BELSIZE ROAD
ABBEY ROAD
Terryson Rd
Priory Park Road
Gengall Road
Victoria Road
Esmond Rd
Hartmore Road
Donaldson Rd
KILBURN
Matro Road
West End Lane
Priory Terr
Priory Road
Rowley Way
Ainsworth Way
Boundary Rd
Willesden Lane Cemetery
Lonsdale Road
Hartland Road
Victoria Road
BRONDESBURY ROAD
Brondesbury Villas
Little Bay
Kilburn High Road Station
Langtry Rd
Kilburn Priory
Mortimer Cres
Greville Place
Greville Road
Carlton Hill
Clifton Hill
Carlton Hill
MAIDA VALE
Kilburn Park
Cambridge Avenue
Oxford Road
Andover Place
Redcliffe Gdns
Greville Road
Hamilton Terrace
Queens Park Station
Albert Road
Denmark Road
Chicester Avenue
Princess Road
Granville Road
Canterbury Road
Cambridge Road
Cambridge Road
Randolph Gdns
Queens Park
CARLTON VALE
Carlton Vale
Randolph Avenue
Lanark Road
WEST KILBURN
Bravington Road
Ashmore Road
Portnall Road
Denholme
Bradiston Rd
Selram Crescent
Malvern Road
Stuart Road
Croxley Road
Fordingley Rd
Lancefield St
Shirland Road
Bravington Road
Portnall Road
Ashmore Road
Fernhead Road
Shirland Mews
Lydford Rd
Warlock
Walterton Road
Chippenham Road
Lanhill Rd
Elgin Avenue
Oakington Rd
Edbrooke Road
Goldney Road
Marylands Road
Sutherland Ave
HARROW ROAD
Woodfield Rd
Amberley Rd
Regent's Canal
KILBURN PARK ROAD
SHIRLAND ROAD
Paddington Recreation Ground
Maida Vale
Grantully Road
Biddulph Road
Ashworth Road
Randolph Road
Elgin Avenue
Lauderdale Parade
MAIDA VALE
Castellain Road
Delaware Road
Sutherland Avenue
Widley Road
Wymering Rd
Morshead Road
Essendine Rd
Red Pepper
Warrington
Formosa St
Formosa St
Warwick Ave
Crescent
See p280

Battersea & Wandsworth

See p279

Battersea Park

BATTERSEA

Pizza Express

ALBERT BRIDGE ROAD

Parkgate Road
Winfield St

River Thames

BATTERSEA BRIDGE ROAD

Battersea Church Rd
Bollingbroke Walk

WESTBRIDGE RD

VICARAGE GR

Parkham St
Surrey Lane

Orbel St
Octavia St
Acanthus St

See p287

Petworth Street

Battersea High Street

Shuttleworth Road

Imperial Road

Bagley's Lane

Townmead Road

L'Antipasto

BATTERSEA PARK RD

Burns Road

Broughton Rd

Stephendale Road

Townmead Road

Galapagos Bistro-Café

LOMBARD RD

William Morris Way

Wye Street

Cabul Road

Longhurst Road

Kerrison Rd

Sheepcote Road

LATCHMERE ROAD

Esere Road

Ingrave Street

Falcon Road

WANDSWORTH BRIDGE

Little Bay

YORK ROAD

PLOUGH ROAD

Darien Road

Stanley Rd

Grant Road

Clapham Junction Station

Pizza Express

See p286

Dorothy Rd

Altenburg Gdns

Lavender Gdns

Mossbury Road

Wynter St

Maysoule Road

Harbut Road

St John's Hill Grove

Cologne Rd

ST JOHN'S HILL

St John's Rd

Eccles Rd

Le Bouchon Bordelais

Wandsworth Town Station

Nantes Close

Rochelle Cl

Ace Fusion

Yardens Rd

Strada

BATTERSEA RISE

Giraffe

Banana Tree Canteen

Nando's

Osteria Antica Bologna

Brady's

Garratt Cl

Birdhurst Rd

Anna Rd

Old York Road

Fullerton Road

Spencer Rd

Elsynge Road

Freemasons

Gourmet Burger Kitchen

NORTHCOTE ROAD

Road

Pizza Express

Frogmore

See p293

EAST HILL

WANDSWORTH

TRINITY ROAD

WINDMILL ROAD

Wandsworth Common Rd

Mallinson

Bannerley

Salcott

Wakehurst

Belleville

Kelmscott

Bramfield

BOLINGBROKE GROVE

Rosehill Rd

Geraldine Rd

Cicada Road

St Ann's Hill

St Ann's Crescent

Heathfield Rd

0   300m

0   300yds

See p285

Broomwood Road

© Copyright Time Out Group 2009

Balham & Tooting

See p284

Wandsworth Common

Wandsworth Common Station

Ciullo's

Nando's

See p286

Harrison's

Pizza Express

Cattle Grid

Fine Burger Company

Fat Delicatessen

Tagine

BALHAM

Balham

Balham Station

Dexter's Grill

Bar Viva

Polish White Eagle Club

Springfield University Hospital

Tooting Bec

Cemetery

Tooting Bec Common

TRINITY ROAD

BALHAM HIGH ROAD

TOOTING BEC ROAD

UPPER TOOTING ROAD

Nando's

Apollo Banana Leaf

Kastoori

Kusinang Munti

Mirch Masala

Harrington's

GARRETT LANE

Dosa n Chutney

Radhakrishna Bhavan

St Georges Hospital

TOOTING

Tooting Broadway

TOOTING HIGH STREET

Sree Krishna

Rick's Café

MITCHAM ROAD

Tooting Station

0   300m
0   300 yds

Clapham & Brixton

See p292

See p287

See p284

See p285

Loughborough Road

Moorland Road

Somerleyton Road

Coldharbour Lane

Railton Road

Talma Road

Rattray Road

Mervan Road

Dalberg Road

Kellet Road

Saltoun Road

Rushcroft Rd

Electric

EFFRA ROAD

BRIXTON HILL

St Matthew's Church

Porden Road

Matthew's Road

Brixton Water Lane

MORVAL ROAD

DULWICH RD

Barwell Road

Milton Road

Shakespeare Road

Spenser Road

Chaucer Road

Elfra Parade

Mayall Road

Canterbury Cres

Wiltshire Road

Villa Road

Atwell Road

St James's Crescent

St James's Crescent

Barrington Road

Gresham Road

COLDHARBOUR LANE

STOCKWELL PARK RD

STOCKWELL RD

BRIXTON RD

St John's Cres

Stansfield Road

Chantrey Road

Gresham Road

Geneva Road

Canterbury

Canterbury Cres

Ballefields

Gately Road

Ferndale Rd

Nursery Road

Brighton Terrace

Brixton

B R I X T O N

Coma y Punto

Franco Manca

Asmara

Nando's

Bamboula

Fiesta-Bar

Rumsey Road

Ramsey Road

Dalyell Road

Mordaunt Street

Hargwyne St

Comberme

Pulross Road

Hubert Grove

Tasman Road

Willington Road

Mayflower Rd

Hembridge

Landor Road

Ferndale Road

Sandmere Road

Timtern St

Stanley St

Raeburn Street

Concanon Rd

Ballater

Corrance Road

Solon Road

Plato Road

Kelpler Road

Hetherington Road

ACRE LANE

ACRE LANE

KINGS AVENUE

BEDFORD ROAD

Trinity Gdns

Rushcroft Rd

Baytree Road

Sudbourne Road

Hayter Rd

Bonham Road

Lambert Road

Branksome Road

Strathleven Road

Horsford Rd

Kildoran Rd

Mandrell Rd

Lyham Road

CLAPHAM ROAD

Chelsham Rd

Clapham High Street Station

Gauden Road

Gauden Road

Edgeley Road

Clapham Manor Street

Aristotle Road

Cato Road

Tremadoc Rd

Kenwyn Road

St Luke's Avenue

Nelson Road

Triangle Pl

Clapham

Larkhall Rise

Cubitt Terrace

Liston Rd

Grafton Sq

Gratton Rd

Rectory Grove

Old Town

The Pavement

CLAPHAM HIGH STREET

CLAPHAM COMMON SOUTH SIDE

LONG ROAD

CLAPHAM PARK ROAD

Nando's

Café Sol

Strada

Café Wanda

Gastro

Breads Etcetera

Eco

Stonehouse

Brown's

Voltaire Rd

Pepper Tree

Macarons

Pizza Express

Dexter's Grill

Newtons

Stonhouse St

Abbeville Road

Northbourne Rd

West Rd

Park Hill

Briarwood Rd

Crescent Lane

Rodenhurst Road

Abbeville Rd

Leppoc Rd

Caldervale Rd

Franconia Rd

Hambalt Road

Abbeville Road

Strachan Rd

Worsopp Drive

St Alphonsus

Clarence Crescent

Fisher Ave

Elms Road

Abbeville Road

Clapham Common

Abbevilles Restaurant

CLAPHAM

Clapham Common

300m

300 yds

© Copyright Time Out Group 2009

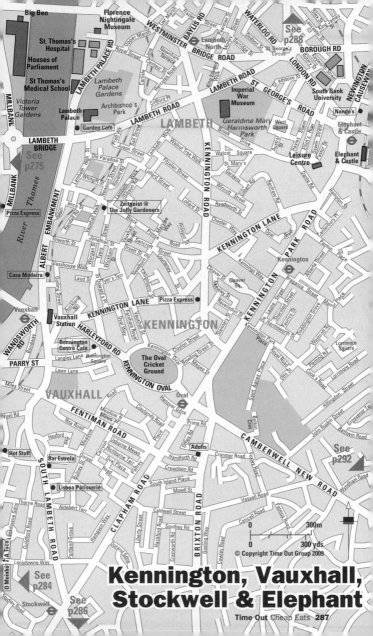

Big Ben
Florence Nightingale Museum
St. Thomas's Hospital
Houses of Parliament
St Thomas's Medical School
Victoria Tower Gardens

WESTMINSTER BRIDGE ROAD
Lambeth North
BOROUGH RD
WATERLOO RD
LONDON RD
South Bank University

LAMBETH PALACE RD
Lambeth Palace Gardens
Archbishop's Park
Lambeth Palace
Garden Café

LAMBETH ROAD
Imperial War Museum
Geraldine Mary Harmsworth Park
West Square

South Bank University
Nando's
Elephant & Castle
Elephant & Castle
Leisure Centre

LAMBETH
MILLBANK
LAMBETH BRIDGE
See p275

Pizza Express

KENNINGTON ROAD
ST GEORGE'S ROAD
KENNINGTON LANE
PARK ROAD

Zeitgeist @ The Jolly Gardeners

Casa Madeira

EMBANKMENT
ALBERT
Glasshouse Walk

Vauxhall
Vauxhall Station

HARLEYFORD RD
KENNINGTON LANE
Pizza Express

Bonnington Centre Café
Bonnington Square

WANDSWORTH RD
PARRY ST
Lawn Lane

KENNINGTON OVAL
KENNINGTON
Kennington
The Oval Cricket Ground

VAUXHALL
FENTIMAN ROAD

Hot Stuff
Bar Estrela

Adulis

Lisboa Pâtisserie

SOUTH LAMBETH ROAD
CLAPHAM ROAD
BRIXTON ROAD
CAMBERWELL NEW ROAD

See p292

See p284
O Moinho
A Toca
See p286
Stockwell

300m
0
300 yds
0
© Copyright Time Out Group 2009

Kennington, Vauxhall, Stockwell & Elephant

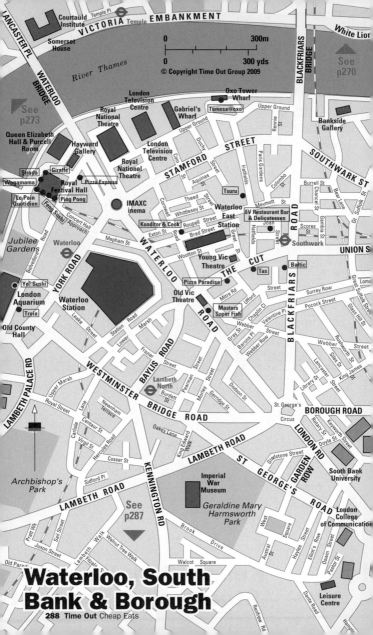

Skinners La

College Row

Queen

High Timber St

Cannon

CANNON ST

CANNON ST

Laurence Pountney La

Arthur St

Martin Lane

Clements Lane

Philpot Lane

Rood Lane

St Mary at Hill

FENCHURCH

HILL

UPPER THAMES ST

Vintners' Hall

Skinners' Hall

Cannon Street Station

Monument

EASTCHEAP

The Monument

LOWER THAMES ST

SOUTHWARK BRIDGE

River Thames

Fishmongers' Hall

See p271

Tate Modern Café: Level 2

Pizza Express

Real Greek

Bankside

Tas Pide

Shakespeare's Globe

Tate Modern

Viva Verdi

Zoar St

Tortilla

SOUTHWARK ST

The Table

Lavington St

Sumner

Emerson

Great Guildford St

Park Street

Rose Theatre

Clink St

Wagamama

Naudo's

Southwark Cathedral Refectory

Feng Sushi

Konditor & Cook

Golden Hinde

Southwark Cathedral

LONDON BRIDGE

DUKE'S HILL

Southwark City Pier

London Bridge City Pier

HMS Belfa

Hay's Galleria

Kwan Thai

Pizza Express

fish! kitchen

Stoney St

Railway App

London Bridge Station

London Bridge St

TOOLEY ST

Thrale St

SOUTHWARK STREET

Keppel Row

Ewer St

Tapas Brindisa

Borough Market

Tas

Tas Café

Tito's

Georgetown

Paul

London Bridge Station

ST THOMAS STREET

Bermondsey Street

UNION STREET

BOROUGH

UNION STREET

BOROUGH HIGH STREET

Pepper St

Copperfield St

Pocock St

Risborough St

London Fire Brigade Museum

MARSHALSEA ROAD

Sturge St

Ayres St

Redcross Way

Little Dorrit Court

Guy's Hospital

Gt Maze Pond

Newcomen Street

Mermaid Ct

Snowsfields

Weston Street

Guy St

Kipling St

Leathermarket St

Morocco St

Lamb Walk

El Vergel

Lant Street

Gt Suffolk St

Borough

St George the Martyr

TABARD ST

Crosby Row

Porlock St

Long Lane

SOUTHWARK BRIDGE ROAD

Stones End St

NEBRASKA ST

Swan Street

Cole Street

Trinity Street

Church St

Merrick Square

GREAT DOVER STREET

Pilgrimage Street

Tabard Street

Manciple St

Hankey PI

Staple St

Wild's Rent

Decima Street

BOROUGH HIGH ST

HARPER ROAD

NEWINGTON CAUSEWAY

BOROUGH ROAD

Tiverton St

Bath Terrace

Rockingham

Avon St

Meadow Row

Trinity St

Avon St

Falmouth Road

Falmouth Rd

County St

Spurgeon St

Burbage CI

Deverell Street

Bartholomew Street

Law Street

Potier St

Tabard Gdn

Prioress St

Alice Street

Rothesay St

M Manze

TOWER BRIDGE D

Webb Street

Leroy Street

Nando's

Elephant & Castle

Elephant & Castle Station

Shopping Centre

NEW KENT ROAD

Deacon Way

Rodney Place

Munton Road

Bath Terrace

Rodney Road

Heygate Street

Hampton St

Chatham St

Peninsula

Westcombe Park
Station

Lessom Street

Old Woolwich Rd

TRAFALGAR ROAD

Blackwall Lane

Humber   Road

ROMNEY ROAD

Maze Hill
Station

Park Vista

Vanbrugh Hill

Foyle Road

Colerane Road

Hardy Road

Brassinghill

Mickenza Road

Westcombe Hill

Pizza Express

GREENWICH

Mase Hill

Westcombe

Park

Road

Vanburgh Park

Vanburgh Park

Greenwich

Croom's   Hill

George Street

Park

Blackheath Avenue

Bower Avenue

Vanburgh Fields

Charlton Way

St
John's

Park

HYDE VALE

Chesterfield Walk

General Wolfe
Road

Pavilion Tea House

Charlton Way

SHOOTERS HILL

Langton

Covington
Way

PRINCE OF WALES RD

St Germans Place

Kidbrook Gardens

SHOOTERS HILL

Blackheath

Long Pond Road

Prince Charles Road

South Row

Wat Tyler Road

Hare and Billet Road

Corkers Road

Mounts Pond Road

Eliot Place

Health Lane

Royal Parade

Chapters

Pizza Express

Strada

Baizdon Road

Laicram

Corner Green

Morden Rd Mews

Park

Gramville

Park

St Joseph's Vale

Blackheath Station

Pond   Road

Blackheath

Brooklands Park

Brookway

Foxes Dale

Parkgate

Boyne   Road

LEE TERRACE

BLACKHEATH

LEE   ROAD

Manor Way

BELMONT HILL

Maristchal Rd

Bessington   Road

Lock Chase

Lee   Park

Dacre Park

Nando's

LEE HIGH ROAD

Chatterton Rise

Gilmore   Road

Belmont Park

Praughman Road

Boone St

Grove

Morley   Road

Wisteria Road

New Cross, Deptford,
Greenwich & Blackheath

Camberwell to Dulwich

La Luna
WJ Arment
Westmoreland Rd

Burgess
Park

St Georges Way

Albany   Road

Lorrimore Road
Hillingdon Street
John Ruskin Street
Grosvenor Terrace

Bethwin Road

See p287

Wyndham Road

CAMBERWELL NEW ROAD

Hooden Rd

Foxley Rd

Paulet Rd

CAMBERWELL

New Church Rd

Bowyer Pl

Lomond Grove

Edmund Street

Southampton Way

Sumner

Commercial Way

Wells Way

Elmington Road

Havil Street

Benhill Road

Peckham

PECKHAM

Camberwell
Green

Caravaggio

CAMBERWELL CHURCH ST

CAMBERWELL ROAD

Dalwood Street

Suya Express

PECKHAM ROAD

M Manze

Mozzarella
e Pomodoro

Warner Road

Denmark Road

Flaxman

Rd

Daneville Rd

COLDHARBOUR
LANE

Nando's

DENMARK HILL

Bessmer Rd

Vestry Road

Sedgmoor Pl

Shenley Road

Bushey Hill Road

Lyndhurst WAY

Talfourd Road

Bellenden Road

Lyndhurst Grove

Peckham Rye
Station

Holly Grove

Ganapati

RYE LANE

De Crespigny Park

Denmark Hill
Station

Camberwell

Grove

McNeil Road

CHAMPION
PARK

Chadwick Road

Petitou

Loughborough
Junction Station

See
p286

Finsen Rd

Herne

Hill

Ferndale Road

Blanchedowne

Champion Hill

Champion Hill

DOG KENNEL HILL

Dayton Grove

Grove Park

Ivanhoe Road

Choumert

Danby St

Avondale Rise

Bellenden Road

Copleston Rd

Oakhurst Grove

Patching Rd

East Dulwich
Station

Melbourne

Grove

GROVE HILL

Ondine Rd

Ebsworth Rd

Nutbrook St

Amott Road

Gowlett

Locale

Adys Road

EAST DULWICH ROAD

PECKHAM RYE

EAST
DULWICH

MILKWOOD ROAD

Poplar Road

Lowden Road

Lilford Road

Hinton Road

Kestrel Avenue

Herne
Hill

DENMARK HILL

Sunray

Red Post Hill

Crossthwaite Ave

Casino Ave

Dunstan's Rd

Townsend Rd

Red Post Hill

HERNE HILL

Herne Hill Station

Lombak

HALF MOON LANE

Sea Cow

Melbourne Grove

EAST DULWICH GROVE

Ashbourne Gr

Melbourne Grove

North Cross Rd

Crystal

LORDSHIP LANE

Palace

Thai Corner Cafe

Blue Mountain
Cafe

Franklins

Whateley Road

Jack's Tea &
Coffee House

Langford Rd

Beauval

Road

BARRY

ROAD

Offley's

North Dulwich
Station

Dulwich

Village

Au Ciel

Carlton Avenue

Townley Road

Woodwarde Road

Franklins

NORWOOD ROAD

Romeo Jopes

Pizza Express

Burbage Road

Turney   Road

Court   Lane

DULWICH
VILLAGE

Pavilion Cafe

Dulwich Park

Peckham Park Road

Benhill Road

Lyndhurst Grove

400m

400 yds

© Copyright Time Out Group 2009

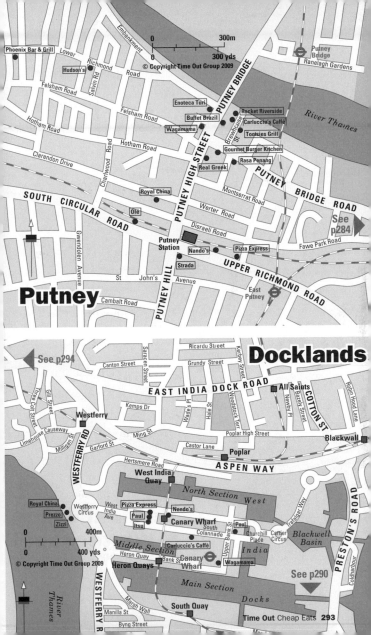

Bethnal Green & Whitechapel

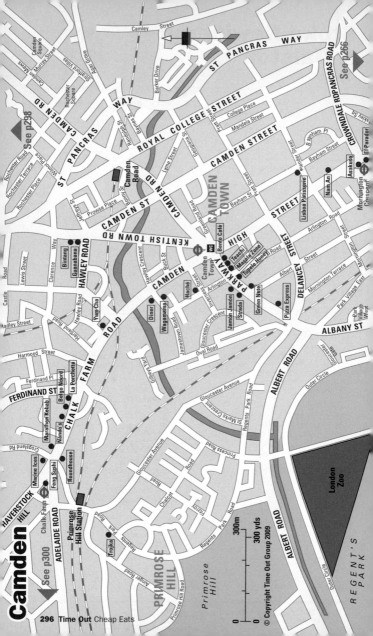

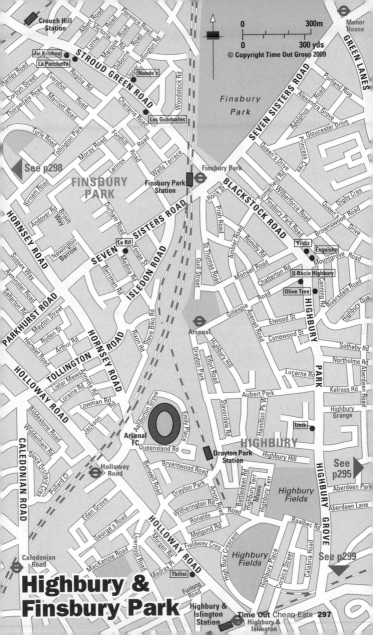

Highbury &
Finsbury Park

Crouch Hill
Station

Jai Krishna
La Porchetta

STROUD GREEN ROAD
Nando's

Los Guadules

Finsbury
Park

SEVEN SISTERS ROAD

Finsbury Park

See p298

FINSBURY
PARK

Finsbury Park
Station

HORNSEY ROAD

SEVEN

SISTERS

ROAD

Le Rif

ISLEDON ROAD

BLACKSTOCK ROAD

Yildiz
Exquisito

Il Bacio Highbury

Olive Tree

HIGHBURY

See p295

Arsenal

PARKHURST ROAD

HOLLOWAY ROAD

TOLLINGTON ROAD

HORNSEY ROAD

CALEDONIAN ROAD

Arsenal
FC

Queensland Rd

Holloway
Road

Drayton Park
Station

HIGHBURY

Iznik

Highbury
Fields

HOLLOWAY ROAD

HIGHBURY GROVE

See p299

Caledonian
Road

Tbilisi

Highbury &
Islington
Station

Highbury
Fields

Highbury &
Islington

© Copyright Time Out Group 2009

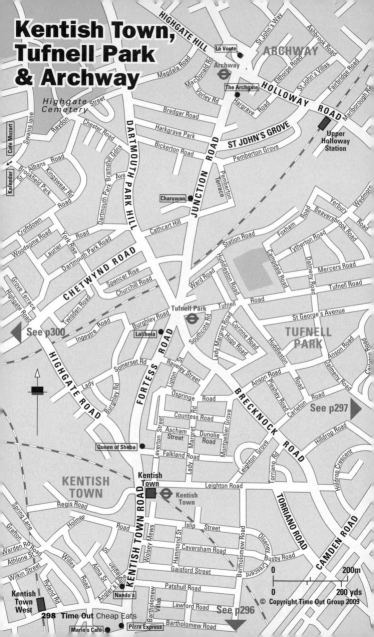

Kentish Town,
Tufnell Park
& Archway

HIGHGATE HILL

ARCHWAY

La Voute

Magdala Road

MacDonald Rd

Archway

HOLLOWAY ROAD

The Archgate

Vorley Rd

Hargrave Road

Highgate Cemetery

Highgate Street

Bredgar Road

ST JOHN'S GROVE

Upper Holloway Station

Reydon

Chester Road

Harkgrave Park

Bickerton Road

Pemberton Grove

St Albans Road

Brookfield Park

Dartmouth Park

Bramshill Gdns

Ave

Pemberton Terrace

Charuwan

Yerbury Road

Beaversbrook Road

Kingswear Rd

DARTMOUTH PARK HILL

JUNCTION ROAD

Station Road

Foxham Road

Wetmore

Croftdown

Woodsome Road

York Rise

Lauriet

Dartmouth Park Road

Cathcart Hill

Ward Road

Huddleston Road

Tytherton Road

Cardinal Road

Dalmeny Road

Mercers Road

Grove Terrace

Highgate Road

CHETWYND ROAD

Spencer Rise

Churchill Road

Tufnell Park

Tufnell

Road

Tufnell Road

St George's Avenue

TUFNELL PARK

Twisden Road

Ingestre Road

Burghley Road

Tufnell Park

Southcote Rd

Lady Margret Road

Corinne Road

Hugo Road

Huddleston

Anson Road

Dalmeny Road

See p300

Lalibela

FORTESS ROAD

Somerset Rd

Burghley Rd

Raveley Street

Upton

Anson Road

Plessey Road

Carleton Road

See p297

HIGHGATE ROAD

Lady

Osprnge

Road

Montpellier Grove

BRECKNOCK ROAD

Leverton Street

Countess Road

Ascham Street

Dunolie Road

Leighton Grove

Torriano Ave

Hilldrop Road

Queen of Sheba

Lady Margret

Falkland Road

Leighton Road

Hilldrop Crescent

KENTISH TOWN

Kentish Town

Kentish Town

Islip Street

TORRIANO ROAD

CAMDEN ROAD

Regis Road

Holmes Road

Wolsey Mews

Hammond St

Caversham Road

Busby Road

Olseney

Sanna Lane

Grafton Road

Warden Rd

Athlone St

Willes Road

Alma St

Anglers Lane

Gaisford Street

Bartholomew

Crescent

Wilkin Street

Ryland Rd

Nando's

Patshull Road

See p296

Kentish Town West

Bartholomew Villas

Lawford Road

Mario's Café

Pizza Express

Bartholomew Road

0   200m

0   200yds

© Copyright Time Out Group 2009

Café Mozart

Kalendar

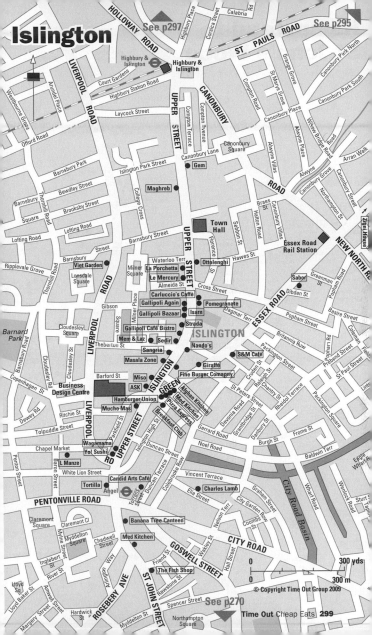

Hampstead to St John's Wood

Brew House

Jack Straw's Castle

HAMPSTEAD

Whitestone Pond

Vale of Health Pond

HEATH

Nautilus

Burrard Rd

Hillfield Road

Mill Lane

Gourmet Burger Kitchen

West End lane

Pizza Express

West Cottages

Nando's

WEST HAMPSTEAD

Sushi-Bar Gen

Banana Tree Canteen

W Hampstead Thameslink Station

W Hampstead Station

West Hampstead

Camden Arts Centre Café

Fenton House

Jin Kichi

Woodlands

dim t

Pizza Express

Louis Pâtisserie

Maison Blanc

Paul

Chaiwalla

Ping Pong

HAMPSTEAD

Giraffe

Carluccio's Caffè

Keats' House

Elephant Walk

Czechoslovak Restaurant

O2 Centre

Hellenic Restaurant

Finchley Road & Frognal Station

Fine Burger Company

Nando's

Yo! Sushi

Mahdi

Pizza Express

Wakaba

Oliver's Village Café

Zara

Hampstead Heath Station

Le Pain Quotidien

ASK

Tootsies Grill

Tapeo

Pizza Express

BELSIZE PARK

Belsize Park

Gourmet Burger Kitchen

Green Cottage

Eriki

South Hampstead Station

BELSIZE ROAD

Swiss Cottage

ADELAIDE ROAD

Chalk Farm

Natural Burger Company

Royal China Club

Pizza Express

Primrose Hill

Primrose Hill Station

ST JOHN'S WOOD

St John's Wood

Carluccio's Caffè

300 Time Out Cheap Eats

Harry Morgan's

Maison Blanc

PRIMROSE HILL

See p283

See p296

0   500m
0   500 yds

© Copyright Time Out Group 2009

Menu glossary

a

accra saltfish cakes.
ackee a fruit that tastes like scrambled eggs when it is cooked; often served with salt cod.
adai fermented rice and lentil pancakes.
adana spicy minced lamb kebab.
agedashidofu fried tofu sprinkled with dried fish, in shoyu (qv) broth.
agedofu fried tofu.
aioli garlic mayonnaise.
albóndigas meatballs in a tomato sauce.
aloo potato.
arnavut ciğeri 'Albanian liver', fried then baked.
avial a mixed vegetable curry in a coconut and yoghurt sauce.
ayam chicken.

b

baba ganoush toasted aubergine purée.
bacalao or **bacalhau** salt cod.
baklava filo pastry with nuts, served covered in syrup.
banh pho rice noodles.
banh xeo Vietnamese crispy filled pancake.
barszcz Polish borscht.
bastilla filo pastry filled with pigeon (or chicken), spices and almonds, and dusted with sugar.
béchamel sauce white sauce made with flour, milk and butter.
bento meal served in a compartmentalised box.
beyti spicy mince and garlic kebab.
bhajee a 'dry' dish of vegetables cooked with various spices.
bhaji vegetables deep-fried in spicy gram flour.
bhaturas puffed discs of deep-fried bread.

bhel poori a snack of puffed rice, deep-fried vermicelli, pooris (qv) and assorted chutneys.
bhindi okra.
bibimbap rice, veg and meat with a raw or fried egg on top.
bifana marinated pork steak in a roll.
bigos hunters' stew.
bindaedok fried savoury pancake of mung bean flour, vegetables and (perhaps) minced beef.
biriani rice cooked with meat or vegetables.
blini a pancake made from buckwheat flour.
bocadillo a crusty roll that is filled with the likes of ham or cheese.
boquerones anchovies.
börek, böreği filo pies with savoury fillings.
borekas Jewish filo pies with fillings such as cheese or spinach.
borscht beetroot soup.
bresaola dried fillet of beef, sliced thinly.
brik fried pastry filled with egg and mince.
brinjal aubergine.
bulgogi marinated beef barbecued at table.
bun rice vermicelli.
burrito a filled cornmeal pancake.

c

cacık diced cucumber with garlic in yoghurt.
calamares squid.
caldo verde cabbage, potato, olive oil and chorizo sausage soup.
calpis, calpico sweet soft drink derived from milk.
calzone folded, stuffed and deep-fried pizza.
ceviche marinated seafood salad.
chaat snack.
cha gio spring rolls

containing vermicelli and herbs.
chakchouka very spicy pepper and tomato stew.
channa chickpea.
chao tom minced prawns barbecued on a stick of sugar cane.
chapati flat bread.
char kway teow rice noodles wok-fried with meat and/or seafood and beansprouts.
char siu marinated barbecued pork.
chermoula a dry rub of herbs and spices.
cheung fun slithery rice flour pasta with various fillings; a dim sum dish.
chirashi sushi (qv) atop a bowl of rice.
cholent a stew of meat and beans.
chollah egg-rich, slightly sweet bread.
chorizo spicy sausage.
churros soft sugared dough sticks.
ciger tava fried liver.
codornices quails.
çöp şiş cubes of lamb.
concasse a pulp of tomatoes and garlic.
couscous semolina; couscous royale is a stew of lamb, chicken and merguez (qv).
crema catalana creamy custard dessert.
crostini savoury toasts.

d

dahi yoghurt.
dahl lentil curry similar to thick lentil soup.
dhansak spicy stew of meat, lentils and vegetables.
dim sum dumplings and other titbits.
dobrada tripe stew.
dolma veg stuffed with rice and pine kernels.
dolmádes stuffed vine leaves.

Menu glossary

donburi bowl of rice with various toppings.
döner sliced lamb (or mince) kebab.
dosa or **dosai** crisp, filled pancakes.

edamame salted soy beans boiled in pods.
empanadillas small savoury pies.
escoveitched fish fish fried then pickled in a tangy sauce.

fajita grilled beef or chicken wrapped in warm flour tortillas.
falafel fried spicy chickpea patty.
falooda thick, sweet milk drink containing vermicelli, nuts etc.
fasólia plakí white beans in a tomato and herb sauce.
feijoada pork and black bean stew.
festival deep-fried, slightly sweet dumpling.
futomaki thick-rolled sushi (qv).
fuul brown broad beans, mashed with garlic, oil and lemon juice.

gado gado vegetable salad with a peanut-based sauce on top.
gajar halwa grated carrots cooked in cardamom milk.
galangal 'lesser ginger', a spice added to South-east Asian dishes.
gambas ajillo prawns with garlic.
garbanzos chickpeas.
gefilte fish poached and fried balls of white fish minced with onions and seasoning; served cold.
gnocchi potato and flour pasta 'dumpling'.
goblaki cabbage parcels, usually stuffed with rice, kasha (qv) or meat.
gohan rice.

gosht lamb.
goulash rich beef soup.
gunkan round sushi (qv) wrapped with seaweed.
gyoza dumplings stuffed with pork and herbs, fried and steamed.

halep usually döner (qv) served over bread with a buttery tomato sauce.
har gau steamed mince prawn dumpling.
harira thick lamb and lentil soup.
harissa hot chilli paste.
hollandaise a hot emulsified sauce of egg yolks and butter.
hoppers saucer-shaped rice-flour pancakes, or **string hoppers** rice-flour noodles, usually served steamed.
houmous creamy paste of chickpeas, sesame seed purée, oil, garlic and lemon juice.

idli steamed sponges of ground rice and lentil; eaten with sambar (qv).
ikan bilis tiny fish, often made into a dry relish with peanuts.
ikura salmon roe.
imam bayıldı aubergine stuffed with onions, tomatoes and garlic in olive oil.
incik slow-roasted knuckle of lamb.
injera spongy Ethiopian flatbread.
iskender döner (qv) kebab with yoghurt, butter and tomato sauce.
ISO maki inside-out sushi (qv) rolls.

jalebis deep-fried spirals of batter, in syrup.
jerk spicy marinated then roasted meat.
jhingri prawns.
jollof rice spicy 'risotto', with tomatoes, onions and (usually) chicken.

kaburga spare ribs.
kadala black chickpea curry.
kaiten zushi 'revolving sushi' on a conveyor.
kalbi marinated beef spare ribs, wrapped in lettuce leaves with chilli sauce and sliced onion.
kaleji liver.
karahi wok-like utensil.
karela bitter gourd.
kasha buckwheat.
katsu breaded and deep-fried meat.
keftédes meatballs.
kenkey maize pudding, eaten with stews.
kheer thick rice pudding flecked with pistachios.
khoresh Persian stews.
kimchi Korean pickles; often taken to signify the classic pickled cabbage.
kısır a mix of parsley, crushed wheat, olive oil, onions, tomatoes and lemon juice.
kléftiko knuckle of lamb, slow roasted.
knedliky bread dumplings.
kneidlach matzo meal dumplings.
köfte, **kofta**, **kafta**, **kufta** minced lamb or beef mixed with spices, egg and onion.
ko sari na mool cooked bracken stalks with sesame seeds.
kothu roti strips of flat bread, pan-fried with vegetables and chicken or mutton.
kratong thong crisp batter cups filled with a mix of vegetables and/or minced meat.
kueh Malaysian cakes.
kulfi ice-cream made from reduced milk.

laap minced meat flavoured with chilli, herbs and lime juice.
lahmacun a 'pizza' of minced lamb on pide bread (qv).

laksa rich and aromatic noodle soup.
lassi sweet or salty yoghurt drink.
latkes fried potato cakes.
liquor milk-free parsley sauce served with pie and mash.
lokma fillet of lamb.
lokshen egg pasta noodles.
lumpia spring rolls filled with meat or veg.

m

makhani cooked with butter and sometimes tomatoes.
maki sushi (qv) with the rice and filling inside a nori (qv) roll.
makki ki roti corn bread.
masala, masaladar 'with spices'.
massaman curry with coconut, peanuts, meat and potato.
masto musir yoghurt with chopped shallots.
mee goreng fried egg noodles with meat, prawns and veg.
mejillones mussels.
melanzane aubergine.
merguez spicy, paprika-rich lamb sausages.
meze or **mezédes** savoury snacks, served either hot or cold.
miso thick paste of fermented soy beans, used in miso soup and some dressings.
mogo cassava.
moussaká aubergines, minced meat and sliced potato, topped with béchamel sauce (qv) and baked.
moutabal aubergine and garlic purée.
mücver courgette and feta fritters.
mung kachori deep-fried spicy bean snack.

n

nabemono cooked in a pot at table.
nan, naan flatbread.
nasi goreng fried rice with shrimp paste.

nigiri lozenge-shaped sushi (qv).
nori dried seaweed.
nuoc mam fermented fish sauce.

o

ocakbası an open grill.
otak otak steamed mousse made of fish, coconut milk and egg.
ouarka pastry thin pastry, very similar to filo pastry.

p

pad Thai fried noodles with shrimps (or meat), beansprouts, salted turnip and peanuts.
paella rice cooked with chicken and/or seafood.
pakora savoury fritters.
panch'an assortment of dishes of pickles, such as cucumber, bracken shoots or perilla leaves.
paneer Indian cheese, similar to beancurd in texture.
pappa pomodoro Tuscan tomato soup made with stale bread.
papri chaat crisp pastry discs, dunked in yoghurt and doused in chutney.
paratha layered flaky fried bread.
parmigiana di melanzane aubergines baked with tomato sauce and parmesan.
pasteis de nata custard tarts.
pastel de feijão pastry with a filling of sweet creamed beans.
patatas bravas cubes of fried potatoes in a spicy tomato sauce.
patlican esme puréed aubergine dip.
patlican salata aubergine salad.
paya curried trotters of lamb in a rich gravy.
pazham pori plantain fried in coconut oil.
pho rice noodle soup with a light, lemony and aromatic beef stock.
phoulorie Trinidadian fried dough balls.

pide flatbread; also the name for Turkish pizza.
pierogi ravioli-style dumplings.
pilau, pillau, pullao flavoured rice, usually spiced with turmeric.
piliç chicken kebab.
piri piri or **peri peri** hot red pepper.
pittu rice flour and coconut steamed in bamboo to make a log.
piyaz white bean salad with onions.
platzel a type of white bread roll.
poh pia dumplings or spring rolls, deep-fried or steamed.
ponzu citrus fruit (ponzu) juice and soy sauce, used as a dip.
pooris puffed up deep-fried discs of dough.
popadom, papad thin wafers made with spicy lentil paste.
prosciutto cured ham, usually thinly sliced.
pulpo a la gallego octopus with paprika.
pyzy potato and flour dumplings.

q

qatme flatbread.
quesadillas pancake stuffed with cheese.

r

raita a yoghurt mix, usually with cucumber.
raki an aniseed-flavoured spirit.
rambutan bright red, oval fruit.
rasam South Indian soup made with tomato and tamarind.
ras malai paneer cheese patties in very sweet, thickened milk.
rendang 'dry' beef curry cooked in coconut milk.
rice and peas rice cooked with kidney beans in coconut milk.
rojak raw fruit and veg in a spicy sauce.
romesco a sauce of hazelnuts, almonds, red peppers and olive oil.

Menu glossary

roti unleavened bread cooked in a tandoor.
roti canai layered fried flatbread with a dip of chicken curry or dahl.

saag, sag spinach.
sabzi fresh herb leaves (often mint and fennel).
saç thin, chewy bread.
saké rice wine.
salad olivieh a potato salad with chicken, eggs and mayonnaise.
salsa verde a sauce of parsley, garlic, olive oil, anchovies and vinegar.
sambar, sambhar spicy lentil gravy made with tamarind and veg.
sambol chilli-hot relishes, often served heated.
sambousek pastries filled with mince, onion and pine kernels.
sashimi sliced raw fish.
satay grilled skewers of meat or fish, served with a spicy peanut sauce.
seekh kebab grilled skewers of minced lamb meat.
shawarma döner kebab.
shoyu Japanese soy sauce.
shish cubes of lamb.
soba noodles made from buckwheat.
shochu a rice spirit.
som tam grated green papaya salad.
soon dae Korean-style black pudding, incorporating rice vermicelli.
sothi coconut milk curry, used as a gravy.
sotong squid.
sujuk spicy sausage made with either lamb or beef.
sumac astringent, fruity-tasting spice.
sunomono seafood or vegetables marinated in rice vinegar.
sushi raw fish, shellfish or vegetables served on vinegared rice.
sütlaç rice pudding.
suya spicy meat kebab.

tabouleh a salad of parsley, tomatoes, crushed wheat, onions and lemon juice.
tagine meat stew, often with olives, almonds, lemon or prunes.
tandoor clay oven.
tapas Spanish snacks.
tarama cod's roe paste.
tarator bread, garlic and walnut mixture.
tavuk beyti spicy minced chicken.
temaki hand-rolled sushi (qv).
tempura fish or veg deep-fried in batter.
teppanyaki grilled on a hotplate (teppan).
teriyaki grilled meat or fish served in a spicy sauce of shoyu (qv), saké (qv) and sugar.
thali set meal with rice, bread, dahl (qv) and vegetable curries.
thoran vegetables stir-fried with curry leaves, mustard seeds, chillies and coconut.
tikka cubes of meat, fish or paneer (qv), marinated in a spicy yoghurt and baked in a tandoor.
tiramisu a rich dessert of sponge soaked in coffee and layered with brandy-flavoured cream.
tolsot bibimbap rice and vegetables, in a very hot stone bowl, mixed with raw egg yolk and chilli sauce at the table.
tom yam, tom yum hot and sour soup, with lemongrass.
tonkatsu breaded and fried pork.
tortilla Spanish-style thick omelette.
twigim batter-fried seafood or vegetables.
tzatsiki yoghurt and cucumber dip.

udon fat noodles.
uramaki inside-out sushi (qv) rolls.

uthappam spicy, crisp pancake usually topped with a mix of tomato, onions and chillies.
uykuluk sweetbread.

vadai, wada spicy vegetable or lentil fritter.
vindaloo hot pork curry from Goa, containing garlic and vinegar; in Britain the term is often misused to signify very spicy dishes.

wasabi a fiery-hot green mustard.
wot thick, dark sauce of slowly fried onions, garlic, butter and spices; used in the aromatic stews of East Africa.

xacuti Goan dish of lamb or chicken, coconut and spices.

yakimono literally 'grilled things'.
yakitori grilled chicken (breast, wings, liver, gizzard, heart) served on skewers.
yaprak sarma vine leaves stuffed with rice, lamb, tomatoes, onion.
yayla yoghurt and rice soup (usually with a chicken stock base).
yoğhurtlu meat (lamb) over bread and yoghurt.
yuk hwe shredded raw beef, strips of pear and egg yolk, served chilled.

zaalouk, zalouk spicy dip of aubergine, tomato and garlic.
zabaglione a pudding of whisked egg, sugar and Marsala (dessert wine).
zensai appetisers.
zeytoon olives.
zrazy beef rolls stuffed with bacon, pickled cucumber and mustard.

Advertisers' index

Please refer to relevant sections for addresses / telephone numbers

Index by cuisine

For branches, see
Index A-Z p312.

Index by cuisine

Index by cuisine

Index by cuisine

Vietnamese

Index A-Z

Entries in **bold** indicate the main review for chain restaurants.

Index by cuisine

Index A-Z

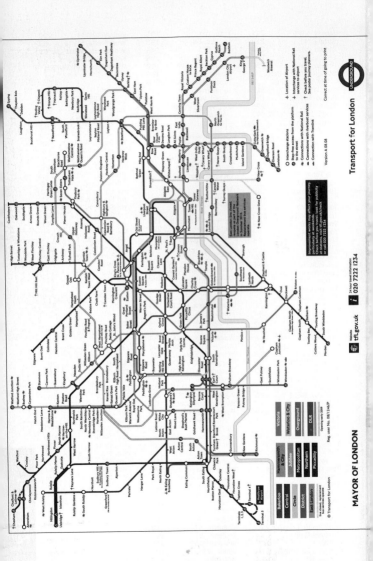

MAYOR OF LONDON

Transport for London

UNDERGROUND

Connect at time of going to print

Version A 08.08

Reg. user No. 08/1246/P

Opening early 2009

© Transport for London

i 24 hour travel information
020 7722 1234

Website
tfl.gov.uk

Bakerloo
Central
Circle
District
East London

Hammersmith & City
Jubilee
Metropolitan
Northern
Piccadilly

Victoria
Waterloo & City
Overground
DLB

line closed, replacement
bus service operates

● Interchange stations
◉ Step-free access from the platform
to the street
+ Interchange with National Rail
services
→ Connections with National Rail
→ Connections with riverboat services
→ Connection with Tramlink
✈ Location of Airport

Improvement works may affect your journey,
particularly at weekends.
Check before you travel: look for publicity
at stations, visit tfl.gov.uk/check
or call 020 7222 1234.

East London (line closed)
reopens as part of the
London Overground network
in summer 2010.
Connecting train and bus services
operate.